A Leisurely Pursuit

Splendid Hardwood Antiquities from the Liang Yi Collection

兩依藏

玩閒談

by Curtis Evarts

Photographs by Alan P.K. Soo
Graphic Design by Eric Lim
Published by United Sky Resources Limited

ISBN: 962-86071-1-1
Printed on recycled paper in Hong Kong

Table of Contents

A Leisurely Pursuit:
Splendid Hardwood Antiquities from the Liang Yi Collection

The phenomenon of antique hardwood furniture streaming into Hong Kong during the late 80's and early 90's will long be cherished as the 'Golden Years' for collecting Chinese furniture. Reduced from a trickle to intermittent drops, the source at the turn of the millennium is all but dry. Still, many treasures gathered away in private hands have yet to be seen, and with each unveiling, knowledge is increased and perspectives broadened. Such is the Liang Yi Collection, which expands into the broad, untrammeled sphere beyond that more narrowly associated with plain, undecorated 'Ming-style' furnishings. Since ancient times, Chinese artisans have drawn upon a rich palette of decorative traditions with stylistic characteristics ranging from the vigorous to the delicate, and from the severe to the ornate. It is variegated splendor that marks the Liang Yi Collection, which being primarily fashioned from two distinguished and noble hardwoods—*zitan* and *huanghuali*—also reflects unity and constraint.

Hardwood furnishings became increasingly popular during the late Ming period, coinciding with the relaxation of foreign trade restrictions in 1572 that permitted the importation of precious timber from resources in the Southeast Asian archipelago and beyond. Throughout the 17th century, economic conditions flourished in cities along the coastal regions, and a burgeoning middle class increasingly sought to surround themselves with the trappings of the elite, including the display of fine hardwood furnishings. Moreover, furniture made from noble hardwoods—with naturally beautiful grain patterns, hard lustrous surfaces, elegant proportions, crisply carved decoration, and high resistance to boring insects as well as waterborne decay—began to rival the long-established decorative lacquer furniture-making traditions.

The transitional 17th century was a period of cultural abandonment and regeneration, and a time when the development of revolutionary new furniture styles and experimental hybrids emerged. For example, while the classical 'recessed-leg' (cf. cat. 7) and 'footed, corner-leg' forms (cf. cat. 8) had been conventions throughout the Ming dynasty (1368-1644), variants such as the 'bamboo-style' (cf. cat. 5) and 'straight-leg, corner-leg' forms (cf. cat. 3, 19, 44) first manifest during this transitional/early Qing period. The high strength and density of tropical hardwoods like *huanghuali* also permitted the delicate shaping of components, achieving unparalleled elegance in line and form. During the Qing dynasty (1644-1911), new, successful patterns were assimilated into the repertoire of traditional furniture. Ming-style furniture following earlier classical themes, such as the *zitan* square tables illustrated as catalogue item 46, also continued to be reproduced and undergo subtle refinement.

One half of the Liang Yi Collection includes full-sized furniture with categories ranging through stools, chairs, tables, cabinets, and screens. The balance is comprised of smaller desktop furnishings including cases, chests, trays and stands, brushpots, and other miscellaneous curiosities. Many of these objects exhibit remarkable quality and provide the field with new and variant objects for reference. They also display an array of styles reflecting regional variation and evolutionary development.

Fine hardwood furniture discovered throughout many provinces in China demonstrates production that was broadly scattered. The Jiangnan region has been well established as one of the primary production centers during the Ming and Qing periods. Including much of modern Zhejiang, Anhui, and Jiangsu provinces, this fertile region was centered about the culturally rich and prosperous cities of Suzhou, Yangzhou and Hangzhou. Significant quantities of hardwood furniture also originated from the Guangdong/Fujian and the north-central Shanxi regions, where enormous wealth was generated from overseas trade and powerful merchant traditions. Variations of forms, construction techniques, and decorative detailing found amongst similar types of furniture often reflect tendencies rising out of the ethos of the diverse ethnic cultures that coexisted throughout China.

Furniture from the north-central regions reflects a heritage of conservative traditions. Aside from its share of those classical patterns that were common throughout the empire, furniture from this region tends toward robust and richly decorated styles. The curvaceous cabriole leg was frequently employed by northern furniture-makers, and it is more than likely that the richly decorated game table (cat. 45) has such regional provenance. The decoration, styling, and workmanship that is evident amongst low kang tables, which are primarily associated the furniture culture of north China, also can be said to reflect northern furniture-making traditions. The yokeback armchair (cat. 10) also exhibits provincial characteristics typical of the Shanxi region, where chairs of similar style with the 'vase-and-bamboo' side post are commonly found, and where Ming-style furniture continued to be produced into the late Qing period.

Furniture from the Beijing region also reflects northern traditions, but was furthermore under the influence of Imperial preference and traditions. The large, ponderous cabinets that stand upon short cabriole legs (cat. 49) as well as the high-waisted kang table (cat. 27), which are both crafted from rare *zitan* and bear late Ming decorative characteristics, may well have served as Palace furnishings during the 17th century. During the Qing period, the unprecedented extravagance for Palace furnishings made from the ever-dwindling inventories of *zitan* compelled new designs of linear style that were material efficient. Thus, the robust, curvilinear patterns characteristic of the Ming period gave way to those of more rigid style with refined and elaborate surface decoration (cf. cat. 32, 42, 48). During and after the Yongzheng period (1723-1735), furniture-makers were recruited from both Guangdong and Jiangnan regions to work in the Imperial Workshops on account of their superior craftsmanship. Thus southern influence was also assimilated into the furniture produced for the Qing court, which in turn, filtered down through the hierarchy.

The decorative arts from the Jiangnan region tends towards elegance and refinement, reflecting characteristics of its people as well as a long history of sophisticated literati traditions. Such distinction is evident in the bamboo-style *zitan* stool (cat. 5) as well as the small *huanghuali* horseshoe armchair (cat. 12), both of which appear to exhibit light, feminine proportions when contrasted to northern counterparts of similar form. The light, spindle-back chair (cat. 17) is also a design commonly found in Jiangsu province. Yangzhou, renown for its decorative lacquer and inlay traditions, was also the origin of much of the Zhouzhi-style inlaid-hardwood furniture, which otherwise exhibits similar characteristics of the Jiangnan region (cf. cat. 13, 81). And while refined in style, furniture from Anhui province can also express an air of nostalgia for elegant Song traditions; such is the rare *huanghuali* side table with out-flared legs and extended-bracket aprons of architectural style (cat. 38).

Woodwork from some areas of Fujian can even reach greater levels of refinement than found in Jiangnan—especially that from Putian and Quanzhou. However, Ming-style hardwood furniture from Fujian and Guangdong region generally tends to be thick in proportion, a characteristic that may reflect its proximity to abundant timber resources. Such is the box-style altar table (cat. 36), discovered in Quanzhou, Fujian province, which is constructed with *huanghuali* frame members of substantial size.

Understanding the puzzle of regional styles is not without entanglements. The recruiting of craftsmen from regions that were renown for their products effectively spread techniques and styles into other regions. High quality furniture was also traded commercially between regions; thus, furniture from production centers like the Suzhou region was also widely distributed through the inland waterways that reached far into the central regions. Furthermore, in the case of the regular relocation of officials or the acquisition by wealthy merchants, furniture was also transported to yet further remote regions. How the pair of large *zitan* cabinets (cat. 49) and *zitan* horseshoe armchairs (cat. 11) found their way to Wuwei, Gansu province is a story that waits to be told.

Range of style aside, the Liang Yi Collection has particularly lent itself to three areas of investigation—*zitan*, Zhouzhi inlay traditions, and brushpots. Over fifty objects in the collection are made from *zitan*, considered to be the noblest of timbers. Dating from the late Ming through the Qing periods, this reference group affords the possibility to examine the characteristics of objects that were made from this rare, precious timber, as well as the various qualities of timber associated with the generic *zitan* family. The collection also includes several objects inlaid with multicolored semi-precious materials. An investigation of this technique, which was variously called Zhouzhi, *babao*, and *baibao* inlay, provides new insights into this decorative tradition. And while an individual brushpot seldom lends itself to more than a short descriptive elaboration, the group of thirty-five hardwood brushpots selected from the Liang Yi Collection also provides a focus for this hitherto unexamined subject. These three topics are explored in the following pages.

Curtis Evarts
May 2000

Zitan: The Noble Hardwood Family of Exotic, Abstruse Origins

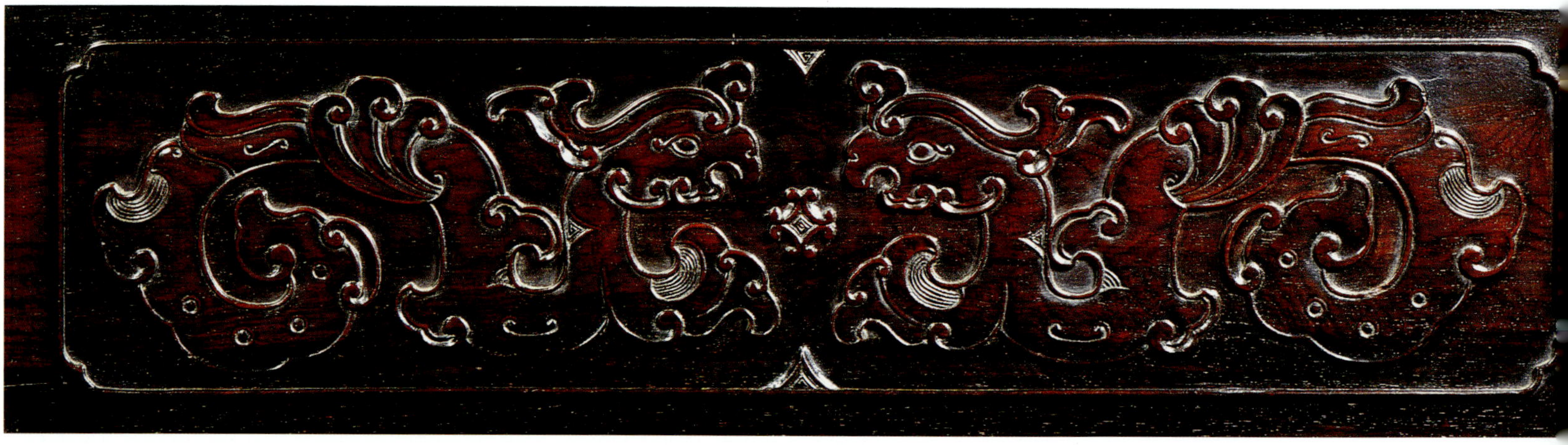

Fig. 1. Detail of relief carving from zitan *cabinets (cat. 52).*

The mystique of *zitan* has captivated the Chinese for centuries. With origins from faraway foreign lands, it has historically been associated with the exotic. With quintessential qualities of deep-red pigmentation, a surface that polishes to a rich, shimmering luster (fig. 2), perfumed fragrance, and massive weight, it reflects virtuous characteristics associated with those of nobility and rank. And with obscure botanical anomalies, *zitan* remains full of intrigue for the modern-minded connoisseur. Having briefly touched upon the subject in a short essay published in 1991[1], the objects of *zitan* in the Liang Yi Collection here provide an opportunity for a more penetrating study. The following distillation of historical facts, recent publications of Chinese authorities, as well as personal observations and speculations, is thus presented here as a fresh attempt to synthesize and organize the myriad of incidental information surrounding the subject.

Sources

Various early compendiums on geography and pharmaceuticals note that *zitan* was imported from abroad. The 3rd century CE *Gujin zhu* cited sources in the historic regions known today as Vietnam and Cambodia, and the Tang dynasty (618 CE-907 CE) pharmacologist Su Gong recorded that *zitan* was imported from the ancient kingdom of Panpan on the Malay Peninsula.[2] Exotic goods such as *zitan* were highly popular amongst the Tang aristocracy during a period when the Chinese empire reached far and wide, and when trade flourished freely across foreign borders. References from this period suggest that *zitan* was primarily used for small luxury items such as game boards, *weiqi* counters, scroll ends, boxes, and musical instruments. Similar Chinese-style objects made with *zitan*, found in the Japanese Imperial collections survive in testimony of the dominant Tang culture.[3] The small size of these objects suggests that early *zitan* was sourced as relatively small-sized timber.

Few records or artifacts of *zitan* are attributable to the following four hundred years. A withdrawal from foreign interest during the Song period (960-1279) may well have influenced the importation of *zitan*, and under the subsequent Yuan dynastic period (1276-1368) of northern Mongol rule, the Chinese aristocracy was largely oppressed. After this lapse, *zitan* appears in the early Ming period connoisseurship treatise *Gegu yaolun* (pub. 1388) as a precious wood with domestic sources in the provincial regions of Hainan, Guangxi and Hunan. However, in a later edition published in 1462, the amended notation "...most suitable use for manufacture of hairpins..." infers a rather diminutively sized timber.[4]

Such limited use stands in sharp contrast to the notion that a hoard of *zitan* was stored away at the capital for Imperial use following the grand naval expeditions of Zheng He during the Yongle period (1403-1424).[5] While not out of the realm of possibility in light of the vast amounts of tribute returning with fleets that voyaged as far as the coast of Africa, actual documentation of *zitan* tribute from these expeditions has yet to be discovered.[6] Following the Yongle reign, isolationist policies were established and remained in effect for over a century until 1567, when maritime trade restrictions were relaxed. The negligible amount of early Ming *zitan* objects and/or literary references until the late 16th century suggest that it remained an extremely rare and exotic material.

This phenomenon is further apparent in the absence of *zitan* objects confiscated from the properties of the deposed prime minister, Yan Song and son, Yan Shifan. In 1562, thousands of luxury items with itemized descriptions were included in a detailed inventory of their holdings—jewelry, clothing, zithers, paintings, jades, bronzes, porcelains, stationery items and miscellaneous furnishings. A sampling of scholar's objects and small furnishings wherein one might expect to discover an object of *zitan* includes a 'brushpot of ivory-inlaid palmwood' (*ya xiang zongmu bitong*)[7]; 'mirror stands of ivory-inlaid *huali*' (*ya xiang hualimu jingjia*)[8]; 'paper weights of jade-inlaid *huali*' (*yu xiang hualimu zhenzhi*)[9], and; 'ebony rulers' (*wumu jiechi*).[10] The absence of *zitan* in such a richly detailed context, and one which also survives as an inventory of luxury items available to one of boundless influence, power and wealth not only suggests rarity, but poses the question of its fundamental availability.

The relaxation of trade restrictions during the Longqing reign (1567-1573) once again permitted the importation of foreign goods. Merchants from different parts of the world immediately responded with the shipment of precious goods to China's coastal cites for trade.[11] Within a matter of a few decades, *zitan* reemerges as a commonly cited precious hardwood. A customs document dated 1567 reveals the importation of *zitan* through portals in Zhejiang province and its relative value at 2.5 times that of *huali*

Fig. 2. 'Golden star' zitan. *Detail from scrollpot (cat. 110).*

and 5 times that of *tieli*.[12]

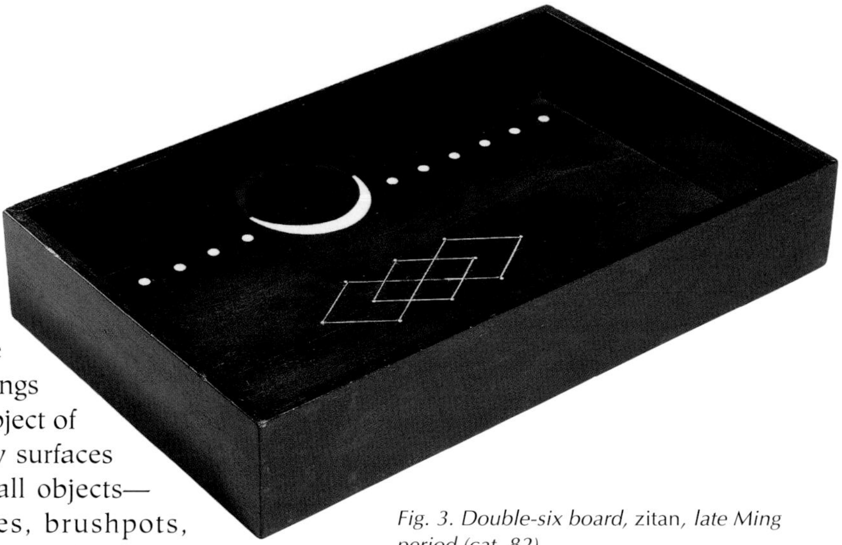

Fig. 3. Double-six board, zitan, *late Ming period (cat. 82).*

Over the next few decades writers from the surrounding region also began noting the marked appearance of fine hardwood furnishings made from *huali* and *zitan*. Nonetheless, the subject of *zitan* as a material for full-sized furniture rarely surfaces in late Ming literature. Rather, it is again small objects—dressing cases, book boxes, inkstone cases, brushpots, brushpot bases, trays, and censer lids—that receive frequent mention throughout the writings of Gao Lian[13], Tu Long[14], and Wen Zhenheng.[15] Liu Ruoyu, who served as a court eunuch during the Wanli period (1573-1620), also recorded small scale productions originating from Imperial Workshops, including *zitan* double-six game boards, chessboards, dominoes, and combs.[16] The double-six game board (fig. 3) in the Liang Yi Collection may well originate from this period, after which time the game gradually fell into obscurity.

Even as late as the late 17th century, it was *small* objects of *zitan* that Cantonese craftsman were producing from resources on Hainan Island which, according to Qu Dajun (1630-1697), were broadly distributed throughout China.[17] Thus, the esteem and rarity of a full-sized piece of *zitan* furniture is revealed when, near the end of his life, Wang Shizhen (1634-1711) recorded the extravagant sum of 120 ounces silver offered in Beijing for an inlaid-*zitan* chair.[18]

At some yet undetermined point, perhaps as tribute during final decades of the Ming period or just after the Manchu overthrow, the Imperial Palace appears to have accumulated a cache of *zitan* timber. Being of sufficient dimension to produce full-sized furniture, this material likely originated from newly discovered resources with large growth trees. Such a scenario would coincide with a significant group of *zitan* furniture that displays discernable 'late-Ming' characteristics in form and decoration. These pieces also typically exhibit an uninhibited use of high quality, uniformly figured timber in their construction, without regard to frugality or restraint associated with a precious material of limited resources. Examples include the kang table (fig. 4) and large cabinets (fig. 5), which could well have been associated with the Imperial Palace during the final years of the Ming period when court eunuchs were said to have "vied with one another in the elegance of their furniture."[19]

While references to *zitan* furniture production are slim through 16th and 17th centuries, material from the 18th century is abundant. Archives dating from the start of the Yongzheng reign (1723-1735) record that *zitan, huali, nanmu*, and decorative lacquer were all being used to produce chairs, tables, cabinets, screens, and other miscellaneous furnishings for the Palace. These were primarily produced in Imperial workshops under the

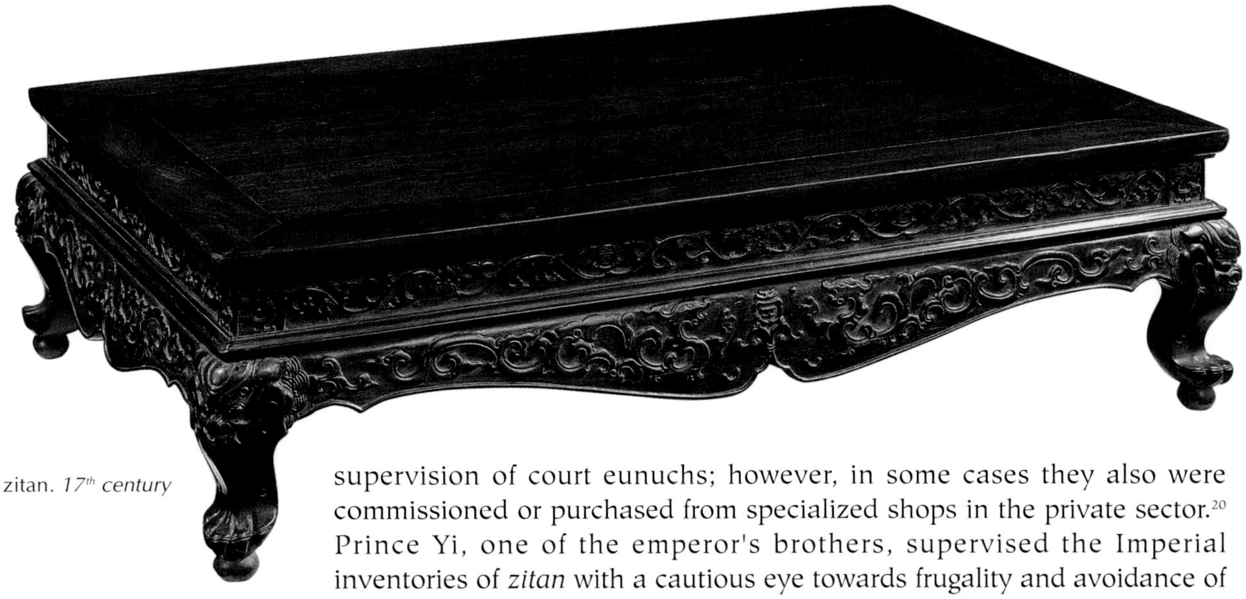

Fig. 4. *Kang table*, zitan. *17th century (cat. 27).*

supervision of court eunuchs; however, in some cases they also were commissioned or purchased from specialized shops in the private sector.[20] Prince Yi, one of the emperor's brothers, supervised the Imperial inventories of *zitan* with a cautious eye towards frugality and avoidance of waste. In one instance, having been informed of its proposed selection for the construction of a throne chair, reprimanded, "It is not necessary to use *zitan*—make it with lacquer!"[21]

As a prized, and perhaps even novel material, *zitan* was sometimes used to reproduce favorite designs from existing pieces of furniture in the palace, a practice that was recorded in several instances. During the 3rd year of the Yongzheng reign (1725), a new table of *zitan* was ordered according to the respective size of an existing red lacquer table and the style of yet another black lacquer table. At the same time, chairs of *zitan* were also reproduced after an old, red-painted lamphanger chair.[22] (Herein also lies one of the difficulties of dating Chinese furniture—the age-old tradition of copies and reproductions, a practice that is deeply ingrained upon the Chinese essence.)

In 1726, a pair of *zitan* incense stands were duplicated from an example that Prince Yi had brought into the Palace.[23] On another occasion in 1727, the court eunuch Cheng Guo arranged for a standing screen of *zitan* with a glass panel to be brought to the Palace; a duplicate was immediately produced with *zitan*, with minor alterations due to the slightly smaller glass panel on hand.[24] Thus, fine *zitan* furnishings were also being produced independent of the Palace with material that was outside of its control. These and other similar instances also further suggest that so-called 'palace-style' furnishings were not devoid of outside influences, but was rather a synthesis of ranging styles deemed suitable for the refined environs of the Court and tastes of the ruling family.

That being said, many new designs were also created in the early Qing palace workshops, which were at times inspired by the Emperor himself or by supervising attendants. Workshop records frequently note the development of prototype models. Such was the case for a small book cabinet, which after approval in 1725, was ordered to be constructed with *zitan* frame members and ivory spandrels.[25] This process ensured that limited supplies were not squandered.

Imperial workshops archives record over thirty *zitan* tables of various size and style that were produced or imported for the halls and apartments of the Imperial palaces during the first six years of the Yongzheng reign. Tables aside, these records indicate that *zitan* was only rarely used for other categories of furniture.

Zitan Tables–Palace Workshop Origin, Yongzheng Period	
several	kang tables, *gaolimu* (oak) frame members with *zitan* panels.
1	low table , *zitan*
1	table, *zitan* frame members with *nanmu* burl panel
8	dining (*shan*) tables, *zitan*
2	tables, *zitan* frame members with *nanmu* panels and silver mounts
6	tables, *zitan* frame members with *nanmu* burl panel and gold mounts
1	*qin* table, *huali* frame members with *zitan* panel and spandrels
1	revolving table, *zitan*
2	incense stands, *zitan*
1	small incense stand with a drawer, *zitan*
1	table, *zitan*
1	table, *zitan* length 2.68, width 1.78 *chi* (1 *chi* = 30 cm)
2	tables, lacquer with *zitan* panels
1	table, *zitan* frame members with *nanmu* panel and *ruyi* decoration, length 2.95, width 1.95 *chi*
1	table, *zitan* frame members with *nanmu* burl panel and inlaid silver mounts with *ruyi* designs

Zitan Tables–Imported, Yongzheng Period	
1	table *hongdou* frame members with *zitan* aprons/length 7.5, width 1.53, height 2.73 *chi*
1	table *hongdou* frame members with *zitan* aprons/length 6.0, width 1.05, height 2.8 *chi*

A number of these Yongzheng period tables employ *zitan* panels in combination with other woods or *zitan* frame members combined with *nanmu* panels. Similar combinations are also evident in the 18th century side table in the Liang Yi Collection (cat. 44) and the pair of *zitan* cabinets (cat. 52), which employ *nanmu* and *huanghuali* as secondary materials. The phenomenon of combined woods, which has generally been considered a fashion of the early Qing period, may well have originated from resourceful management of rare material. Regardless, the harmonious combination of *zitan* and *nanmu* burl has also survived as a classical pairing.

An account of *zitan* during the Qianlong period (1735-1796) appears in a well-documented study by Tian Jiaqing.[26] The Qianlong emperor was directly involved with the Imperial furniture-making workshops, as he was with the jade workshops and others. Under his influence, a refined style of jade carving, inspired from archaic motifs, was highly popularized—a style that was also transmitted to works in *zitan* produced during this period. Such is the exquisite relief carving of *chi* dragons on the pair of cabinets (fig. 1) and kang table (fig. 6), the latter of which are raised against a flat ground and enhanced with concave profiling. Such exquisite handling has given rise to the term '*zitan gong*', a superlative which generally reflects exquisite workmanship matched with the potential of dense *zitan* for fine detailing and smooth, lustrous polishing.

A good deal of *zitan* furniture was produced during the 18th century, not

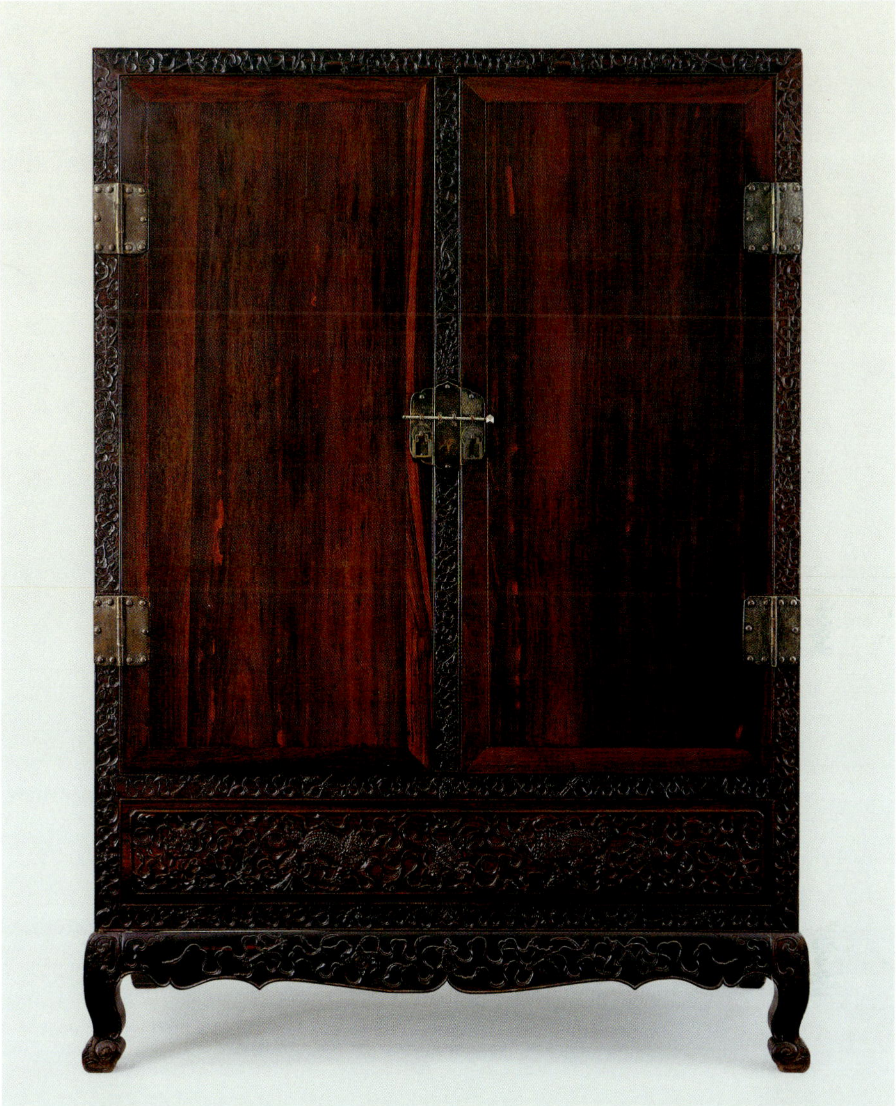

Fig. 5. Cabinet, one of a pair, zitan*.*
17th century (cat. 49).

only for the Palace, but also for those of sufficient means. An inscription on a pair of *zitan* cabinets records an expense exceeding 300 ounces of silver paid out by a Cantonese gentleman in the year 1747; as Tian noted, such lavish expenditure would have far exceeded the expense of an architectural structure to house them.[27] Sumptuous *zitan* furniture was also described in the 18th century novel *Hongloumeng*, which documents the semi-fictional daily life of an extended family bestowed with Imperial favor. One of the main halls of the family estate was set out with a "large *zitan* table carved with *chi* dragons" that was of sufficient dimension to place "a huge bronze *ding* nearly three feet in height with a smaller antique gilt bronze vessel and crystal bowl on either side."[28] In consideration of the preponderance of small-timber *zitan*, that required for such massive cabinets and tables must have been exceedingly rare.

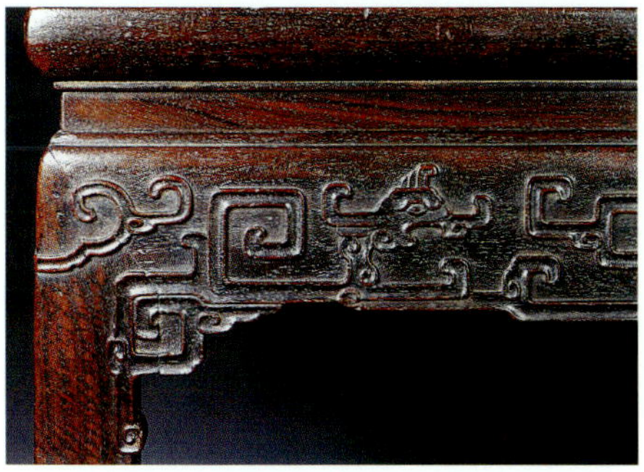

Fig. 6. Detail of relief carving of kang table illustrated as catalogue item 32.

It is widely accepted that increased use of *zitan* for Palace furnishings during the Qianlong period gradually depleted Imperial reserves. This situation was further compounded as court fashion trickled into the broader realms of aristocratic society, which resulted in increased private competition for premium materials. Shortage of *zitan* timber at the Palace was no clear indication that material was not available elsewhere. During

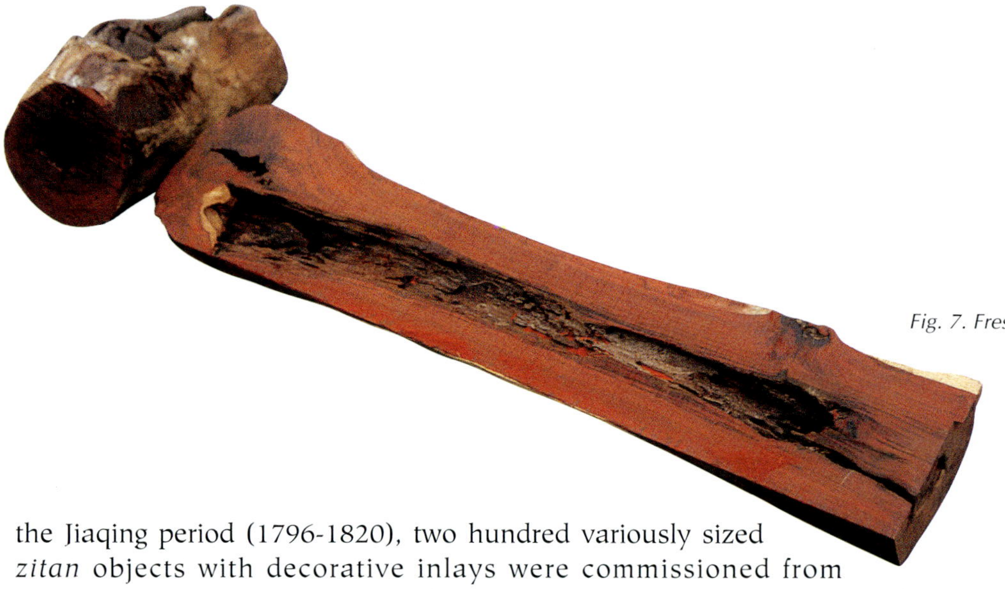

Fig. 7. Freshly cut zitan *timber with pithy center.*

the Jiaqing period (1796-1820), two hundred variously sized *zitan* objects with decorative inlays were commissioned from Yangzhou workshops for renovations to the Yuanmingyuan.[29] As noted above, there is little evidence of a strict or effective Imperial monopoly on the supply of *zitan*. And indeed, even with attempts at control, the major ports of entry in Guangdong and Zhejiang were located at great distances from the capital. Given the prevalence of corruption and smuggling, a good deal of material also likely found its way around custom houses.

With demand running high, entrepreneurs were also actively seeking new supplies from further abroad during the 18th century. The Spanish Jesuit priest Juan Jose Delgado, who having been posted to the Philippines in 1711 for over forty years, noted the predilection of the Chinese sea traders for a local hardwood resembling *zitan*, known as *tindalo*.

> "...in China, they say *tindalo* sells for its weight in silver and is valued as such; they make from it many curious desks, chairs and stools. They also know how to preserve in the wood a blood red color, washing it frequently in salt water. In time, if care is not taken, it changes to a dark color, but is very lustrous; it can be polished to such a degree that one's face can be seen in it...."[30]

Such are the typical characteristics of *zitan* which, when freshly cut, reveals the concentrated, deep-red color of its pigmentation (fig. 7). However, within a few months after exposure to light, the color of this freshly cut surface shifts toward darker and darker tonalities.

The Chinese had been frequenting Manila since the removal of trade restrictions in 1567, trading porcelain and silk for much needed silver, which the Spanish were shipping from Central and South America. The virgin tropical forests in the Philippines and elsewhere throughout the southeastern archipelago also provided a rich resource of precious hardwoods suited to the demand in China. Delgado as well as those others who followed throughout the 18th and 19th centuries as forestry administrators in the Philippines noted the purchasing patterns of the 'Chinese mestizos':

> ..... the Chinese never buy wood by invoice and attach little importance to names. Their methods of buying are very crude, the principal factors of importance to them are, that the wood does not float, and that it is of a dark color, when as a matter of

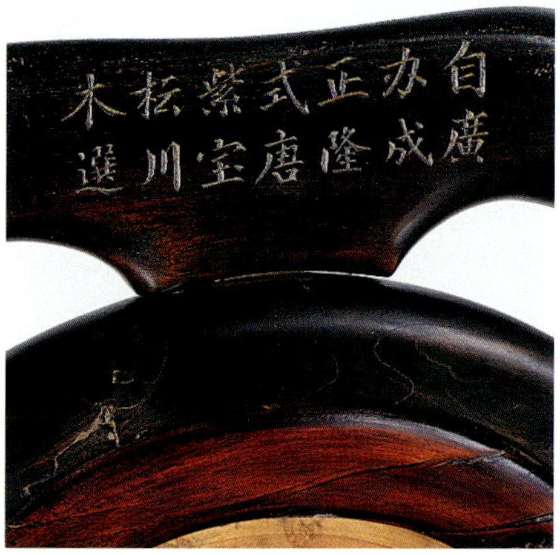

Fig. 8. Detail of inscription from rocking chairs (cat. 22).

> fact, many of the Filipino woods of the first class, when well-seasoned, float. Their methods of buying is by inspection, cutting the wood with an ax and examining it. The woods which they prefer are the Molave, Narra, Bansalaguin (highly prized), Yacal, Dungon, Supa, Tindalo, Betis, Mangachapuy, Camagon, Acle and Ipil.[31]

These empirical methods recorded by Dominic Vidal late in the 19th century likely reflect longstanding, traditional patterns. As premium sources became depleted, selections were compromised with alternate materials of similar characteristics. This is in part why botanists have great difficulty with the identification of *zitan*, and why connoisseurs struggle at odds to categorize and differentiate its qualities.

Thus, *zitan* furniture from the 19th and early 20th centuries appears as a mixed lot, reflecting diverse sources and uneven standards. Quality of workmanship and materials are reflected in the 19th century altar side table and incense stands (cat. 42, 48). More often, however, the fine line between *zitan* and *hongmu* becomes difficult to distinguish as one material blends into the other and workmanship degenerates. Such are the stools illustrated as catalogue item 4, whose material reflects characteristics of gold flecked *zitan* as well as dark *hongmu*. Perhaps it was this murky situation that inspired the discerning inscription, "Directly imported real *zitan*......." (fig. 8) on the rocking chairs illustrated as catalogue item 22. Nevertheless, even the quality of this material does not match that of earlier pieces in terms of uniformity of color and consistency of grain patterns. Material aside, late Qing and Republican period (1912-1949) works generally falls short of the superior '*zitan gong*' that distinguishes earlier works. Such compromised standards are often visible in the uneven ground of relief carved decoration and/or beading of inconsistent uniformity.

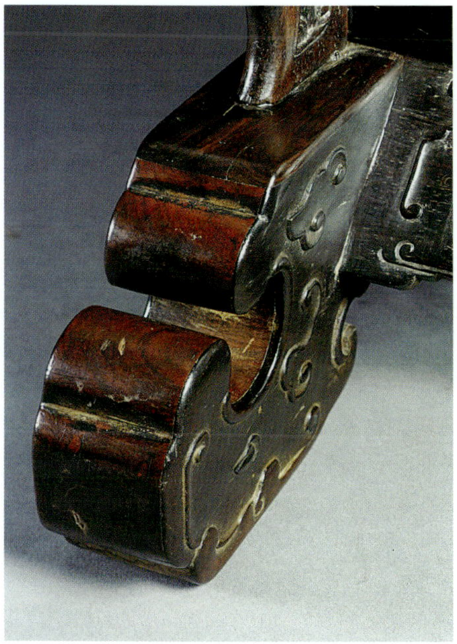

Fig. 9. Detail of laminated material from table screen (cat. 57).

In circumstances of popular demand and limited supply, *zitan* furniture from the late 18th, 19th, and early 20th centuries was also commonly fabricated from deficient timber requiring laminated construction or the use of patched, piece-work components. Most *zitan* is harvested as a small, twisted, and crooked timber with a pithy, hollow core, giving rise to the common saying "100% *zitan*, 90% hollow" (*shi tan jiu kong*) (fig. 7). While suitable for the manufacture of small objects, the use of dwarfed timber for larger pieces required that individual components first be built up through various processes of laminating, splicing, and patching. Such are several of the pieces catalogued herein, including a table screen constructed with thin veneers of *zitan* laminated to a *hongmu* core (fig. 9). The use of patched material is also evident in the side table (cat. 47) and chairs (cat. 18, 20), which also date from the mid- to late Qing periods.

A summary of these historical literary references tallies more or less with the surviving body of *zitan* objects. Given the hardness, durability, and esteem of *zitan*, there is no reason to doubt the survival of a few small objects from the Tang dynasty; more realistically, a significant percentage of small objects may date from the late Ming period. On the other hand, with the exception of the small group attributed to the 17th century, few pieces of full-sized *zitan* furniture can be securely dated to the Ming period. The 18th century can be considered the 'golden age' for *zitan* furniture, when the material was highly valued, and when the highest standards of workmanship were demanded. During the late Qing and Republican periods, the production of *zitan* furniture becomes blurred with the late Qing traditions of *hongmu* furniture.

It has long been accepted as traditional knowledge amongst Hong Kong furniture dealers that sets of *zitan* furniture were produced for wealthy Cantonese families during the early part of the 20th century. However, while many dealers simultaneously perpetuated the 'rarity-to-the-point-of-extinction' myth, new sources of *zitan* also continued to be discovered. Today, *zitan* timber is still available (see fig. 7) and is selectively used by reproduction workshops as well as by those with less scrupulous intentions who sell fakes throughout Southeast Asia and elsewhere. The timber merchant Gu Yongqi, who is based in Nantong, Jiangsu province, regularly advertises sizeable *zitan* logs in the Chinese antiquities magazine *Shoucangjia* (Collectors). One grade is available in small logs ranging 16-20 cm in diameter, and 120-160 cm in length; price: 35,000 RMB/ton. A higher grade is available in slightly larger logs ranging 20-26 cm in diameter, and 120-240 cm in length; price: 45,000 RMB/ton. The recently opened Zitan Museum in Beijing features reproductions of Ming and Qing furniture crafted in new *zitan*. More interesting is the signature series inspired from classical Ming designs employing new *zitan* produced by the workshop of Tian Jiaqing, of which a group was successfully sold at auction in Beijing.[32] Western furniture designers are also finding ways to employ this ancient, noble timber—an exquisitely crafted jewelry case made with *zitan* and Brazilian rosewood by the English cabinet-maker David Linley is one of the most recent additions to the Liang Yi Collection (fig. 10).

Connoisseurship and Botanical Studies

With regard to the identification and appraisal of *zitan*, divergent opinions arise from different viewpoints. Studies based in connoisseurship and those in botany communicate with different languages, each employing terminologies that address distinct concerns. Connoisseurship studies are primarily focused upon the 'after-the-fact' visual appearance of the polished surface, and secondarily with density, surface hardness, durability, fragrance, etc. These studies show little interest in the tree of origin nor any in attributes associated with its microscopic cellular world. Relative to a visual aesthetic, such a prioritization is appropriate, as that which is imbued with intrinsic and

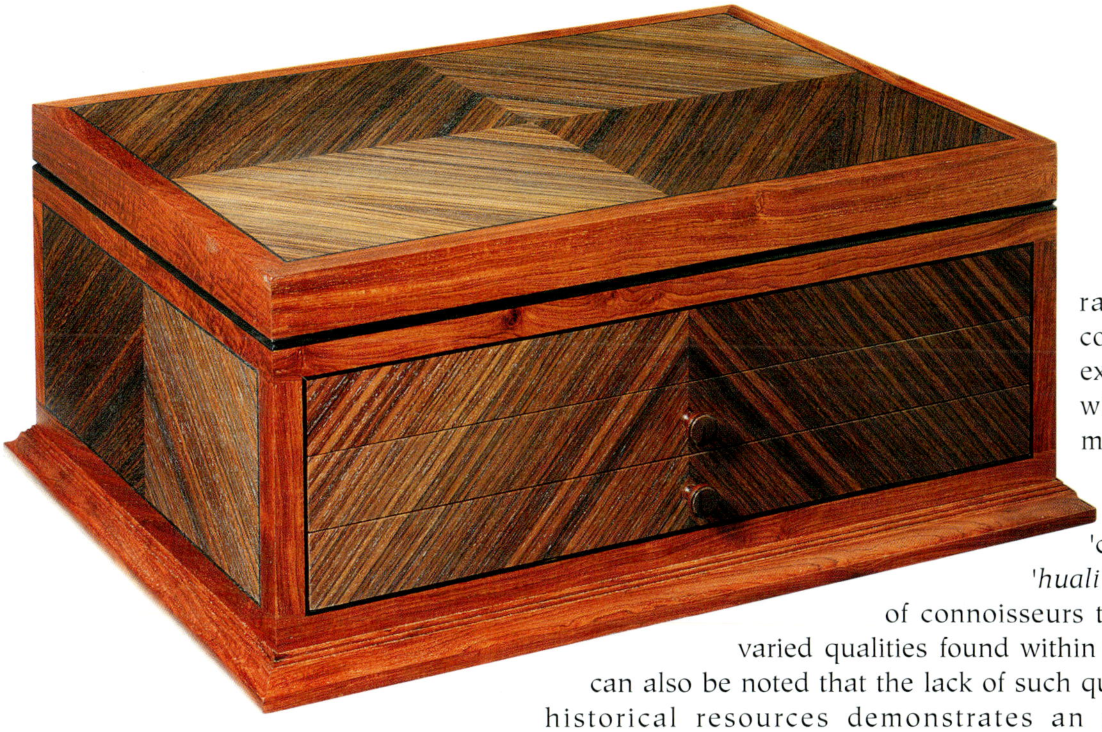

Fig. 10. Jewelry case. New zitan and Brazilian rosewood. 48 X 33 X 20 cm H. David Linley, cabinetmaker 1999. Liang Yi Collection.

rarified beauty will consistently produce a more exalted experience than that which earns a 'precious material' title from laboratory analysis. Thus, the terms 'golden star' (*jinxing*)-, 'chicken blood' (*jixue*)-, and '*huali*'-*zitan* reflect the attempts of connoisseurs to distinguish between the varied qualities found within the generic *zitan* family. It can also be noted that the lack of such qualifying distinctions in any historical resources demonstrates an unprecedented level of connoisseurship that now exists around the subject.

On the other hand, viewed through the scope of botanical analysis, the visual appearance of a finished timber is only one of its many identifiable characteristics, and one that is influenced by many extenuating and often, unpredictable factors. For instance, because the composition of timber follows a layered pattern of concentric growth, a square-cut timber will exhibit significant grain pattern variations due to the orientation of its surface to these growth rings. Thus, it is in the tangentially orientated surface where so-called 'cow hair' open-pore grain pattern is found (see fig. 12). In the radially oriented surface from the same timber, these same pores appear like short, whisker shavings, and an oscillating striped or ribbon grain pattern appears due to the manner in which light reflects from the interlocked grain. Trees of the same species also have differences in density, color, texture, grain patterns, and may be more or less subject to the phenomenon that produces the sparkling *jinxing* effect. These variations can all result from tree gender, soil conditions, exposure, magnetic field orientation, altitude, etc. Two distinct species may also produce material of similar appearance.

In Chen Rong's *Classification of Chinese Woods* (pub. 1959), two varieties of *zitan* are noted, including *pterocarpus indicus* (*qiangwei mu*), which grows in India, the Philippines, the Malay Peninsula, and Guangdong, and *pterocarpus santalinus*, with origins in India and Ceylon, and also grows in Guangdong and on Hainan Island.[33] These two varieties were recently substantiated and further elaborated upon by Gu Yongqi, the Nantong timber dealer mentioned above. Accordingly, *pterocarpus indicus* is native to southern China and its bordering regions; it is a broadleaf deciduous tree that mostly grows as a small shrub with crooked branches, it has a hollow pithy center, and its red pigmentation is not water soluble (fig. 7). *Pterocarpus santalinus* is native to the islands of the Indian Ocean; it is an evergreen broadleaf tree that grows with a straight trunk, generally has a solid center, and its red pigmentation is water soluble. While these two botanical types have distinct characteristics, Gu notes that a material of similar quality is yielded from both species.[34]

For the connoisseur, the general inadequacy of the botanical species classification system is demonstrated by its inability to target and distinguish between the subtle differences of woods like *hongmu* and *zitan*. From a botanical point of view, these woods remain indistinguishable members of related rosewood families. While this has led some venturous Chinese scholars to begin using the term *hongmu* as a broad category inclusive of *zitan* as well as *huanghuali*,[35] the association with inferior *hongmu* is unthinkable to connoisseurship methodology. While the refined qualities of *zitan* remain incognizant to modern science, developed visual sensitivities tempered with some basic botanical knowledge can aid in critical appraisal and supplement the casual, romantic appreciation with a deeper level of understanding. Accordingly, the following characteristics of *zitan* commonly cited by connoisseurs are elaborated upon below.

Categories

- 'Golden star' (*jinxing* 金星) *zitan* (fig. 11), also called 'golden thread' (*jinsi* 金絲), is considered to be a marker of the finest quality *zitan*. The term describes the fine thread-like strands of golden-yellow to vermilion-red color that appear embedded within the surface. According to a recent study by Gu Yongqi, these flecks of material are a residual of silicate that crystallized from the original tree sap and settled into the open grain pores.[36] After the surface has been polished, the translucence of this substance is highlighted and produces a sparkling effect. Gu has further pointed out that this so-called *jinxing* characteristic appears randomly in two distinct species from the Islands of the Indian Ocean and Southeastern Asia.

Fig. 11. 'Golden star' zitan. *Detail from chest illustrated as catalogue item 78.*

- 'Cow hair' (*niumao* 牛毛) (fig. 12) describes the pattern of elongated open pores with fine pointed ends that appear like strands of cow hair. This characteristic is primarily evident in the tangential surface, such as in the surface of a brushpot (cf. cat. 101) or alternately, a flat surface that has a more or less tangential orientation to the growth rings. Conversely, these same pores appear as short, whisker-like markings in the radial surface. In some types of material, the grain pores appear as curling S-shapes. Because of the interlocked grain structure, these open pores will also exhibit a 'herring-bone' pattern, which has also been described as 'crab-claw markings' in traditional historical references.

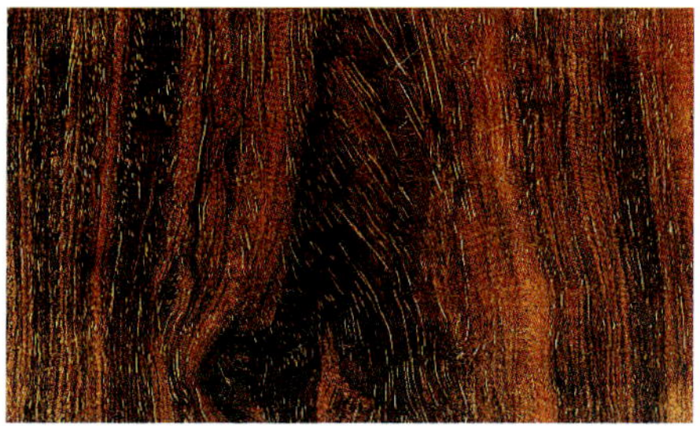

Fig. 12. 'Cow hair' zitan. *Detail from chest illustrated as catalogue item 79.*

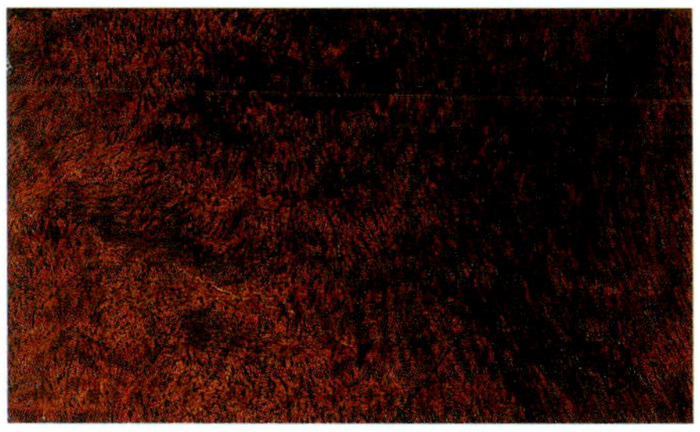

Fig. 13. 'Satin' zitan. *Detail from stool illustrated as catalogue item 5.*

• 'Satin' (*duanmian* 緞面) *zitan* (fig. 13) describes the lustrous quality of shimmering satin. Like satin, velvet, or the hologram embossed upon a credit card, a shimmering effect is produced when the surface is viewed from shifted positions. This effect results from the play of light reflecting from multi-faceted structure of the interlocked grain. In the radial surface orientation, this effect appears as a shimmering striped or ribbon pattern.

Fig. 14. 'Chicken blood' zitan. *Detail from balance stand illustrated as catalogue item 94.*

• 'Rooster blood' (*jixue* 雞血) *zitan* (fig. 14), sometimes called 'ox blood' (*niuxue*), bears deeply pigmented striations of dark and red-colored stripes. Because the material is usually found with relatively straight grain, it can be easily confused with *hongmu*.

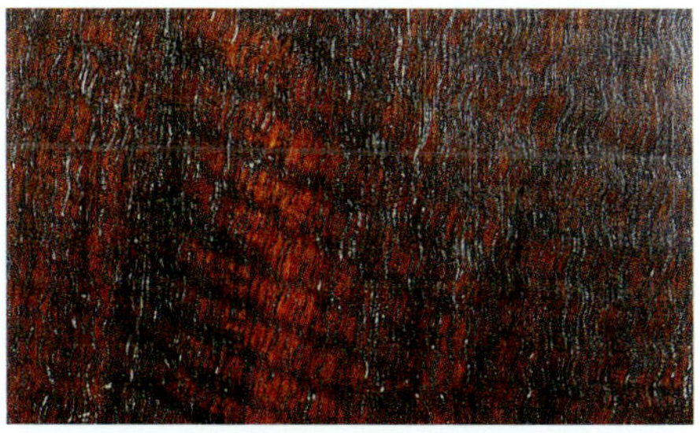

Fig. 15. Wavy-grain zitan. *Detail from box with sliding cover illustrated as catalogue item 73.*

• 'Burl-like (*douban* 豆瓣) *zitan*' (fig. 15) loosely describes various mottled, wavy, or curly figures, the causes of which are generally unknown. In some cases they appear to result from internal stresses that cause the cellular growth to develop a rippled, or washboard-like structure. When cut and polished to a flat plane, curly wave-like stripes appear across the grain that shimmer with reflected light. The intensity of this characteristic varies from that only visible under strong light, to a more distinct 'tiger-striped' (*huban*) figure. An example of the latter is strongly pronounced in the side panels of the small box illustrated as catalogue item 73.

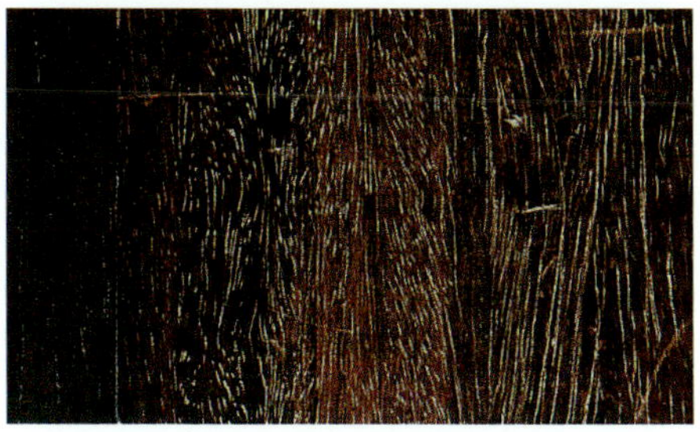

Fig. 16. Huali zitan. *Detail from chairs illustrated as catalogue item 19.*

• '*Huali* 花梨 *zitan*' (fig. 16) describes a material that, as Ma Weidu notes, "barely qualifies as a member of the generic *zitan* family, only to 'filling in to make up the numbers' (*lan yu chong shu*)."[37] The material is dense, and has an open pore structure that is relatively large. The tonality is grayish-black, and the luster appears dull when compared to superior types. The style of furniture with which it is commonly associated suggests a use that emerges during the late Qing and Republican periods. Such material is represented in the single stool and pair of chairs illustrated as catalogue items 3 and 19.

• *Chawu* 茶烏 describes an inferior ebony with brown-toned figuring, which according to Zhang Dexiang, may also be confused with *zitan*, but can be distinguished by its very fine pore structure.[38] Qu Dajun noted Hainan as a source for this timber along with characteristics of "strength without the brittleness [of a true ebony]", and "sinking in water".[39] Such material may also relate to Camagon (*maoshi mu*) which, according to early 20th century customs documentation, was also imported from the Philippines. It is further characterized as ebony-like, "brownish-black to black in color with reddish-brown steaks, very fine-grained, extremely hard, dense and durable, and rarely attacked by insects. Used by the Chinese for carvings, pipe-stems, fine quality furniture, chopsticks, and various ornaments".[40]

Notes:
See Bibliography for full citations.

[1] Evarts, Curtis. "A Pair of Zitan Southern Official's Hat Armchairs". *Journal of the Classical Chinese Furniture Society,* 1:4 (Autumn 1991), pp. 4-9.

[2] Schafer, Edward H., "Rosewood, Dragon's Blood, and Lac". *Journal of the Classical Chinese Furniture Society* 1:4 (Autumn 1991), p. 65.

[3] Shoso-in Office. *Treasures of the Shoso-in: North Section,* pls. 1, 5, 7. *South Section,* pls. 129, 131.

[4] David, Sir Percival. *Chinese Connoisseurship, The Ko Ku Yao Lun, The Essential Criteria of Antiquities,* p. 153.

[5] Tsai C. Y. *Zitan: The Most Noble Hardwood,* p. 9. Also see, Gu Yongqi. "Zitanmu de banzhi yu dingming" (The identification and terminology of *zitan*), p. 40.

[6] In personal communication with Tian Jiaqing, who has yet to discover such evidence.

[7] *Tian shui bing shan* (A Record of the Waters of Heaven Melting the Iceberg), in *Biji xiaoshou daguan,* Vol. 6:6, p. 3646.

[8] Ibid., p. 3643.

[9] Ibid., pp. 3643, 3646.

[10] Ibid., p. 3642.

[11] Wang Shixiang. *Connoisseurship of Chinese Furniture,* vol. 1, p. 16.

[12] Ibid., vol. 1, p. 148.

[13] Gao Lian. *Zunsheng bajian* (Eight Discourses on the Art of Living) (ca 1591), *juan* 15:52.

[14] Tu Long. *Qi ju ji fu qian.* (Notes on Utensils and Clothing for Daily Life) (pub. 1606), pp. 201, 205.

[15] Wen Zhenheng. *Zhangwuzhi* (Treatise on Superfluous Things), p. 247 (*juan* 7:1); p. 315 (*juan* 7:57).

[16] Wang Shixiang, ibid., vol. 1, p. 145.

[17] Qu Dajun. *Guangdong xinhua* (New Remarks on Guangdong), Hainan wenmu (Figured woods from Hainan), *juan* 25, p. 655.

[18] Wang Shizhen noted that he had recently heard of such an offer in *Fen Gan Yu Hua,* published in 1709. Trans. in Wang Shixiang, Ibid, vol. 1, p. 145.

[19] Wang Shixiang, ibid., vol. 1, p. 16.

[20] Zhu Jiajin. "Yongzheng nian de jiaju zhizao kao" (A Study of the Yongzheng Imperial Furniture Workshops) *Mingjia tan jianding,* pp. 353-363.

[21] Ibid., pp. 361-362, 356.

[22] Ibid., p. 355.

[23] Ibid., p. 354.

[24] Ibid., p. 360.

[25] Ibid., p. 359.

[26] Tian Jiaqing. "Zitan and Zitan Furniture," pp. 43-49.

[27] Tian Jiaqing, ibid., p. 45.

[28] Cao Xueqin. *Honglou Meng* (Dream of the Red Mansion), Chapter 3:46.

[29] Qian Yong. *Fuyuan conghua* (preface dated 1825). *Biji xiaoshuo da guan* 2:5, *juan* 12:7b.

[30] Ahern, Captain George P., *Compilation of Notes on the Most Important Timber Tree Species of the Philippine Islands,* pp. 81-82.

[31] Ibid., p. 97.

[32] China Guardian. *Classical Chinese Furniture,* October 27, 1999, Beijing, lots 1187, 1188.

[33] Wang Shixiang, ibid., vol. 1, p. 149.

[34] Gu Yongqi. "Zitanmu de banzhi yu dingming" (The identification and terminology of *zitan*), pp. 40-42.

[35] Ibid., p. 42.

[36] Ibid., p. 41.

[37] Ma Weidu. "Chenmu yongsu de zitan jiaju" (Elegant Zitan Furniture), p. 25.

[38] Zhang Dexiang. "Zhongguo gudai jiaju muzhi de shibie ji jianding yiyi" (The discernment and appreciation of antique Chinese furniture woods, Part 1), p. 38.

[39] Qu Dajun, ibid., pp. 654-55.

[40] Watson, Ernest. *The Principal Articles of Chinese Commerce,* p. 338.

The Zhouzhi Tradition and Inlaid Hardwood Furnishings of the Late Ming and Qing Dynasties

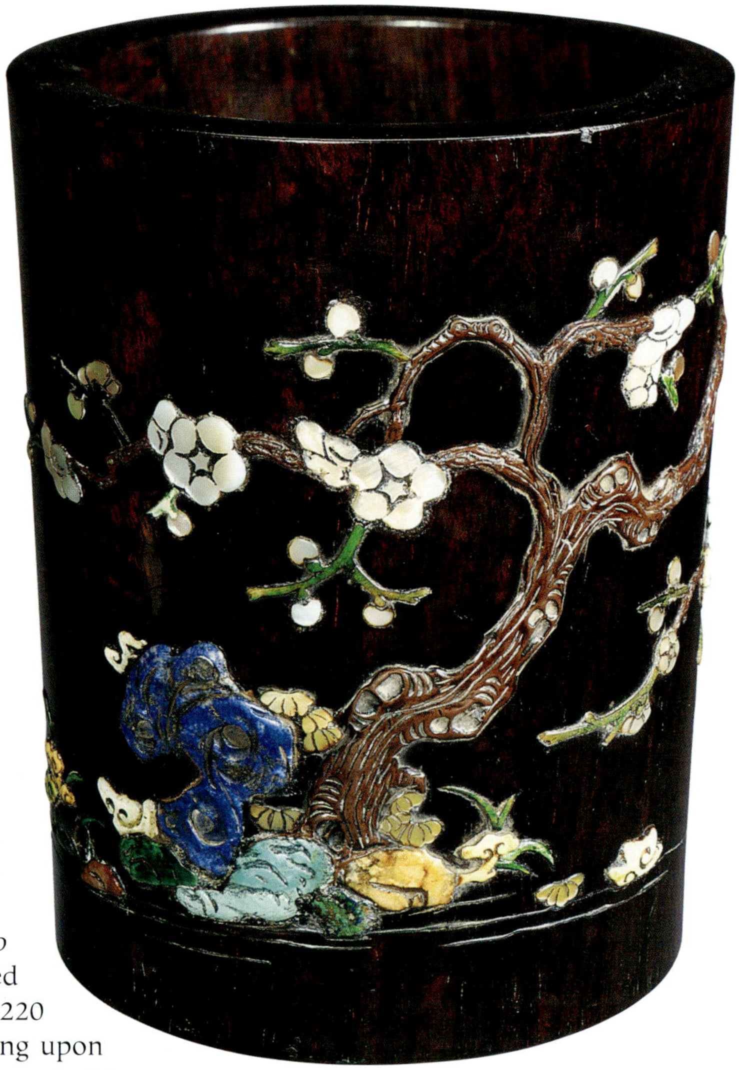

Fig. 1. Brushpot, zitan *with Zhouzhi inlay (cat. 117).*

The art of inlay is rooted in China's ancient past and has flourished throughout the ages. During the late Ming period, a new branch developed with techniques employing intricate, multi-colored inlays to compose painterly imagery upon lacquer and wood panels. According to tradition, this novel technique was created by a craftsman named Zhou Zhu 周柱; thereafter, the celebrated style of his works thrived throughout the Qing dynasty with increasing popularity under the hallmark of Zhouzhi 周製—an appropriation drawn from the style of 'Zhou's work (*zhi*)'. The group of inlaid-hardwood objects in the Liang Yi Collection (cat. 13, 59, 66, 77, 81, 117) provides an opportunity to investigate the history and characteristics of the Zhouzhi inlay tradition.

History

Zhouzhi, *babao*, and *baibao* are three Chinese terms that are somewhat interchangeably used to describe inlay work comprised of variegated semi-precious materials. What distinguished Zhouzhi works from earlier *-bao* traditions may have simply been the stature of artisan Zhou. Nevertheless, the term came to be more closely associated with artistic inlays of a compact, intricate style that were applied to hardwood and lacquer objects (fig. 1), and for which the terms *babao* and *baibao* are also shared today.

Qibao (seven treasures), a precursor to the terms *babao* (eight treasures) and *baibao* (one-hundred treasures), was used to describe the decorative inlays of Han dynasty (202 BCE-220 CE) sitting platforms.[1] Representations of court ladies sitting upon stools elaborately studded with semi-precious stones appear in Tang dynasty (618 CE-907 CE) paintings[2], and allusions to splendid furnishings decorated with glass, tortoise shell, and jade are also found amongst contemporary poetry from the period.[3] Tang-style game boards and musical instruments housed in Imperial Japanese collections since the 8th and 9th centuries also exhibit exquisite inlays with ivory, mother-of-pearl, tortoise shell, and exotic woods.[4] Moreover, their intricate geometric patterns, scrolling floral designs, and complex compositions—with hunting scenes, birds and wild animals, and camel-mounted travelers—rival the finest inlay work from the Ming and Qing periods.

During the Song dynasty (960-1279), a somewhat more painterly style of inlay decoration developed with compositions of landscapes, figures, birds and flowers set out with mother-of-pearl against a black lacquer ground. This technique continued to evolve through the Yuan (1276-1368) and Ming (1368-1644) periods. Luxurious inlaid-lacquer furnishings were markers of status, and were appraised at exceedingly high values.[5]

The adaptation of intricate, color-variegated inlays to compose yet more splendid imagery may be seen as a natural development from the duo-tone mother-of-pearl/lacquer traditions, and parallels the earlier development of polychrome *doucai* porcelain during the Chenghua period (1465-1487). By the Longqing period (1567-1573), *baibao* inlay was established as a highly esteemed technique which, according to the contemporary lacquer manual *Xiushu lu*, incorporated carved inlays of coral, amber, agate, pearl, tortoiseshell, mother-of-pearl, ivory, and rhinoceros horn to decorate lacquered panels with intricate and colorful compositions.[6] Today, a few rare examples are found in the Palace Museum, Beijing.[7] Of similar style is the inlaid lacquer brushpot illustrated in figure 2, with colorful scenes of flowers and birds displaying unique charm and naïve innocence that has taken leave in later works.

According to one account, the related Zhouzhi technique had developed under the patronage of the Prime Minister Yan Song during the Jiajing period (1522-1567) by the artisan Zhou Zhu, who was said to create colorful inlaid scenes for objects of lacquer as well as hardwood. However, nearly two hundred years had lapsed when the reputed Zhou Zhu/Yan Song relationship was recorded by the Qing artist/scholar Wu Qian (1733-1813). Wu further speculated upon the absence of original works, explaining that "upon Yan's disgrace, Zhou's works were all sequestered and entered the Palace; thus, extremely few pieces are still in circulation."[8]

The corruption case against Yan Song and son, Yan Shifan was well publicized. In 1562, they were stripped of illegally begotten wealth and personal properties. However, amongst the extraordinary published account of these properties—extending from vast real estate to embroidered clothing and jade hairpins—it is the absence of traditional Zhouzhi objects that raises some questions concerning Zhou's involvement with the Yan family and/or the original style of his inlay work. The few items that can be sifted out from the voluminously detailed inventory—brushpots of palmwood with ivory inlays[9], mirror stands of ivory-inlaid *huali*[10], and paper weights of jade-inlaid *huali*[11]—suggest a more elementary inlay style than is normally associated with the intricate, variegated inlays of traditional Zhouzhi works.

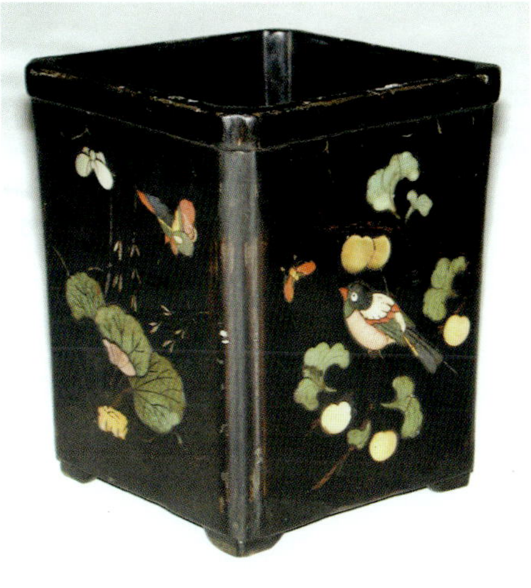

Fig. 2. Brushpot, lacquer with semiprecious inlays. Late 16th/early 17th century. 13 x 13 x 16cm H. Private collection.

The life of Zhou Zhu and the attributes of his work were undoubtedly embellished over the centuries; that his full name has been recorded with no less than five different, albeit similar homophonic variations indicates a legacy of oral tradition. The most immediate characterization of Zhou's inlay work is found in Gao Lian's *Eight Discourses on the Art of Living* (*Zunsheng bajian*) (pub. 1591). Hangzhou-based Gao extolled the early, unrivaled inlay work of Zhou; but without citing specific attributes,

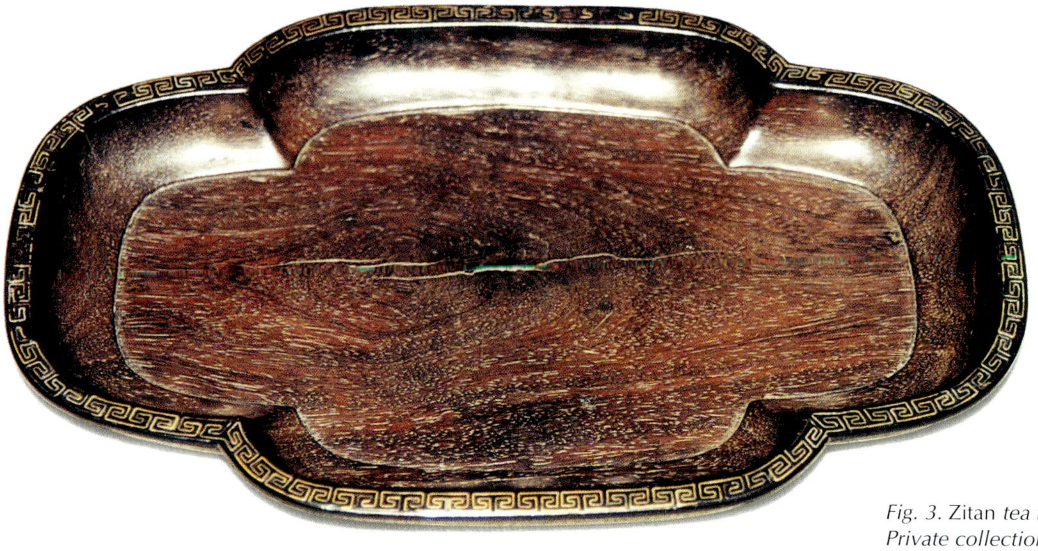

Fig. 3. Zitan tea tray with Wumen Zhou Zhu inscription. Private collection.

contrasted them against the marginally inadequate works that had since become commonplace:

> As for the various objects of *zitan* inlaid with carved, semi-precious jewels, they are not worth considering. Although they may be of short-term merit, the inlay work will not survive more than a few decades. Either because the adhesive lacquer will lose its strength, and/or because the small case (*xia*) will expand and contract with changes in humidity, I am afraid there is little chance of the inlays surviving repeated handling and polishing over time. The inlay work that is now widespread is distantly removed from inspired, early work of Zhou, and moreover, far below its value.[12]

In distinguishing later works in *zitan* from the early work of Zhou, Gao singles out the inadequately attached inlays. While the characteristics of 'the early work of Zhou' is here unspecified, such distinction can be seen to be related to different techniques used for inlaid lacquer and inlaid hardwoods. Inlays that were embedded with lacquer floated around them after they were set in place were secure and difficult to remove; those fit within cavities carved into hardwood panels and merely attached with adhesive were more likely to loosen and fall out.

Elsewhere in *Eight Discourses on the Art of Living*, Gao comments favorably on hardwood inkcases and book boxes inlaid with jade belt plaques or other archaic jade panels[13]—such uncompounded style is also contrasted to the intricacy of typical *Zhouzhi* works. A small *zitan* tea tray with a Zhou Zhu inscription may reflect an early work (fig. 3). The rim is inlaid with a simple key-fret pattern in gold wire, which was also used for the seal script inscription 'Wumen Zhou Zhu' (吳門周柱) (Zhou Zhu of Suzhou) on the underside (figs. 3ab). Interestingly, this inscription is more or less identical to that on the inkstone box in the National Palace Museum, Taipei, which also features variegated inlay work more characteristic of the Zhouzhi tradition.[14] That such inscriptions were copied is also not out of the question, as similar inscriptions found on other inferior works may well have been reproduced during the later vogue of fashion.[15]

Two *zitan* brushpots and a *zitan* vase published by Zhu Jiajin and

Fig. 3a. Details of inscription and inlaid gold-wire border.

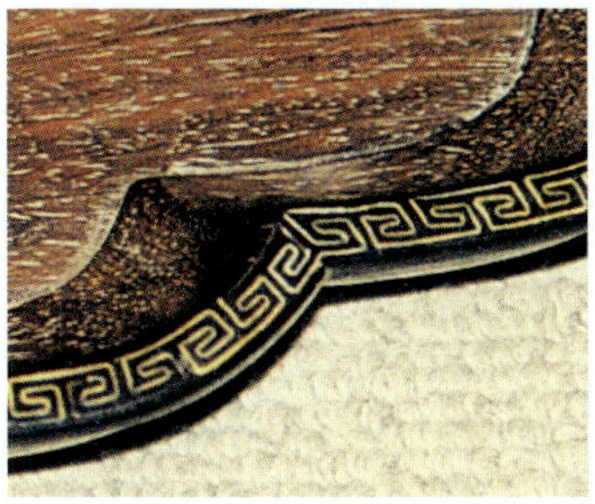

Fig. 3b. Details of inlaid gold-wire border.

Wang Shixiang also exhibit early inlay styles.[16] The rims of the two brushpots are bordered with colorful inlays of auspicious animals and flowers linked with scrolling patterns of silver wire. T-shaped key-fret patterns inlaid with silver wire border the rim and foot of the *zitan* vase, which was excavated from a Wanli period (1573-1620) tomb in the Shanghai region. Dating no later than the Wanli period and possibly somewhat earlier, these three examples also exhibit rather elementary inlay techniques relative to the intricate compositions that followed.

It was well into the 19th century when Qian Yong's (1784-1844) *Fuyuan conghua* (preface dated to 1825) fully detailed the characteristics and scope of what had by that time become known as Zhouzhi inlay work.

> The technique of Zhouzhi work is unique to Yangzhou. During the late Ming period a man named Zhou created the technique, which is the reason it is called Zhouzhi. The method variously employs gold, silver, gemstones, pearls, red coral, nephrite (*biyu*), Burmese jade (*feicui*), crystal, agate, tortoise shell, sea shell (*cheju*), lazurite (*qingjin*), turquoise, mother of pearl, ivory, amber and eagle wood. These are carved to render to compositions of landscapes, figures, trees, pavilions, flowers, birds, and animals, which are then inlaid into the surface of [*zi*]*tan*, [*hua*]*li*[*mu*], and lacquered objects. Large objects include screens, tables, chairs, windows, and bookcases; small ones, brushrests, teaware, inkstone cases, and small cases for books. With variegated colors beyond description, they are indeed rare novelties unknown in ancient times. During the Qianlong period, Wang Guoshen (1736-1795) and Lu Yingzhi were quite skilled at this technique. Nowadays [Lu Yingzhi's] grandson Kuisheng (1780-1850) is still quite talented.[17]

This passage is perhaps the most frequently cited reference to Zhouzhi work, and has been variously quoted to support late Ming attributions of similarly styled work. However, with further investigation into the subject, it becomes increasingly clear that Qian was also describing a technique that was in its zenith at the time of his writing during the early 19th century.

Yangzhou, traditionally associated with the Zhouzhi inlay tradition, was a major city north of Suzhou along the Grand Canal renown for its artisan traditions during the Ming and Qing periods. This historical city was devastated during the Qing overthrow, when the least of which was destroyed may have included many late Ming Zhouzhi works. Nevertheless, the spirited populace and its lively, artistic culture quickly recovered. The early Qing playwright/publisher Li Yu, who also amused himself with furniture design, went so far as to express the opinion that the furniture-making traditions of Yangzhou were superior to those of Suzhou.[18] Also renown for its excellence in jade-working, Yangzhou was the source of the most important Imperial commissioned works during the Qianlong period (1735-1976). The skills associated with polishing jades and other hardstones were also an essential component to the complex art of Zhouzhi inlay.

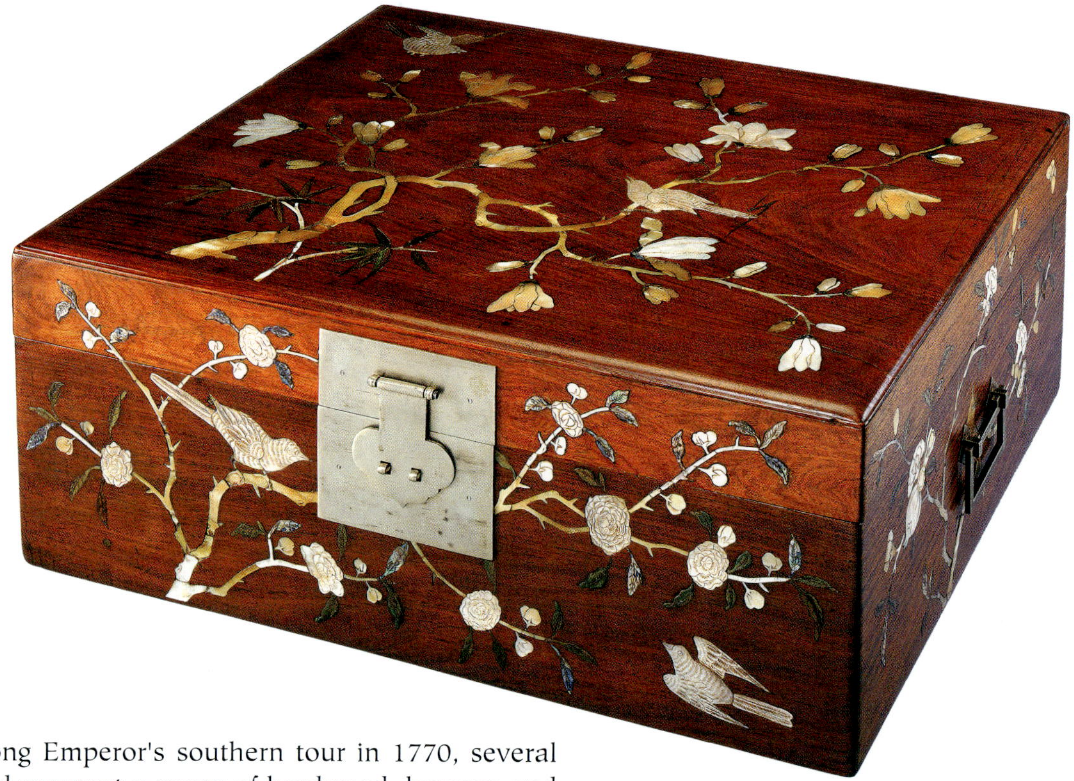

Fig. 4. Huanghuali *clothes chest with inlaid decoration (cat. 81).*

Shortly after the Qianlong Emperor's southern tour in 1770, several inlaid objects were included amongst a group of hardwood, lacquer, and bamboo furnishings sent to the Palace as tribute by the Yangzhou Salt Commissioner.[19] These objects were qualified with the variant hallmark of Zhouzhu 周鑄, which was also in use amongst Yangzhou craftsman at that time[20]—a term that provides the literal meaning of 'cast (*zhu*) by Zhou' and is also homonymous with Zhou's given name. Amongst these tribute items were table screens and hanging screens inlaid with poems and paintings, as well as an inlaid-*zitan* clothing chest (*zhuangxiang*)—the latter perhaps being of similar style to the inlaid-*huanghuali* example in the Liang Yi Collection (fig. 4).

The Lu family of Yangzhou was at the leading edge of inlaid lacquer work during the Qianlong, Jiaqing (1796-1820), and Daoguang (1821-1851) periods. Besides their renown skills in the lacquer arts, Lu Yingzhi [Ang] and his grandson Lu Dong [Kuisheng] (1780-1850) were both known to have produced extremely fine Zhouzhi work.[21] Qian Yong was a contemporary of Lu Kuisheng and native of nearby Wuxi, situated along the Grand Canal between Yangzhou and Suzhou. Thus, Qian was well positioned to be familiar with their inlay works as well as with the lore that had passed along through the successive generations of Zhouzhi craftsmen in Yangzhou who continued to develop and refine the art.

Qian Yong also recorded that on separate occasions during the years of 1814 and 1817 late in the Jiaqing reign, the Yangzhou Salt commissioner was asked to supply several hundred *zitan* objects with Zhouzhi inlay for various new constructions at the Yuanmingyuan Palace. Both small and large furnishings were produced. Large objects included display cabinets, floor-length friezes (*dizhao*), and some two hundred window screen panels each measuring over nine feet tall; the latter of which alone required the labor force of more than twelve hundred craftsman. These were only a trifling of the treasures that vanished when the Yuanmingyuan was sacked and burnt to the ground by Western aggressors in 1860. Notwithstanding, an inlaid-*zitan* frieze surrounding a kang bed in the Yangxin Pavilion at the Forbidden City may well be representative of the lost Yangzhou productions; the *zitan* panels are decorated with jades and other variegated *Zhouzhi*-style inlays.[22]

With thousands of craftsmen skilled in the refined art of inlay during the late 18th and early 19th centuries, it may be that the Qianlong, Jiaqing and Daoguang periods should be considered the Golden Age of *Zhouzhi* inlay. This well-established tradition also survived into more recent times. During the early 20th century, workshops in Beijing were actively producing inlaid-lacquer furniture that were sold as antiques.[23] In 1999, this author was shown several works of an elderly Beijing craftsman who was obviously quite skilled at embellishing old hardwood brushpots and boxes with inlays. While recently forced to retire due to the loss of his once steady hands, his skills have been passed on to his son. And according to the modern scholar Zhang Yan, artisans in the Yangzhou region have also maintained hard- and softstone inlay traditions.[24]

Characteristics of Zhouzhi Inlay Work

A. Forms and Decoration

While the 19th century writings of Qian Yong cite the application of Zhouzhi inlay to a wide range of large and small furnishings, those produced during the late Ming period appear to have been limited in scale. Wu Qian, an 18th century artist/scholar from Zhejiang province, recorded that Zhou's original work included 'various types of dressing cases (*lian*) and small boxes (*xia*).'[25] Similar small objects, including *zitan* or lacquer library cases and dressing cases decorated with inlays of jade, agate, and mother-of-pearl, were noted during the early years of the 17th century by Wen Zhenheng, who generally found such embellished works suitable only to the quarters of the opposite sex.[26] Gao Lian and Tu Long had also extolled the ink cases and book boxes made from precious woods with jade inlays.[27] It was small inlaid objects that were excavated from the Wanli period tomb in the Shanghai region which, aside from the *zitan* vase cited above, also included hardwood ink cases, rules, paperweights and vase that were variously inlaid with jade and mother-of-pearl.[28] Standing out in the absence of references to larger objects, these examples support the opinion that the late Ming Zhouzhi inlay works were generally of small scale.

It is not until the Qing period (1644-1912) when full-sized hardwood furniture with Zhouzhi-style inlay work appears with support in literary and visual reference materials. In a publication dated 1709, Wang Shizhen (1634-1711) cited the exorbitant price of 120 ounces silver offered in Beijing for a chair of *zitan* with semi-precious inlays.[29] That such rarified objects were more commonly found within the domain of the Imperial Palace is evidenced by the stools, tables and lamps decorated with multi-colored inlays that appear in early 18th century court paintings portraying within richly furnished apartments at the Yuanmingyuan of the Yongzheng prince's concubines (fig. 5).[30] Records from the Yongzheng period (1722-1735) Imperial workshops fail to mention any significant production of inlaid hardwood furniture. Notwithstanding, in 1726 a *huali* table was commissioned with specific instructions to decorate the frame members according to 'the exquisite patterns of inlaid silver and mother-of-pearl' that were found on a *huali* screen in one of the existing pavilions[31]—perhaps this was a rare, early work.

The application of Zhouzhi inlay to objects of larger scale is found on almost all types of furniture, including screens, cabinets, couch-bed railings, chairs, tables, washbasin stands, mirror stands and cosmetic boxes. The *huanghuali* eight-panel screen, illustrated as catalogue item 59, was decorated with inlays of auspicious flowers and antiquities. Unfortunately, as forecast by Gao Lian, most of the original inlays loosened and disappeared, leaving only hollowed cavities (fig. 6). During the early 19th century, Xie Kun (1784-1844) had also lamented the loss of inlays in Zhouzhi works, noting "....foolishly valuing the trade price of coral and gemstones, the real ones are removed and replaced with fakes, leaving the original object worthless."[32] Whether replaced or fallen out, the surviving inlays of the screen are of secondary quality materials including color-stained ivory and soft soapstone. Nevertheless, the substitution of artificially colored materials and imitation ceramics for semiprecious stone had already become common by the early 17th century, an economical practice recorded in annotations to the lacquer manual *Xiushilu*.[33]

Given the prevalence of poorly preserved inlay work, the inlaid-*huanghuali* wardrobes housed at the Metropolitan Museum of Art are deserving of special mention. Each of the eight door panels exhibits spectacular displays of flowers and birds executed in bold compositions and stunning colors, the effect which further contributes to balance the otherwise imposing

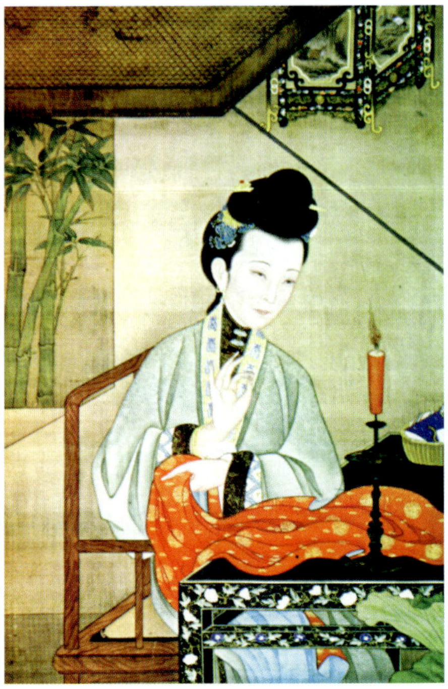

Fig. 5. Inlaid court furniture. Detail from Twelve Beauties of the Yuanmingyuan, *early Qing period. Palace Museum Collection, Beijing.*

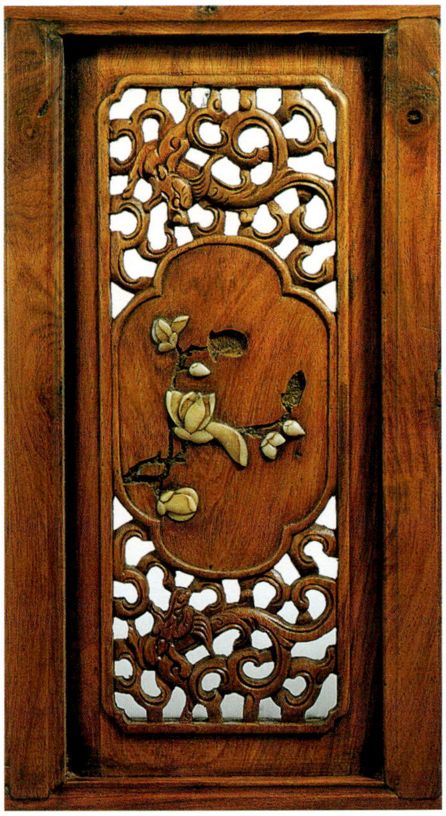

Fig. 6. Inlays and cavities from huanghuali *screen (cat. 59).*

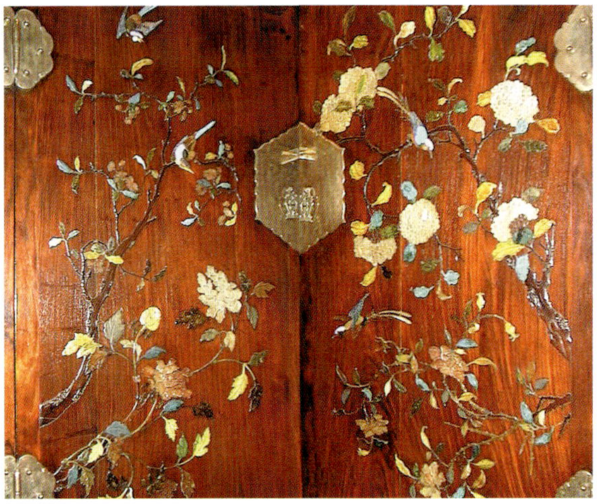

Fig. 7. Detail from wardrobes. Huanghuali *and semi precious inlays 17th century, Metropolitan Museum of Art, New York.*

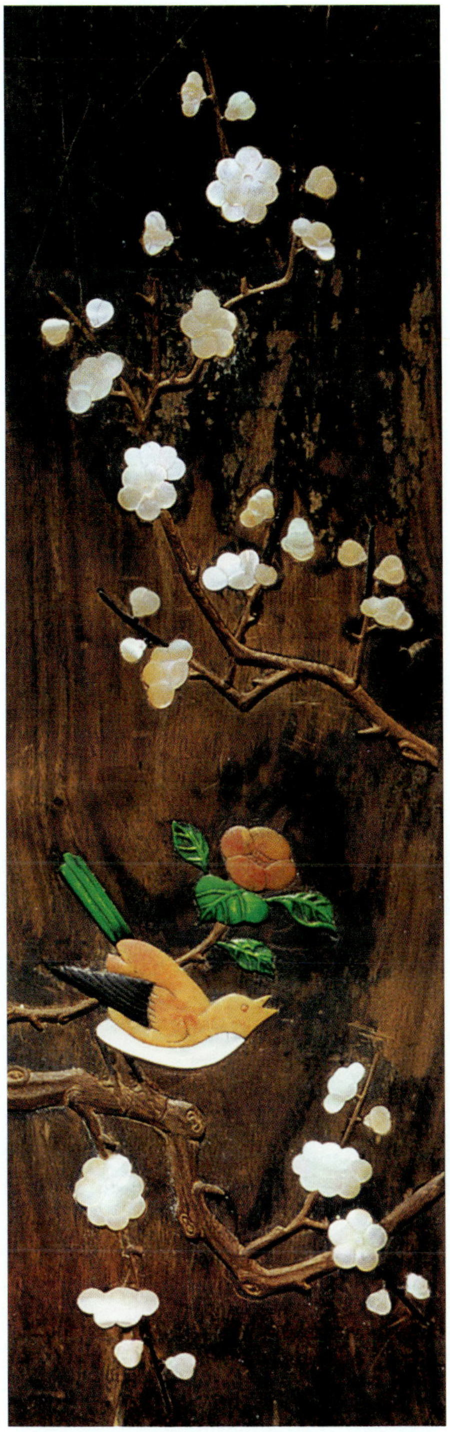

Fig. 8. Detail of backrest from a 17th huanghuali *yokeback armchair with restored inlays.*

stature of the colossal cabinets. Having survived in remarkable condition, the splendid inlay work is truly one of the masterpieces of the *Zhouzhi* tradition (fig. 7). A few lacquered cabinets with inlaid compositions surviving from the 17th century[34] suggest the period during which this genre had become established.

Backrests of chairs were also decorated with delightful compositions of birds and flowers, of which several Ming-style *huanghuali* examples have recently been published.[35] Figure 8 illustrates the backrest panel from a 17th century *huanghuali* yokeback armchair that was recently restored by a Tianjin artisan who refitted the crisply outlined cavities with variegated inlays carved from traditional materials. The backrests of the *huanghuali* chairs illustrated as catalogue item 13 were also discovered with similar hollowed patterns, and now exhibit an interim restoration with colorless mother-of-pearl.

Due to the intricacy of the inlay compositions as well as the expense of semi-precious materials, smaller chests, cases, brushpots were the most popular forms for such inlay work. Dressing cases for females were especially well-suited for such embellished decoration, which often carried symbolic associations related to the responsibility of bearing male children. Such is the *huanghuali* case illustrated as catalogue item 66, with the 'one-hundred boys' imagery on the two front panels; the lid is decorated with ripe pomegranates exposing their inner seeds, which form a rebus for the auspicious blessing 'Ripe pomegranates revealing one hundred seeds (boys)' (fig. 9).

According to Qian Yong, the several thousand inlaid-*zitan* objects commissioned for the Yuanmingyuan during the Jiaqing period were all decorated such with auspicious themes, including:

'Pomegranates revealing one hundred seeds (boys)' (*liu kai bai zi*)
'Ten thousand generations and everlasting spring' (*wan dai chang chun*)
'The immortal *lingzhi* promises longevity' (*zhi xian zhu shou*)
'Eternal longevity and everlasting spring' (*wan shou chang chun*)
'Shared autumn blessings' (*jiu qiu tong qing*)
'May your fortune increase with riches and sons' (*fu zeng gui zi*)
'Longevity promised by the flowering orchid' (*shou xian lan sun*)[36]

Small items with such decoration would have been especially appropriate as gifts or as receptacles for gift exchange. Such is the *huanghuali* case (cat. 77), which is somewhat more randomly decorated with miscellaneous precious treasures, auspicious flowers, and antiquities—emblematic of manifold blessings.

The finest example of Zhouzhi artistry in the Liang Yi Collection is the small inlaid-*zitan* brushpot (fig. 1). The compact composition depicts a plum tree with twisted, gnarled truck rooted in a rocky outcropping along a waterside embankment. *Lingzhi* and grasses appear freshly sprouted about, and a pair of butterflies flutter above the blossoming plum flowers.

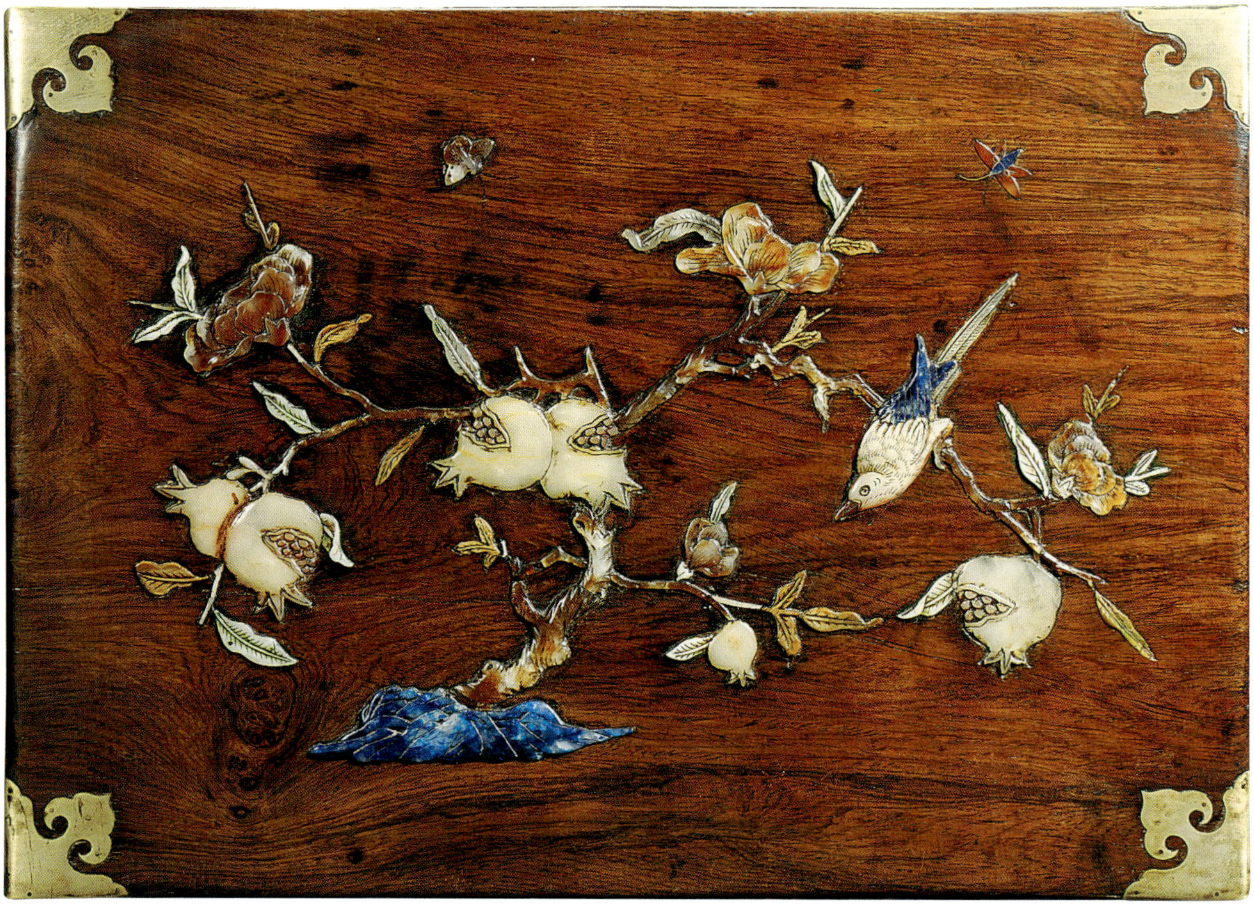

Fig. 9. Top of huanghuali *chest with pomegranates (cat. 66).*

New growth at the tip of the plum branches is realistically highlighted with a green hardstone, foretelling of fresh leaves yet to sprout. Silver wire was used to impart the smooth ripples of the watery foreground. While many of the inferior Zhouzhi works use artificial materials to achieve a multi-colored effect, these inlays are naturally colored gem stones, including emerald, malachite, turquoise, and coral. The imagery, which breathes with animation, is a delight to behold.

B. Materials

The variegated materials used for Zhouzhi inlays were selected not only for their intrinsic value, but moreover, for suitable color, pattern, and texture as elements subordinate to an overall composition. These materials can be broadly categorized as semi-precious stones, shells, bone, wood, metals, and other miscellaneous materials. Some of the more common materials are outlined below:

Semi-precious stone

- Agate (*manao*)

- Nephrite (*biyu*)
- Jadeite (*feicui*)
- Lapis lazuli (*qingjin*). Ultramarine or azure blue color of varying intensity, 5.5 hardness, and vitreous luster. Imported from India, Afghanistan, Pakistan, and Russia's Lake Baikal region.
- Rock crystal (*shuijing*). Transparent variety of quartz, colorless, hardness of 7, and found in China and Japan.
- Turquoise (*lusong*). Opaque, blue to green in color, waxy luster hardness of 6. Imported from Persia, Central Asia, India,
- Soapstone. Soft stone easily carved. Qingtian and Changhua stone from Zhejiang, and Shoushan stone from Fujian.

Shell

- Sea shell (*cheju*). Large sea shell from India, one of the seven precious treasures.
- Mother-of-pearl (*luotian*). Lining of oyster shell as well as other mollusks, or mussels that has an iridescent, lustrous lining. Found near Japan and South China.
- Pearls (*zhenzhu*).
- Coral (*shanhu*). Hard, red color. Imported from Japan

Bone

- Ivory (*xiangya*). Elephant tusk imported from Southeast Asia.
- Cow tooth, horn and bone (*niuya, niujiao, niugu*). Ivory substitutes.
- Rhinoceros horn (*xijiao*). Traditionally from Yunnan and south eastern Asia
- Tortoise shell (*daimao*). Soft pliable material. Much was imported from the Indian Ocean and the seas of the Malay Archipelago.

Wood

- Aloeswood/eaglewood (*chenxiang*). A wood with a high amount of resin, high density, very hard, dark reddish-brown or blackish-brown. Takes a very high polish, fragrant.
- *Hongmu*
- Boxwood (*huangyang*)
- *Jichimu*

Metal

- Gold wire
- Silver wire

Others

- Amber (*mila, hupo*). Fossilized resin from conifer trees, hard brittle 2.0-2.5 hardness, semi-translucent, generally pale yellow in color, ranging from orange red, to brownish red. Very brittle when cold and is usually heated before carving.
- Coconut shell
- Glass
- Porcelain

C. Technique

Zhouzhi inlay work demanded artistic skills in composition as well as the ability to handle a wide range of materials. Due to the general tendency towards specialization, few individual artisans may have possessed such a full arsenal of skills. It is more likely that most productions were accomplished in closely supervised workshops, with those skilled in the art of composition managing a team of specialized craftsmen.

Skilled painters sometimes worked in concert with inlay workshops to create artistic designs, as was the case for the Lu family workshops in Yangzhou.[37] Artisans also relied upon material amongst the copious illustrated publications and manuals that appeared during the 17th century. Amongst these, the *Mustard Seed Garden Painting Manual* (*Jiezi yuan huazhuan*) included step-by-step compositional techniques, with illustrations of perched and flying birds, flowers, plum blossoms, grasses[38], any of which could easily have been adapted for inlay patterns.

After a design was created, suitable raw materials were selected according to their size, color, pattern, and texture as elements in the overall composition. These were then worked to the required profiles. The shaping and polishing of hard stones required the use of abrasive tools associated with jade-working, while softer materials like soapstone, ivory, and wood, were carved with sharp-edged tools. The individual pieces were shaped to protrude or fit flush with the surface according to design, and were finished with fine incised detailing and smooth polishing. The profile of the finished inlays was then accurately traced onto the surface of the object, which was then carved with cavities into which the inlays were snuggly fit and adhered with glue.

The Zhouzhi inlay tradition is one of the outstanding achievements in the art of inlay. It draws from painting traditions the art of composition and theme to combine with the highly skilled craftsmanship of specialized trades working with precious materials. While the difficulty of coordinated effort and complicated technique is reflected in the fragility and short life of these creations, those that have survived reveal an unparalleled art.

Notes:
See Bibliography for full citations.

1 Cui Rongxue. *Zhongguo jiaju shi-zuoju bian*, p. 61

2 Lin, Lina. *Special Exhibition of Furniture in Paintings*, 1996, p. 77.

3 Handler, Sarah. "The Chinese Screen: Movable Walls to Divide, Enhance, and Beautify," *Journal of the Classical Chinese Furniture Society* 3:3 (Summer 1993), p. 12.

4 *Shoso-in Office. Treasures of the Shoso-in*: The North Section, pls. 1-8, 55-60, 64-74.

5 Such were the stools, chairs and tables confiscated from Shen Wansan, a wealthy Suzhou landowner during early Ming period; see David, Sir Percival. *Chinese Connoisseurship, The Ko Ku Yao Lun, The Essential Criteria of Antiquities*, pp. 148-49. Detailed assessments from properties confiscated from the fallen prime minister Yan Song in 1562 also demonstrate that mother-of-pearl inlaid furniture was of far greater value than other types; see Clunas, Craig. "Furnishing the Self in Early Modern China", pp. 24-25.

6 Wang Shixiang. *Xiushilu jiehshou* (An introduction to the Ming dynasty lacquer manual *Xiushilu*), p. 151.

7 Zhu Jiajin, Xia Gengqi, eds. *Zhongguo qiqi quanji: 5 Ming*, pls. 188, 198, 199.

8 Watson, William, ed. *Chinese Ivories from the Shang to the Qing*, 1984, p.128.

9 *Tian shui bing shan*, 6:6, pp. 3643-3646.

10 Ibid., p. 3643.

11 Ibid., pp. 3643, 3646.

12 Gao Lian. *Zunsheng bajian* (Eight Discourses on the Art of Living), *juan* 14:76a.

13 Ibid., *juan* 15:51b, 53b-54a.

14 Chi Jo-hsin. "Zhou Zhu yu Zhouzhi gongyi" (Chou Chu and the Craftsmanship of Chou Chih works), p. 676, figs. 1-2.

15 This author was recently shown another small *zitan* tea tray with Zhouzhi inlay work of inferior quality and with a gold-wire inlaid seal sealscript inscription also reading 'Wumen Zhou Zhu'.

16 Zhu Jiajin and Wang Shixiang. *Zhongguo meishi quanji* Vol.11 *Gongyi meishu bian*, pls. 67-69.

17 Qian Yong. *Fuyuan conghua* (preface dated 1825). Biji xiaoshuo da guan 2:5, *juan* 12:7ab.

18 Wang Shixiang, *Connoisseurship of Chinese Furniture*, vol. 1, p. 23.

19 Zhang Yan. *Yangzhou qiqi shi* (History of Yangzhou Lacquerware), pp. 122-126.

20 Ibid., p. 214.

21 Ibid., pp. 90, 109-119 discusses the Lacquer Workshop of the Lu family.

22 Palace Museum Ancient Architecture Department. *The Illustrated Catalogue of the Architecture and Decoration of the Imperial Palace: Interior Design*, p. 278.

23 Lee, Yu-kuan. *Oriental Lacquer Art*, pp. 340-341.

24 Zhang Yan, ibid., pp. 216-17.

25 Chi Jo-hsin, ibid., p. 665.

26 Wen Zhenheng. *Zhangwuzhi* (Treatise on Superfluous Things), pp. 311, 315. According to Wen, library cases and dressing cases made of *zitan* or lacquer and variously inlaid with jade, agate, and/or mother of pearl were inelegant and to be avoided.

27 Tu Long. *Wenfang qiju qian*. (Notes on Utensils for the Studio) (published 1606), p. 205.

28 Shanghai shi wenwu guanli weiyuanhui. "Shanghai Baoshan Ming Zhu Shoucheng fufu hezang mu." *Wenwu* 1992:5, pp. 63-65, pl. 5, figs. 5-6.

29 Wang Shifen, Fen Gan Yu Hua. Trans. in Wang Shixiang, *Connoisseurship of Chinese Furniture*, vol. 1, p. 145.

30 Tian Jiaqing. *Classic Chinese Furniture of the Qing Dynasty*, figs. 1, 4, 8-11.

31 Zhu Jiajin. "Yongzheng nian de jiaju zhizao kao" (A Study of the Yongzheng Imperial Furniture Workshops). *Mingjia tan jianding*, p. 354.

32 Xie Kun. *Jinyu suosui*, p. 233.

33 Wang Shixiang. *Xiushilu jiehshou*, p. 151.

34 Ellsworth, Robert Hatfield. *Chinese Furniture: One Hundred Examples from the Mimi and Raymond Hung Collection*, pl. 78. Also see Clunas, Craig. *Chinese Furniture*, p. 93.

35 Berliner, Nancy. *Beyond the Screen: Chinese Furniture of the 16th and 17th Centuries*, pl. 10; National Museum of History. *Splendor of Style: Classical Furniture from the Ming and Qing Dynasties*, p. 86; Nicholas Grindley, pl. 8. Yip Shing-Yiu and Grace Wu Bruce. *Chan Chair and Qin Bench: The Dr. S. Y. Yip Collection of Classic Chinese Furniture II*, pl. 3.

36 Qian Yong, ibid., p. 7b.

37 Zhang Yan, ibid., p. 110.

38 Sze, Mai-Mai. *The Tao of Painting: A Study of the Ritual Disposition of Chinese Painting.*

Elegant Empty Containers: Hardwood Brushpots

The brushpot varies in its capacity and style, and was produced from a wide range of materials including bamboo, ivory, wood, lacquer, porcelain, bronze and precious stone. Its functional use was generally associated with the desktop where it served as practical container for brushes and hand scrolls; as a decorative base stand, it also housed those loftier implements like horsehair dusters, peacock feathers, and *ruyi* scepters. The extent of fine, hardwood brushpots in the Liang Yi Collection affords the opportunity to examine the history and characteristics of these uniquely Chinese stationery accessories which, as elegant empty containers, also came to be viewed as works of art.

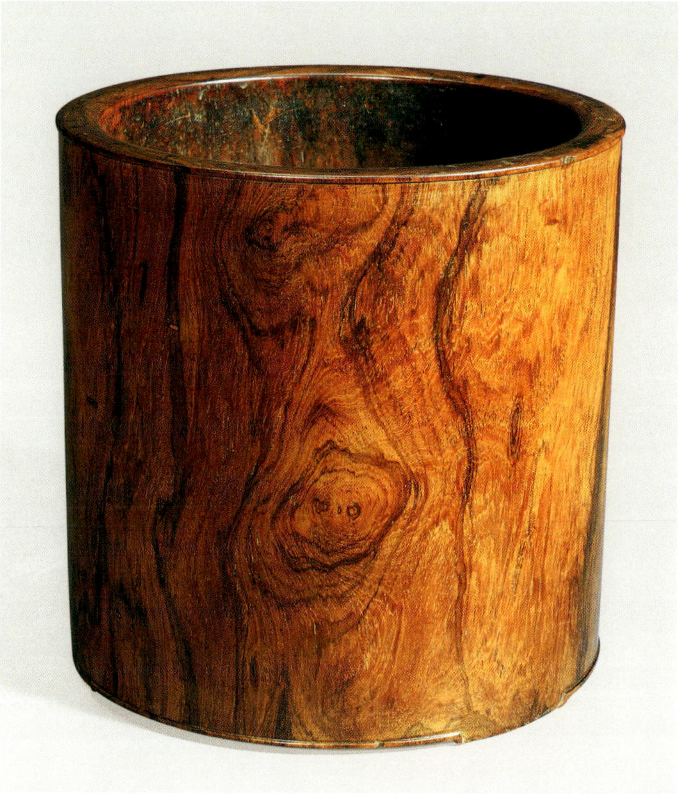

Fig. 1. Huanghuali *brushpot (cat. 106)*

The primary function of the brushpot was to hold brushes in an inverted position to protect their delicate tips. Prior to the use of hollowed, cylindrical vessels, brush holders existed as a small rack. Such is the form noted by the Southern Song (1127-1279) connoisseur, Zhao Xigu (1170-1242):

> Use ivory or ebony to make a small stand with four holes in the top and a pedestal base. Then, after rinsing, the inverted brush is inserted into the stand. Any remaining moisture moves downward towards the base, and the tip of the brush is prevented from harm.[1]

Similar brush stands—patterned with an ancient rack pattern that can be traced to the Shang dynasty (ca 1600-1000 BCE)[2]—appear in numerous Song (960-1279) and Yuan (1271-1368) paintings as writing and painting table accessories (figs. 2a-c).

Such brush racks gradually faded out of use during the Ming dynasty. During the late 16th century Gao Lian attempted to revive the tradition by extolling its archaic form, which at that time was termed *bichuang* 筆牀.[3] Gao also elaborated upon the 'brush screen' (*biping* 筆屏), which was

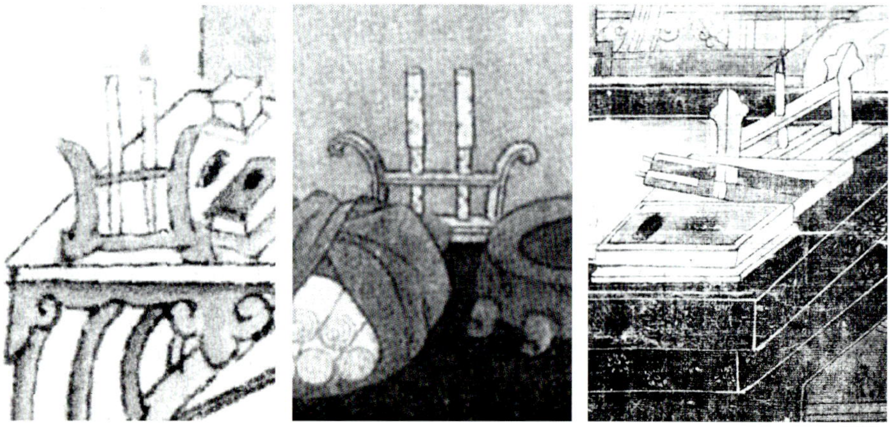

Fig. 2. Early brush racks. left) Detail from Odes of the State of Pin, *Anonymous, Southern Song dynasty; right) Brush rack. Detail from* Eighteen Scholars of the Tang, *Attributed Liu Songnian, Song-Yuan periods, National Palace Museum, Taipei. center) Brush rack. Detail from album leaf* Whiling Away the Summer Beneath a Locust Tree, *Anonymous, Song dynasty.*

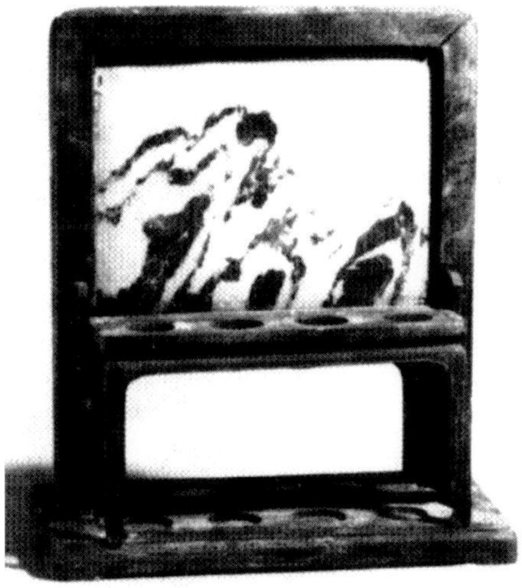

Fig. 3. Brush screen. Zitan *and Dali marble, 17 x 8 x 20 cm H, Wanli period (1573-1620). Excavated from tomb of Zhu Shoucheng and spouse at Shanghai, Baoshan. After* Wenwu *1992:5.*

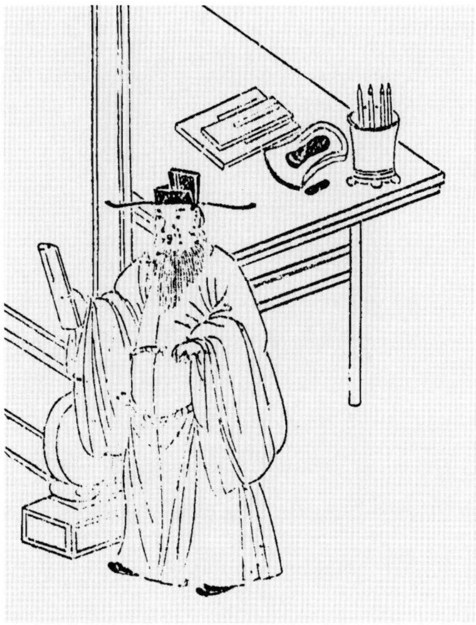

Fig. 4. Brushpot with base. Detail from woodcut illustration to Yangzheng tujie. *Illustration by Ding Yunpeng. Ming, Wanli period, 1594.*

constructed like a small table screen with a brush rack mounted to one side and accordingly, had once been popular at the Song Imperial court.[4] A rare example of this type, made from *zitan* with a Dali marble panel, was excavated from a Wanli (1573-1620) period tomb (fig. 3).[5] However, late Ming attitudes concerning the inelegant style of both types can be found in the writings of Wen Zhenheng[6], and Gao's efforts to preserve the outdated tradition were ignored.

Thus, the 'old-fashioned' racks gave way to the cylindrical brushpot which, by the late Ming period, had come into widespread use. From where and when this new form emerged is uncertain. Examples in the Palace Museum Collection fashioned from *zitan* and carved red lacquer have been attributed as early as the mid-Ming period.[7] However, discussions of the subject in traditional texts on connoisseurship do not emerge until the late 16th and early 17th centuries, which is also when brushpots simultaneously appear with frequent depictions in paintings and book illustrations. An early rendering found in a mid-16th century painting depicts a brushpot of rare quatrefoil form seated upon a base, the style of which is related to the lobed *huanghuali* brushpot with integrated base in the Liang Yi Collection (see cat. 99 and accompanying illustration).

Brushpots with base stands frequently appear in late Ming paintings and book illustrations (fig. 4), and the Liang Yi Collection is fortunate to include a few extant examples of this rare, early style (cat. 97-100). This period/style relationship is further supported by examples at the Palace Museum, Beijing[8] as well as an excavated piece from a Wanli period tomb at Baoshan, Shanghai (fig. 5).[9] The excavated piece—a small *zitan* brushpot molded with a wide, flat beading around the rim and fitted with a footed, convex-molded base—can be compared to one of remarkably similar form in the Liang Yi Collection (fig. 6), the latter with a variant-styled square base with *kunmen* openings. A cylindrical form with a square-base, which plays on the cosmological theme 'round Heaven above, square Earth below', is also evident in catalogue item 100. Brushpots that have been shaped with base moldings of substantial profile may also simulate this early style (cf. cat. 102, 105, 118).

The discourses of Gao Lian (pub. 1591)[10] and Tu Long (pub. 1606)[11] extolled brushpots of speckled bamboo, a rarified species whose surface is patterned with finely delineated spots of reddish-color. Tu Long furthermore noted, "when inset in a lipped base made from *zitan* or *wumu* they are exceptionally elegant—inserting anything else is unnecessary!" Here is early inference to the brushpot as a work of art. While extant brushpots of speckled bamboo are quite rare, examples of carved bamboo have survived from the late Ming period.[12] The naturally hollow form of bamboo easily lent itself for such use; furthermore, the modest material, which was full of virtuous connotations, was a traditional favorite amongst the literati.

Wen Zhenheng, heir to a family steeped in literati traditions, also critiqued the subject in *Zhangwu zhi*, a work that was completed circa 1620. Wen echoed the earlier praise of speckled-bamboo brushpots, and further cited those of the coir palm (*pinglu*) as being amongst the most beautiful.[13] In 1562, nearly sixty years earlier, it was brushpots of palm, ivory, and cowhorn that had been amongst the luxurious holdings confiscated from the fallen minister Yan Song.[14] It may well be that the earliest brushpot materials were those with naturally hollow or pithy cores, which were readily fashioned into empty containers.

Wen also pronounced, "....*Zitan*, *wumu*, and *huali* [brushpots] are also acceptable, but avoid the eight-sided ones of foliated style..."[15] These remarks coincide with the popular fashion for tropical hardwoods that spread by the 17th century. Pithy-cored *zitan* would have naturally suggested itself as a brushpot material. Moreover, the rich patterning of *huanghuali* was best revealed in the smooth, tangential surfaces of the cylindrical brushpot, where the prized imagery of landscapes and ethereal ghost faces was fully manifest (fig. 1). Wen's dismissal of those shaped in a foliated style also provides a period benchmark for this type. A related example in the Liang Yi Collection is also further enhanced with *chi* dragons and auspicious flowers that exhibit decorative characteristics of the late Ming period (fig. 7). Wen's further comments on the use of inlaid bronze and various types of porcelain points to the expanding range of brushpot materials.

The 18th century brought about tendencies toward refinement and imitation in brushpot styles—tendencies that are also reflected throughout the decorative arts. Yongzheng (1723-1735) and Qianlong period (1735-1796) porcelains, for instance, display a marked refinement of decoration when compared to those of the preceding Kangxi period (1662-1722). Such corollary can perhaps be found in the *huanghuali* brushpot with finely beaded lip and base (fig. 1) and that of unusual, bellied form (cat. 105), both of which mirror developed refinement. The art of imitation reached unprecedented heights during the Qianlong and Jiaqing (1796-1820) periods in the faux creations made from precious jade, lacquer, and porcelain that simulated more common material. Such imitative style is also reflected in the bamboo- (cat. 120) and wicker-style brushpots (fig. 8) that were fashioned from *huanghuali* wood.

Of magnificent 18th century Imperial style is the *zitan* brushpot carved with dragons writhing through clouds and waves (cat. 122). A *zitan* brushpot with *huanghuali* base illustrated by Wang Shixiang and Zhu Jiajin exhibits a similar decorative theme, but is clearly of an earlier style—attributed not later than the Jiajing period (1522-1567) (see accompanying illustration cat. 122).[16] Such work may well have provided inspiration for the example in the Liang Yi Collection, whose dragon decoration is more typical of the mid-Qing period, and whose carving

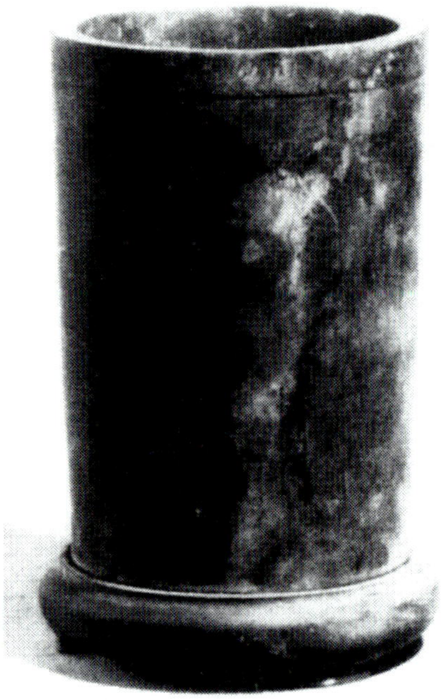

Fig. 5. Brushpot. Zitan, *15.7 diameter x 20 cm H, Wanli period (1573-1620). Excavated from the tomb of Zhu Shoucheng and spouse at Shanghai, Baoshan. After* Wenwu *1992:5.*

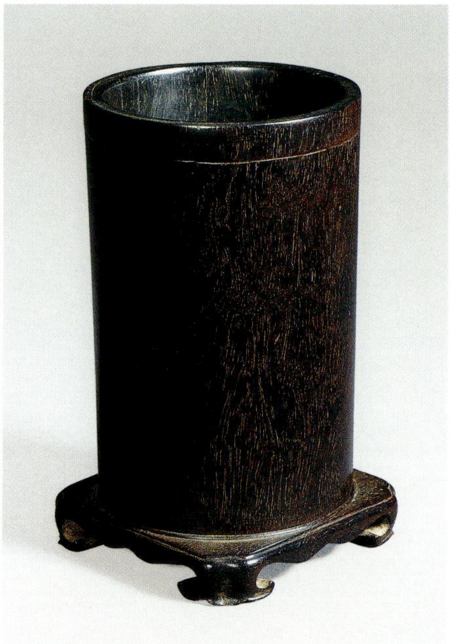

Fig. 6. Brushpot. Zitan, *17th century. Liang Yi Collection (cat. 97).*

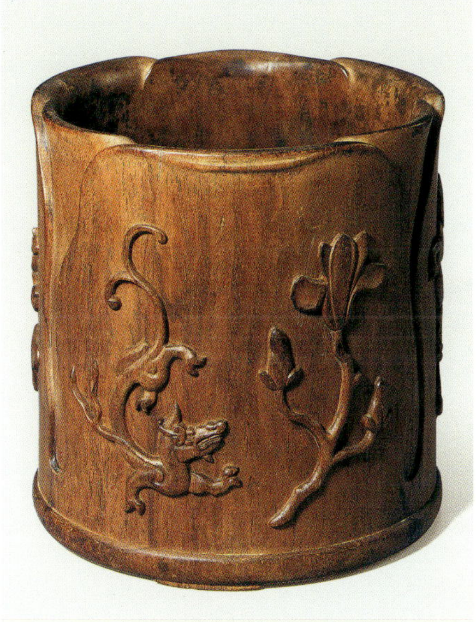

Fig. 7. Foliate-style brushpot. Huanghuali, *17th century. Liang Yi Collection (cat. 118).*

technique displays exceptionally fine relief work.

Hardwood brushpots were also carved in a fine, low relief style that was typical of bamboo carving. Such is the example illustrated as catalogue item 121, which depicts a rather untraditional scene wherein an inebriated lady composes herself upon a garden bench; complementary lines of poetry incised in running script read "Drunken Repose in the Peony Garden."

While brushpots are commonly associated with the male dominated literati culture, women skilled in the arts of the brush also required their use. A passage from the semi-fictional, 18th century novel *Hong Lou Meng* describes the room of a teenage girl who was so inclined:

> A large *huali* table with a Dali marble panel stood at the center of the room and was heaped with calligraphy manuals, and scattered with dozens of inkstones, brushrests, and a small forest of writing brushes stood in an array of variously styled brushpots and scrollpots (*bihai* 筆海).[17]

The style and decoration of brushpots belonging to women, whose desk accessories are regularly depicted in illustrative art (cf. supplementary woodcuts cat. pls. 106, 113, 115), may also reflect the strong gender distinctions that existed during the Ming and Qing periods.[18]

Various types of inlay were also applied to brushpots, including mother-of-pearl, ivory, wire, as well as the Zhouzhi type of variegated semi-precious materials. A particularly fine example of the latter is found in the Liang Yi Collection (cat. 117). Its animated imagery depicts a plum tree rooted in a rocky outcropping along a waterside embankment with two butterflies fluttering above an outstretched branch with blossoming plum flowers. The charming style of this decoration along with its auspicious rebuses for longevity and immaculate beauty may well reflect a material culture that existed for women cultivated in the arts.

Notwithstanding such association, the above-mentioned *zitan* brushpot carved with dragons—of probable Ming period Imperial provenance—was also decorated with a band of semi-precious inlays around the rim.[19] And of refined, scholarly air are the rarified *zitan* brushpots that occasionally appear with fine key-fret or scrolling-grass patterns inlaid with silver, gold, or bronze wire around the rim,[20] a decorative technique also common to the late Ming period.[21]

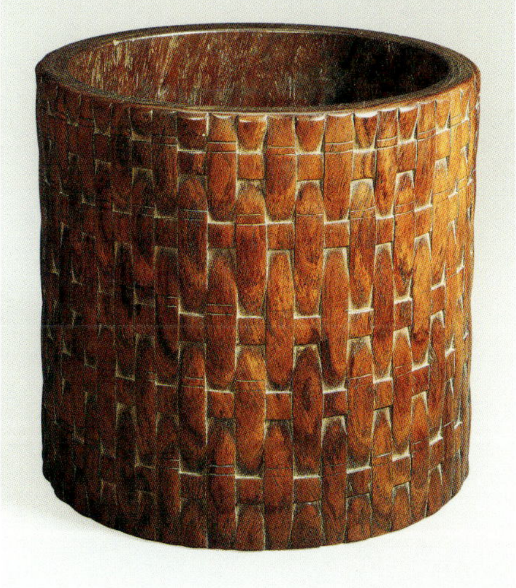

Fig. 8. Wicker-style brushpot. Huanghuali, *17th century. Liang Yi Collection (cat. 119).*

Brushpots contrived as naturalistic tree trunks appear with notable frequency in paintings and woodcut illustrations dating from the mid- to late Qing period, from which era many examples of such style also likely date. The source of this tradition, however, had begun much earlier, and by the Song dynasty, stands and chairs were contrived from tree trunks, roots or rattan. These earliest objects reflected Buddhist and Daoist ideals, which rejected materialism and strove towards humility through natural simplicity. By the late Ming period, fashionable objects of naturalistic style had become mingled with those of refined and leisurely lifestyles. Relative to brushpots

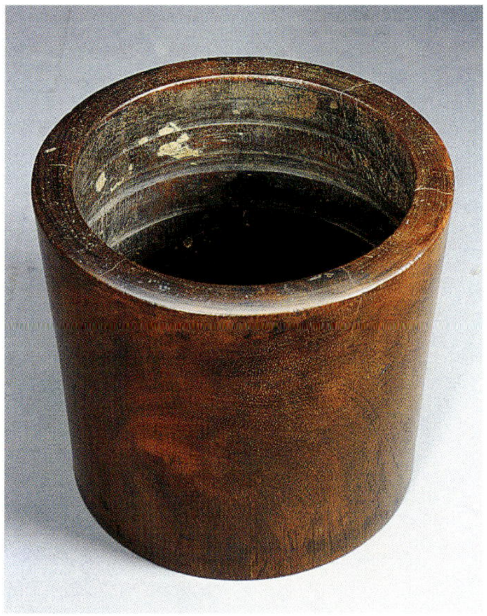

Fig. 9. Tool marks left by lathe turning on the interior walls of tielimu *brushpot (cat. 104).*

that are finely carved as tree trunks, an early tradition is evident in bamboo and hardwood examples bearing late Ming and early Qing inscriptions.[22] The small *zitan* brushpot in the Liang Yi Collection (cat. 98) is shaped as a smooth trunk with branches of pine, bamboo, and prunus clinging in relief, of which the decorative theme and style both exhibit characteristics typical of 17th century. The imitation of knubby pine tree trunks was also a popular theme for hardwood brushpot carvers (cf. cat. 114, 115, 116). Emblematic of longevity, steadfastness, and ability to endure under adverse conditions, the noble pine was also a favorite of the literati.

Poetic verse also was used to enhance the surface of brushpots and to display the skills of the artisan carver. Favorite themes amongst the literati included the idealization of the unfettered recluse, songs of praise to the virtue of wine, and romances to the glorious past. Such are literary-inspired inscriptions on the *tieli* wood (cat. 104) and *zitan* (cat. 107) brushpots in the Liang Yi Collection. Both feature calligraphic stanzas in clerical script that are skillfully incised, and the application of bronze-toned pigment further has created a pleasing, subtle contrast.

Whether at an owner's request or due to shortage of material and changes in fashion, the later reshaping or enhancement of old brushpots was also practiced. In some cases, the reworked surfaces of an otherwise uninteresting brushpot improved its marketability—a situation that can be especially difficult to distinguish in the case of an original work that has been over cleaned. An original work should reveal uniform patination (aged appearance due to exposure, wear and damage) on interior as well as exterior surfaces. Relief or incised carving that appears without the inevitable chipped or softly worn edges resulting from several generations of handling with periodic negligence should be suspect.

During the late Qing period, tea caddies (cf. cat. 93) were also resourcefully produced from older brushpots with slight modifications and added decorative wings, lid, and handle. These add-ons were often selected from alternate material and/or exhibit different qualities of patination.

Relative to its production, the typical hardwood brushpot of cylindrical form starts from a short section of a tree trunk or branch. The use of primitive wood-turning lathes is occasionally evident by traces of tool marks on inner walls and/or base, which appear as ring-shaped grooves that were not entirely removed with polishing (fig. 9). The interior was quickly hollowed out by the spinning action of the blank section against a sharp tool, which also yielded a uniform cylindrical form. It is likely that brushpot-turners initially produced a crudely hollowed blank with thick walls and base which, after undergoing a period of drying and reestablishment of equilibrium, underwent a secondary turning to achieve a final shape and fine polish. Additional carving, incising, and or inlay work was accomplished by specialists.

The bottom of the pot varies according to the condition of the material. Some have a solid bottom that is simply shaped from the original timber; others are fitted with a small plug inserted at the center; for some, the bottom is comprised of an entirely separate piece that is inset, or exists as a separately shaped base unit. The principal reason for these various methods is related to the condition at the center of the timber. As a tree develops, its central core often decays into a pithy material. This phenomenon occurs to a greater or lesser extent according to species of tree (see fig. 7, p.16). There is an old saying about *zitan* that 9 parts of 10 are hollow (*shi tan jiu kong*)[23]; however, varieties of *zitan* are also found with solid cores. While some value is placed upon a brushpot with a solid timber bottom, this characteristic should be considered secondary to primary aesthetic characteristics. In fact, the earliest use of an independent base may well have been associated to techniques that only later developed to preserve the fragile end grain at the bottom of the brushpot.

Notes:
See Bibliography for full citations.

[1] *Dongtian qinglu*, (Song, mid 13th century). Huang Binhong, Deng Shi eds. *Meishu Congshu*, Vol. 5, p. 255.

[2] Ecke, Gustav. *Chinese Domestic Furniture*, p. 11, fig. 12.

[3] Gao Lian. *Zunsheng bajian* (Eight Discourses on the Art of Living) (ca 1591), *juan* 15:42ab.

[4] Gao Lian, ibid, *juan* 15:42b.

[5] Shanghai shi wenwu guanli weiyuanhui. "Shanghai Baoshan Ming Zhu Shoucheng fufu hezang mu." *Wenwu* 1992:5, pp. 63-65.

[6] Wen Zhenheng. *Zhangwu zhi* (Treatise on Superfluous Things). 12 juan. Compiled ca. 1620. Annotated edition by Chen Zhi, *juan* 7, p. 257.

[7] Zhu Jiajin and Wang Shixiang. *Zhongguo meishi quanji* Vol. 11. Gongyi meishu bian, pl. 67. Zhu Jiajin and Xia Gengqi, eds. *Zhongguo qiqi quanji: 5 Ming*, pl. 54.

[8] Zhu Jiajin and Xia Gengqi, eds. ibid., pl. 145. Zhu Jiajin and Wang Shixiang, ibid., pl. 67.

[9] Shanghai shi wenwu guanli weiyuanhui, ibid., pp. 63-64.

[10] Gao Lian, ibid., *juan* 7:30a.

[11] Tu Long. *Qi ju ji fu qian*. (Notes on Utensils and Clothing for Daily Life) (published 1606). Meishu congshu 2:9, p. 201.

[12] Zhu Jiajin and Wang Shixiang, ibid., pls. 3, 8.

[13] Wen Zhenheng, ibid., *juan* 7, p. 258.

[14] *Tian shui bing shan*, in *Biji xiaoshou daguan* 6:6, pp. 3644-3645.

[15] Wen Zhenheng, ibid., *juan* 7, p. 258.

[16] Zhu Jiajin and Wang Shixiang. *Zhongguo meishi quanji* Vol. 11. *Gongyi meishu bian*, pl. 67, also see p. 13.

[17] Cao Xueqin. *Honglou Meng* (Dream of the Red Mansion), ch. 40, p. 540.

[18] A general discussion of gender distinction related to the material culture of the late Ming period is found in Clunas, Craig. *Superfluous Things: Material Culture and Social Status in Early Modern China*, pp. 54-56.

[19] This and another similar, yet somewhat later brushpot with inlaid rim are both illustrated in Zhu Jiajin and Wang Shixiang, ibid., pls. 67, 68.

[20] National Museum of History. *Splendor of Style: Classical Furniture from the Ming and Qing Dynasties*, p. 204.

[21] A small *zitan* vessel with wire-inlaid fret designs that was excavated from the Wanli period tomb at Baoshan, Shanghai is illustrated in Zhu Jiajin and Wang Shixiang, ibid., pl. 69.

[22] A bamboo brushpot that is finely carved as a tree trunk with pine branches, which also bears a Ming Jiajing period inscription of Zhu Songlin, father of the Jiading school of bamboo carving, is illustrated in Zhu Jiajin and Wang Shixiang, ibid., pl. 3; a small boxwood brushpot that is exquisitely carved as a prunus trunk bears a Kangxi period inscription. Tsang, Gerard and Hugh Moss, *Arts of the Scholars Studio*, pl. 59.

[23] Zhang Dexiang. "Zhongguo gudai jiaju muzhi de shibie ji jianding yiyi" (The discernment and appreciation of antique Chinese furniture woods, Part 1). *Shoucangjia* (Collectors) 27, 1998:1, p. 38.

Stools

杌凳

1

Square Stool with C-Curved Leg

紫檀有束腰馬蹄穀腿彭牙方凳

Zitan
Late 17th/Early 18th Century
Jiangnan Region
63 x 63 x 52.7 cm H

This stool exhibits a pleasing style and neat construction; the *zitan* material is uniform and generously portioned throughout. The three-piece flush-panel seat is supported with two transverse braces below. The concave waist section is separate from the aprons, the latter being decorated with large scrolling cloud patterns carved in a softly modeled style. The bulging C-curved legs were generously sculpted from large precious timber; notwithstanding, small spandrel-like flanges carved from the same timber were resourcefully integrated at the juncture where the aprons and legs meet, adding critical support to the mitered corner-leg joint.

Previously exhibited and illustrated in:
- National Museum of History. *Splendor of Style: Classical Furniture from the Ming and Qing Dynasties*, p. 70.

Similar examples are also found in:
- Wang Shixiang. *Classic Chinese Furniture: Ming and Early Qing Dynasties*, pls. 20, 21.

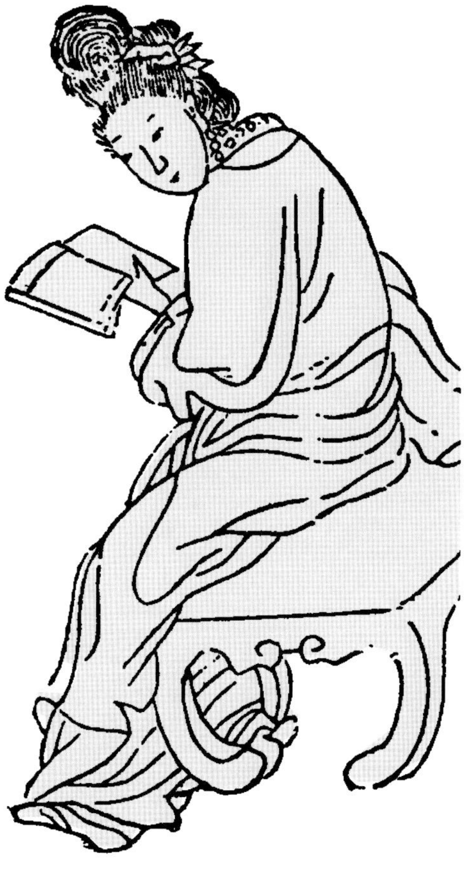

Stool with C-curved legs. Woodcut illustration from Hong lou meng, *Qing Daoguang period (pub. 1831).*

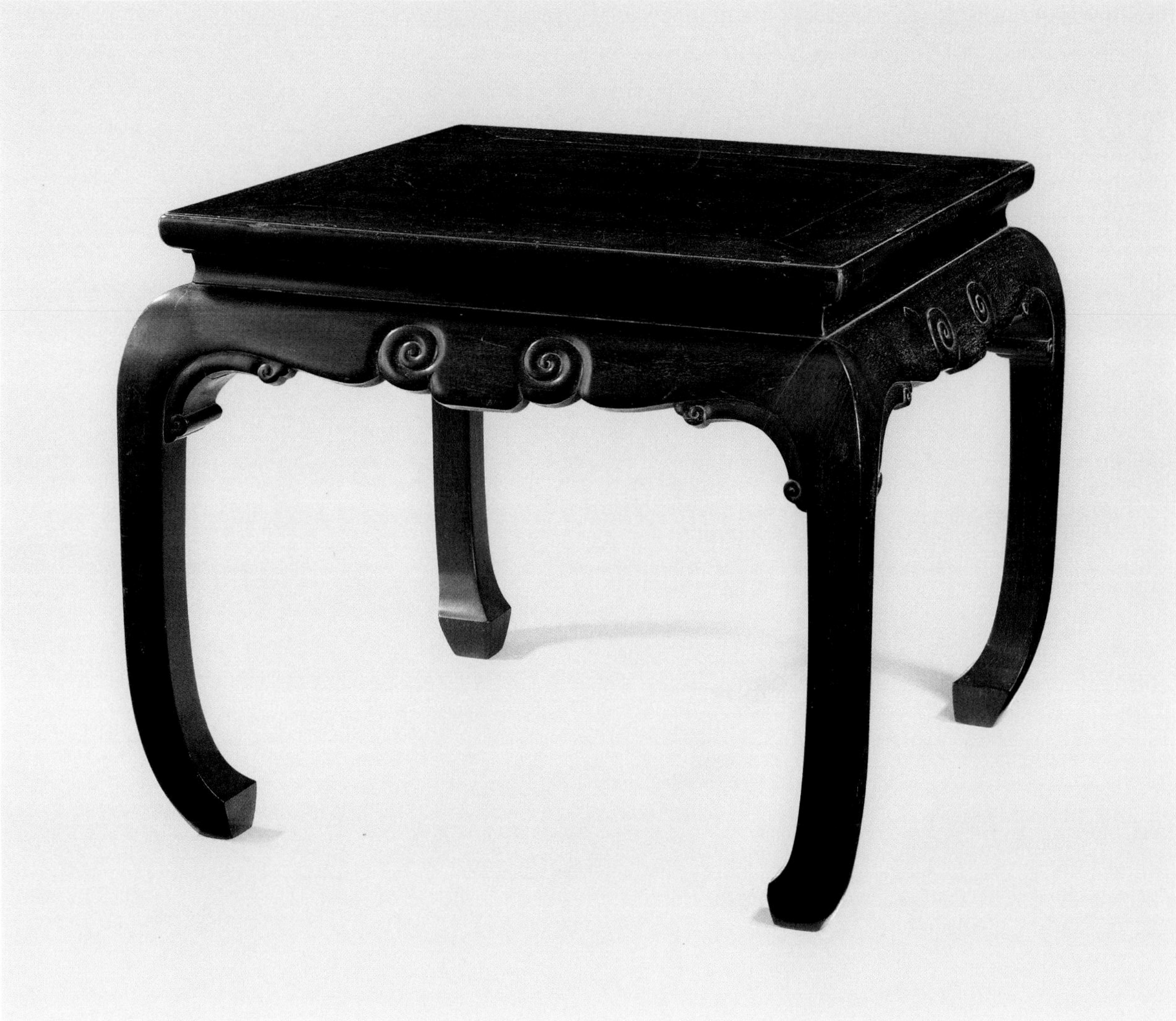

2

Square Stool with Articulated Leg

紫檀楠木有束腰三彎腿方凳

Zitan and *Nanmu* Burl
18th Century
Jiangnan Region
54.5 x 54.5 x 52.5 cm H

This stool is finely constructed from high quality *zitan*. The top panel, which was originally fit with a stone panel, has been replaced with a suitably sized remnant of old *nanmu* burl. The aprons are neatly joined to the waist section with a small dovetail peg that tenons through the waist into the underside of the seat frame. The spandrels are carved with cloud scrolls, which combine with the carved detailing on the upper part of the leg to form a *taotie* mask. The articulated cabriole legs terminate with scrolled *ruyi*-shaped feet. A hexagonal stool with articulated legs that was illustrated in an early Qing period album painting (see figure below) provides an early benchmark reference for the dating of this style.

Stools of similar style with more elaborately carved surfaces are illustrated in:

- National Museum of History. *Splendor of Style: Classical Furniture from the Ming and Qing Dynasties*, p. 72.
- Tian Jiaqing. *Classic Chinese Furniture of the Qing Dynasty*, pl. 7.

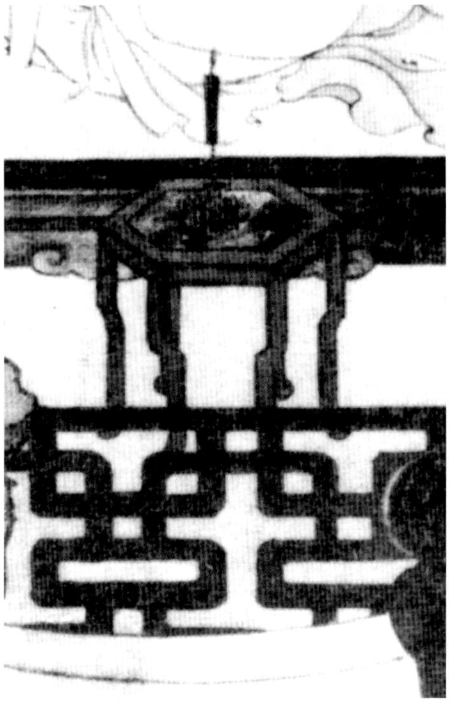

Hexagonal stool with articulated leg. Detail from Bai mei tu, *an album leaf set depicting scenes from the novel* Jin Ping Mei. *Early Qing period.*

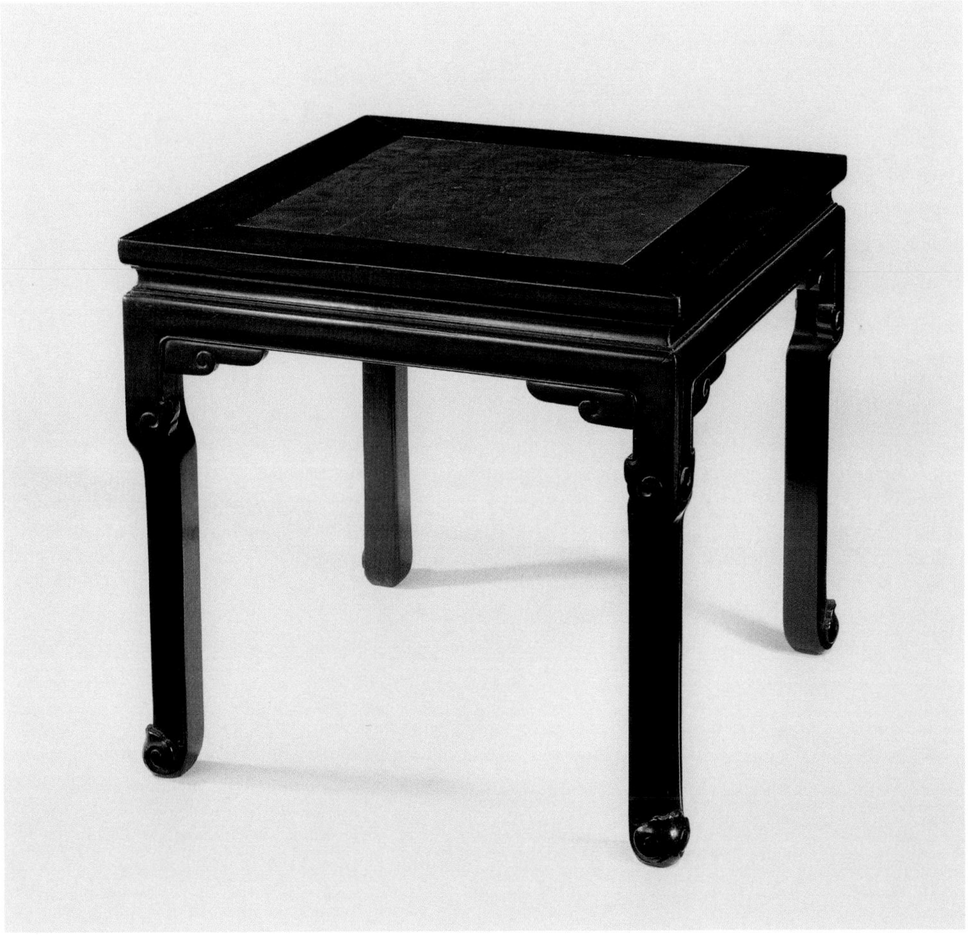

3

Square Stool with Humpback Stretchers

紫檀有束腰羅鍋棖方凳

Zitan
Late 18th/Early 19th Century
55 x 55 x 52 cm H

The linear design of this stool reflects a development in furniture-making during the Qing period, before which time evidence has yet to be discovered. This linear style, which was popular throughout the Qing period, also appears in the chairs and table illustrated in catalogue items 19 and 44.

This stool is of waisted corner-leg construction with straight legs, and the frame members are shaped with convex surfaces and indented corner moldings. The *zitan* material is of a uniform and somewhat coarse texture, reflecting the characteristics of '*huali zitan*'; moreover, the single piece apron/waist members indicate plentiful materials.

Stools of closely related style are illustrated in:

- National Museum of History. *Splendor of Style: Classical Furniture from the Ming and Qing Dynasties*, p. 68.
- Ellsworth, Robert H. *Chinese Furniture, Hardwood Examples of the Ming and Early Ch'ing Dynasties*, pl. 111.

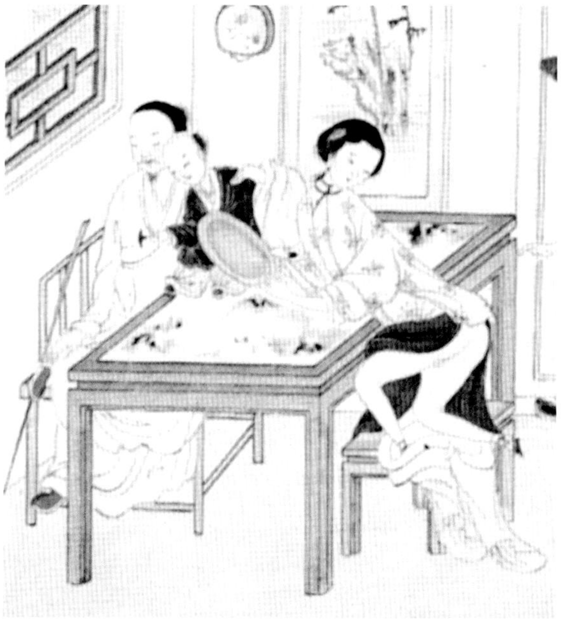

Stool. Detail from erotic album leaf depicting a scene from short story 'The Blind Man with Sharp Ears', late 18th century. After Dreams of Spring: Erotic Art in China.

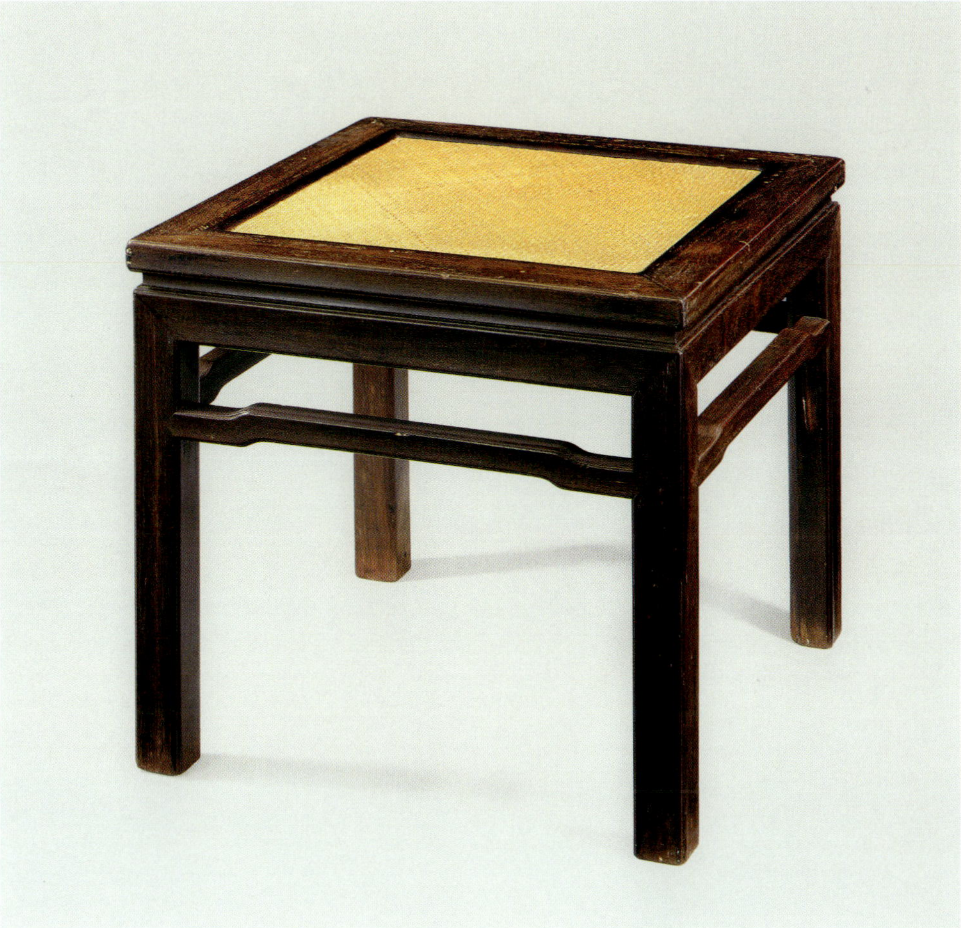

4

Pair of Rectangular Stools

紫檀有束腰馬蹄長方凳一對

Zitan
19th Century
North China
47.5 x 47.5 x 52.5 cm H

These square stools are crisply styled with straight legs and angular scrolled hoofs. The wide seat-frame members house a recessed, hard panel with caning attached to the surface. The aprons and shoulders of the legs are carved in relief with leafy foliage in a style that reflects Western decorative influence introduced during the latter half of the 18th century. Scrolling humpback stretchers attached below the aprons appear as two S-shaped brackets that are banded together at the center. The undersides retain traces of thin lacquer coatings.

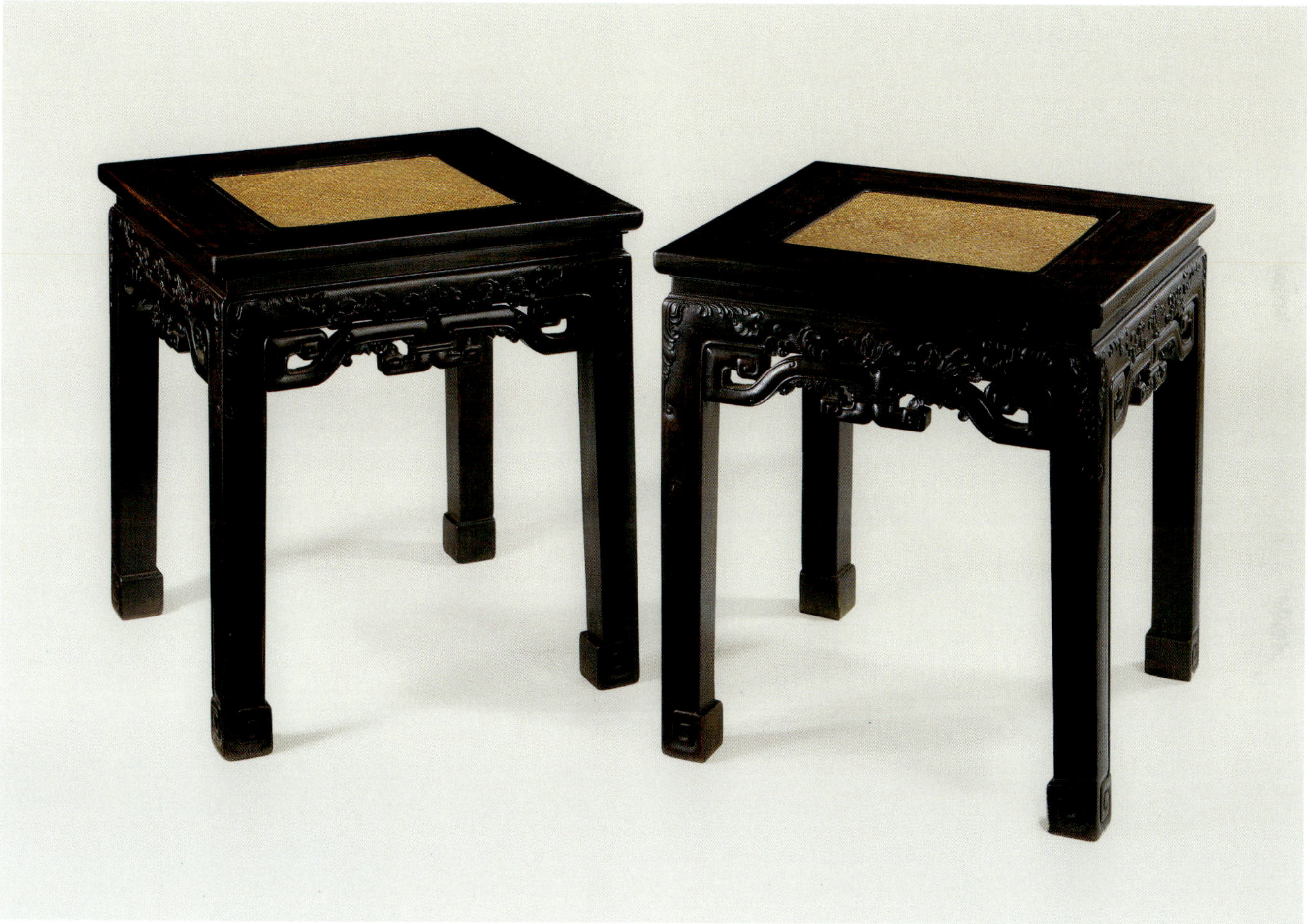

5

Square Bamboo-Style Stool

紫檀仿竹式方凳

Zitan
18th Century
Suzhou Region
52 x 52 x 53 cm H

The layered convex moldings frame and the wrap-around stretchers of this stool imitate bamboo-style construction in the refined medium of hardwood. Early evidence of this newly developed style is found in an album leaf set dated to the early Qing period (see illustration below), after which it flourished with popularity throughout the Qing dynasty.

This square stool exhibits excellence in style and construction. Contrary to the normal pattern of construction, the legs are splayed, which imparts an impression of visual stability. The seat frame is also unusually joined with a dovetail mortise-and-tenon arrangement, the complexity of which disappears when fully assembled. The original round-cornered, stone-panel seat has since been replaced.

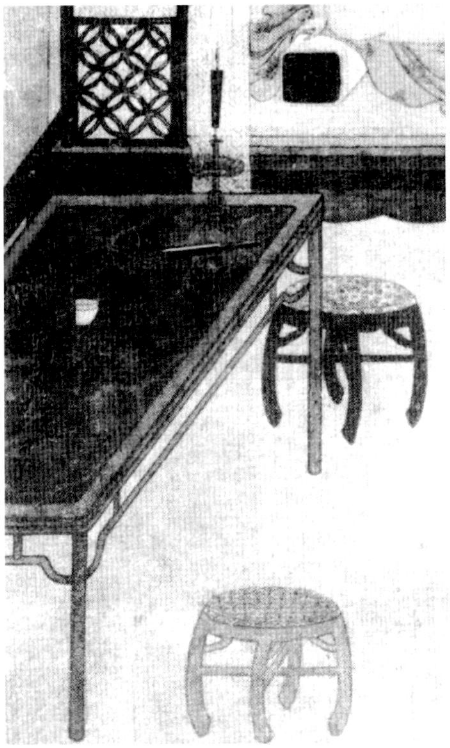

Round-leg table. Detail from Bai mei tu, *an album leaf set depicting scenes from the novel* Jin Ping Mei. *Early Qing period.*

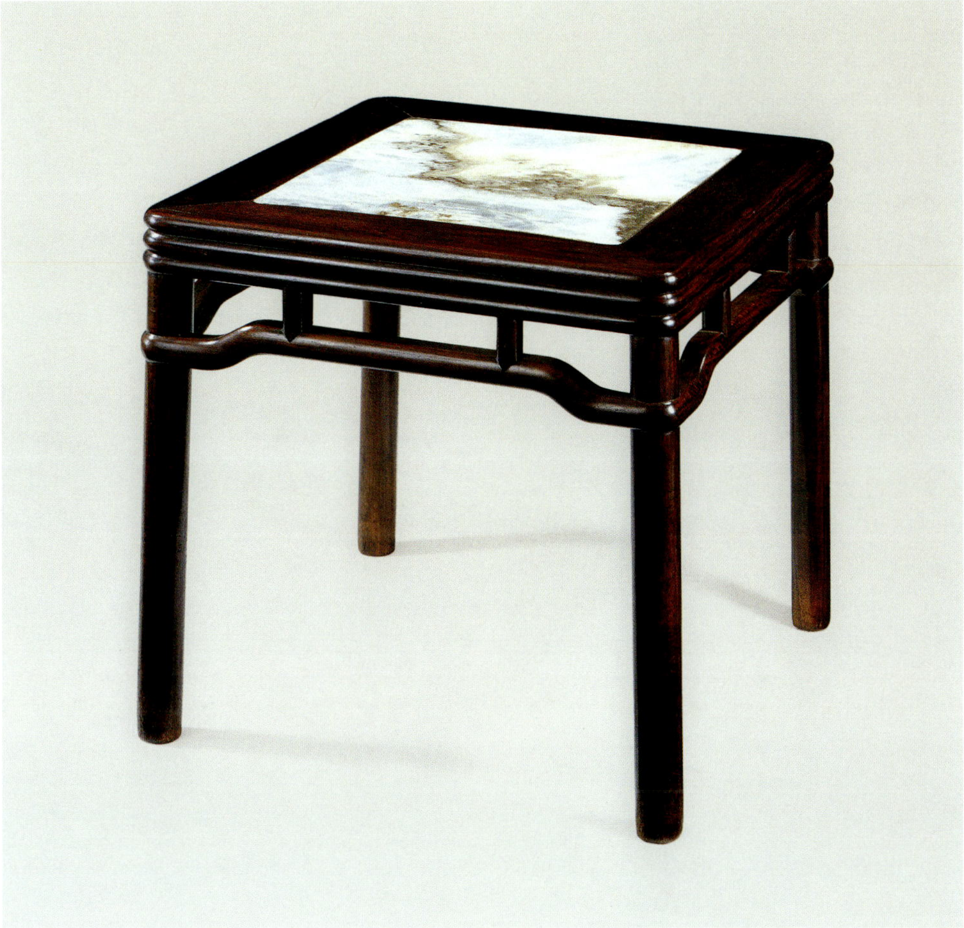

6

Bench

黄花梨夾頭春凳

Huanghuali
17th Century
Jiangnan Region
88 x 38 x 35.5 cm H

The seat of this small bench is woven with soft cane. The aprons are fit with cloud-shaped spandrel heads and finely beaded. Innovative styling is evident in the single stretchers shaped with spandrel heads and feet that gently flare outward to provide a relaxed stance.

The front edge of the seat frame is softly rounded over from multiple generations of use. The various components have mellowed to a uniform patination. The underside retains traces of a red lacquer with fabric underlayment. Such are the components of genuine age.

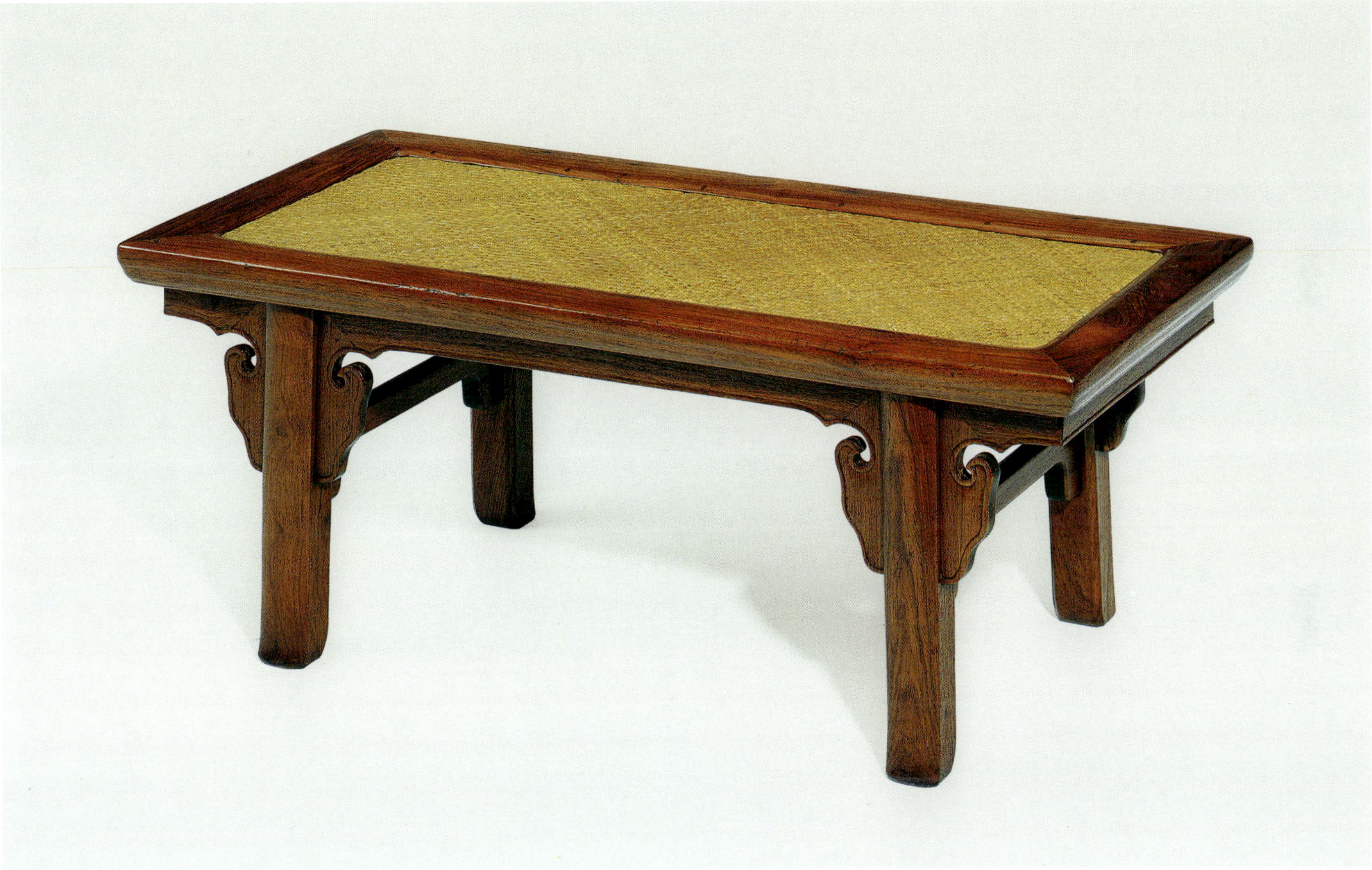

7

Bench/Stand

黃花梨夾頭春凳

Huanghuali
17th Century
North China
190 x 50.5 x 46 cm H

The original function of this recessed-leg bench is undetermined. While resembling a common bench, the unusual top is constructed as a hollow core panel—a technique that is occasionally employed on musical instrument tables for tone amplification. Exquisite workmanship is also apparent in the pillowed surfaces of the single-piece aprons as well as their fine beading.

A bench of similar style and size is illustrated in:
• Ecke, Gustav. *Chinese Domestic Furniture*, pl. 42.

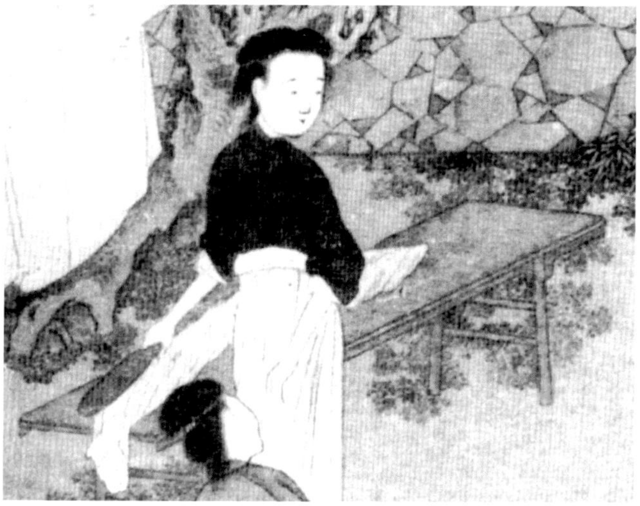

Recessed-leg bench. Detail from Bai mei tu, *an album leaf set depicting scenes from the novel* Jin Ping Mei. *Early Qing period.*

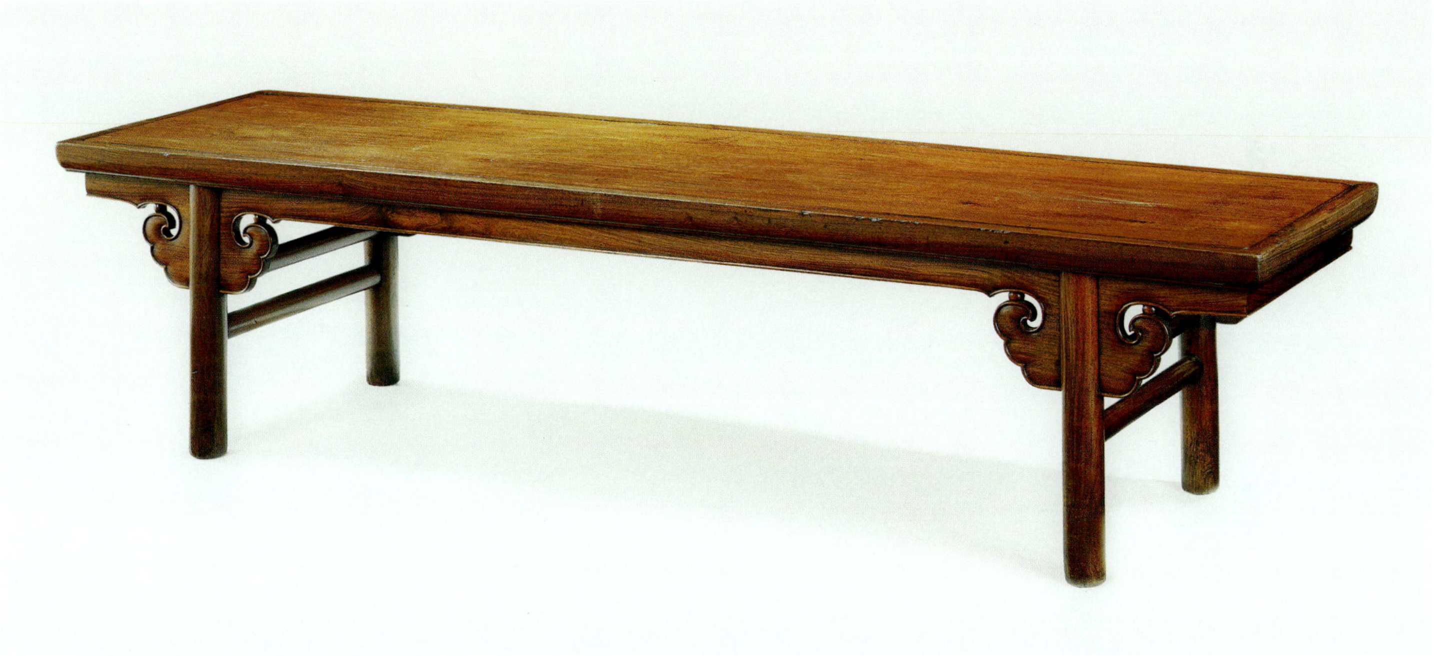

8

Bench

黃花梨有束腰馬蹄春凳

Huanghuali
Late 16th/Early 17th Century
161 x 44 x 48 cm H

This long bench displays a classical Ming dynasty style, and its elegance of line belies underlying solidity and mass of construction. The seat frame houses bookmatched panels and is shaped with a sharply profiled 'ice-plate molding'. Below, thick aprons (4.5 cm) provide girder-like strength to support the long seat span, and their mass at the critical corner-leg joint insures a strong connection to the otherwise unreinforced leg. The smooth aprons are shaped with a concave waist, and their curvilinear *kunmen* line sweeps gracefully into the legs.

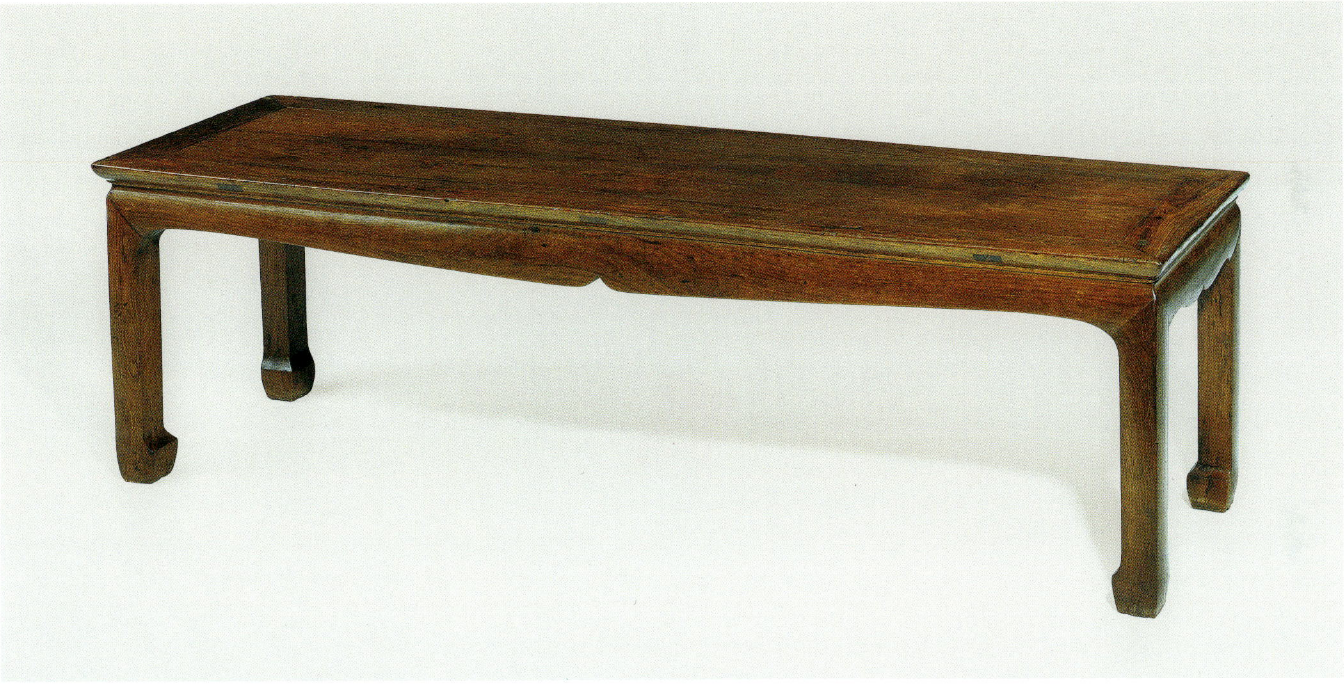

9

Bench

黃花梨有束腰羅鍋棖馬蹄春凳

Huanghuali
17th Century
Jiangnan Region
139.5 x 41 x 46.5 cm H

Benches are traditionally termed 'spring bench' (*chundeng*), with connotations similar to the Western 'love seat'. Fine hardwood benches are relatively rare. The stout and slightly bowed legs of this example impart a robustly animated character. The seat frame is woven with soft caning. Below, humpback stretchers reinforce the legs and are decorated with oval struts. The surfaces are well patinated and exhibit natural wear from age.

A bench of similar style is illustrated in:
- Ecke, Gustav. *Chinese Domestic Furniture*, pl. 4.

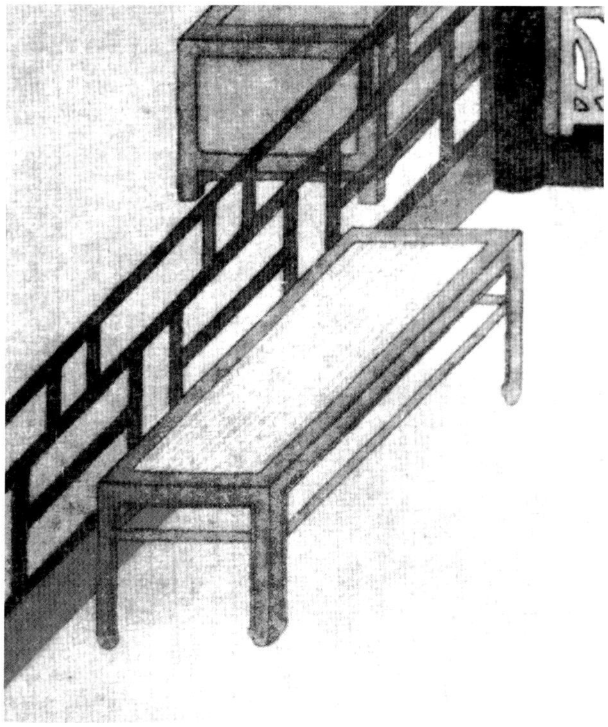

Waisted corner-leg bench. Detail from Bai mei tu, *an album leaf set depicting scenes from the novel* Jin Ping Mei. *Early Qing period.*

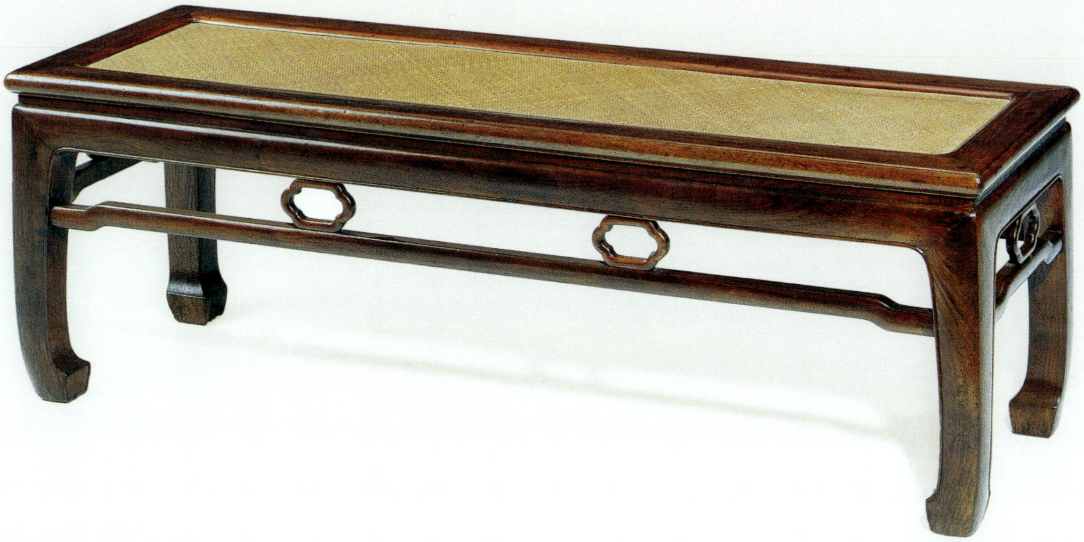

Chairs

椅

10

Yokeback Armchair

黃花梨四出頭官帽椅

Huanghuali
17th Century
North China
51 x 62 x 112.5 cm H
Seat Height 49 cm

This yokeback armchair is distinguished by long curvilinear flanges that flank the framed backrest and 'vase-and-bamboo' armrest supports. Chairs with a similarly styled backrest and sideposts depicted in late Ming woodcuts published in Fengyang, Anhui demonstrate decorative conventions of the period (see illustration below); however, *huanghuali* examples of this style are typically from North China.

The upper panel of this chair's backrest is pierced with a *fu* character; the central panel features richly patterned burlwood; and, a high-arched 'base-brightening' (*liangjiao*) panel is fit at the base. The secondary armrests supports shaped like bamboo rising from a vase suggest the rebus *zhubao pingan*, or 'may bamboo bring peace'—a convention that is commonly found on Ming and Qing armchairs from the Shanxi region. The seat frame is woven with cane matting that is trimmed with unique finishing strips shaped with radiused corners. Lacquer with fabric underlayment is found on the underside of the seat frame.

This chair belongs to a group of related *huanghuali* chairs that that were likely produced by a single workshop. For a detailed survey, see:

- Evarts, Curtis, "From Ornate to Unadorned: A Study of a Group of Yokeback Chairs", *Journal of the Classical Chinese Furniture Society* 3:2 (Spring 1993), pp. 24-33.

Other similar chairs have since appeared in:

- Ellsworth, Robert Hatfield. *Chinese Furniture: One Hundred Examples from the Mimi and Raymond Hung Collection*, pls. 8, 10.
- Jacobsen, Robert D. *Classical Chinese Furniture in the Minneapolis Institute of Arts*, pl. 46.

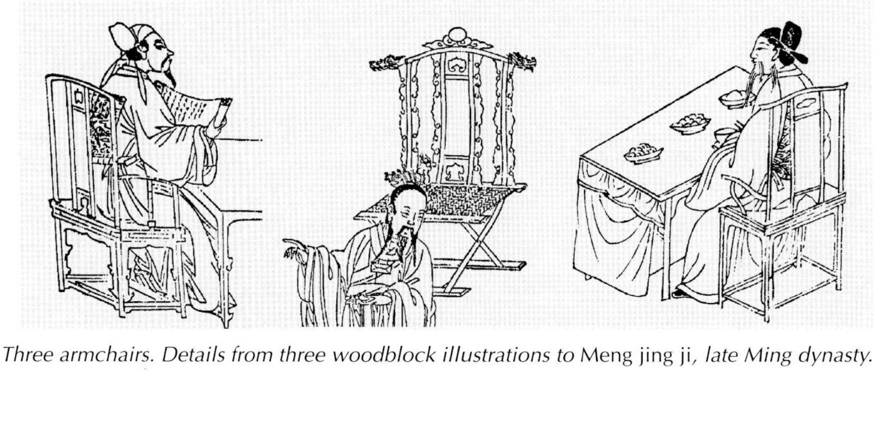

Three armchairs. Details from three woodblock illustrations to Meng jing ji*, late Ming dynasty.*

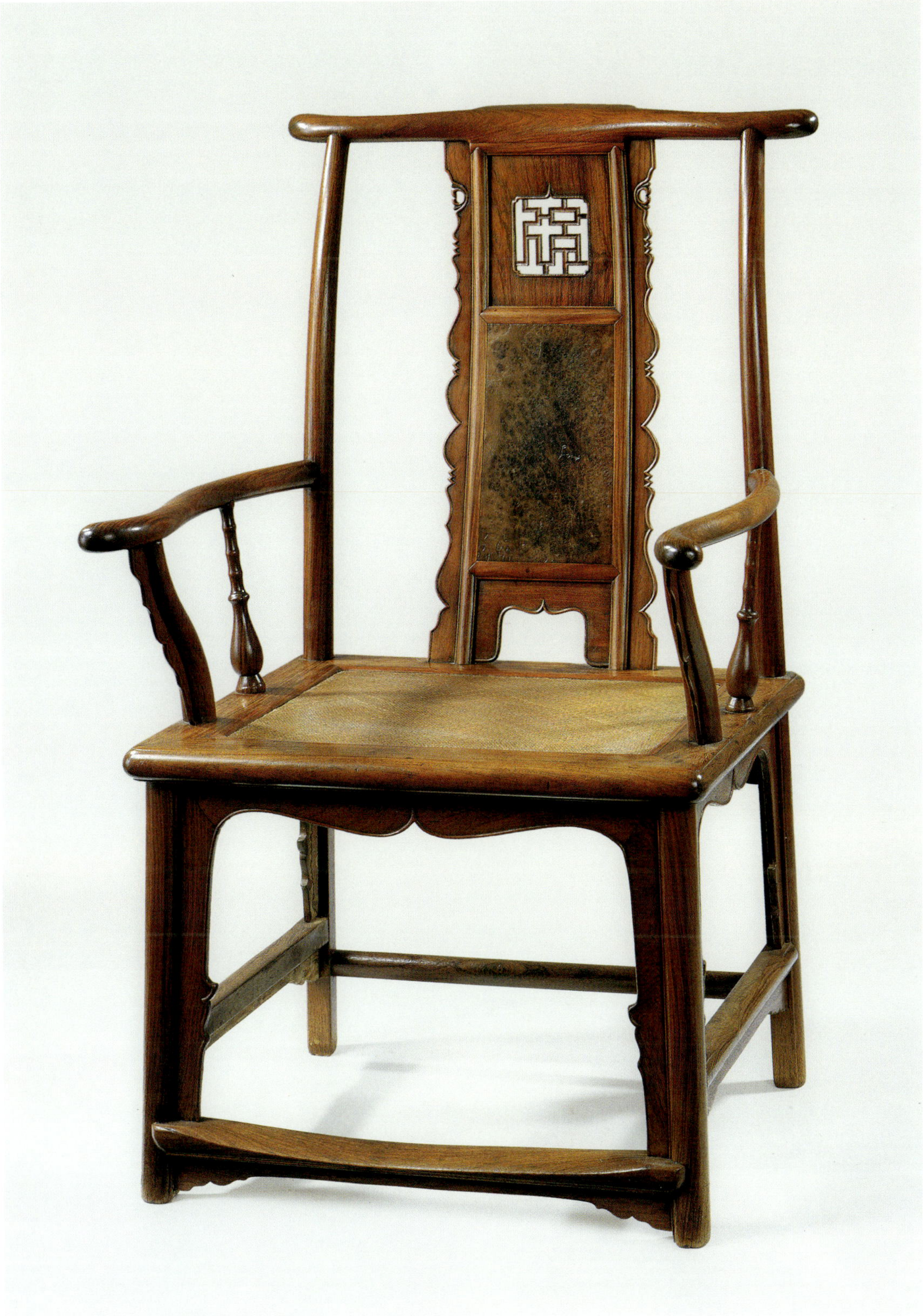

11

Horseshoe Armchair

紫檀圈椅一對

One of a Pair
Zitan
17th Century
North China
61 x 47 x 102 cm H
Seat Height 52 cm H

These chairs were discovered together with the large *zitan* cabinets (cat. 49) in Wuwei, an important trading center at the intersection of the Silk Route and Great Wall in Gansu province. It is highly improbable that they were local products, but were rather brought by a high official or wealthy merchant from the capital.

The armchairs exhibit a perfected classical style. The circular armrest is well rounded and finishes with neatly scrolled handgrips. The backrest is shaped with flanges, and is carved with a medallion at the top and a *liangjiao* motif at the base. The style and patination of the medallion, which is inconsistent with that at the base, appears as a later embellishment. The seat frame is woven with soft caning. Below, full aprons carved in relief decorate the openings on fronts and sides. Traces of nail holes along the top of the footrest stretcher indicate the previous fitting of a protective plate.

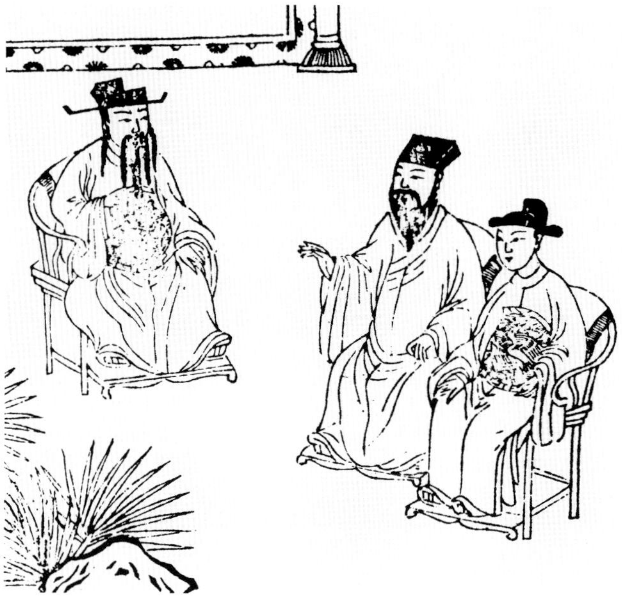

Horseshoe armchairs. Detail from woodcut illustration to Shan'gong cao, *Qing Kangxi period (1662-1722).*

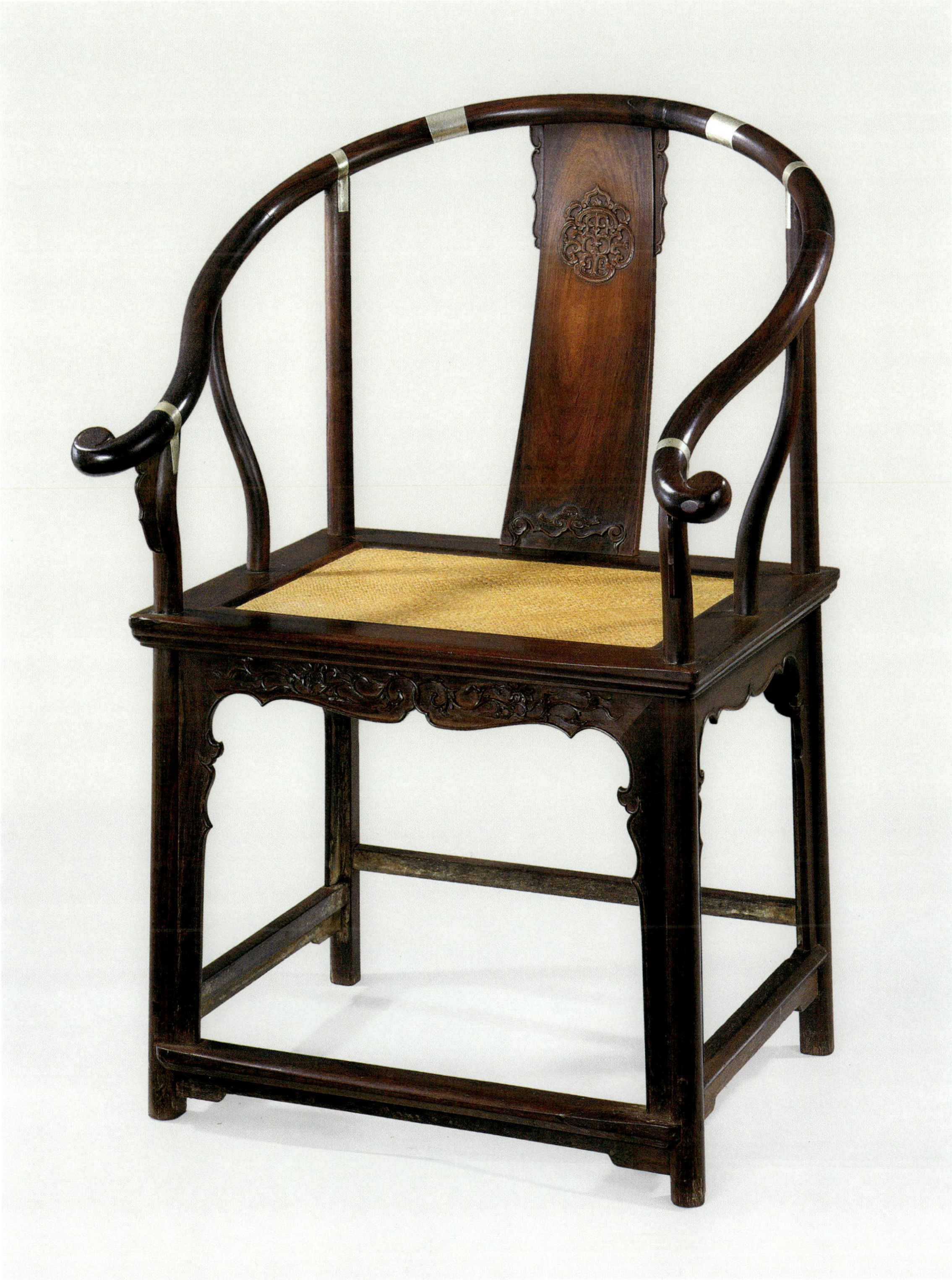

12

Horseshoe Armchair

黄花梨圈椅

Huanghuali
17th Century
Suzhou Region
59 x 44.5 x 98 cm H
Seat Height 51.5 cm

This horseshoe armchair exhibits a light, elegant style. The solid panel backrest is carved to simulate a framed three-panel construction, the central panel of which is decorated with a blossoming plum sprig, a *ruyi* in a vase, and a *lingbi* rock on a stand. The five-piece armrest follows a graceful curve that terminates in neatly scrolled handgrips. The seat frame is woven with a soft caning.

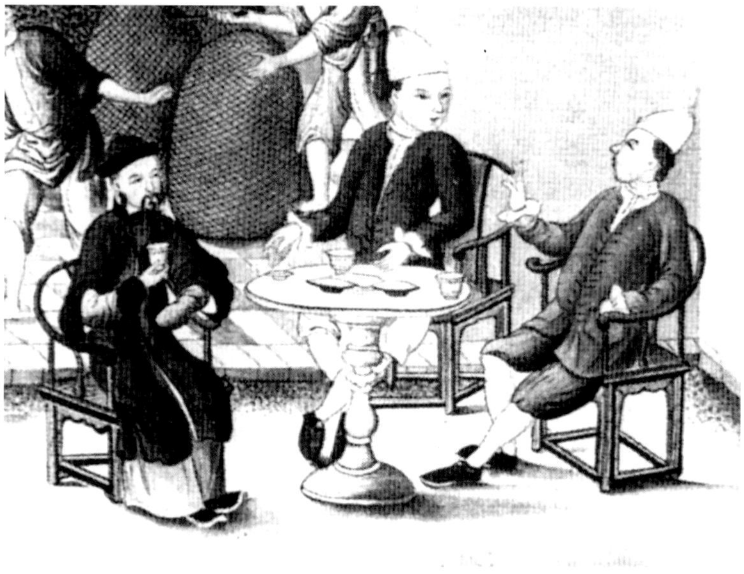

Horseshoe armchairs. Detail from watercolor painting, Qing dynasty 1780-90.

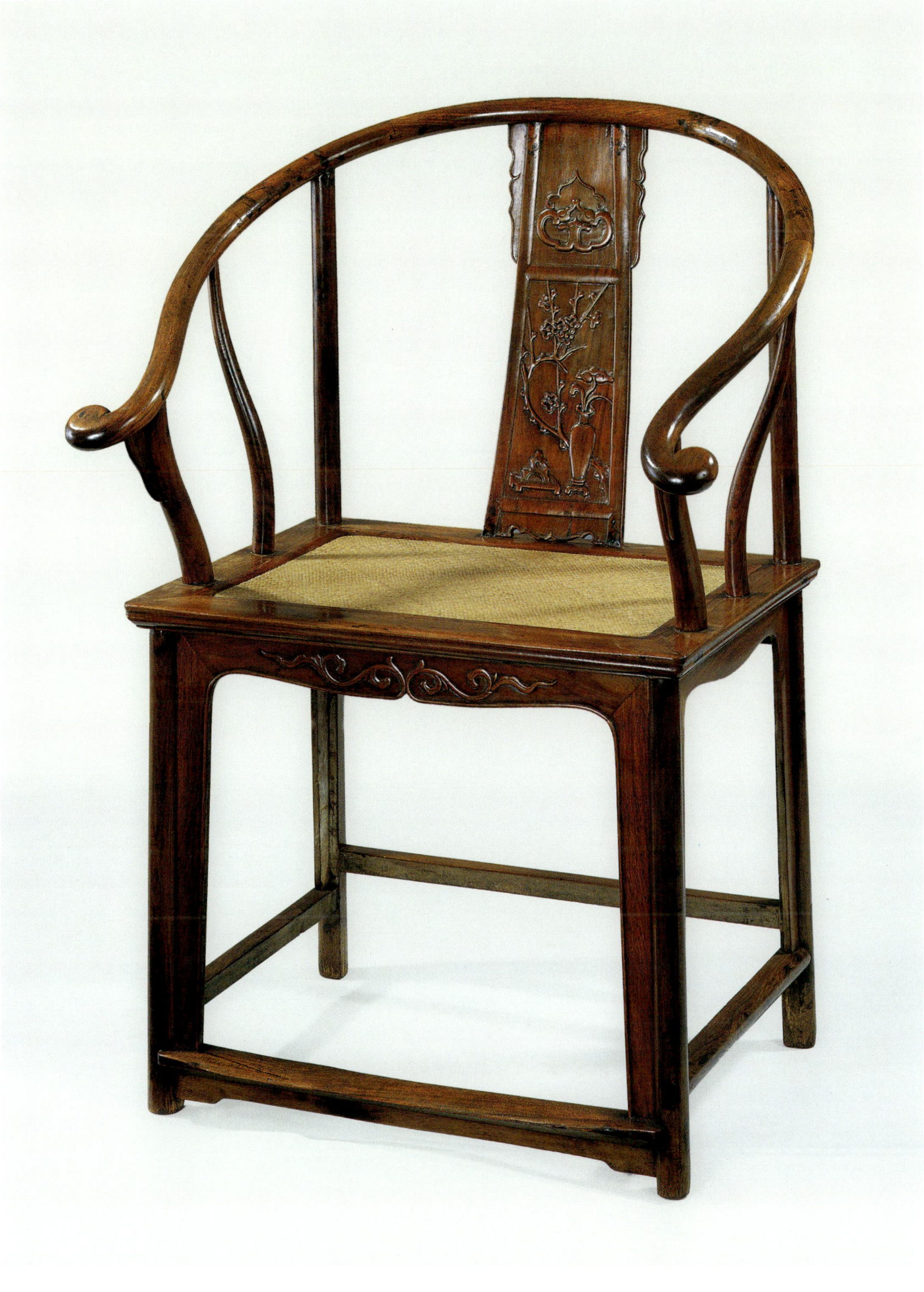

13

Southern Official's Armchair with Inlaid Backrest

黄花梨嵌百寶南官帽椅一對

One of a Pair
Huanghuali
17th Century
Jiangnan Region
61.5 x 44 x 121 cm H
Seat Height 52.5 cm

These chairs exhibit a traditional, high-back southern official's pattern, and their elegantly shaped lines reflect a southern, Jiangnan style. The inlaid 'flower-and-bird' designs decorating the back splats, which have been restored with mother-of-pearl, were originally inlaid with semi-precious stones—a technique traditionally associated with Yangzhou and commonly called Zhouzhi inlay. One chair is decorated with plum blossoms and birds; the other, with pomegranates and birds.

Similarly styled chairs with Zhouzhi inlay backrests have been published in:

- Berliner, Nancy. *Beyond the Screen: Chinese Furniture of the 16th and 17th Centuries*, pl. 10.
- National Museum of History. *Splendor of Style: Classical Furniture from the Ming and Qing Dynasties*, p. 86.
- Yip Shing-Yiu and Grace Wu Bruce. *Chan Chair and Qin Bench: The Dr. S. Y. Yip Collection of Classic Chinese Furniture II*, pl. 3.

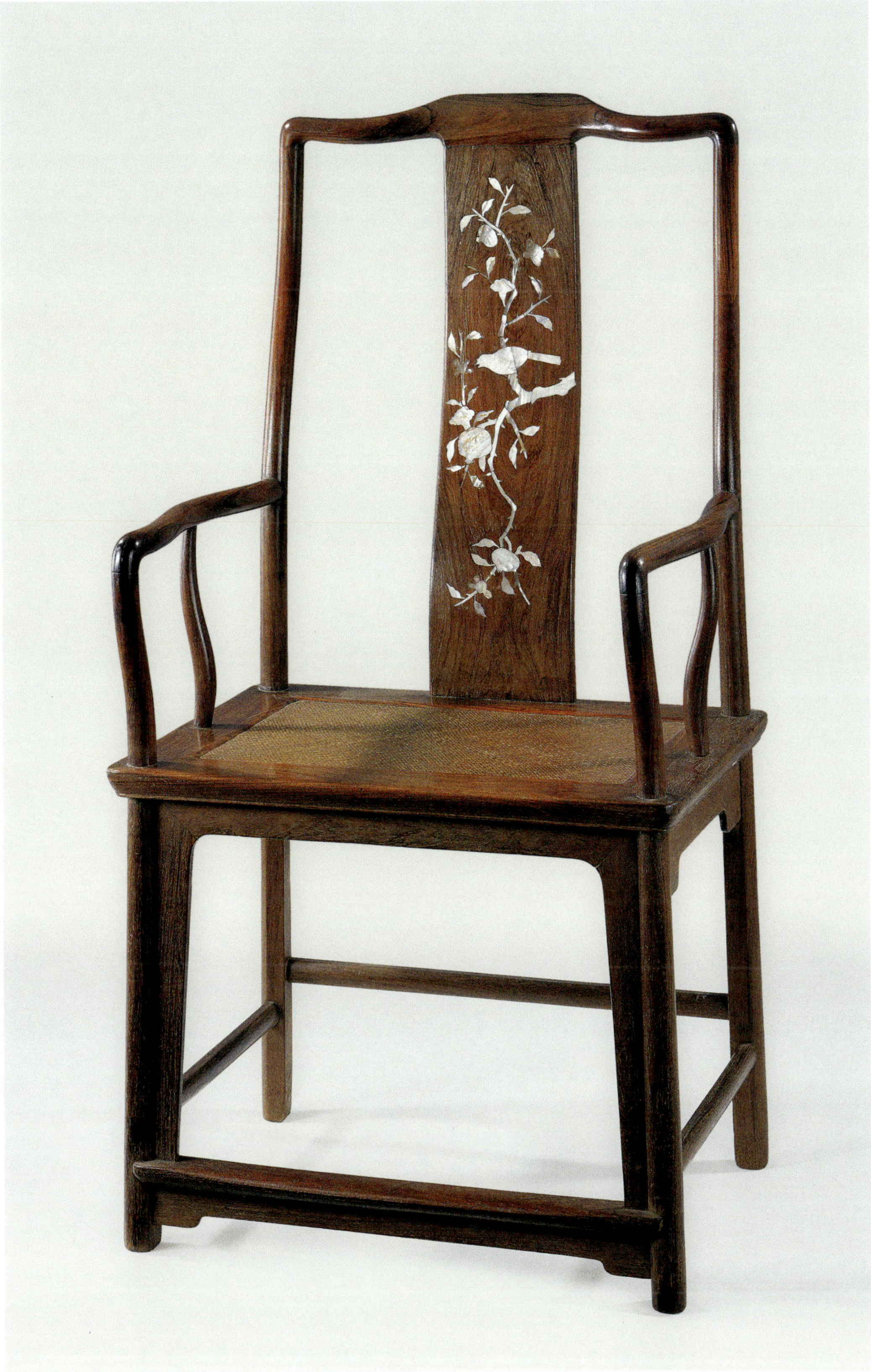

14

Southern Official's Armchair

黄花梨南官帽椅

Huanghuali
17th Century
Northern Jiangsu (Subei)
69.5 x 46 x 99.5 cm H
Seat Height 49.5 cm H

This chair is constructed with thickly shaped members in a plain, undecorated style. The frame members above the seat surface are shaped to fluid, sinuous lines and round in section; below, the squared members of the linear base are profiled with convex-shaped surfaces. This piece, illustrated here with unpolished surfaces only having been lightly cleaned, reveals the muted appearance of unrestored *huanghuali*.

Previously exhibited and illustrated in:

- National Museum of History. *Splendor of Style: Classical Furniture from the Ming and Qing Dynasties*, p. 89.

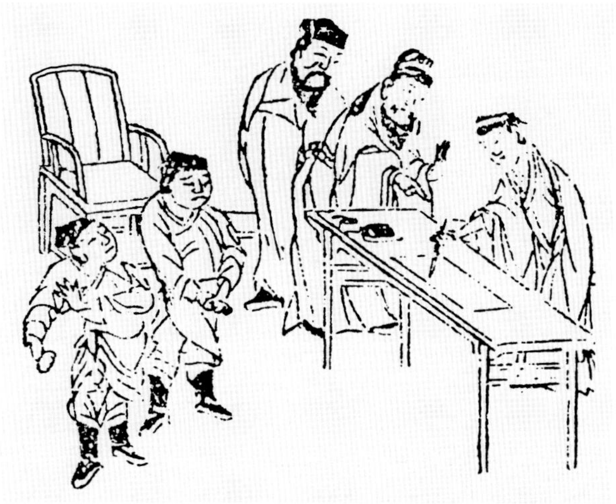

Southern official's armchair. Detail from woodcut illustration to Yong tuan yuan, *late Ming period.*

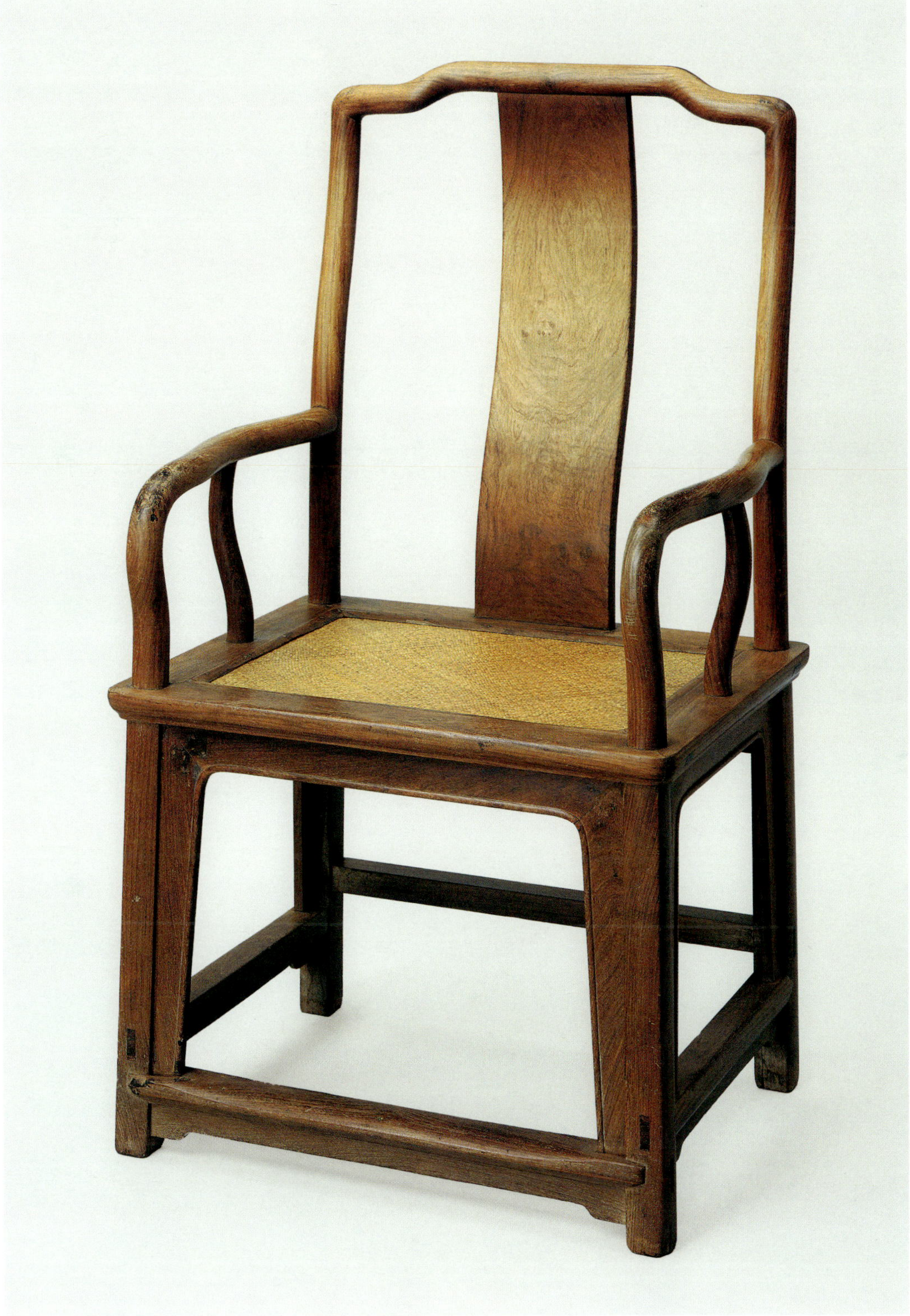

15

Southern Official's Armchair

紫檀南官帽椅

Zitan
Late 18th/Early 19th Century
Tianjin
59.5 x 45.8 x 99.5 cm H
Seat Height 51.5 cm

This chair exhibits a substantial structure, exquisite craftsmanship in its fluid curvilinear structure, and fine decorative carving. The backrest is fashioned like a *meiping* vase on a stand. The surface decoration is finely carved in relief as a pendant suspending a bat, endless knot, and pair of fish. Signifying 'wealth', 'longevity', and 'multiple abundance', such auspicious motifs were common for chair splats during the mid- to late Qing period. The squared frame members are shaped to sinuous lines, and modeled with softly rounded surfaces. The seat frame is fit with a hard panel. The aprons below are raised with fine beading that scrolls with archaic cloud designs against a flat ground.

Previously exhibited and illustrated in:

- National Museum of History. *Splendor of Style: Classical Furniture from the Ming and Qing Dynasties*, p. 88.

Mid-to-late Qing period chairs with similar backrest decoration are illustrated in:

- Tian Jiaqing. *Classic Chinese Furniture of the Qing Dynasty*, pls. 35, 36, 37, 41, 50.

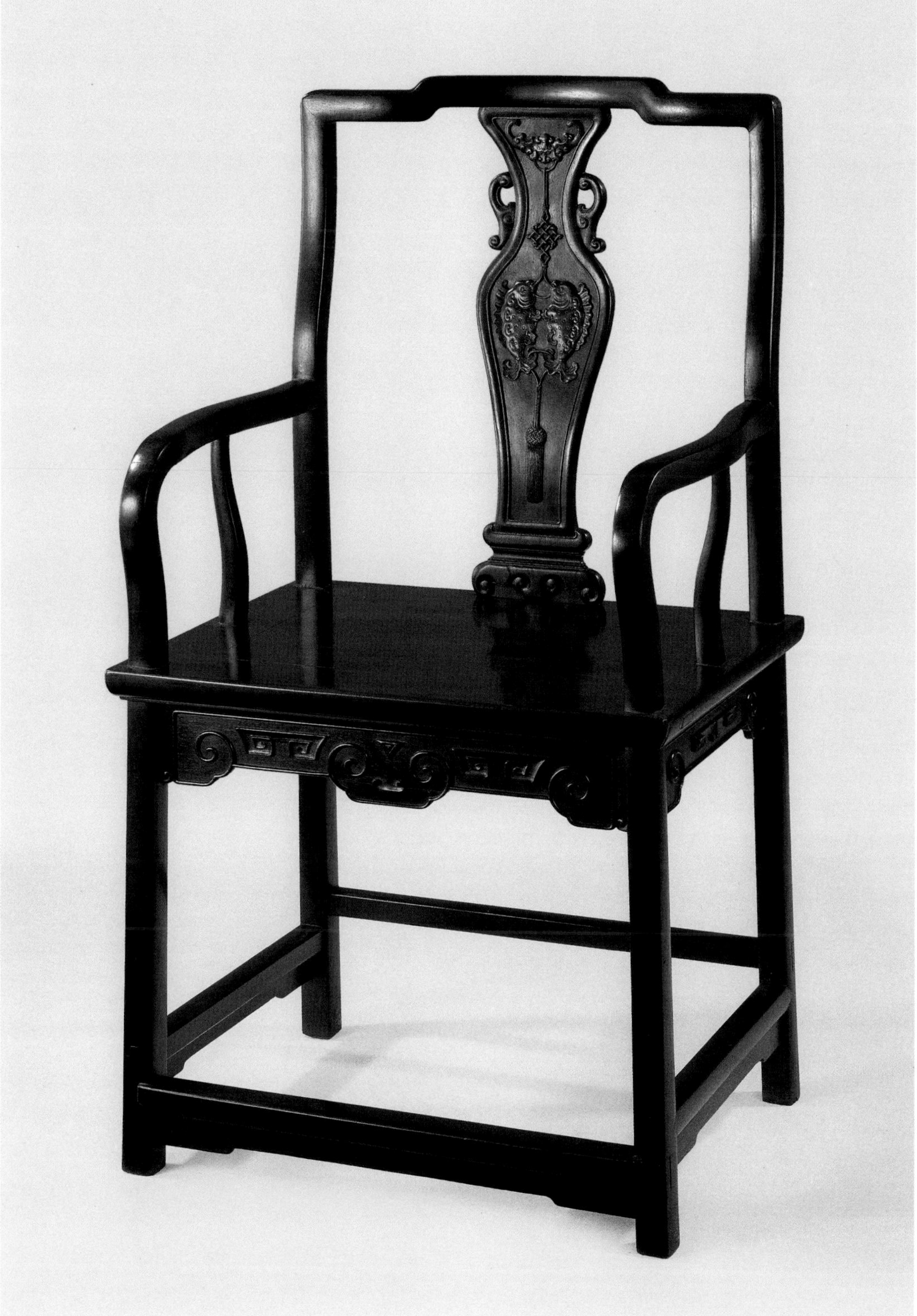

16

Rose Chair

黃花梨玫瑰椅一對

One of a Pair
Huanghuali
18th Century
North China
57.5 x 44 x 88 cm H
Seat Height 52 cm

The somewhat petite 'rose chair' is characterized by the angular construction of its straight-member back- and armrests. The spaces that are delineated above the seat of the chair are typically framed with aprons or filled with various lattice patterns, resembling bamboo chairs of similar form. Unlike most other chairs of traditional style, the back of the rose chair is devoid of a comfortable back splat.

Although many hardwood and softwood rose chairs have survived, there is curiously little evidence for the existence of this form in traditional reference sources. Wang Shixiang has compared it to large chairs of angular style that are occasionally depicted in Song paintings; however, the overall style and proportions of these examples is only vaguely approximate to the characteristic style and proportion recognizable amongst the large number of surviving rose chairs. Those illustrated in Ming period woodcuts generally appear with backrests. More traditionally styled 'rose chairs' appear in an early Qing edition of *San Guo zhi* (see illustration below). The angular form is immediately identifiable and the back and armrests are filled with a traditional lattice pattern; moreover, the small size of the chair is contrasted by the size of the seated characters.

These rose chairs are constructed with *huanghuali*. The backrest is fit with an inner apron-like frame that is carved in relief with angular scrolling. A low railing at the sides and back may have retained a seat cushion. The aprons below the seat frame are carved in relief with a thick pattern of scrolling grass. The surfaces of the chairs exhibit wear from natural age and retain good patination.

A rose chair of similar style is illustrated in:

- Pu Anguo. *Ming Qing Sushi jiaju* (Suzhou-style furniture from the Ming and Qing dynasties), pl. 194.

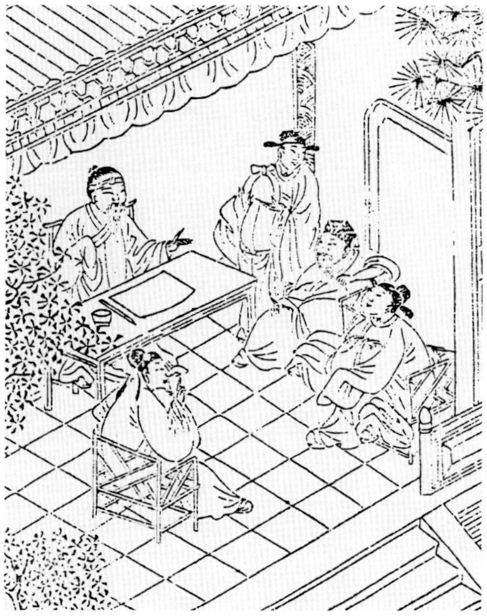

Rose chair. Detail from woodcut illustration to San Guo zhi, *Early Qing period.*

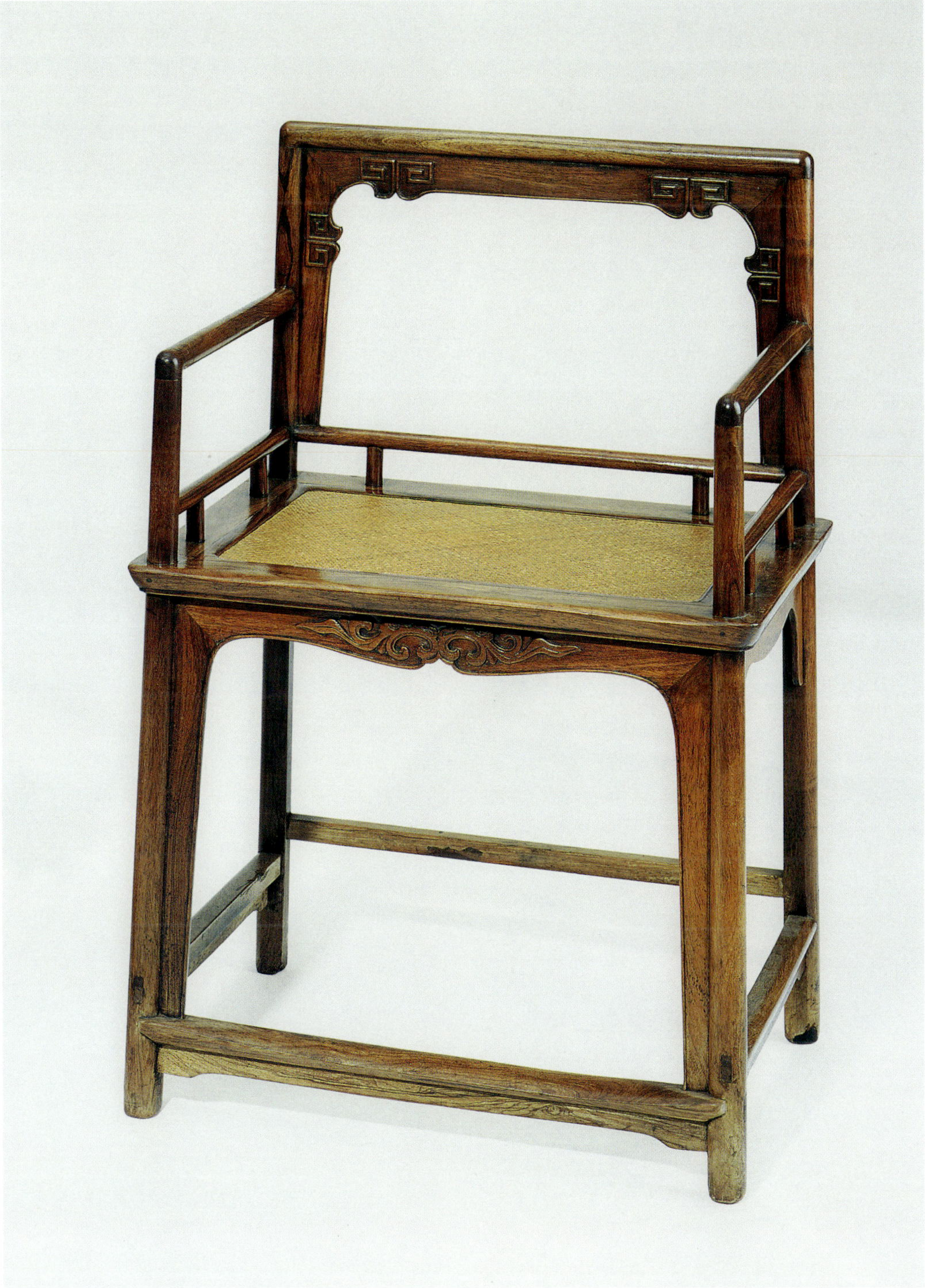

17

Spindle-Back Chair

黄花梨梳背扶手椅

Huanghuali
Late 18th/Early 19th Century
Jiangnan Region
52.5 x 43 x 84 cm H
Seat Height 48 cm

This chair reflects a Suzhou style typical of the mid-to-late Qing period, and one that is more commonly produced in *hongmu*. The design exploits the use of vertical spindles as well as horizontal elements with humpback lines. The spindle- or 'comb-back' (*shubei*) railings are each constructed as independent panels that are attached to the top of the seat frame. Unlike a traditional rose chair, the backrest here is shaped with a subtle arch-backed curve to provide the sitter with a comfortable back support. The seat frame is woven with soft matting, and refined humpback stretchers with pillared struts are fit below. The concealed joinery also reflects refined Suzhou workmanship.

Similar examples are published in:

- Ellsworth, Robert Hatfield. *Chinese Hardwood Furniture in Hawaiian Collections*, pl. 61.
- Beurdeley, Michel. *Chinese Furniture*, pp. 80, 188.
- Tian Jiaqing. *Classic Chinese Furniture of the Qing Dynasty*, pl. 42.
- Pu Anguo. *Ming Qing Sushi jiaju* (Suzhou-style furniture from the Ming and Qing dynasties), pls. 39, 59.

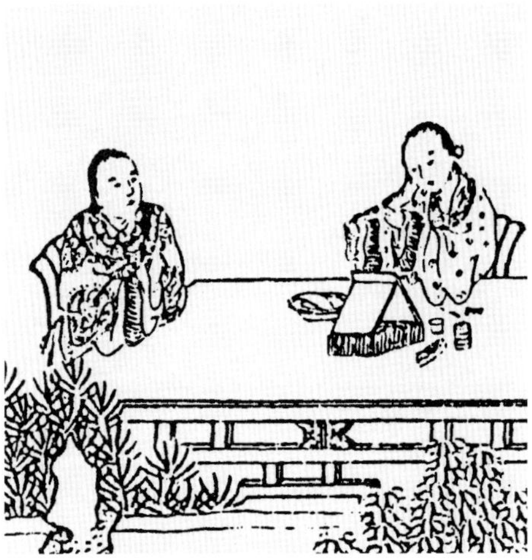

Spindle-back chairs. Detail from woodcut illustration to Shitou ji*, Qing Guangxu period (1875-1908).*

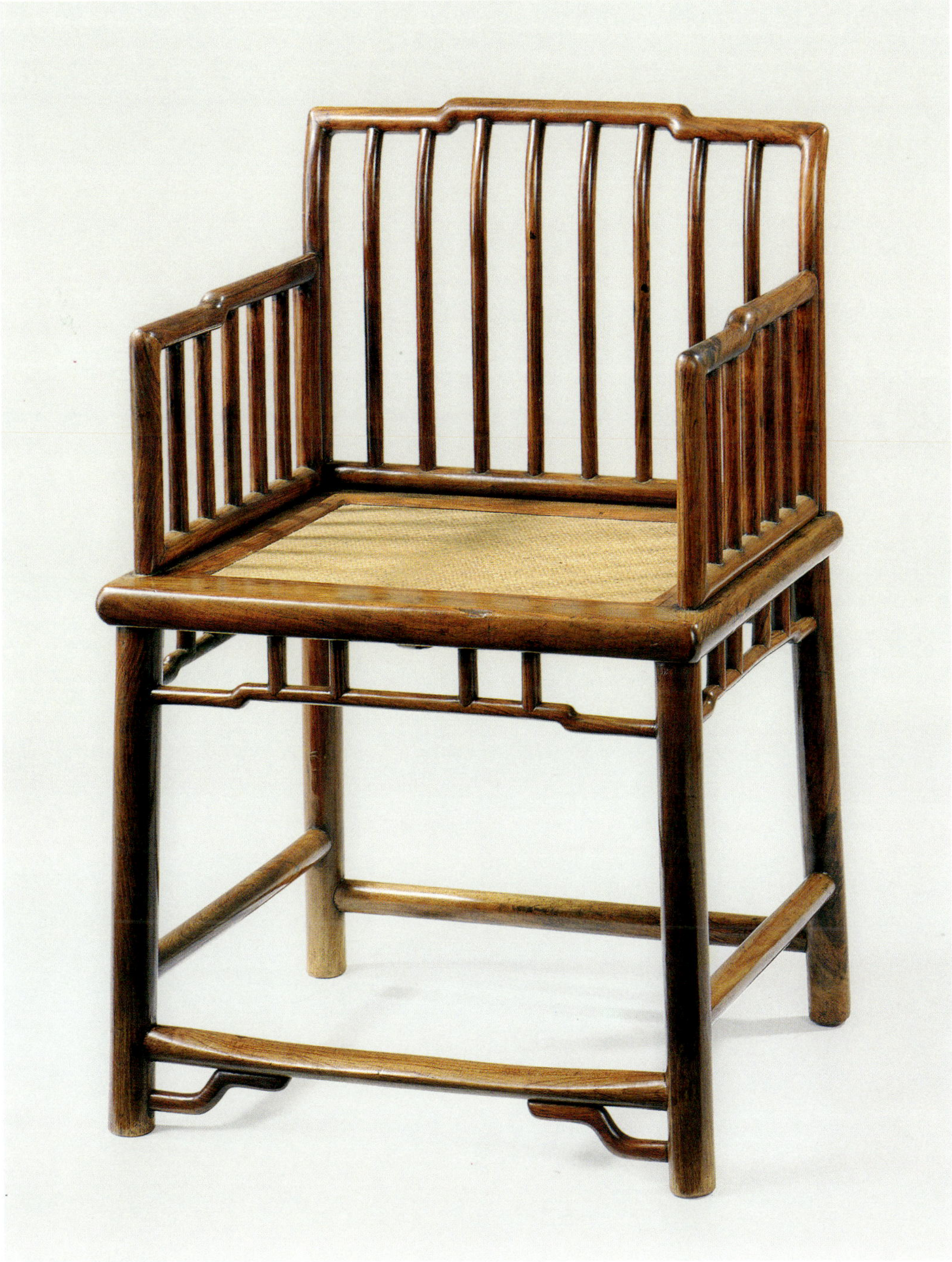

18

Low-Back Southern Official Armchair

紫檀梳背扶手椅

Zitan
Late 18th/Early 19th Century
Jiangnan
56 x 42 x 91 cm H
Seat Height 48.5 cm

This low back southern official's chair is styled with graceful, fluid lines. Closely spaced spindles in the backrest arch back in alignment with the profile of the backposts; those under the armrest fan outward under the curvilinear line of the armrests. Decorative oval-shaped struts are fit between the humpback stretchers and the soft woven seat frame. The joints at the armrests, backrests, seat frame and lower stretchers are all reinforced with plain metal straps inset flush to the surface, and small metal caps are found around the feet. Reused material is found throughout—a practice suggesting a date of construction towards the latter part 18th century or later when supplies of high quality *zitan* were scarce.

Previously exhibited and published in:

- National Museum of History. *Splendor of Style: Classical Furniture from the Ming and Qing Dynasties*, p. 87.

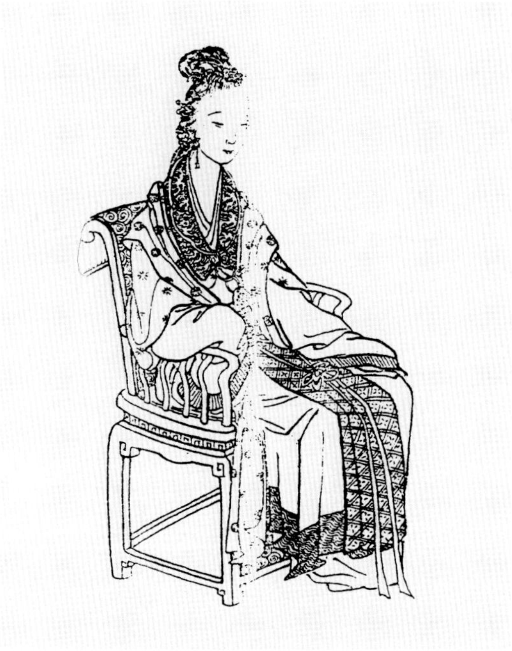

Armchair with spindles. Woodcut illustration to Shitou ji, *Qing Guangxu period (1875-1908).*

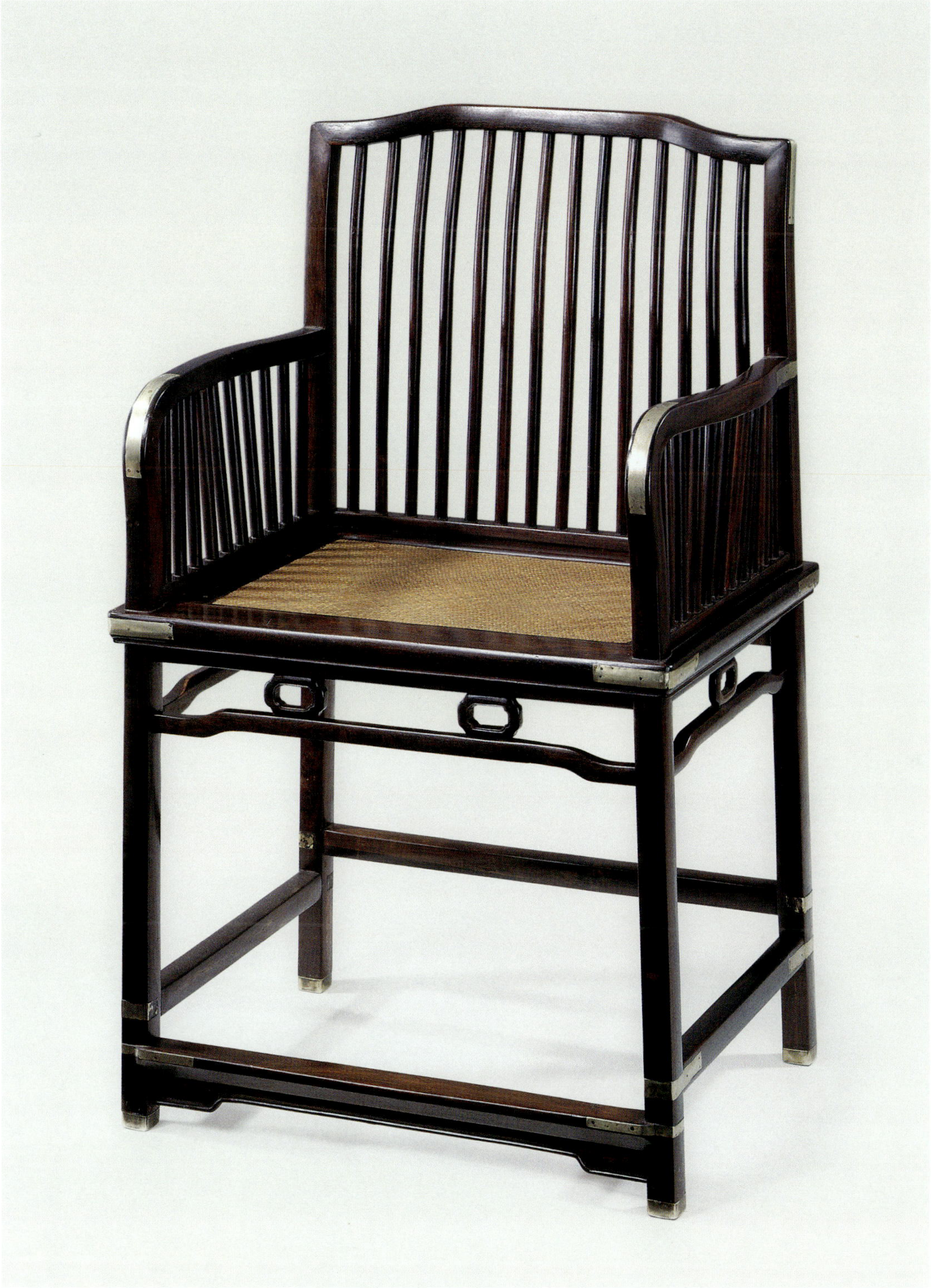

19

Qing-Style Armchair with Marble Panels

紫檀崁大理石清式扶手椅一對

One of a Pair
Zitan and Dali Marble
Late 18th/Early 19th Century
Zhejiang/Fujian
63 x 49 x 92 cm H
Seat Height 50.5 cm

Qing-style chairs are characterized by a construction that appears as a large stool with railings attached above. These chairs also exhibit a pleasing linear style that was popularized during the 18th century, and one which also appears in the stools and tables illustrated as catalogue items 3 and 44. The railings each feature select marble panels with mountainscape scenes, each of which are framed with a vivid arrangement of panels pierced with rectangular beaded openings. The frame members of the railings above and stool-like base are all uniformly shaped with concave surfaces and indented corner moldings. The *zitan* material of their construction is evenly textured with a relatively coarse, open grain, and uniformly muted color–characteristics of '*huali zitan*'.

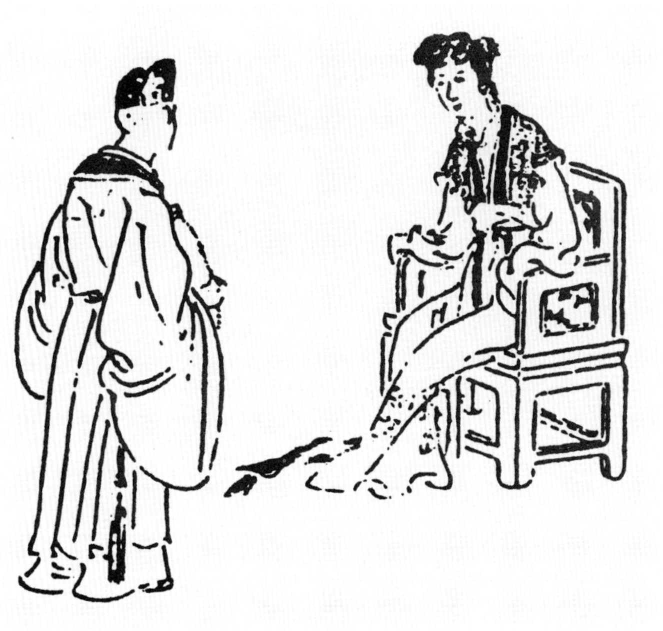

Qing-style armchair with marble panels. Woodcut illustration from Hong lou meng, *Qing Guangxu period (pub. 1882).*

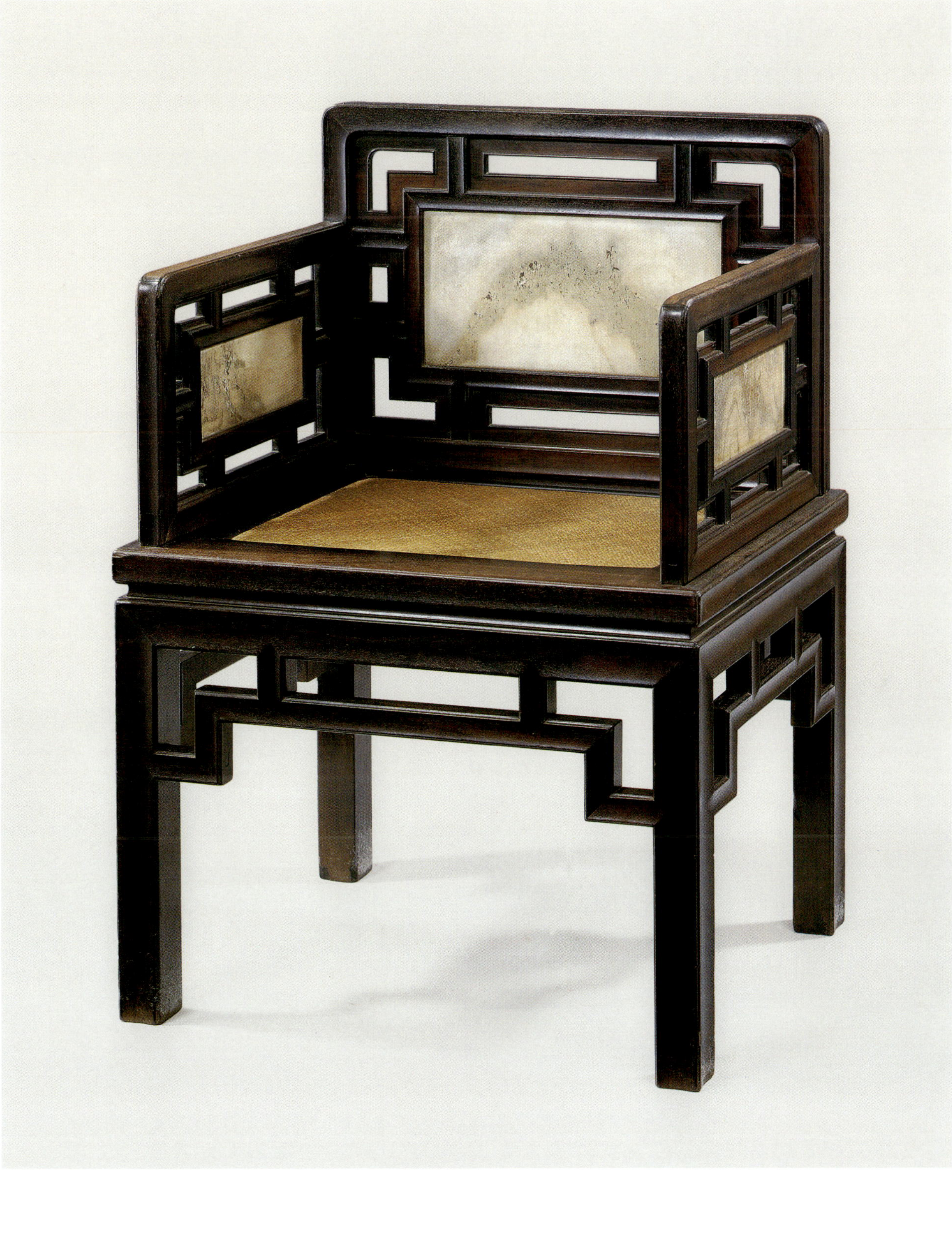

20

Qing-Style Chair with Marble Panel

紫檀崁大理石清式長椅

Zitan and Dali Marble
19th Century
Guangdong
101 x 55 x 93.5 cm H
Seat Height 50 cm

This broad-seated Qing style chair exhibits an elegant southern style. It is constructed as a waisted platform with neatly assembled angular railings attached above. The back railing also features a landscape panel of Dali marble with mountain peaks and misty clouds. The side rails are fitted with flattened armrest supports, a characteristic that appears somewhat commonly amongst 19th and 20th century Cantonese furniture made with *hongmu*.

Blackwood chairs of similar style are published in:

- Cai Yi-An, *Qingdai guangshi jiaju* (Qing dynasty Cantonese furniture), p. 18 fig. c6, p. 19 fig. c8, and p. 39 fig. c53.

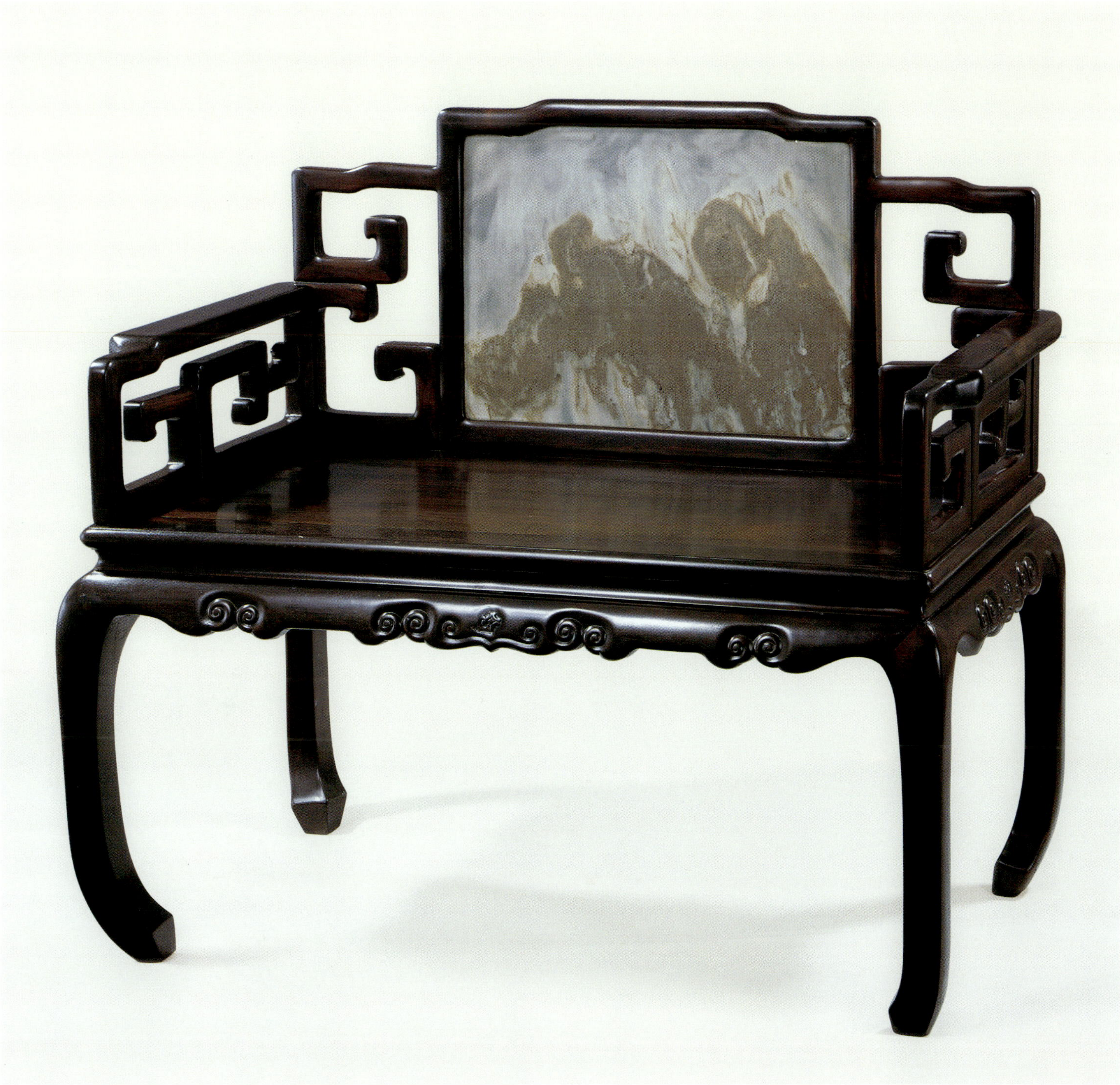

21

Lounge Chair with Retractable Footrest

紫檀梳背躺椅

Zitan
19th Century
Southern China
67.5 x 98.5
(145.5 extended) x 101 cm H
Seat Height 52 cm

Deep-seated chairs were generally accompanied with an adjustable sloping backrest or a soft, cushioned mat for comfortable lounging; erotic paintings also demonstrate their compatibility for lovemaking. Chairs of similar style were commonly made from bamboo; a closely related example is clearly evident in a depiction of 19th century Canton workshop (see detail below). The style of this rare *zitan* chair with spindle-back railings clearly imitates that of the bamboo chair, as well as the detailing that is found in panels of the other bamboo chairs and tables. The retractable footrest assembly is a replacement that was refitted according to the traces of the original design found in the underside, and also corresponds to that detailed in the watercolor painting.

A deep-seated chair of similar form is illustrated in:

- Ellsworth, Robert Hatfield. *Chinese Furniture: One Hundred Examples from the Mimi and Raymond Hung Collection*, pl. 27.

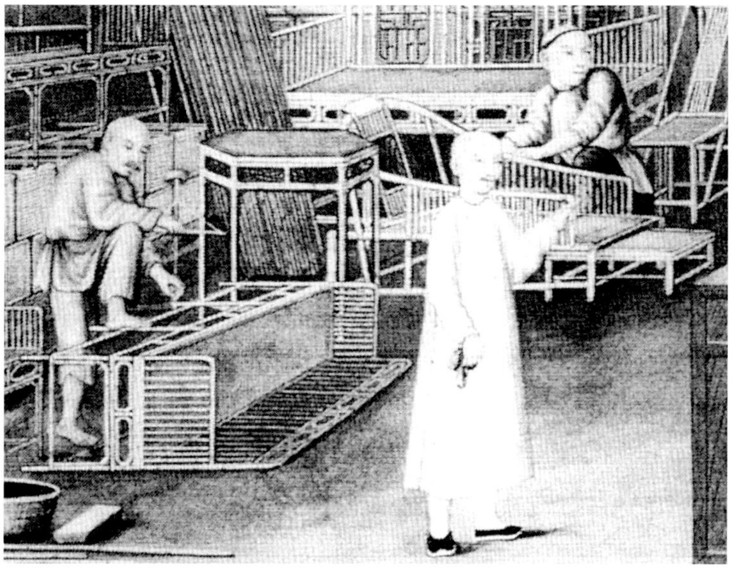

Bamboo lounge chair. Detail from a watercolor painting of a bamboo furniture making shop in Canton, Qing dynasty (ca. 1830).

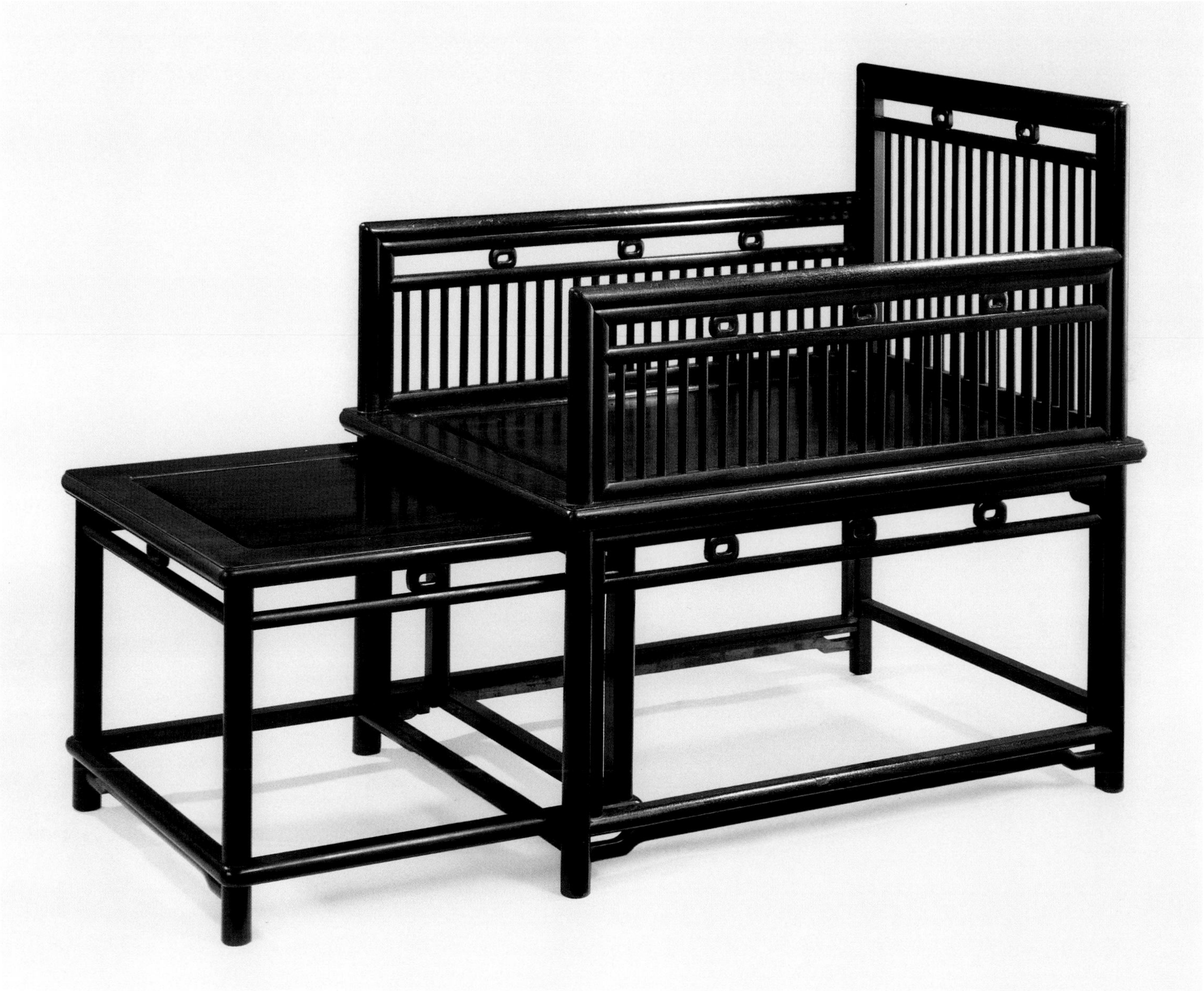

22

Rocking Chair

紫檀崁癭木搖椅一對

One of a Pair
Zitan and Burlwood
19th Century
Guangdong
45.5 x 92.5 x 83.5 cm H

The rocking chair, a category which is on the fringe of traditional Chinese furniture, was likely introduced by Westerners during the mid- to late Qing period. This rare pair of rocking chairs is finely constructed of *zitan*. The curvilinear crestrail is shaped from a single piece, and carved in relief with a pair of bat heads. A large panel of burl wood is fit within the oval-framed backrest. The soft woven seat frame is made as a removable panel. All of the mortise-and-tenon joints are securely locked with wood pins. An inscription incised on the back of each headrest reads, "Directly imported real *zitan*, selected by Tang Baochuan at Guang Chenglong (workshop name)" (see fig. 8, p. 16).

Previously exhibited and published in:

- National Museum of History. *Splendor of Style: Classical Furniture from the Ming and Qing Dynasties*, p. 103.

A chair of related design is illustrated in:

- Pu Anguo. *Zhongguo Hongmu Jiaju* (Chinese Hongmu Furniture), p. 58, fig. 134.

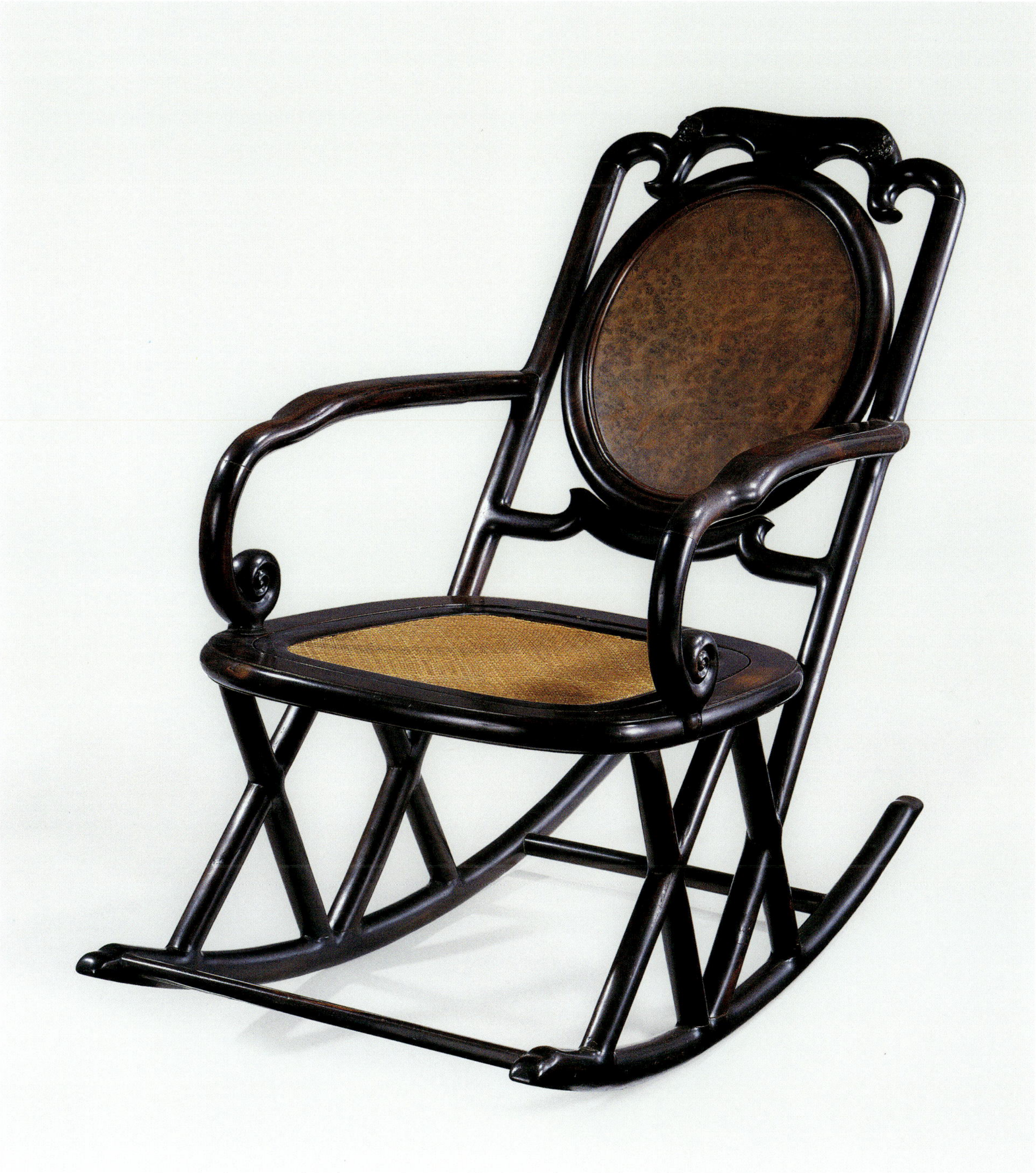

Beds

床榻

23

Daybed

黄花梨有束腰三彎腿榻

Huanghuali
17th Century
North China
214.5 x 105 x 52 cm H

The multi-functional daybed evolved from the ancient platform upon which priests and officials of rank were elevated. They served as a platform for sitting or reclining, and the surface was also used much like a tabletop.

Of waisted corner-leg form, this daybed has cabriole legs that terminate in cloud scroll. The front apron is decorated with scrolling grass raised in relief, and all four are shaped with a thick, rounded beading that continues down the inside of the cabriole legs. The convex molded seat frame is woven with soft caning. The arrangement of stretchers below is comprised of two curved braces of *tieli* that span the mid-section, and straight stretchers at each end that are joined to the short side frame members with two short perpendicular struts.

A similar example is illustrated in:

- Wang Shixiang and Curtis Evarts. *Masterpieces from the Museum of Classical Chinese Furniture*, pl. 4.

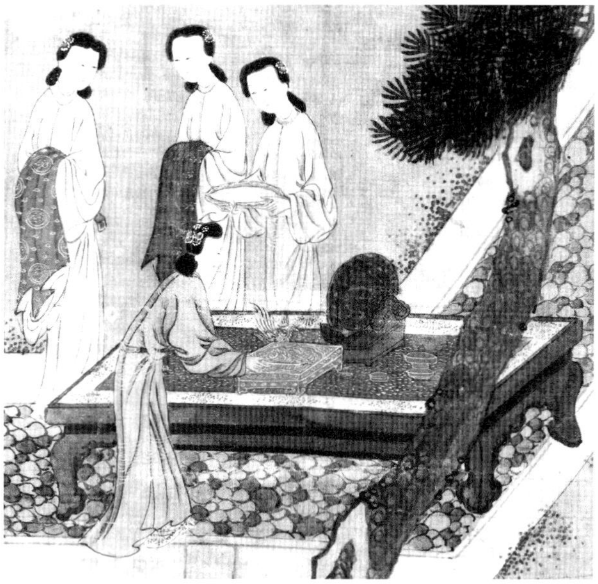

Cabriole leg daybed. Detail from handscroll attributed to Wang Zhenpeng, probably Ming dynasty. National Palace Museum, Taipei.

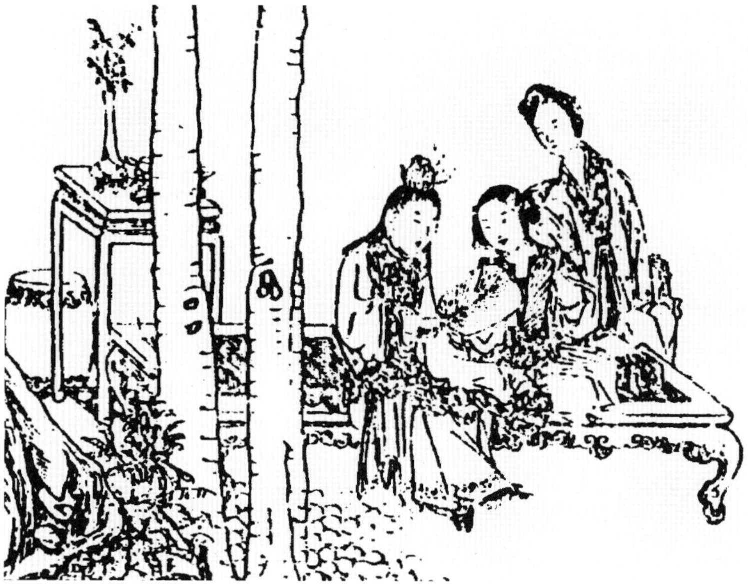

Cabriole leg daybed. Detail from woodcut illustration to Hong lou meng, *Qing Guangxu period (pub. 1879).*

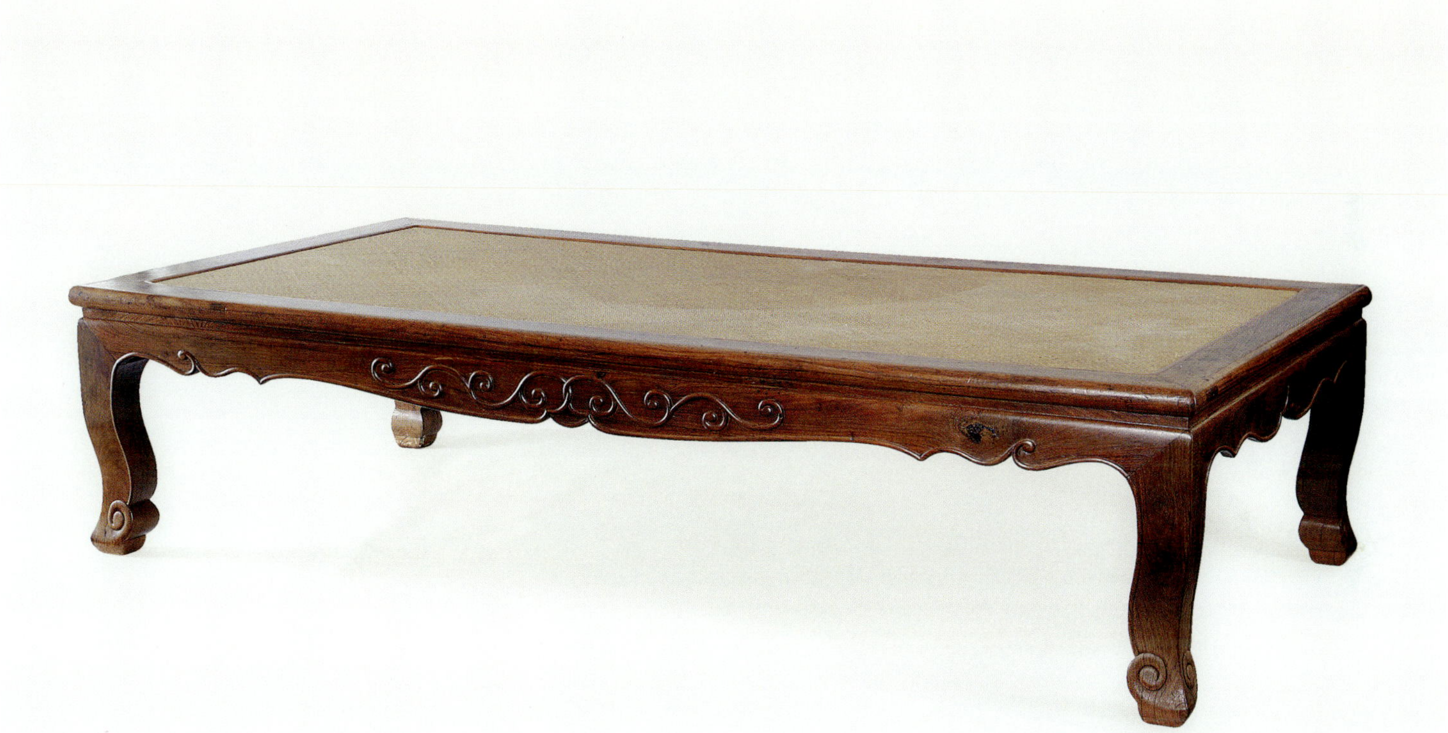

24

Canopy Bed

黄花梨透雕架子床

Huanghuali
18th Century
North China
227 x 157 x 221 cm H

This northern-style canopy bed belongs to a family of six-post canopy beds that share common construction techniques. Although variations are found in their pierced openwork carving, characteristics that identify these beds include: 1) an open-frame top; 2) rich decorative quality of the pierced open work, and; 3) high-waisted platforms, often with bamboo-shaped struts.

The super structure of this bed is supported with six posts of square section with rounded-over corners. The corner posts support an open framework over which silk curtains were draped for privacy as well as to provide insulation from drafty rooms. The frieze of narrow panels and spandrels surrounding the top is pierced with *chi* dragons and *shou* characters. Below, the railings display dragons, auspicious wealth (*fu*) and longevity (*shou*) characters. The rhythm and fluidity of this patterned openwork creates decorative effect that resonates with visual interest. The architecturally styled platform base is solidly constructed. The continuous panels of the high waist are decorated in relief with *chi* dragons and *shou* characters. The stout cabriole legs are carved with *sichituntou* animal masks and clawed feet.

For further discussion on this family of related canopy beds, see:

- Evarts, Curtis. "The Furniture Maker and the Woodworking Traditions of China." Catalogue essay in *Beyond the Screen: Chinese Furniture of the 16th and 17th Centuries*, pp. 58-61.

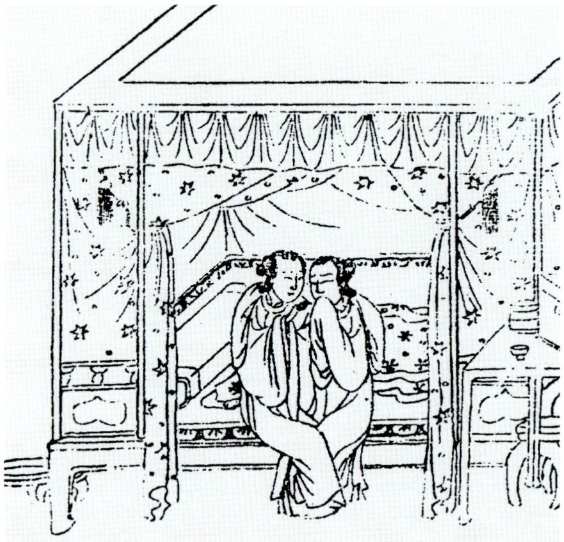

Canopy bed. Detail from woodcut illustration to Xing shi heng, *Ming Tianqi period (1621-1627).*

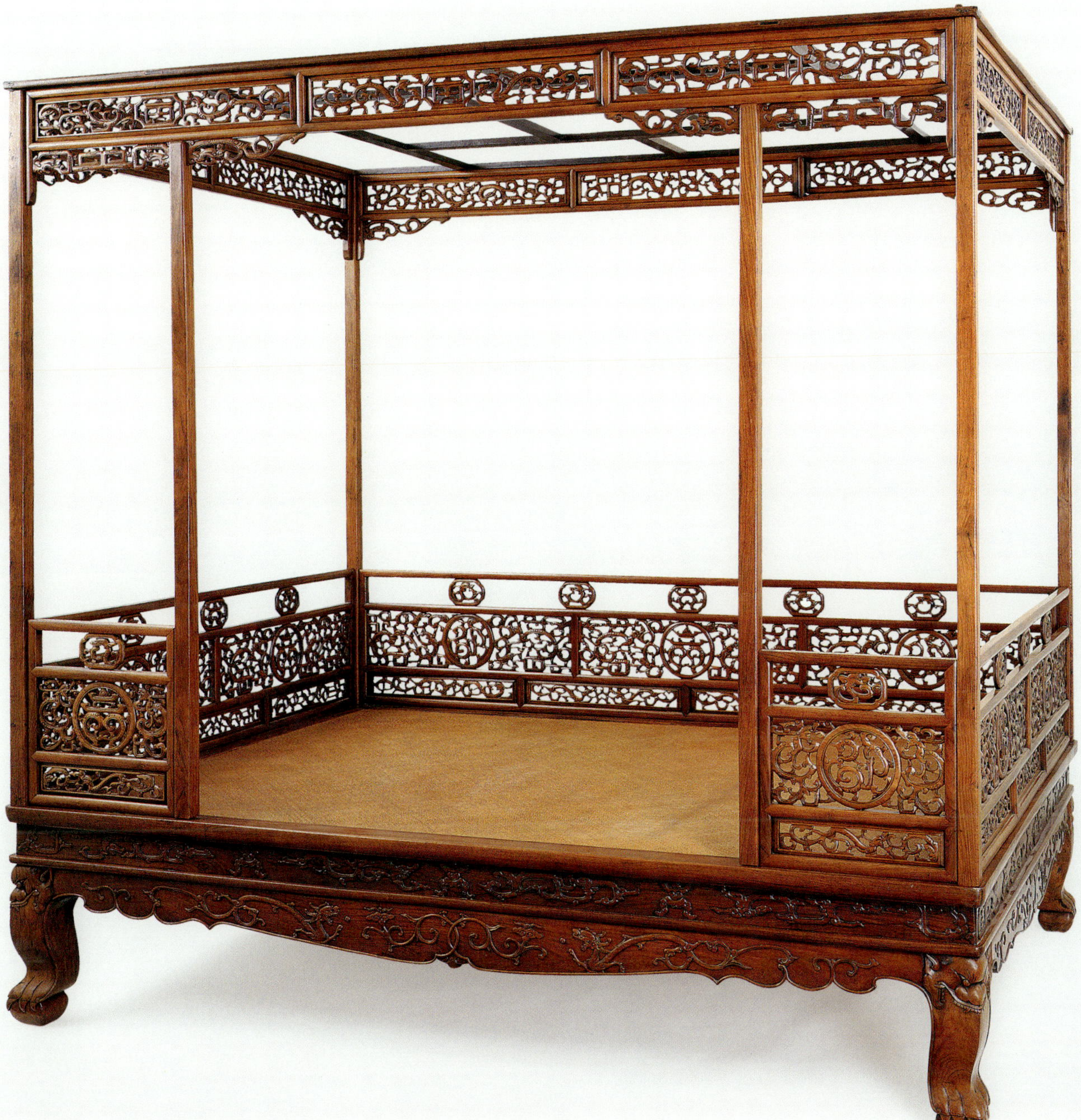

25

Footrest

黄花梨腳踏

Huanghuali
18th Century
North China
110 x 51.5 x 17 cm H

Large footrests were placed in front of a bed or under a large desk where they served as a small step for getting onto the bed, and/or elevated the feet off the cold floor. The scroll-like form of this footrest frame terminates in crisply shaped horsehoof feet. The open frame houses six slats, which are further reinforced with two thin stabilizing braces that pierce through the slats.

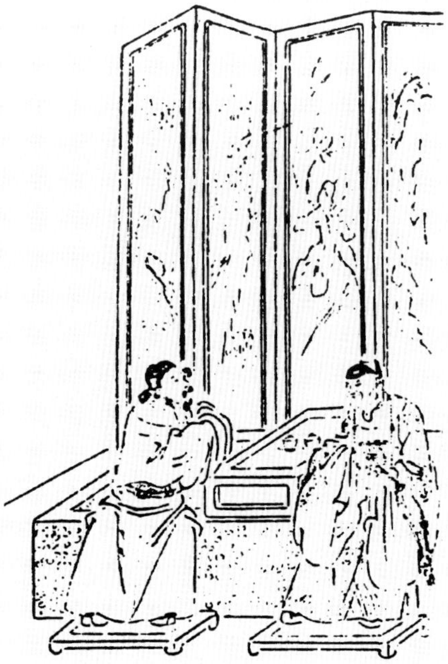

Footrests. Detail from woodcut illustration to Hong lou meng. *Republican period (pub. 1922).*

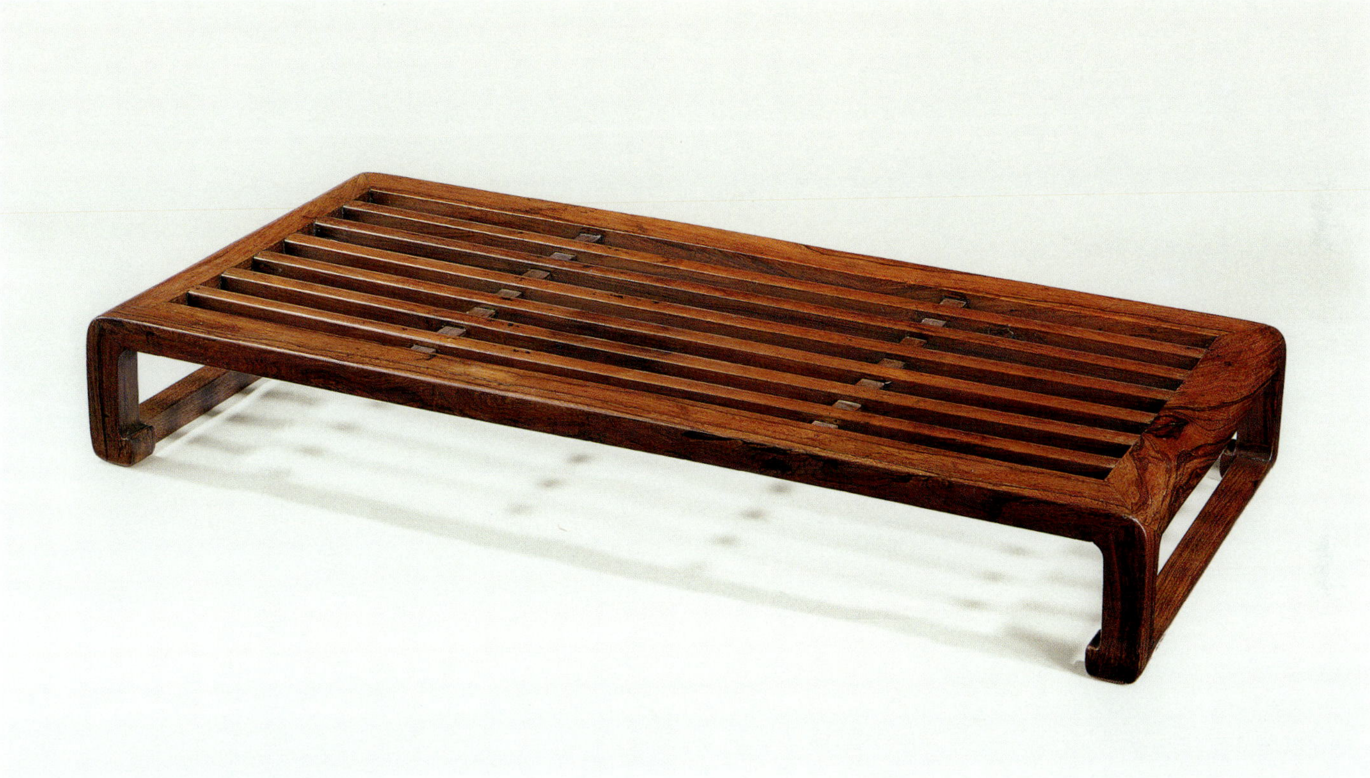

Tables

26

Folding Kang Table

黃花梨折疊炕棹

Huanghuali
16th Century
Shanxi Region
76 x 51.5 x 27 cm H

Small portable tables were convenient for travel, and were especially well suited for boating along the inland waterways or excursions into the mountains. A kang table of similar style depicted in a portrait of the Kangxi Emperor also demonstrates the use of folding-leg kang tables at the Palace (see illustration below).

The legs of this table are joined with double stretchers and hinged to fold under the tabletop within the shallow enclosure of the box-like apron frame. The aprons are finely carved in low relief with winged dragons and lotus blossoms. Such dragons appear in mid-to-late Ming porcelain decoration and stone carving, but rarely as furniture decoration. The finely shaped cabriole legs terminate with a leaf embracing ball and rest upon lotus-shaped pads carved with *ruyi*.

The underside of the table and aprons retain much of an old lacquer coating layered with red and black lacquer. Reinforcing cloth strips are embedded along the joints, and hemp-like fiber distributed throughout the thin plaster-like undercoating.

Previously exhibited and published in:

- National Museum of History. *Splendor of Style: Classical Furniture from the Ming and Qing Dynasties*, p. 116.

Closely related tables are illustrated in:

- Ellsworth, Robert Hatfield. *Chinese Furniture: One Hundred Examples from the Mimi and Raymond Hung Collection*, pl. 36.
- Wang Shixiang and Curtis Evarts. *Masterpieces from the Museum of Classical Chinese Furniture*, pl. 40.

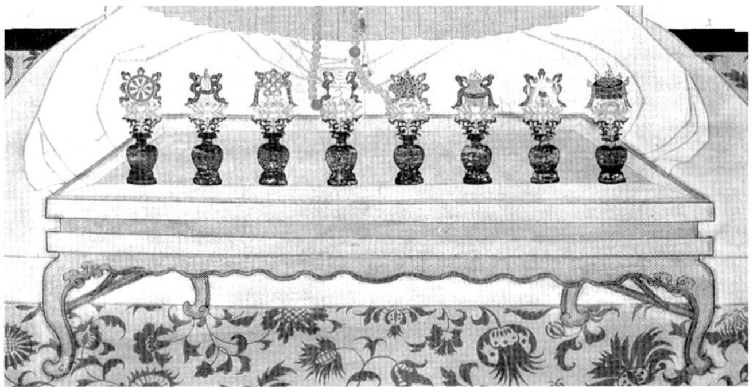

Folding kang table. Detail from portrait of the Kangxi Emperor. Oil painting, early Qing dynasty.

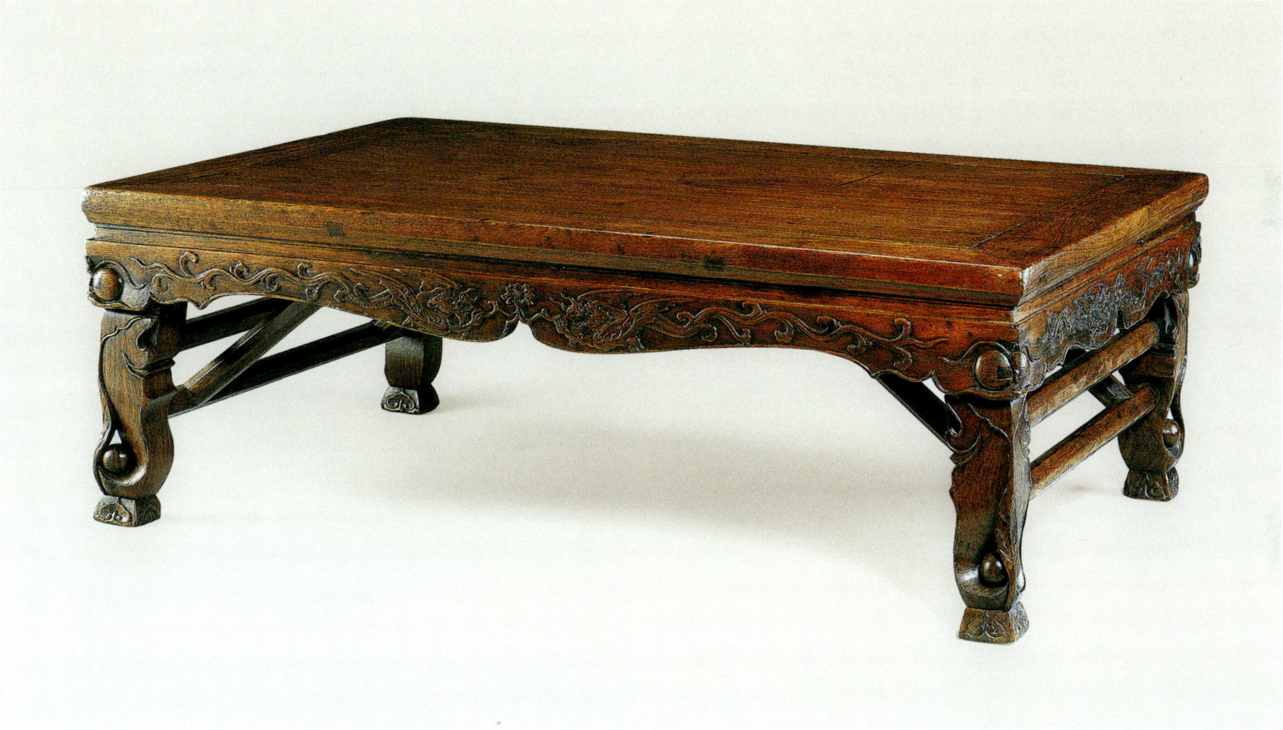

27

Kang Table

紫檀高束腰炕桌

Zitan
17th Century
North China
101 x 65.5 x 27.5 cm H

Low 'kang' tables were typically used in northern China where the widespread use of the kang—a raised, hearth-like platform—provided warmth for family members during the long cold winters. This table exhibits an archaic, high-waisted corner-leg form, and the surfaces are richly decorated in an ornate, northern style. The long narrow waist panels feature scrolling lotus and longevity characters, and the short struts at the corners are decorated with *chi* dragons. The aprons are shaped to a deep curvilinear profile and carved in relief with *chi* dragons and *shou* characters. The shoulders of the short cabriole legs are sculpted with 'four-fanged swallowing heads' (*sichituntou*) and terminate with clawed feet resting upon round pads.

Previously exhibited and published:

- Hong Kong Museum of Art. *In Pursuit of Antiquities*, pl. 281.
- National Museum of History. *Splendor of Style: Classical Furniture from the Ming and Qing Dynasties*, pp. 118-119.

A *huanghuali* kang table with similar decoration and likely produced by the same workshop is illustrated in:

- Wang Shixiang. *Classic Chinese Furniture: Ming and Early Qing Dynasties*, pl. 66.

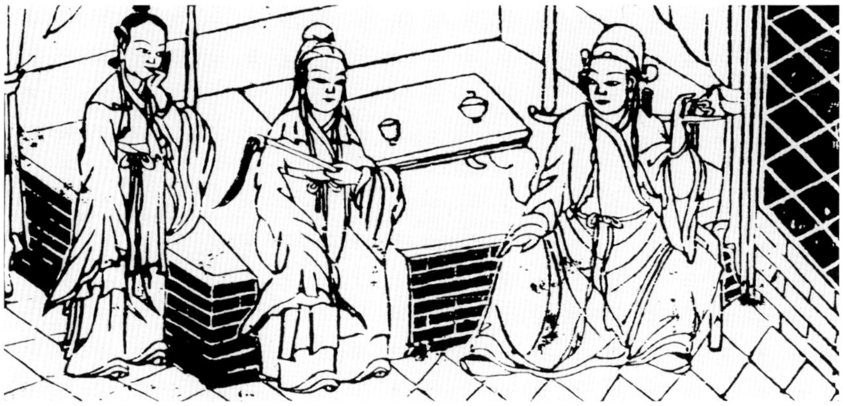

Kang Table. Woodcut illustration from Wang jiang ting, *Qing dynasty.*

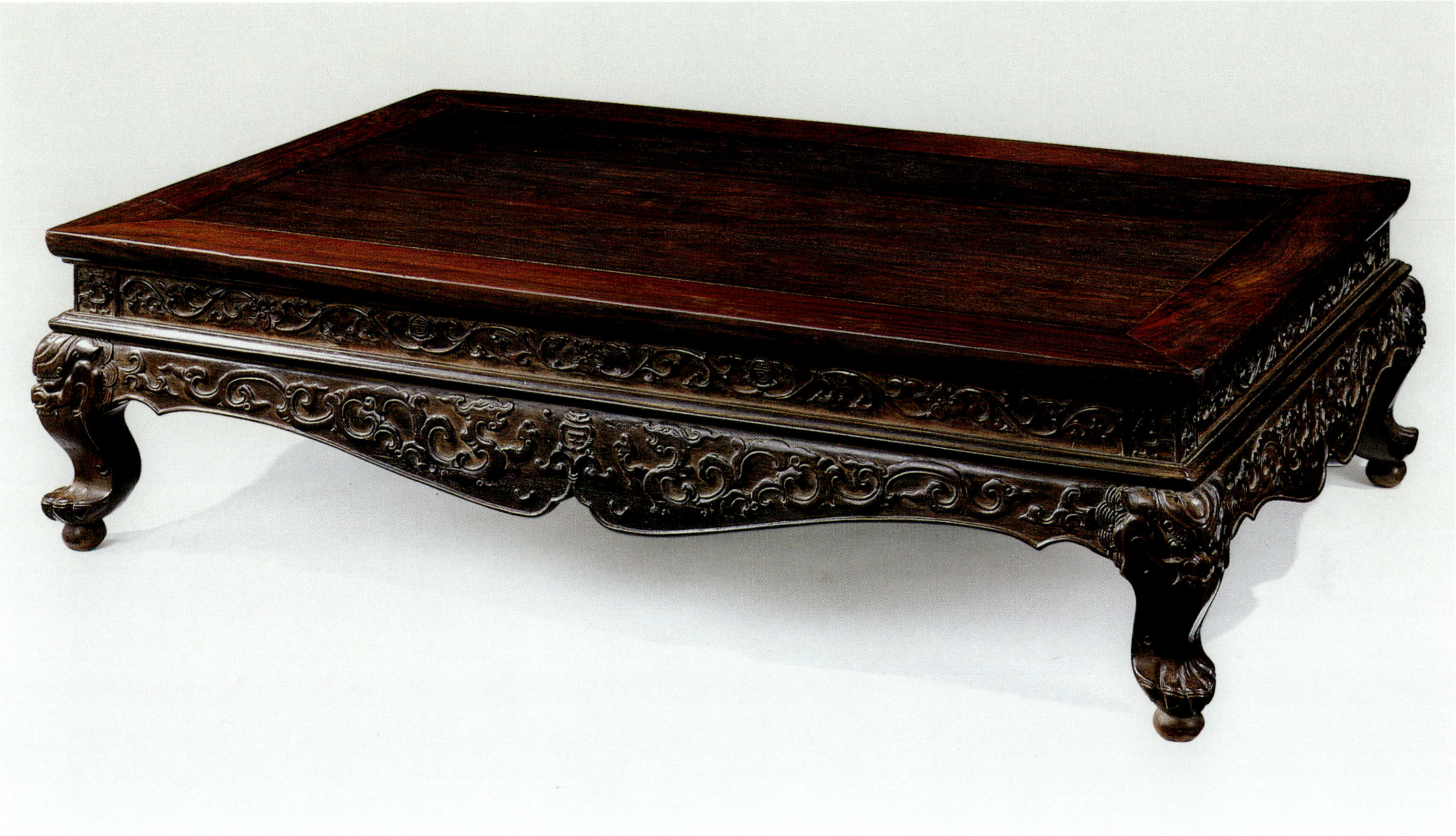

28

Kang Table

紫檀有束腰三彎腿炕桌

Zitan
17th Century
North China
58 x 48 x 16 cm H

Small kang tables were typically placed on beds and couches. This table exhibits a robust, spirited form, expressed through the traditional *kunmen* profiling of the aprons that curve neatly into the short cabriole legs; this seamless line is further accentuated by a wide, rounded beading that terminates in cloud scroll feet. Amongst the various types of *zitan* material, this can be further characterized for its relatively high density and uniform texture. This piece has survived in excellent condition.

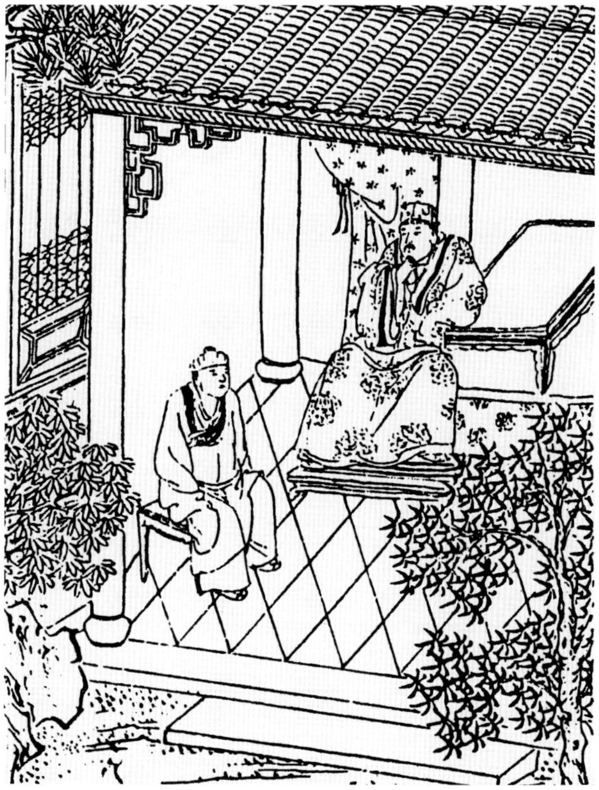

Kang table. Detail from woodcut illustration to Shitou ji, *Qing Guangxu period (1875-1908).*

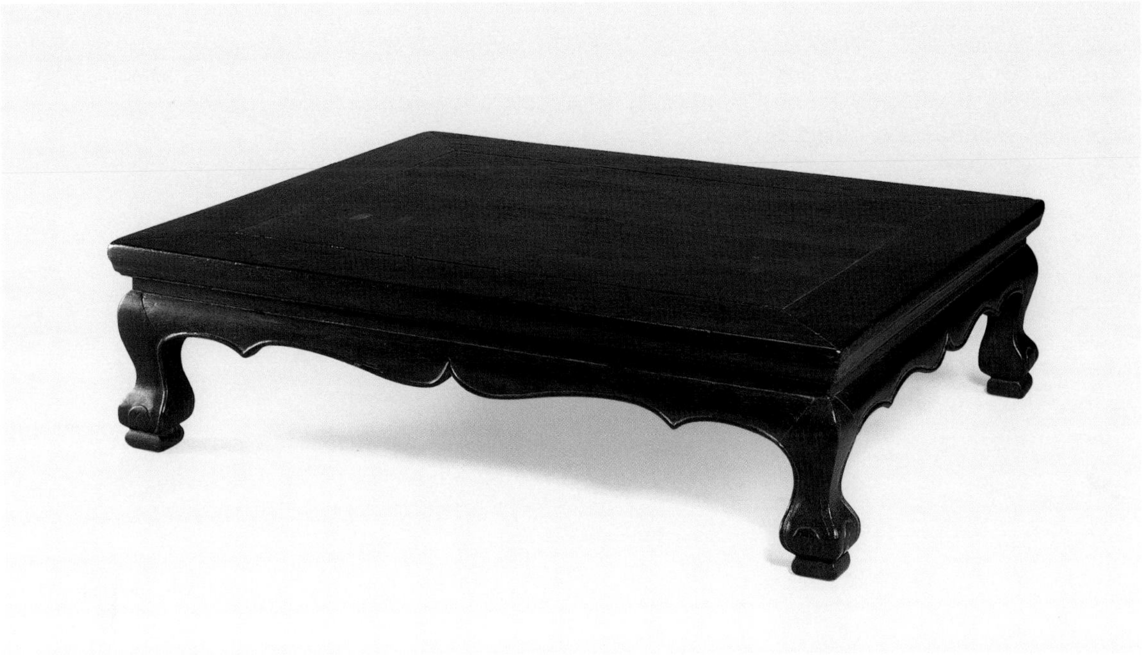

29

Kang Table

紫檀有束腰三彎腿炕棹

Zitan
17th Century
North China
70.5 x 43 x 29 cm H

This *zitan* kang table exhibits a traditional 17th century style, which is further evident in its construction techniques, use of uniform, high quality material, and deep, dark patination. The tabletop frame houses a two-board panel, and the mitered mortise-and-tenon employs a small additional stabilizing tenon at the corner that is exposed. The straight aprons are shaped together with the concave waist, and each section is reinforced from the backside with wedge-shaped dovetail tenons. Beading along the lower edge of the aprons continues down the short cabriole legs, which terminate with a scrolled, *ruyi*-shaped foot.

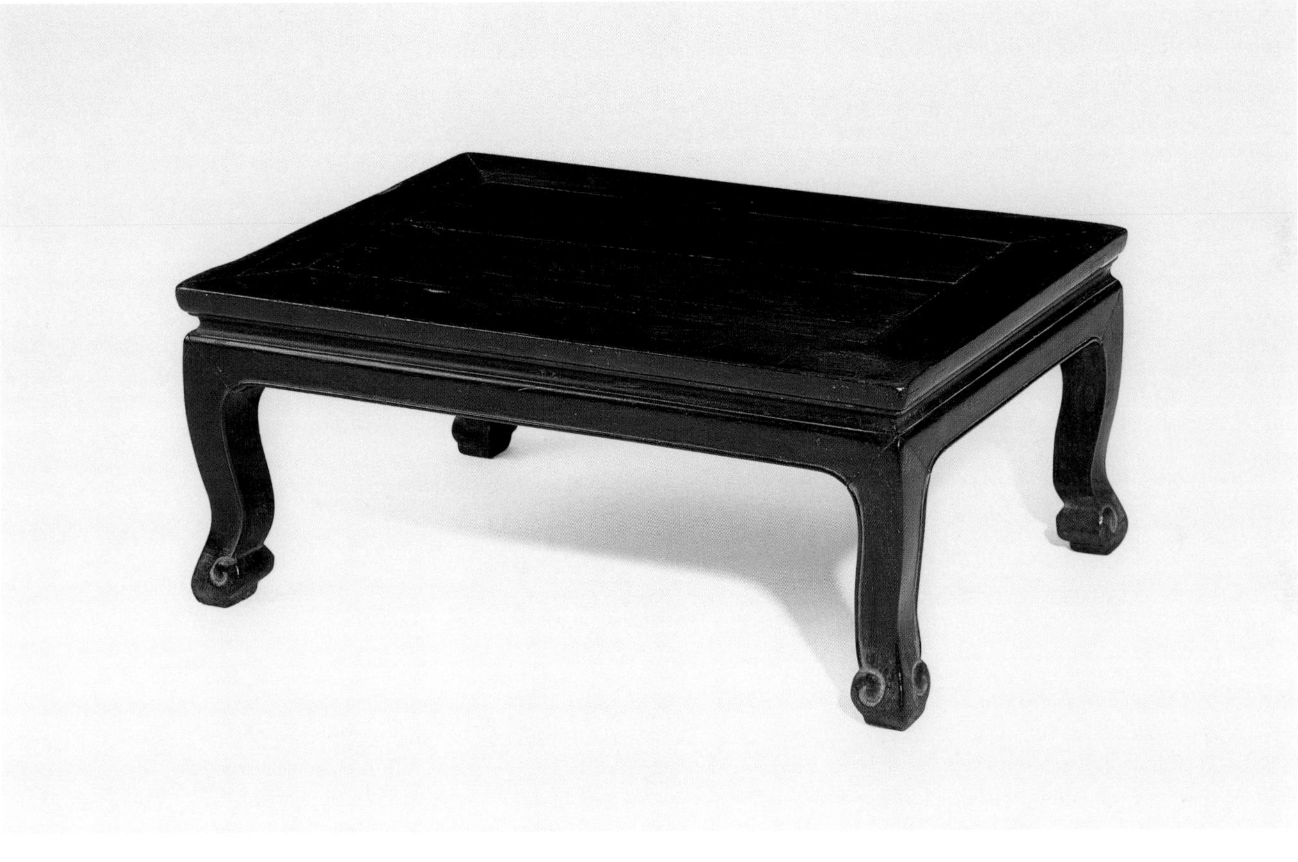

30

Square Kang Table

黄花梨有束腰三彎腿方炕棹

Huanghuali
17th Century
North China
57 x 57 x 24 cm H

This small square table exhibits a light, elegant style with plain, undecorated surfaces. The aprons are shaped to a traditional *kunmen* curvilinear profile and flow into the cabriole legs with a smooth, uninterrupted curve. The tabletop is made up with two panels surrounded by a frame with drip-edge molding. The underside retains traces of an old lacquer undercoating.

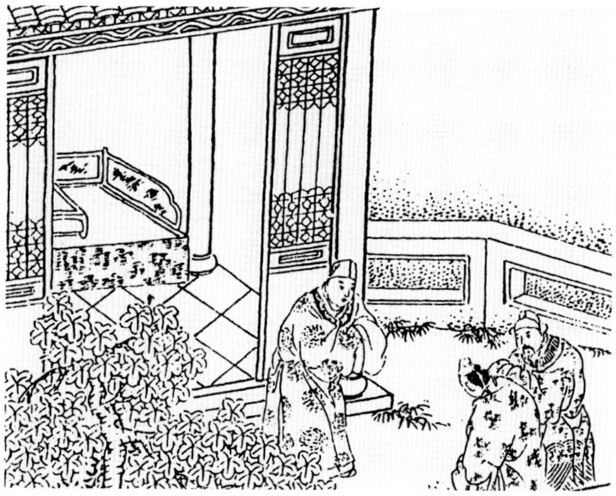

Kang table. Detail from woodcut illustration to Shitou ji, *Qing Guangxu period (1875-1908).*

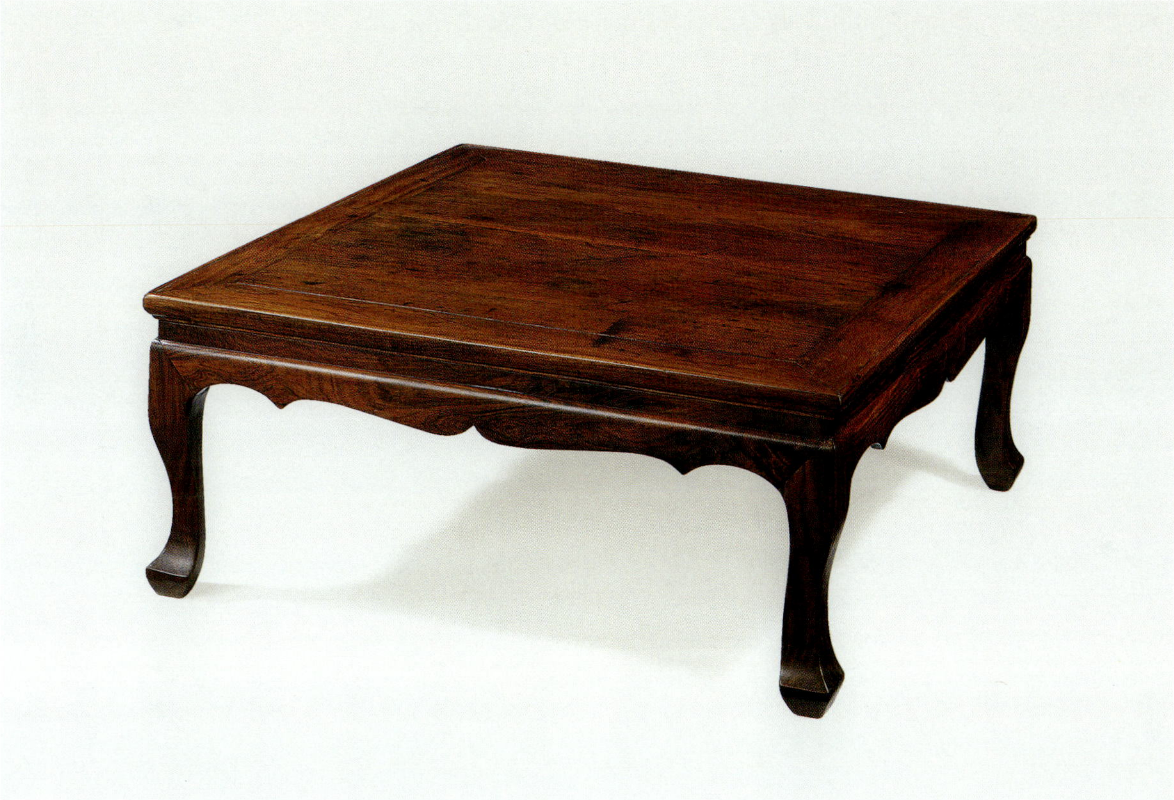

31

Square Kang Table

黄花梨有束腰三彎腿方炕棹

Huanghuali
Late 17th/Early 18th Century
North China
78.5 x 79.5 x 28 cm H

This kang table exhibits a formal, decorative style. Dragons with angular scrolled tails face a standing *ruyi* on each of the aprons, and the four corners are sculpted as guardian beasts. Those on two of the legs as well as the dragonheads on one apron were pared away—perhaps during the Cultural Revolution; these have since been restored. The short cabriole legs terminate in claw feet.

A kang table of similar decorative style is illustrated in:

- Wang Shixiang and Curtis Evarts. *Masterpieces from the Museum of Classical Chinese Furniture*, pl. 39.

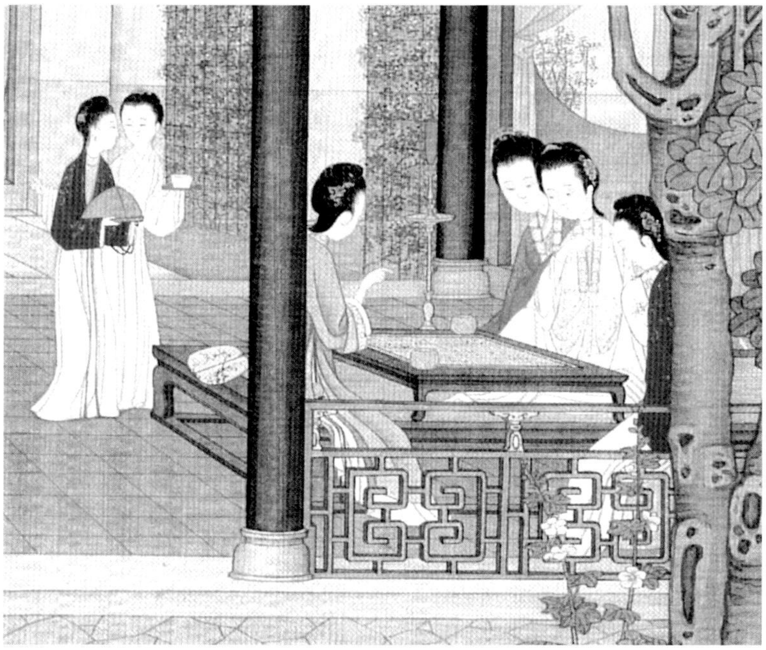

Square kang table. Detail from album leaf set Classical Ladies *by Jiao Bingzhen. Yongzheng period (1723-1735).*

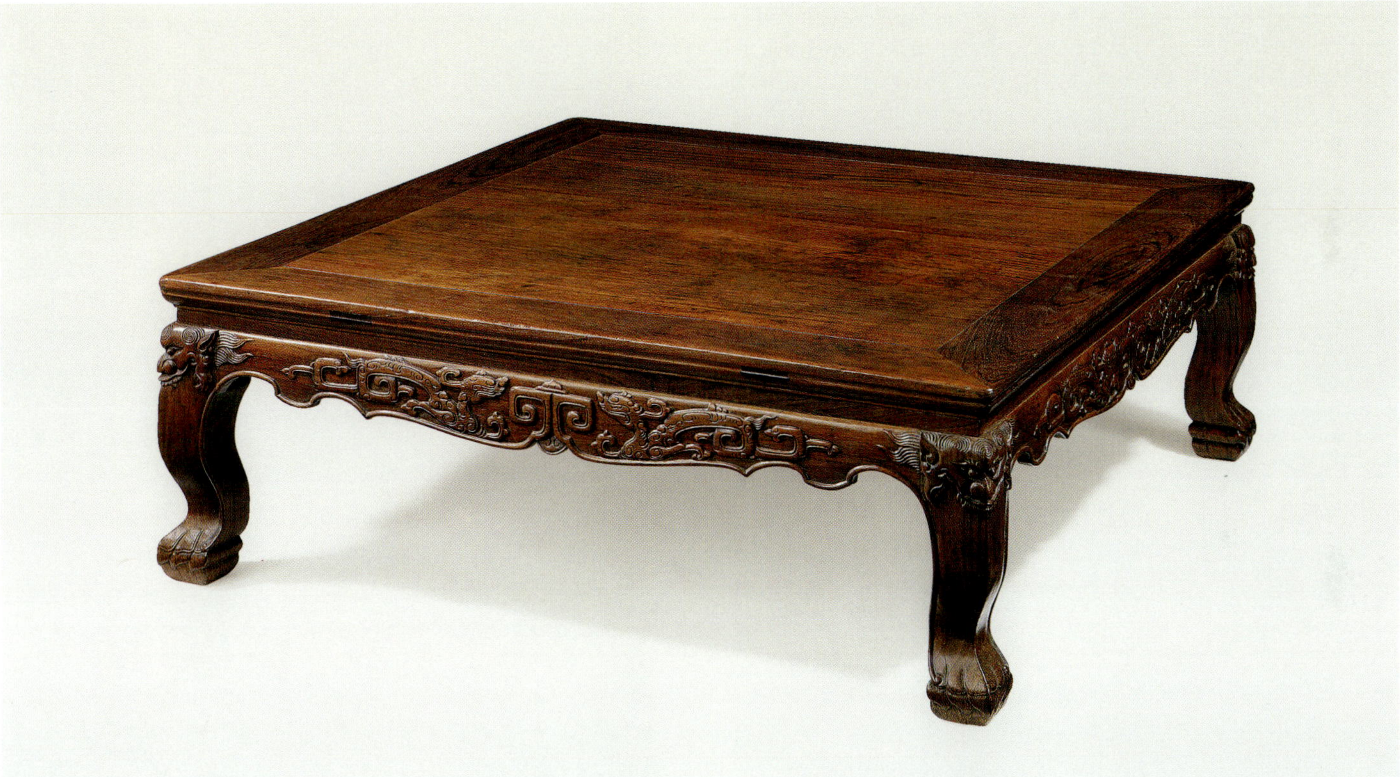

32

Kang Table

紫檀有束腰炕棹

Zitan
Mid 18th Century
North China
87 x 54.5 x 32 cm H

This kang table exhibits a court style associated with middle Qing period. The *zitan* material is of high, uniform quality, and the workmanship exquisitely refined. The carved aprons display a unique technique whereby the *chi* dragons, angular scrolling and *ruyi*-shaped corner lappets all appear raised against a flat ground, with the relief work then worked to a concave profile (see fig. 6, p. 15). Such decorative effect is also found amongst archaic jades produced during the middle Qing period.

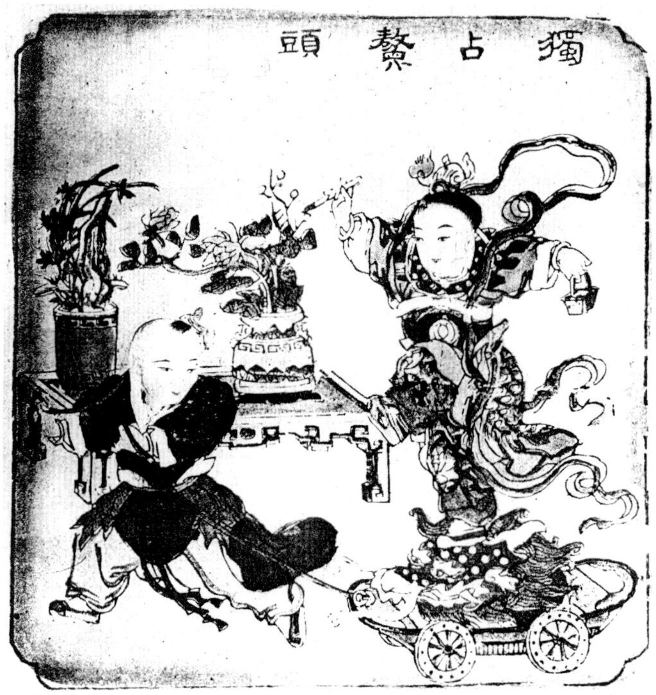

Low table. New Years woodcut illustration by Yang Liuqing. Late 18th/early 19th century.

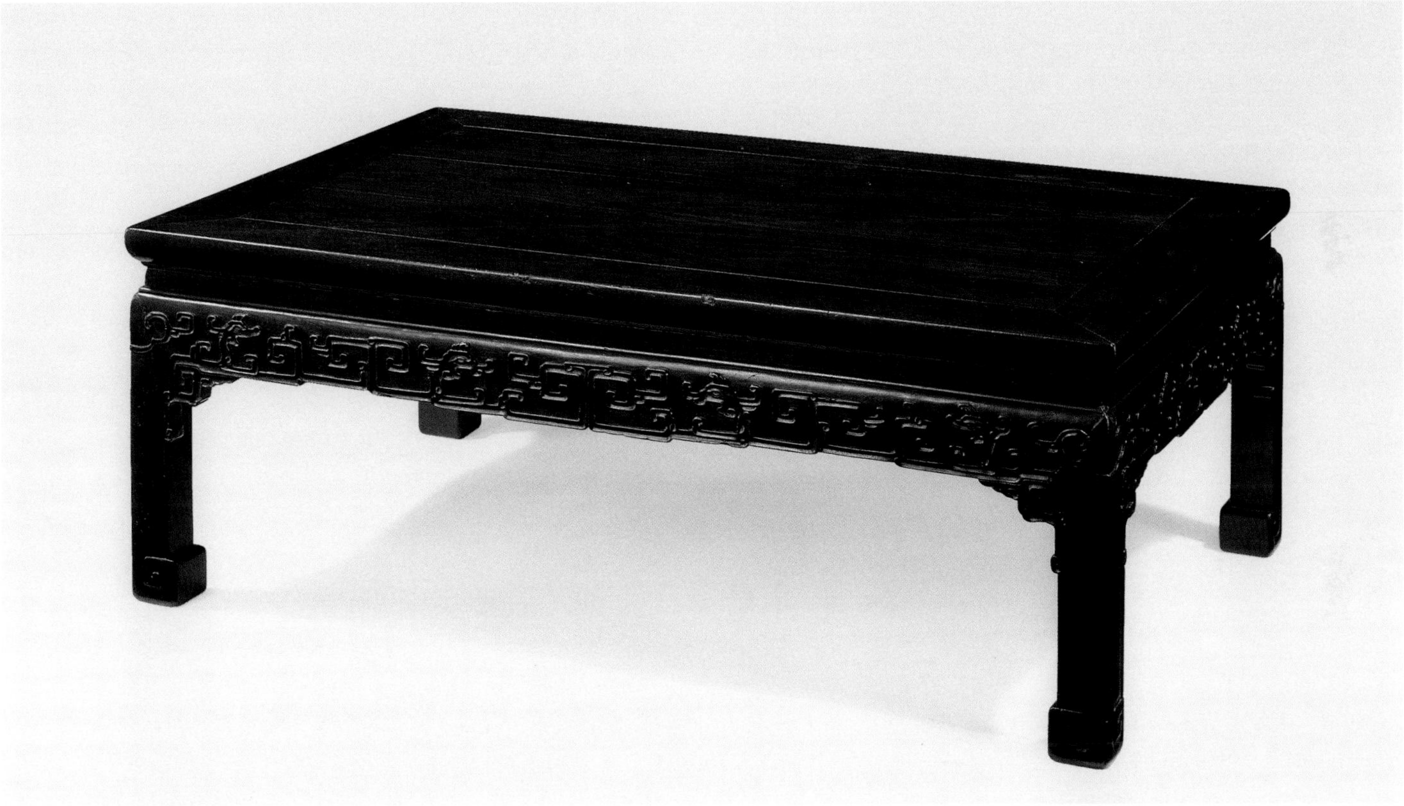

33

Low Scroll Table

黄花梨炕几

Huanghuali
17th Century
Beijing
156 x 33 x 41 cm H

This elegantly shaped low table may have served as a *qin* table. The simple linear form was achieved with three planks of finely figured *huanghuali* timber assembled with invisible dovetail joints. Solid boards of additional thickness were required to achieve a radiused-corner effect as well as to shape the scrolled feet, which are not laminated, but one with the end panels. Compact round medallions pierced and carved with angular dragons complement the minimalistic form.

A low scroll table made from solid *zitan* timber is illustrated in:

- National Museum of History. *Splendor of Style: Classical Furniture from the Ming and Qing Dynasties*, p. 132.

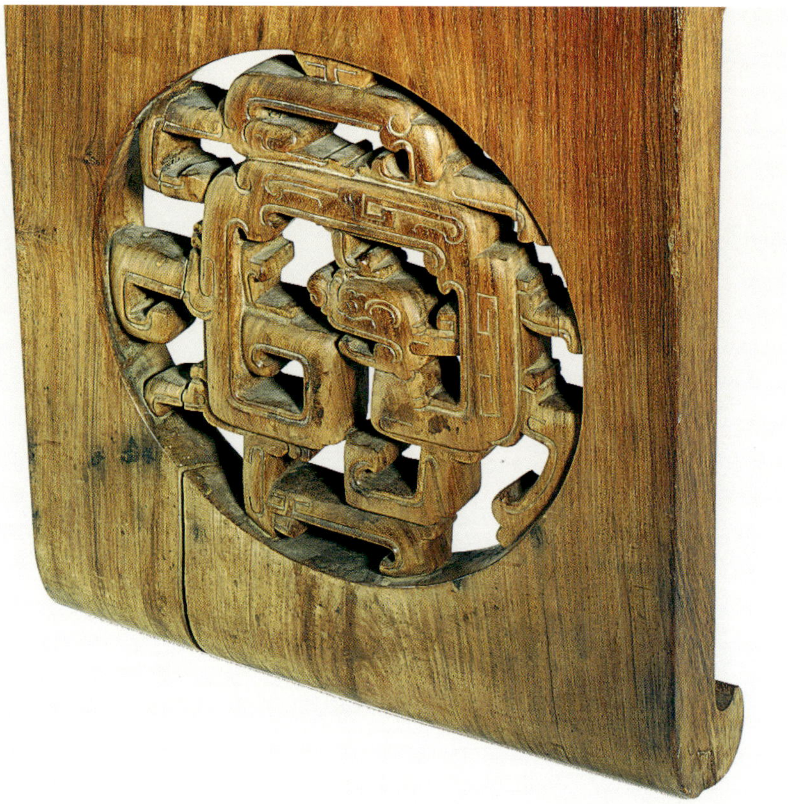

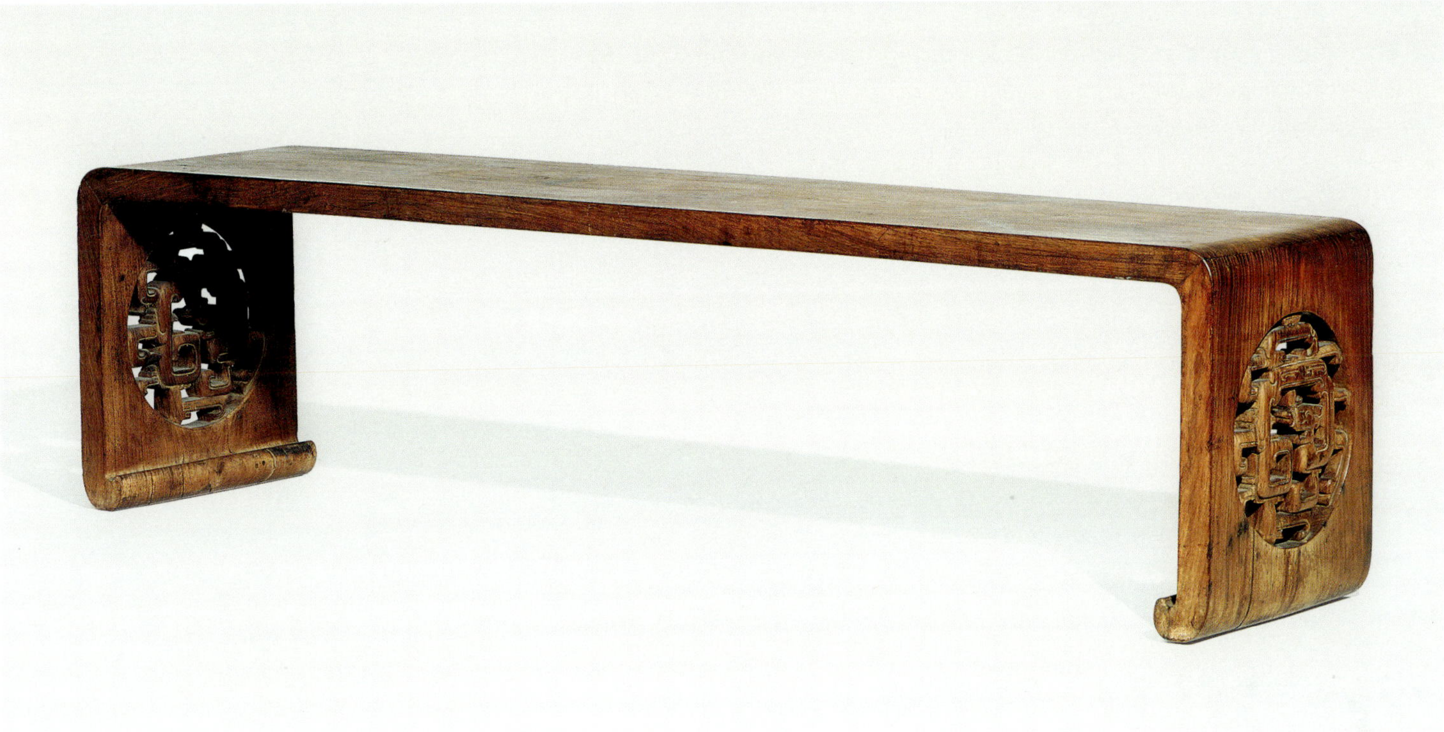

34

Low Scroll Table

黃花梨雕雲紋炕几

Huanghuali
Early 18th Century
Beijing
85.6 x 32.8 x 35 cm H

The sides and top of this low table are fabricated with solid timbers of finely figured *huanghuali*. A molding attached around the inner edge of the table imparts the appearance of additional thickness, and the joint is cleverly concealed within the finely carved key-fret border. Additional material is also laminated at the base for the scrolled foot design, the ends of each which are embellished with a dragonhead in fine relief work. The end panels are pierced and carved with bracketed decoration that supports a medallion decorated with a *ruyi* cloud head and *wanzi* motif. The quality of workmanship of this piece may reflect an Imperial Workshops origin, and its refined decorative style corresponds with an early 18th century attribution.

Previously exhibited and published in:
- National Museum of History. *Splendor of Style: Classical Furniture from the Ming and Qing Dynasties*, p. 126.

Previously published in:
- Wang Shixiang. *Connoisseurship of Chinese Furniture*, B16 and fig. 4.19e.

A table of related style is illustrated in:
- Ellsworth, Robert H. Chinese Furniture. *Hardwood Examples of the Ming and Early Ch'ing Dynasties*, pl. 99.

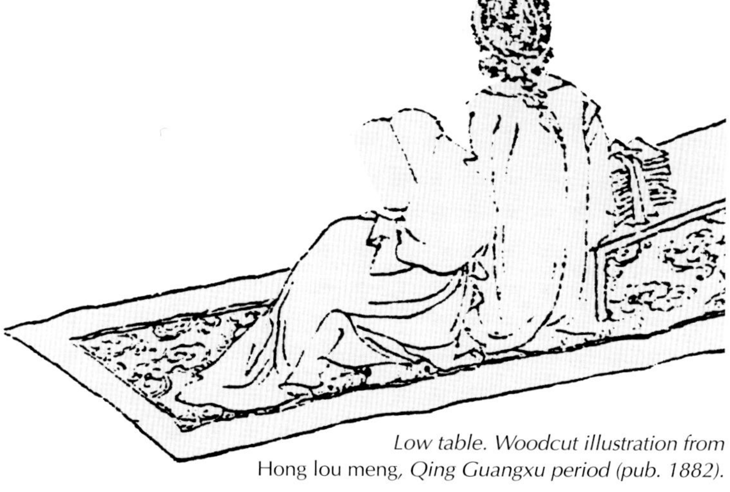

Low table. Woodcut illustration from
Hong lou meng, *Qing Guangxu period (pub. 1882).*

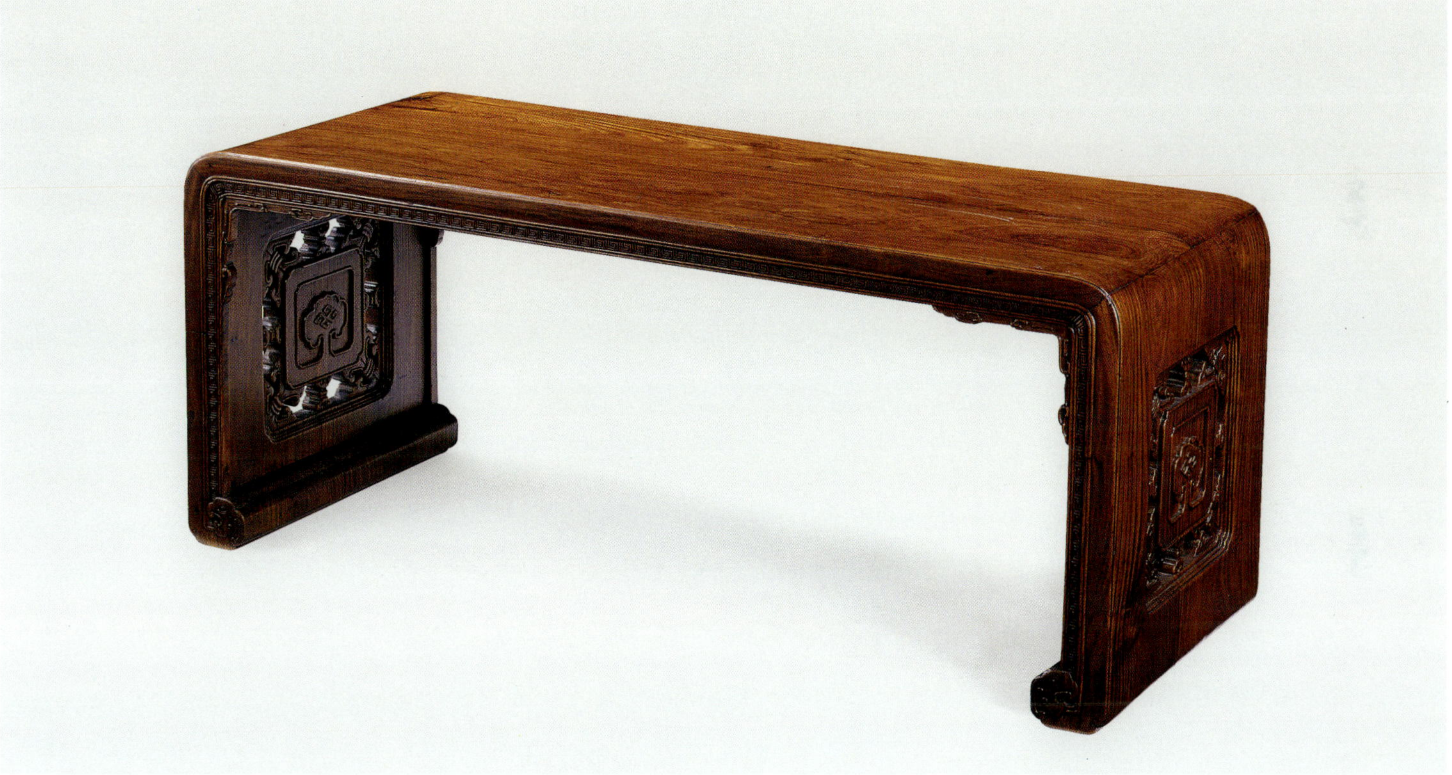

35

Low Altar Table

黃花梨矮夾頭翹頭案

Huanghuali
Early 18th Century
North China
94 x 32 x 51 cm H

Within a temple setting, a secondary table of smaller scale was often placed in front of the large altar table. The reduced proportions of this altar table suggest that it was made for such purpose or perhaps a confined space.

Quality workmanship is evident throughout this piece, which is further reflected in its well-preserved condition. The solid-timber top is fit with rounded-over everted flanges. The aprons are neatly carved in low relief with angular scroll designs, and the end panels are pierced and carved with round longevity (*shou*) characters.

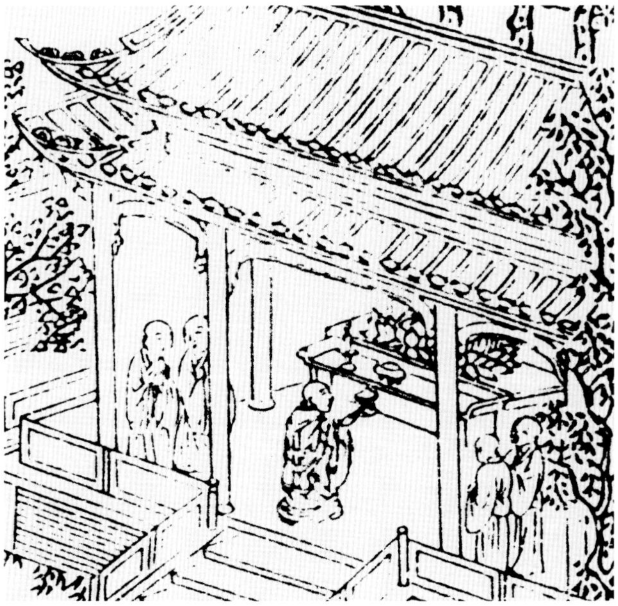

Stepped altar tables. Woodcut illustration, late Ming period.

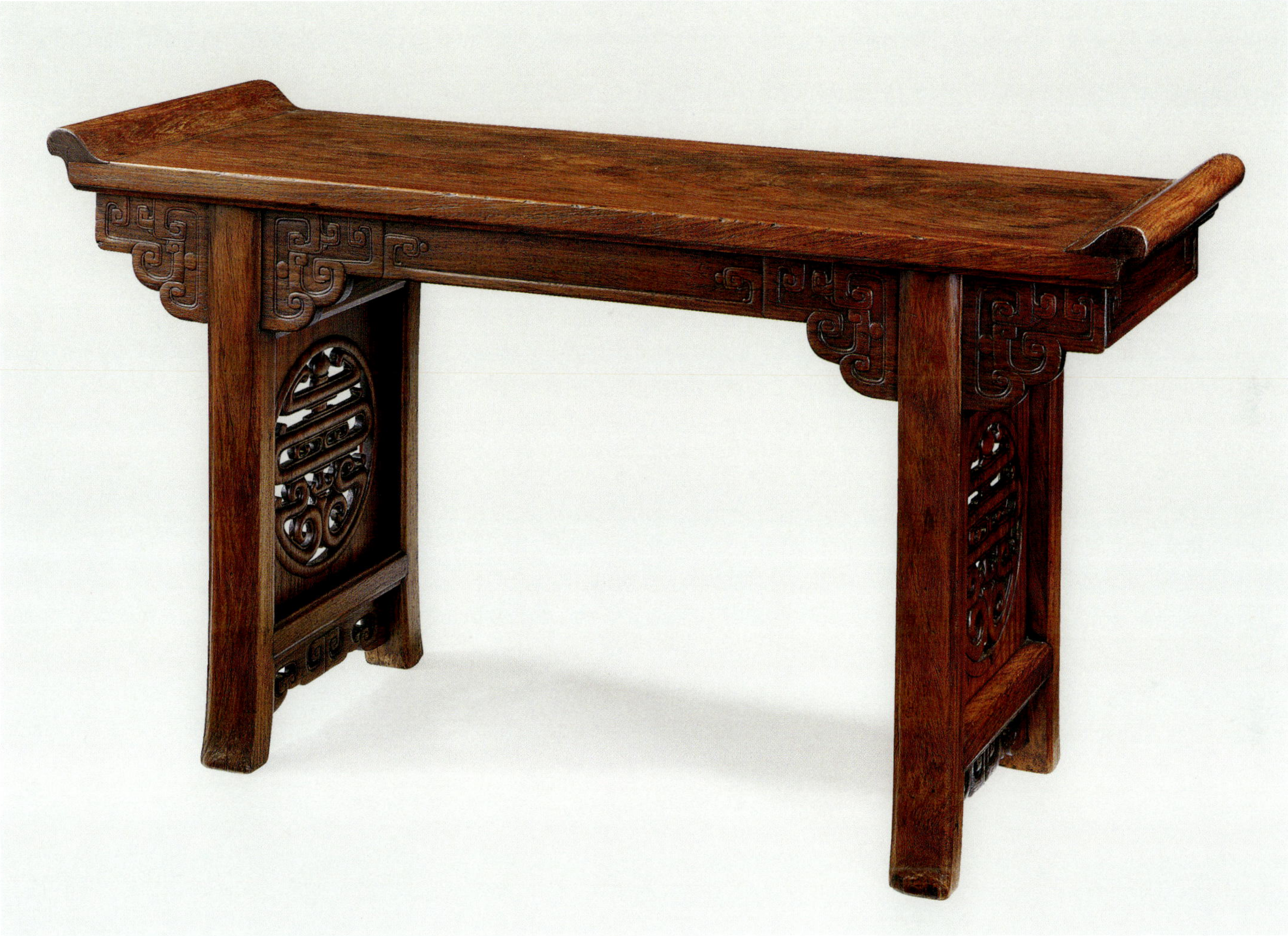

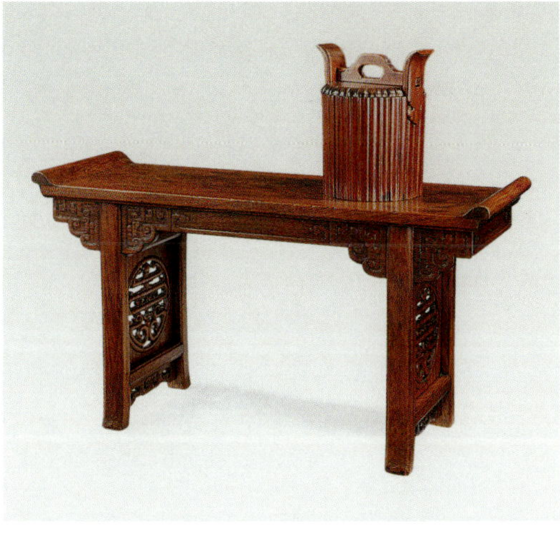

36

Box-Style Altar Table

黄花梨壽子供案

Huanghuali
18th Century
Fujian
105 x 65 x 87 cm H

Serving as a platform to display ritual objects and to set out offerings, the altar table existed in various forms. As depicted in the woodcut illustration below, this box-style altar table may have been similarly arranged with a censer, candlesticks, and vases. The longevity (*shou*) character decoration suggests an origin from an ancestral hall.

This table was discovered in Quanzhou, Fujian province along with the renowned screen formerly in the Museum of Classical Chinese Furniture collection and now with the Minneapolis Institute of the Arts. The use of thick *huanghuali* timber for the construction of its framework may also reflect proximity of Quanzhou to sources of prized tropical hardwoods such as *huanghuali*, *tielimu*, and *jichimu*. Hardwood furniture from the southeastern region is frequently characterized by a generous use of timber.

The *simianping* box-like form is rare amongst extant altar tables. The top is shaped with a thick lip and is profiled with corner indentations that continue down through the massive front legs. The lattice panels, which feature round longevity (*shou*) characters and angular *chi* dragons, exhibit an 18th century decorative style.

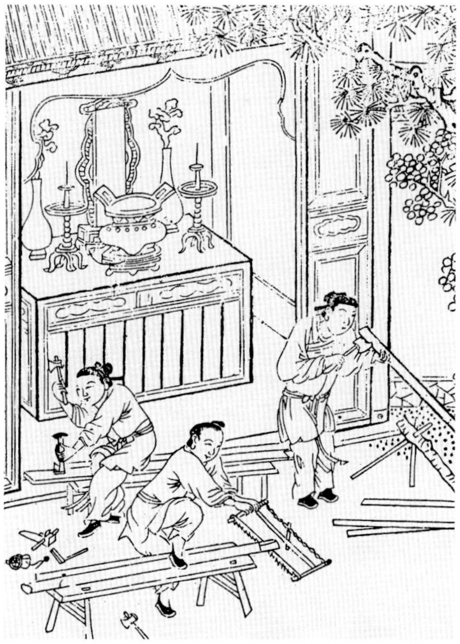

Altar table. Detail from woodcut illustration to Lou li lang, *Ming Wanli period.*

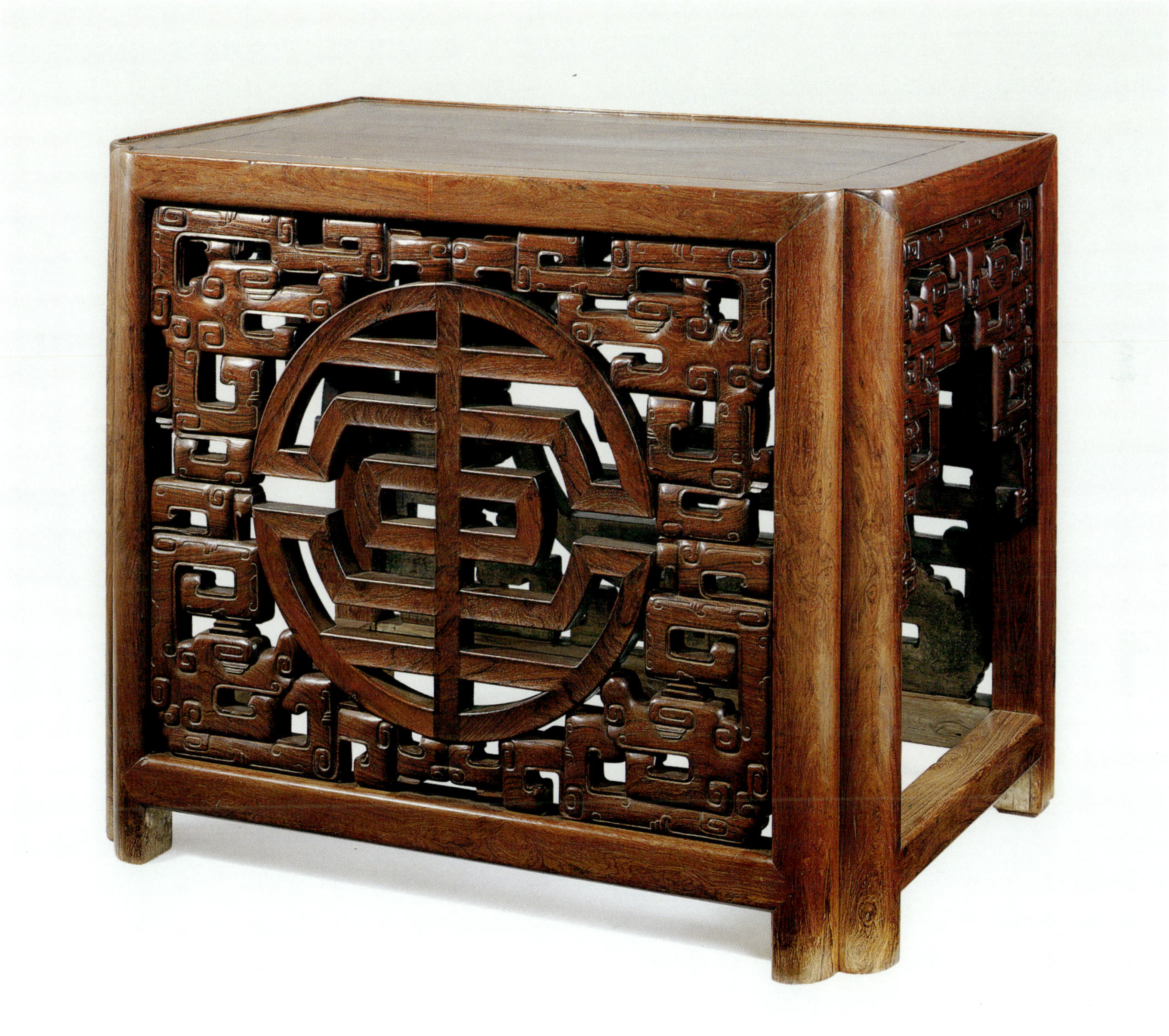

37

Formal Side Table

黃花梨夾頭翹頭案

Huanghuali
17th Century
North China
208 x 39.7 x 85.3 cm H

This recessed-leg side table features a solid timber top with everted flanges attached at each end. The aprons are also made from single boards, and the cloud scroll relief carving on each of the spandrel heads appears as an animal mask (*taotie*) design. The end panels are each pierced and carved with a standing *ruyi*, which is bracketed by four small *ruyi* around the edges.

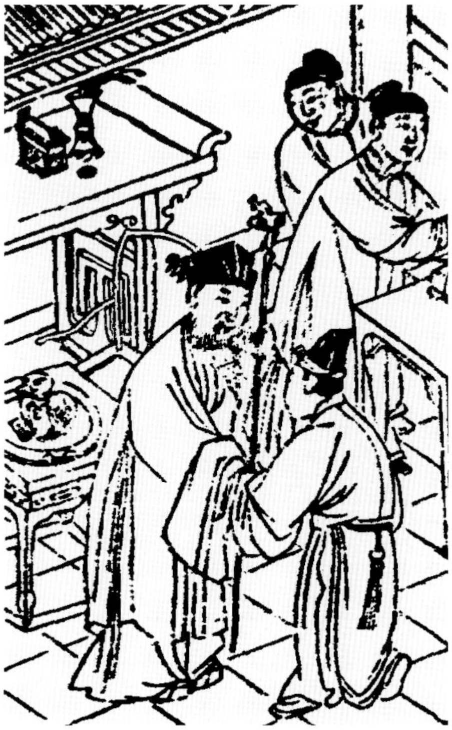

Formal side table. Detail from woodblock illustration to Yangzhou meng, *Qing Kangxi period (1662-1722).*

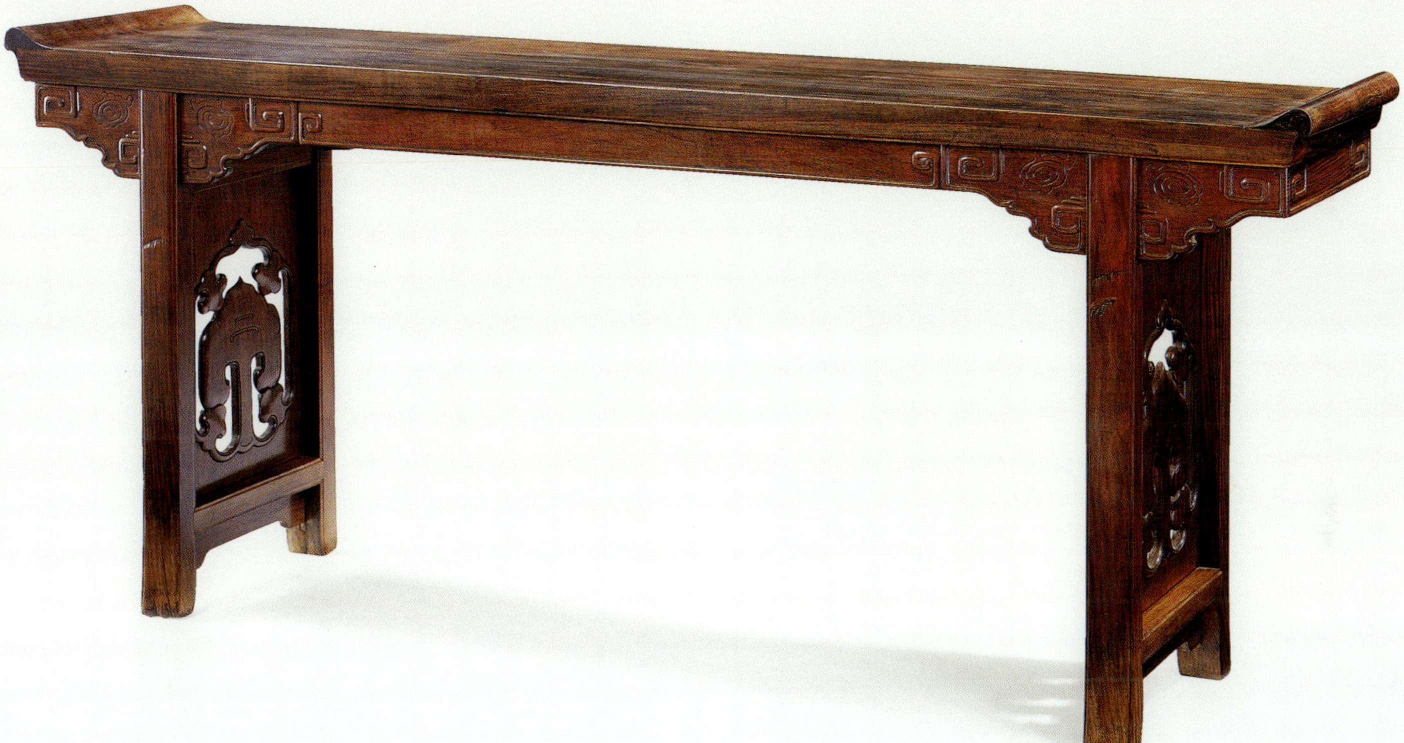

38

Formal Side Table

黃花梨夾頭翹頭案

Huanghuali
Early 17th Century
Anhui
213 x 36.5 x 86.5 cm H

This table exhibits a light, lyrical style and reflects decorative characteristics of the Anhui region. The solid plank top is highly figured and fit with lively upturned ends. Bracket-like aprons extend through the legs as long, reinforcing supports. The spandrel heads are neatly carved with scrolling grass and ruyi heads.

The legs splay outward more than normal, and additionally flare outward near the base. A panel with an open-carved *ruyi* of scrolling grass is framed between the legs; below, there is a narrow horizontal panel with a beaded *haitangshi* cutout, and a curvilinear apron at the base.

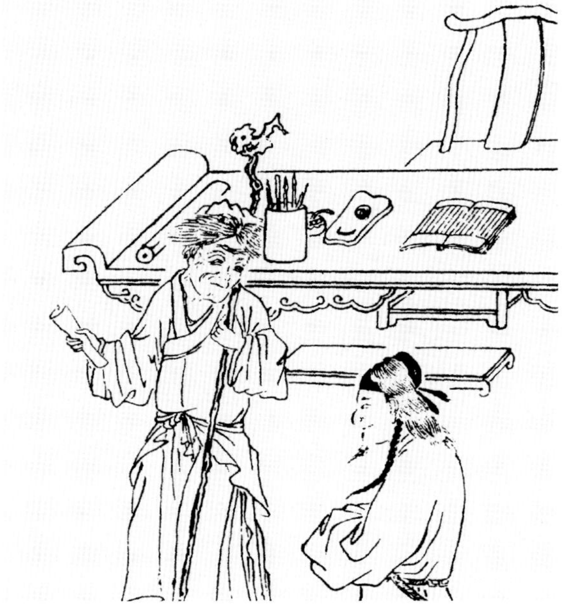

Formal side table. Detail from woodcut illustration to Imperial Edicts, *Qing Kangxi period (1662-1722).*

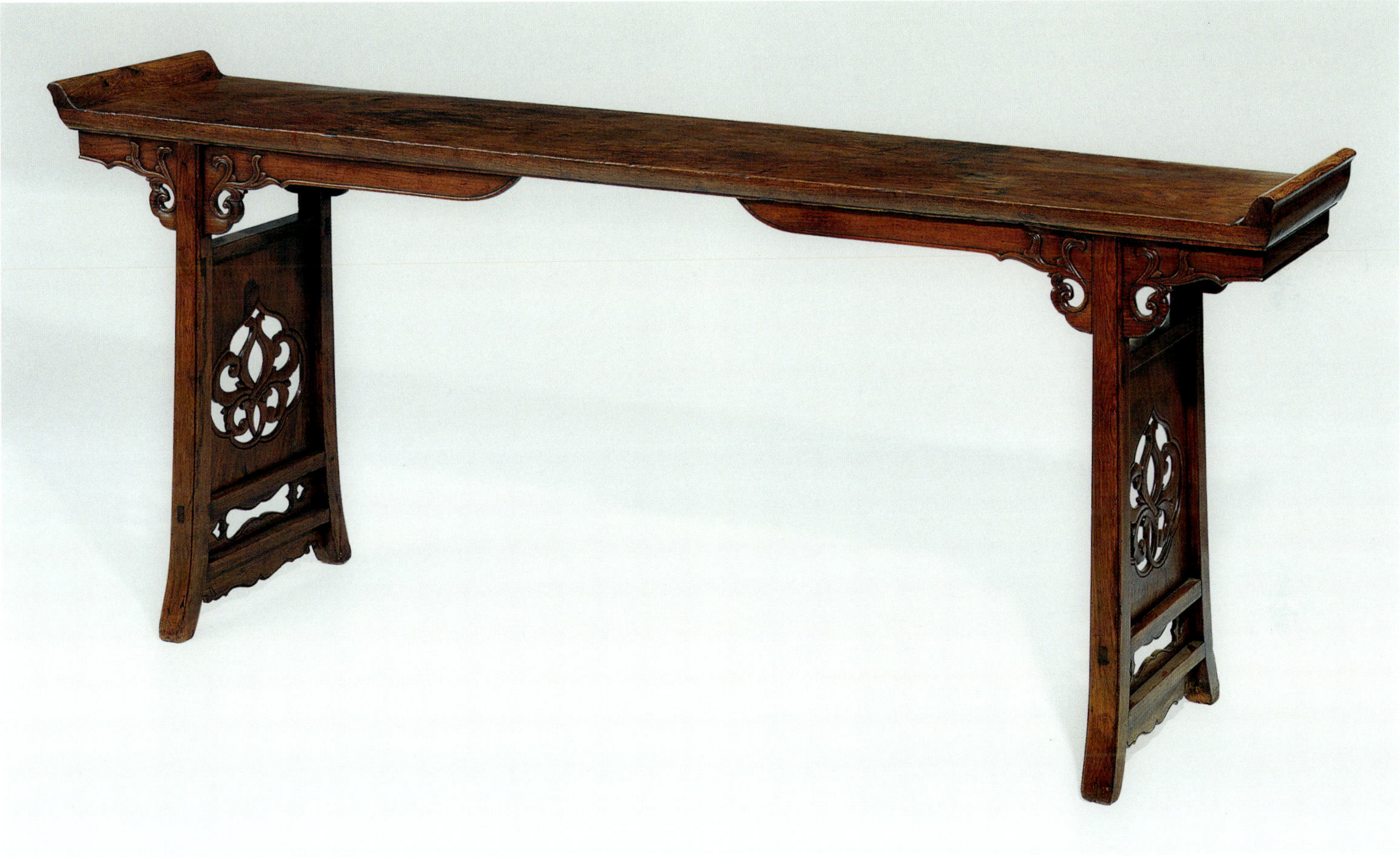

39

Formal Side Table

黃花梨夾頭翹頭案

Huanghuali
Late 17th/Early 18th century
North China
199.5 x 36 x 91 cm H

A solid panel of richly figured *huanghuali* fit with gently upturned flanges gracing the ends of this altar table. Below, the table is more elaborately decorated; the surfaces of the long aprons are filled with immature *chi* dragons carved in relief, and the end panels are pierced and carved with a lively pattern of dragons and *qilin*.

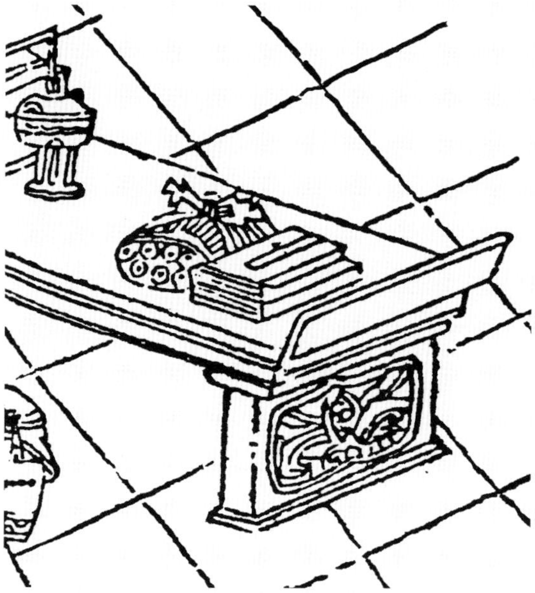

Formal side table. Detail from woodcut illustration to Lie Gou Zhi, *early Qing period.*

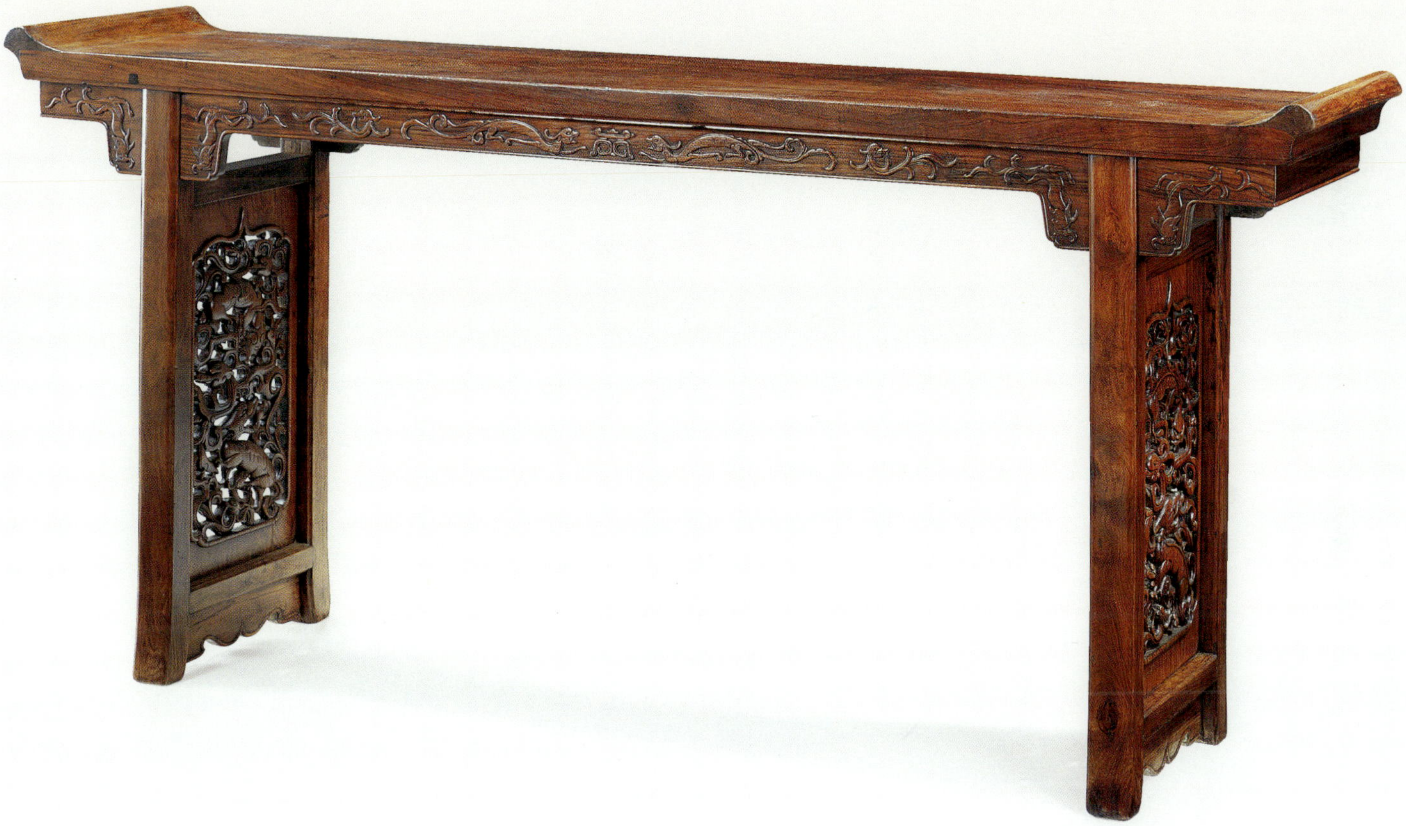

40

Table with Drawer

紫檀夾頭翹頭抽屜案

Zitan
Late 17th/Early 18th century
Jiangnan Region
129 x 52.5 x 88 cm H

This small recessed-leg table is fitted with a drawer. The top is comprised of a four-board panel framed on the ends with everted flanges. The aprons are decorated with angular scrolling; the central apron section on one side is the face of a drawer that fits invisibly below the tabletop.

Wide double beading runs down the face of each leg and neatly loops near the foot to return up along the outer edges. The feet gently flare out near the base and are decorated with angular scrolled beading. Lattice panels of geometric design are fit between the legs.

This piece has excellent patination on the original surfaces. Although the drawer has been replaced, it has survived as a fine example of early Qing furniture.

Previously exhibited and illustrated:

- National Museum of History. *Splendor of Style: Classical Furniture from the Ming and Qing Dynasties*, p. 140.

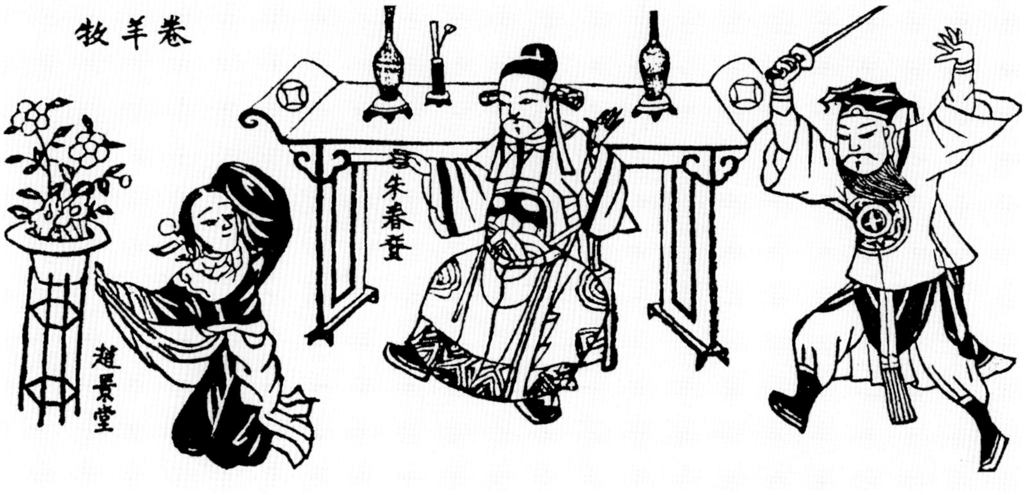

Side table. Detail from woodcut illustration to Muyang juan, *Qing period.*

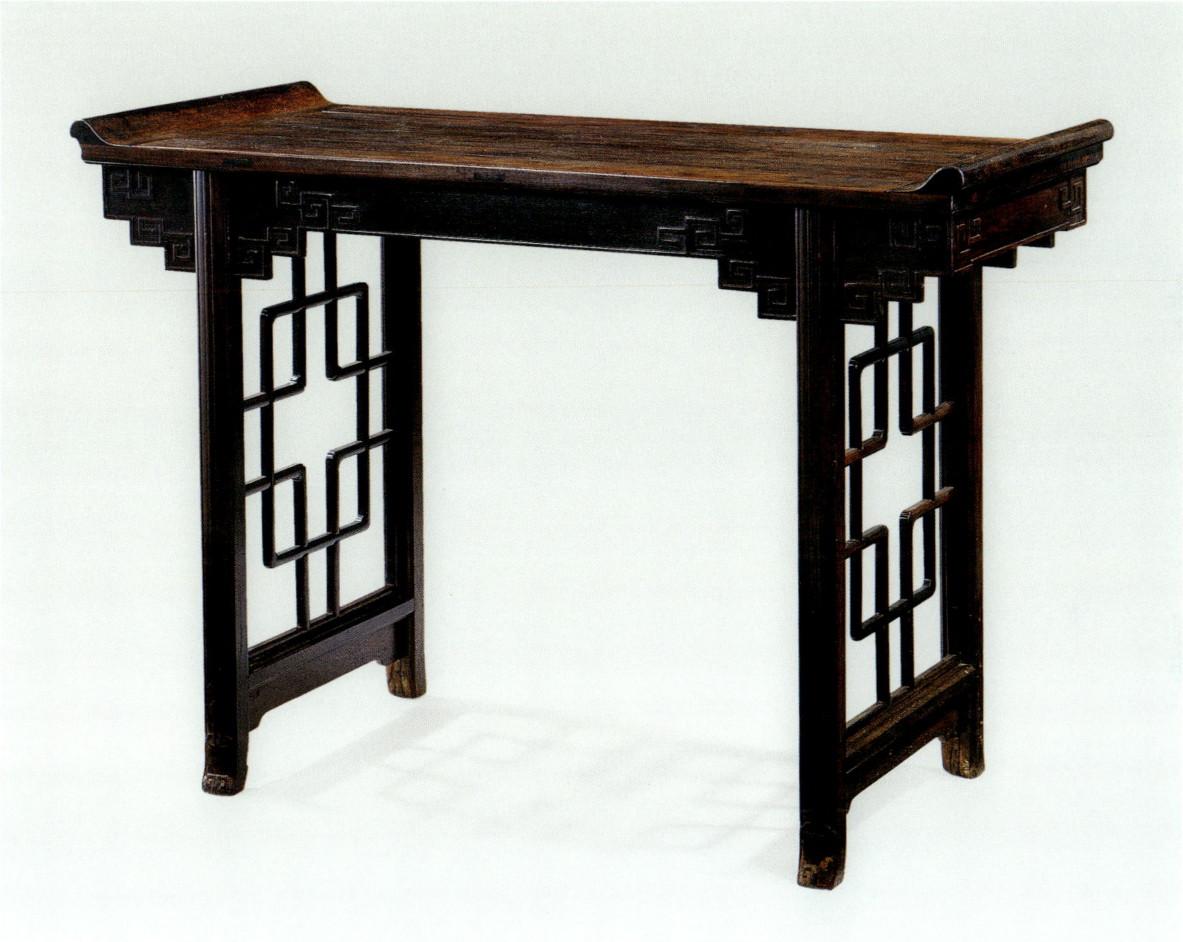

41

Painting Table

黃花梨夾頭平頭畫案

Huanghuali
Late 17th/ Early 18th Century
Jiangnan Region
210 x 66 x 85 cm H

The relatively broad two-board panel of this painting table is shaped with round corners and housed within a wide frame. The style—with large bracket-like spandrels and no connecting aprons—varies from the traditional recessed-leg pattern. Each of the spandrels is decorated in low relief with a *ruyi* that alternately appears as the flared nostrils of a guardian animal mask. 'Bamboo-like' inner frames decorate openings between the legs and further enhance the light, ethereal quality.

Similar treatment with bamboo-like frames decorating the openings can be found on a *huanghuali* stool illustrated in:

- Ecke, Gustav. *Chinese Domestic Furniture*, pl. 77.

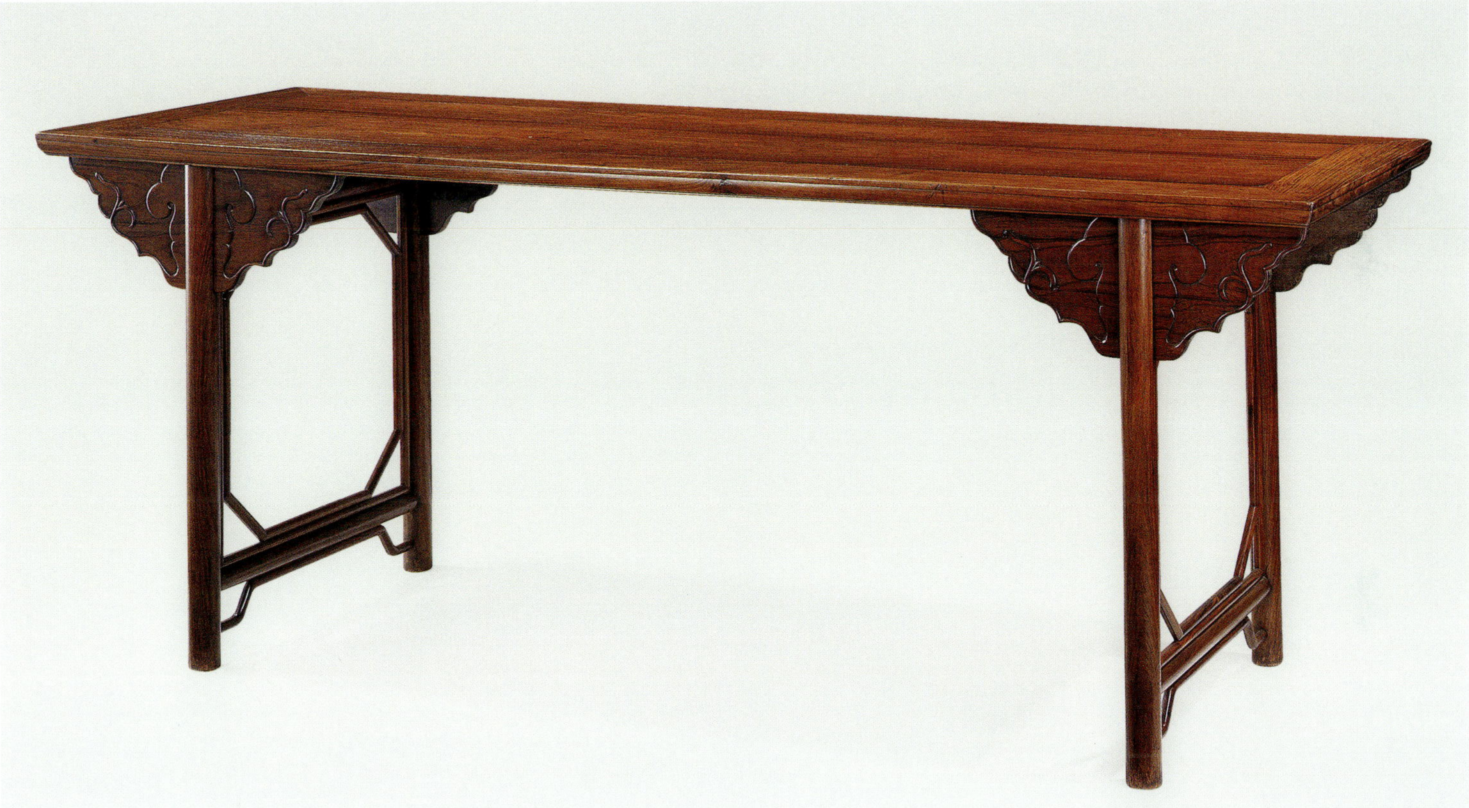

42

Formal Side Table

紫檀夾頭平頭案

Zitan
Early 19th Century
Northern Jiangsu (Subei)
177 x 45.5 x 87 cm H

Constructed of quality *zitan*, this mid-Qing period table also exhibits an archaic recessed-leg style with large bracket-like spandrel heads (cf. cat. 41). The artisan/designer also realized dynamic visual effect by contrasting the plain tabletop with intricately carved aprons and end panels below, which exhibit popular mid-to-late Qing period decorative themes. The spandrels are carved in relief with bats and clouds, and the end panels are pierced with five bats soaring in the clouds above the Isle of the Immortals.

Previously exhibited and illustrated:
- National Museum of History. *Splendor of Style: Classical Furniture from the Ming and Qing Dynasties*, p. 148.

A *zitan* table of similar style is illustrated in:
- Tian Jiaqing. *Classic Chinese Furniture of the Qing Dynasty*, pl. 81.

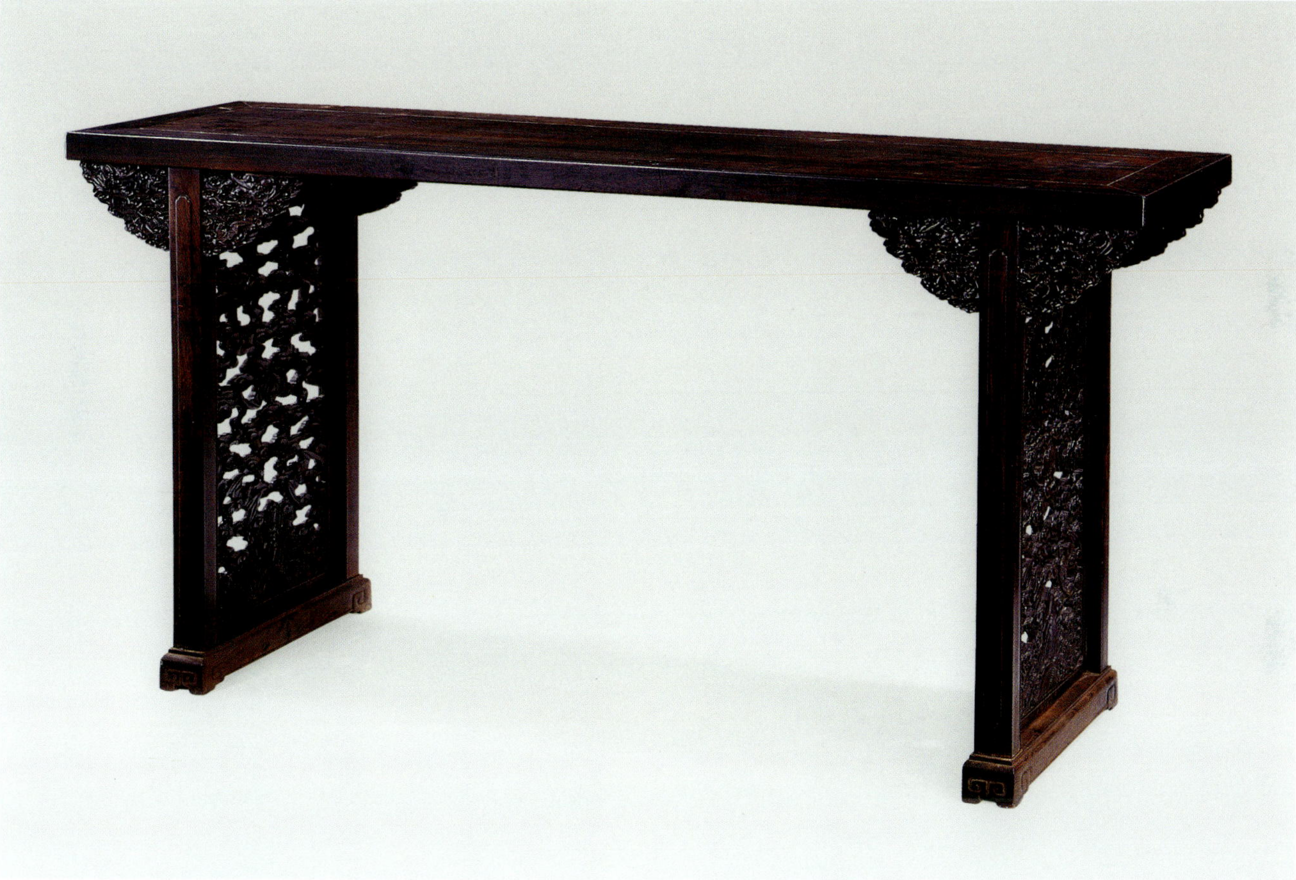

43

Bamboo-Style Side Table

紫檀竹節式條桌

Zitan
18th Century
Suzhou
147 x 54 x 85 cm H

This side table exhibits a light, elegant style with frame components of precious *zitan* each shaped like common bamboo. The joinery is concealed throughout—a characteristic of fine Suzhou workmanship. The old, patinated surface was renewed in the early 90's previous to concern for the conservation of original surfaces.

A table of similar style is illustrated in:

- Wang Shixiang. *Connoisseurship of Chinese Furniture*, Vol. 2, B67.

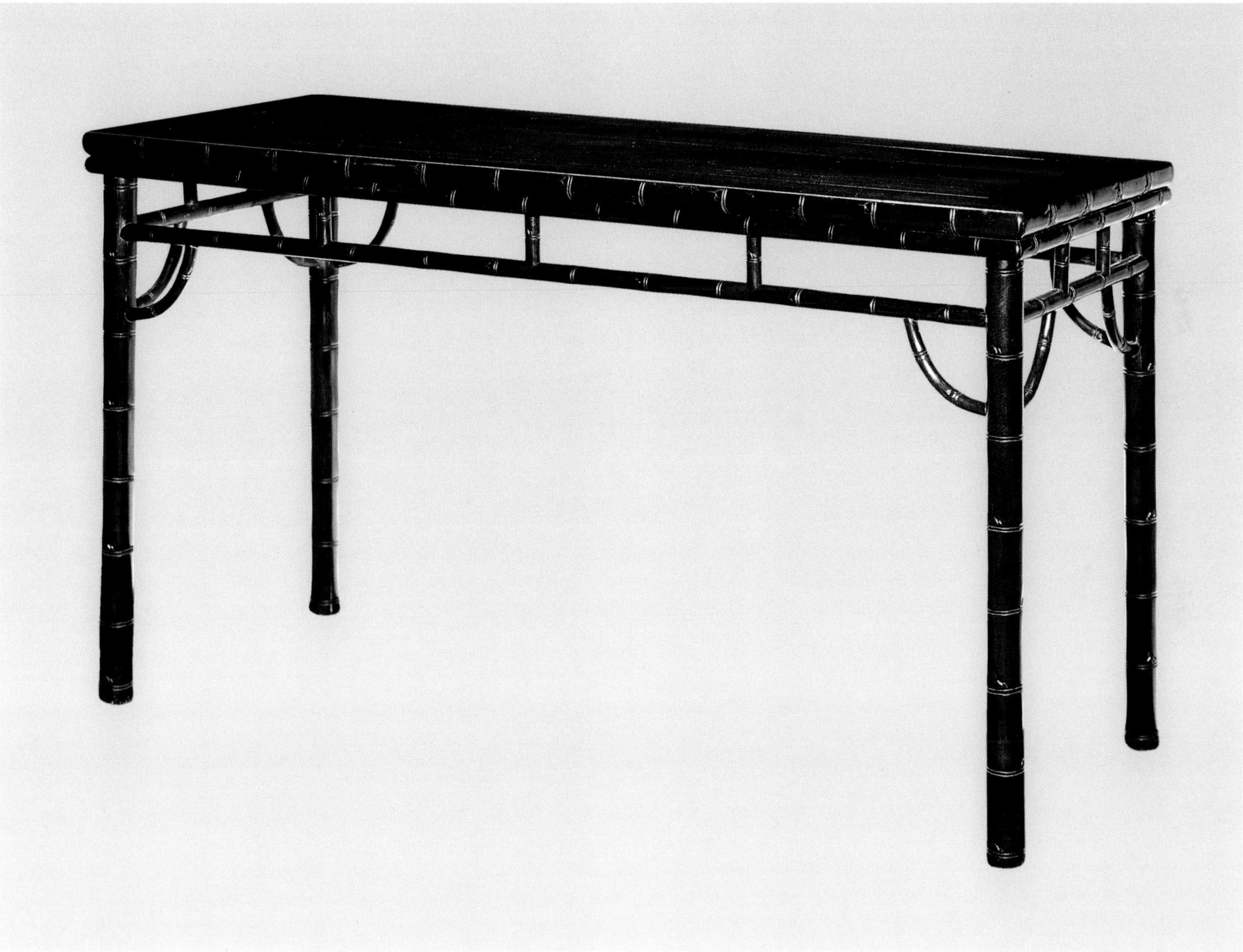

44

Side Table

紫檀楠木直足條桌

Zitan and *Nanmu*
18th Century
Jiangnan/Guangdong
211.5 x 63 x 88 cm H

This table exhibits a 'square-corner straight-leg' pattern of construction. A square table of comparable style drafted by the Englishman William Chambers when in Canton during the first half of the 18th century (see illustration below) suggests an approximate date for the development of this pattern; earlier evidence has yet to be discovered. The linear style, which is characteristic of early Qing design, is further highlighted by the uniform shaping of the frame members with indented corner moldings and concave surfaces. The workmanship is of consistent, fine quality. The tabletop is fit with a 'round-corner' *nanmu* panel—a technique commonly employed by Suzhou furniture-makers.

Tables of similar style and size are illustrated in:
- Tian Jiaqing. *Classic Chinese Furniture of the Qing Dynasty*, pls. 74, 85.
- National Museum of History. *Splendor of Style: Classical Furniture from the Ming and Qing Dynasties*, p. 146.

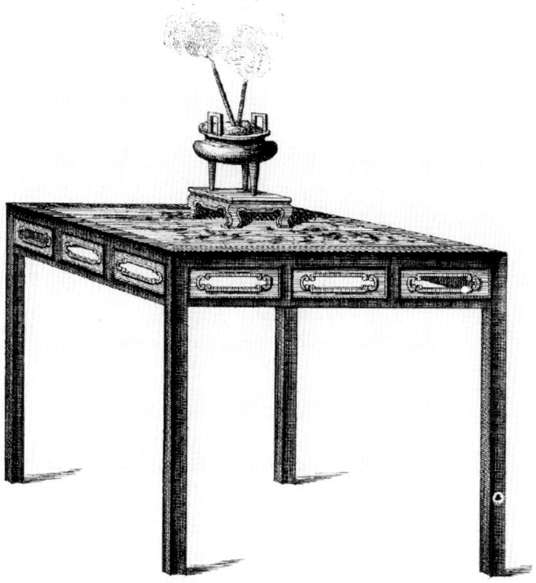

Engraving after William Chambers, Designs of Chinese buildings, furniture, dress, machines, and utensils, *published in 1753.*

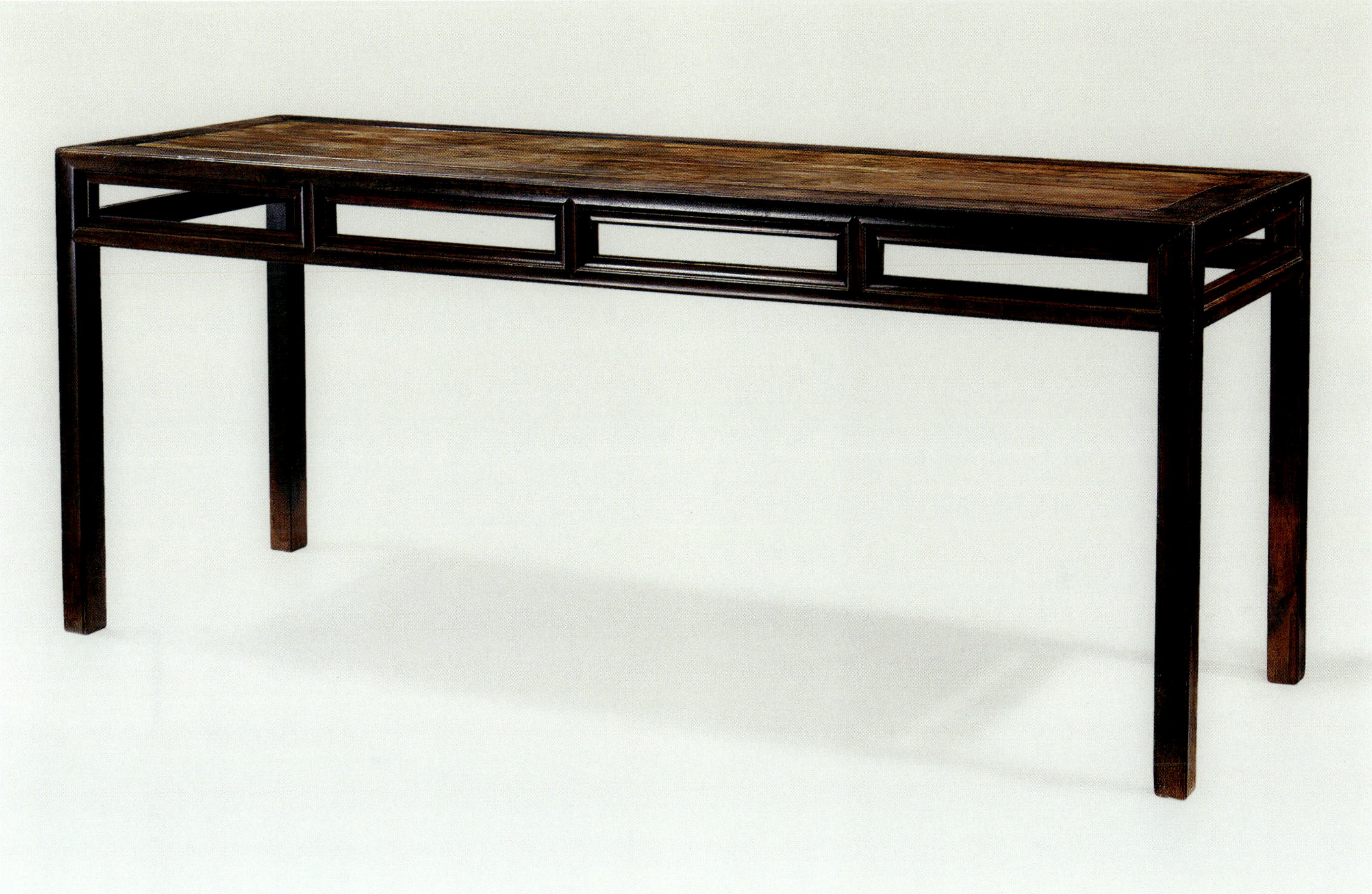

45

Square Game Table

黄花梨有束腰三彎腿方棋棹

Huanghuali
18th Century
North China
91 x 91 x 89 cm H

Square tables with cabriole legs are rare; moreover, this example is configured as a game table. Drawers are concealed on the four sides, and chess, *weiqi*, and double-six gaming boards were originally fitted under the removable top. The aprons are carved with dragons and *lingzhi* in a deep relief style that is smoothly polished. Dragon-shaped spandrels reinforce the long, elegantly shaped legs.

This table was previously exhibited and published in:

- National Museum of History. *Splendor of Style: Classical Furniture from the Ming and Qing Dynasties*, p. 130.

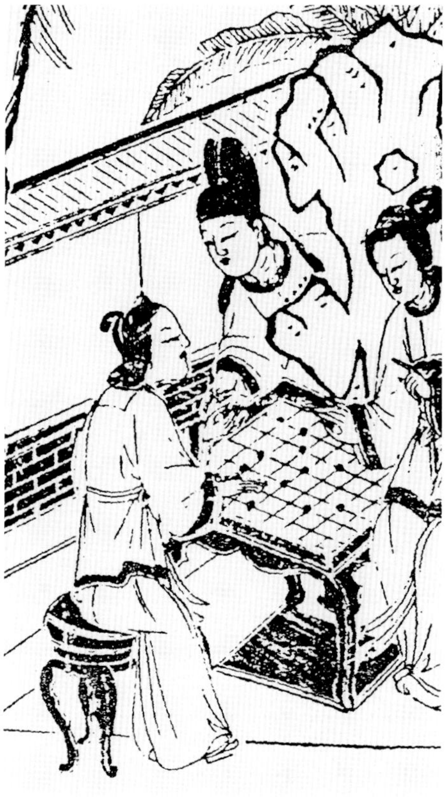

Game table. Detail from woodcut illustration to Xixiang ji, *Ming dynasty.*

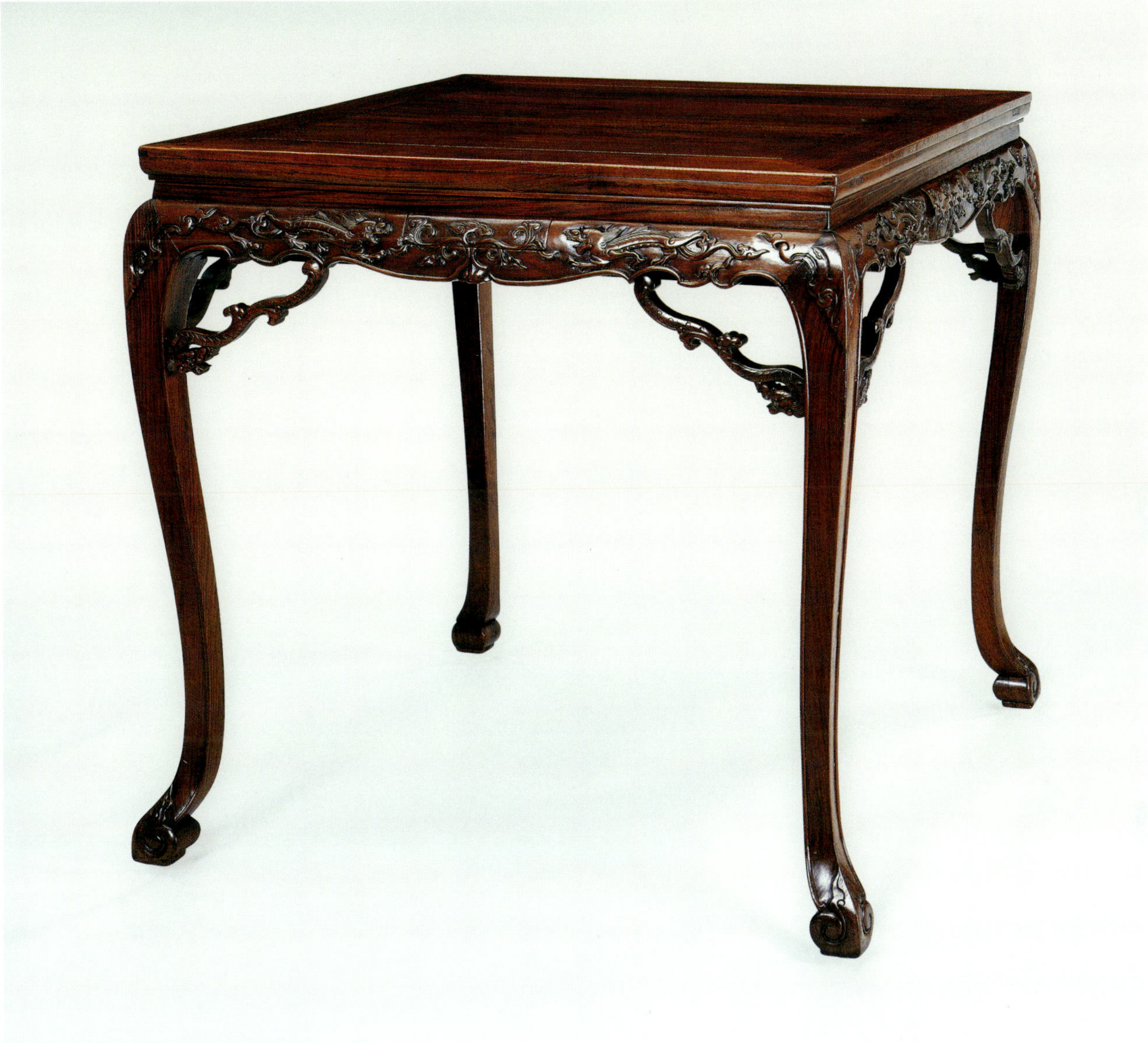

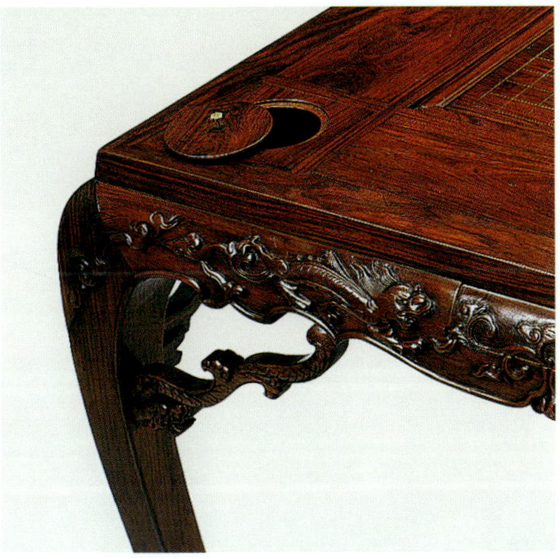

46

Square Table

紫檀有束腰羅鍋棖加卡花方桌一對

One of a Pair
Zitan and Boxwood
18th Century
Jiangnan Region
90.5 x 91 x 88.5 cm H

This rare pair of *zitan* square tables exhibits refined workmanship and precious material of uniform, high quality. Decorative struts of boxwood and carved in the shape of stylized longevity characters (*shou*) are fitted between the humpback stretchers and aprons. The aprons, legs and stretchers are all finely beaded, and the legs terminate with angular scrolled feet.

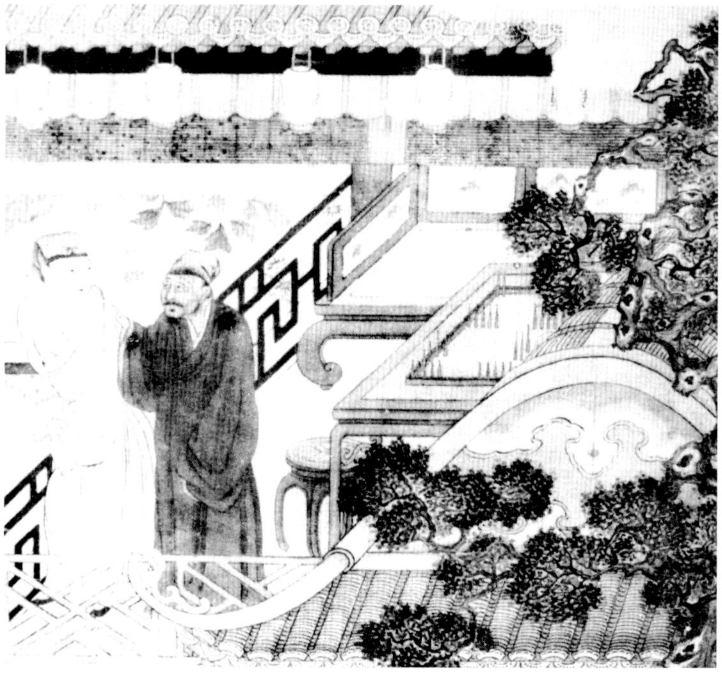

Square table. Detail from the album leaf set Bai mei tu *depicting scenes from the novel* Jin Ping Mei, *early Qing period.*

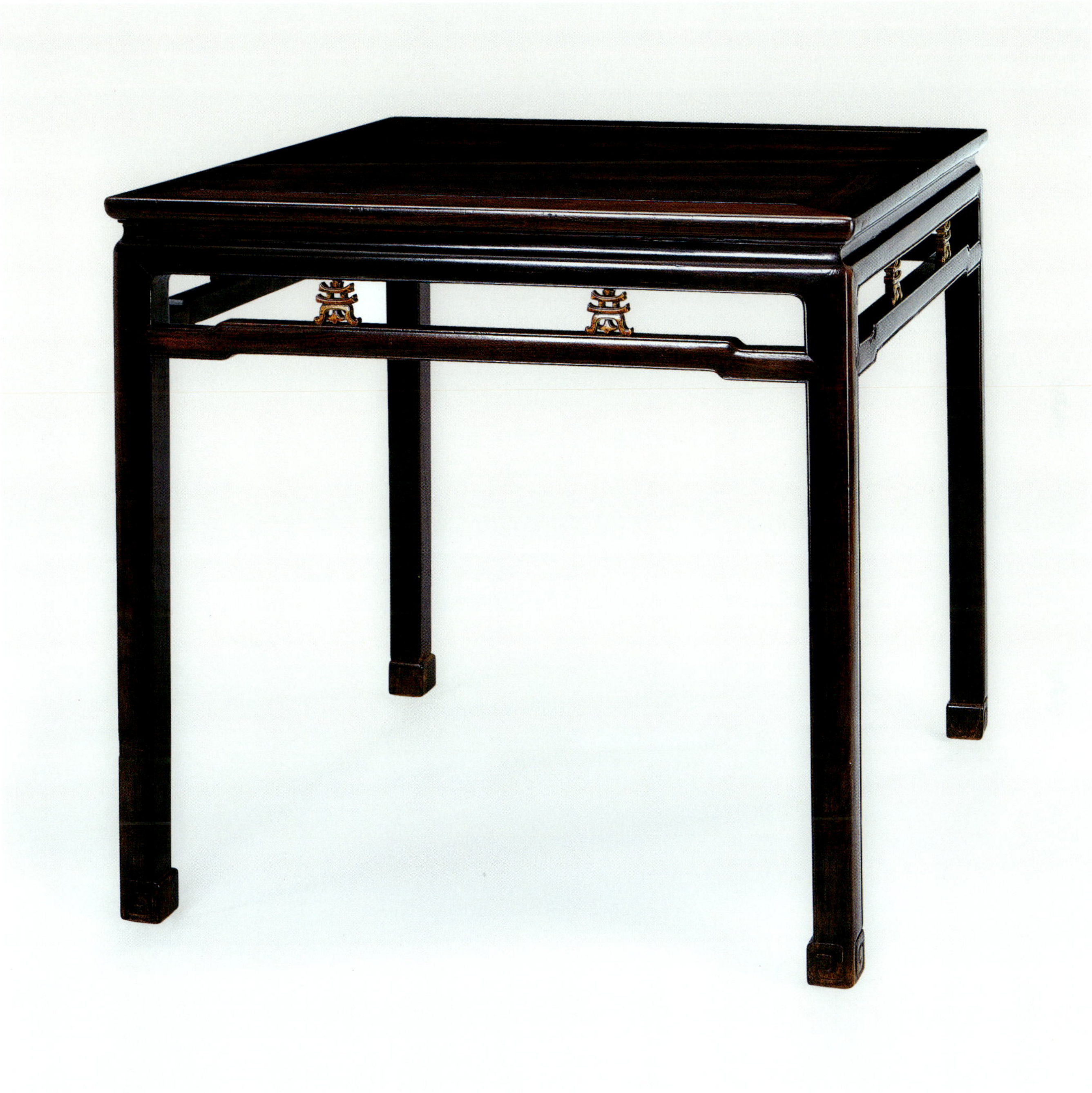

47

Waisted Corner-Leg Table

紫檀有束腰馬蹄棹

Zitan
Late 18th/Early 19th Century
Jiangnan Region
94 x 58 x 86.5 cm H

This waisted corner-leg table exhibits a decorative style typical of the middle Qing period. Refined workmanship and elegant styling are particularly evident in the detailing of the waist, which is shaped to a double ogival profile and sits upon an additional *tuosai* molding; cloud scrolls are also finely raised in relief upon the aprons. Decorative brackets are joined to the legs with double miters while 'giant's arm' braces more invisibly provide the basic reinforcement. The use of patched material corresponds to conditions that existed during the late 18th and early 19th centuries, when low inventories of *zitan* material were noted in the Imperial workshops, and when available material was largely limited to small growth timber.

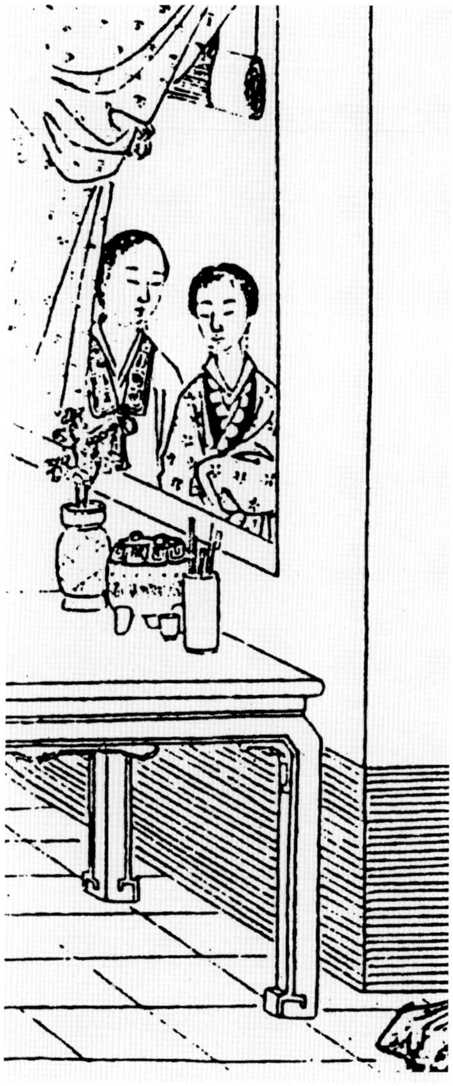

Waisted corner-leg table. Woodcut illustration from Hong lou meng, *Qing Guangxu period (pub. 1882).*

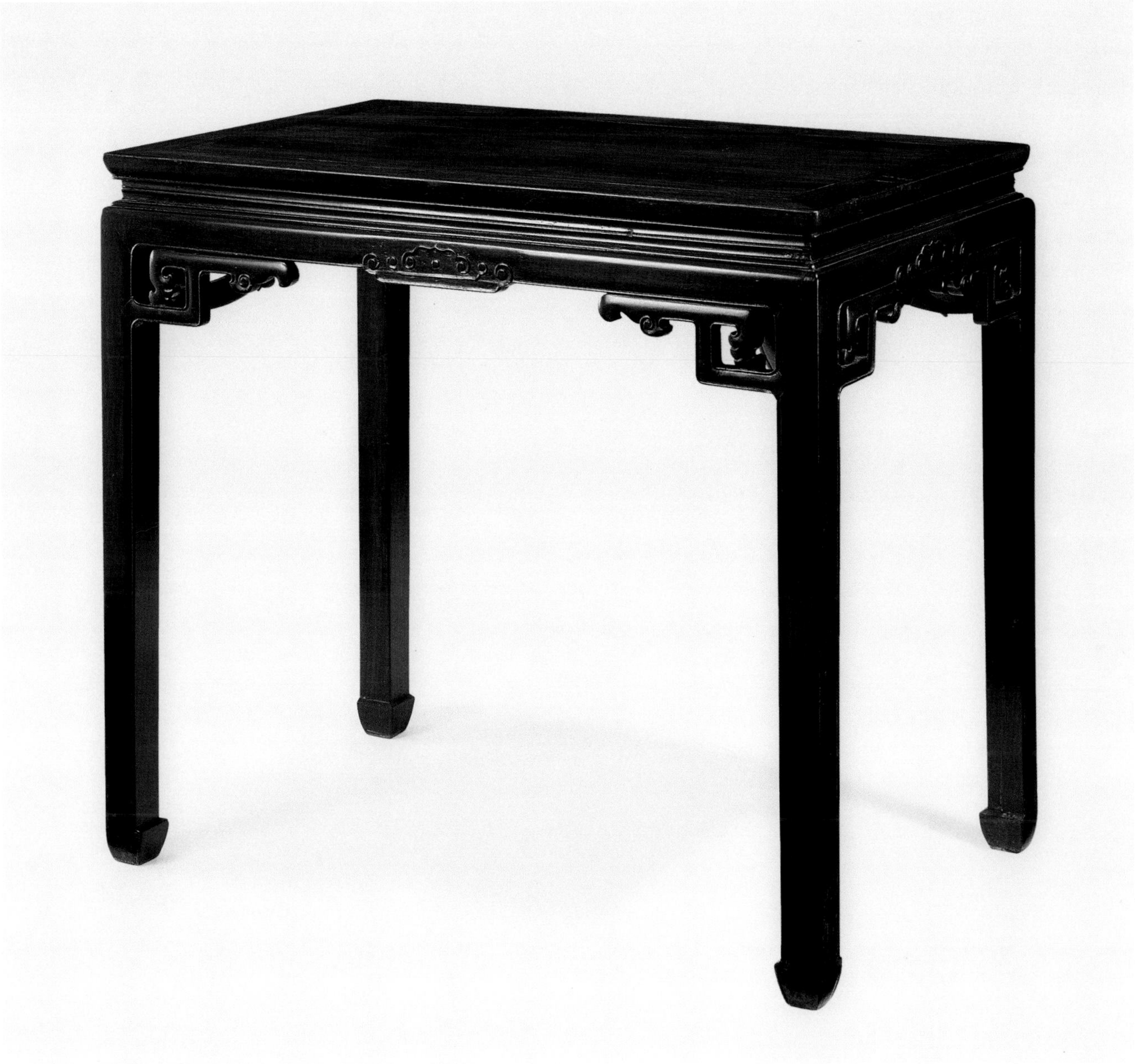

48

Pair of High Stands

紫檀有束腰馬蹄長方花几一對

Zitan
Early 19th Century
Tianjin
45 x 45 x 89 cm H

The angular form and decorative style of these stands reflect a mid-to-late Qing period origin. The high waist is pierced with cloud designs, and below, each apron is elaborately carved in relief with five bats flying about scrolling clouds—an auspicious rebus for bringing fruitful blessings into the household (cf. with *zitan* table cat. 42). The straight legs terminate with angular scrolled hoof feet of laminated construction, and stand upon replaced floor stretchers.

Previously exhibited and published in:

- National Museum of History. *Splendor of Style: Classical Furniture from the Ming and Qing Dynasties*, p. 155.

Stands and tables of similar style and period are illustrated in:

- Tian Jiaqing. *Classic Chinese Furniture of the Qing Dynasty*, pl. 66.
- Shanghai Museum. *Chinese Ming and Qing Furniture Gallery*, pp. 31-31.

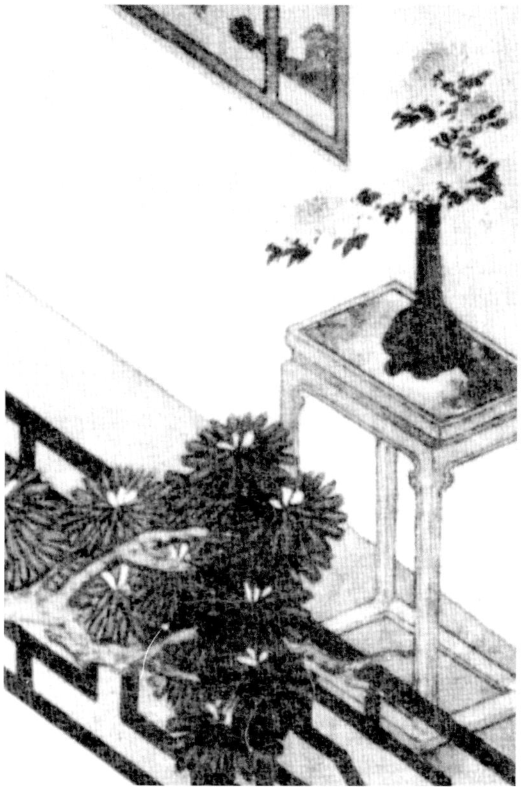

Incense stand. Detail from album leaf set Bai mei tu *depicting scenes from the novel* Jin Ping Mei, *early Qing period.*

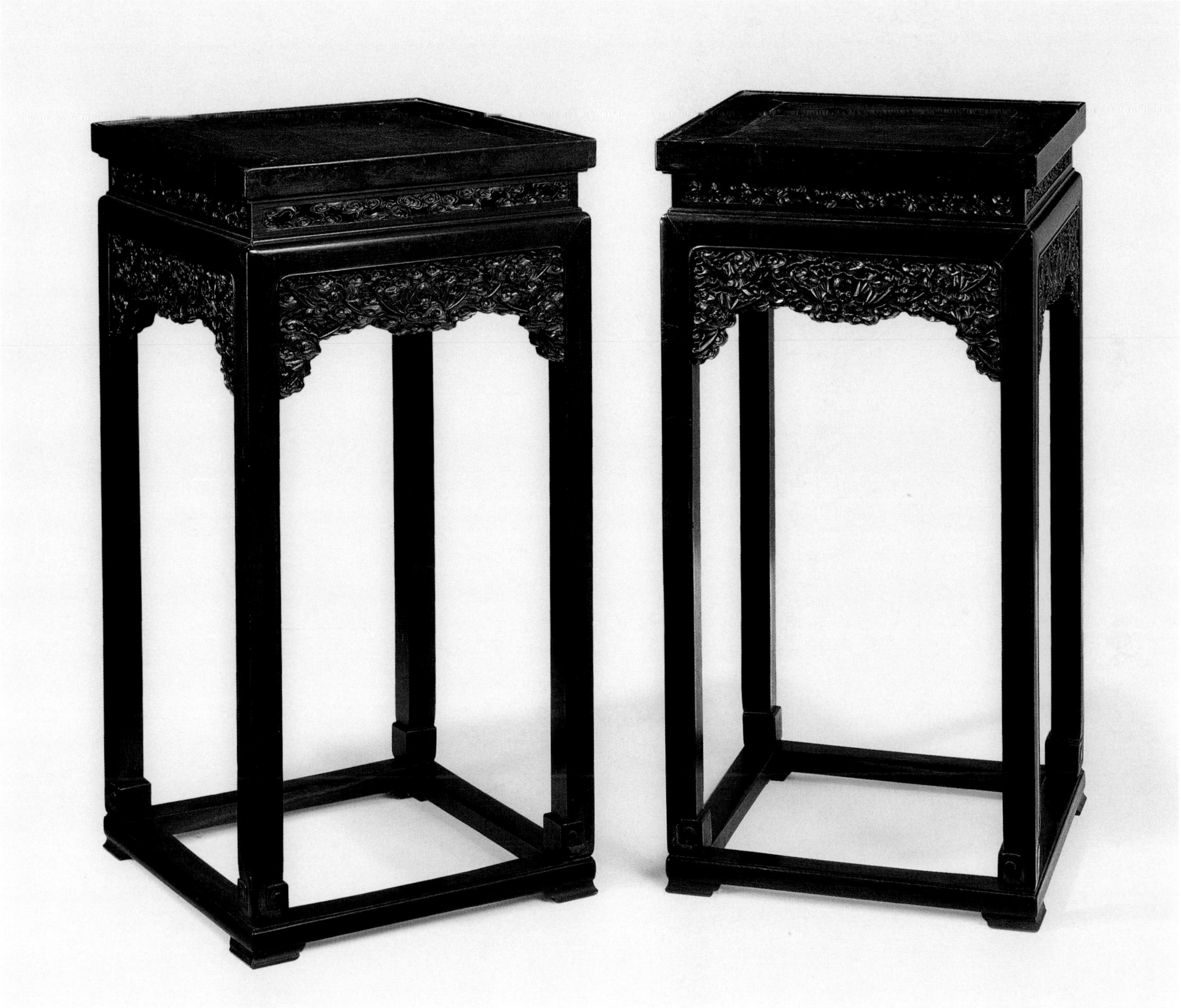

Cabinets

櫥櫃

49

Large Cabinet

紫檀三彎腿方角櫃一對

One of a Pair
Zitan and *Huanghuali*
Early 17th Century
North China
137.5 x 62.5 x 201 cm H

These large *zitan* cabinets were discovered together with the horseshoe armchairs (cat. 11) in Wuwei, an important trading center at the intersection of the Silk Route and Great Wall in Gansu province. It is highly improbable that they were local products, but rather originated from a production center elsewhere in northern China and were brought to Wuwei by a high official or wealthy Muslim merchant. Location marks—both carved and inked—are found on numerous components, which facilitated disassembly and reassembly for tranport (see detail).

The massive, square-corner cabinets stand upon stout cabriole legs shaped from the continuous vertical frame members. The face of the frame members and front aprons are carved in relief with fluttering ribbons interspersed with various precious treasures, and mythical lions with an embroidered ball decorated the panel at the base. Such ornamentation was characteristic of the late Ming period.

While primarily constructed of *zitan*, secondary *huanghuali* was employed for the shelves, drawer interiors, removable back panels, bottom and top of each cabinet. The original hardware is attached with large boss head pins. The inside of the cabinet has a traditional arrangement of shelves and drawer unit.

Aside from minor replacements, these cabinets have survived in remarkably good condition. Of grand style and made with bountiful precious materials, they could well have been associated with the Imperial Palace during the final years of the Ming period when court eunuchs were said to have "vied with one another in the elegance of their furniture."

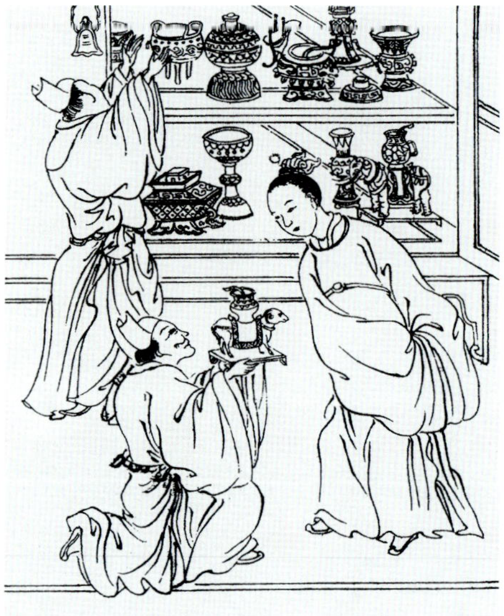

Large cabinet. Detail from woodcut illustration to Imperial Edicts*, Kangxi period (1662-1722).*

Previously exhibited and published in:

- National Museum of History. *Splendor of Style: Classical Furniture from the Ming and Qing Dynasties*, p. 169.

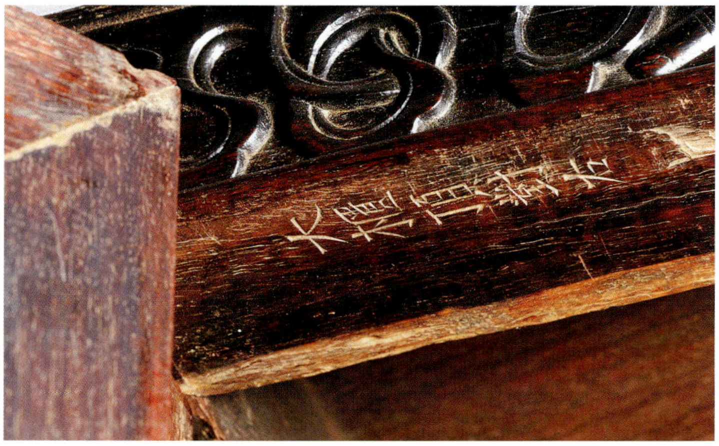

Detailed. Inscribed assembly marks on the underside of top rail.

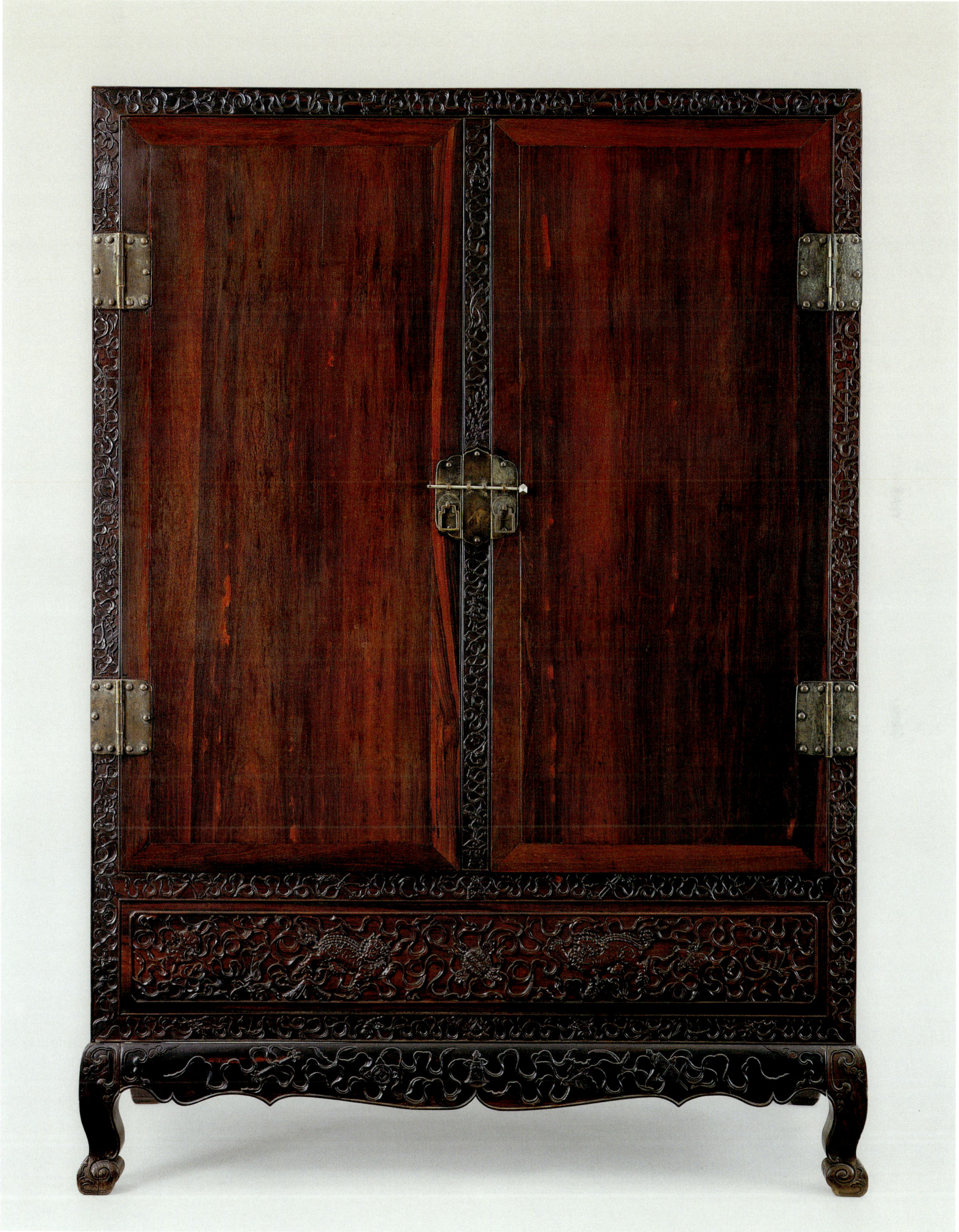

50

Cabinet

黄花梨圓角櫃

Huanghuali
18th Century
North China
127.5 x 61 x 181.5 cm H

This stoutly proportioned cabinet exhibits a round-corner construction pattern without any splay imparted to the legs. Thick *huanghuali* panels and frame members were used throughout, resulting in an exceptionally heavy piece of furniture that is difficult for two men to handle. The back is made up of two framed panels that are also neatly finished. The interior is fit with a built-in shelf, a shelf unit with two drawers, and a lidded storage compartment at the bottom. The entire cabinet has survived in excellent condition and also retains its original paktong hardware.

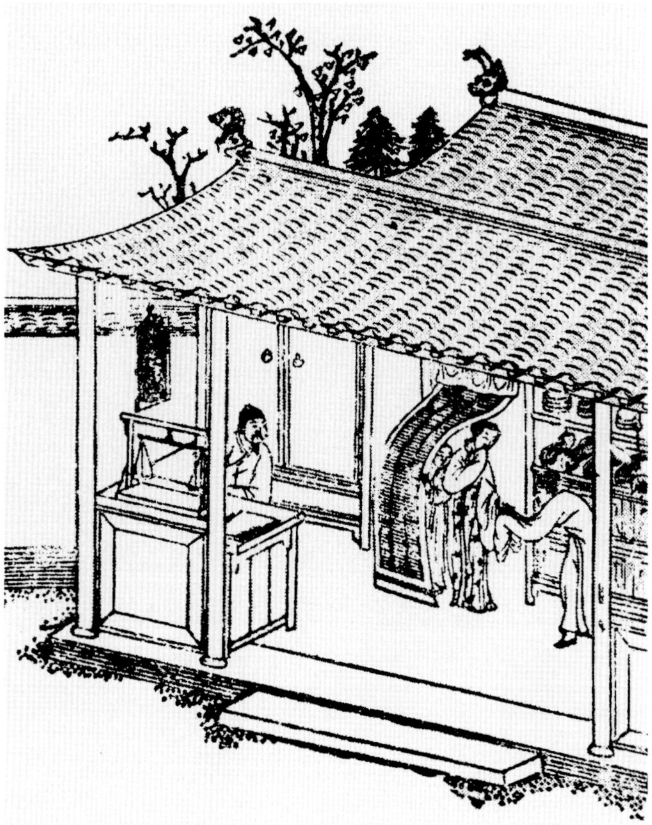

Tapered Cabinet. Detail from woodcut illustration to Jingshi tongyan, *late Ming period.*

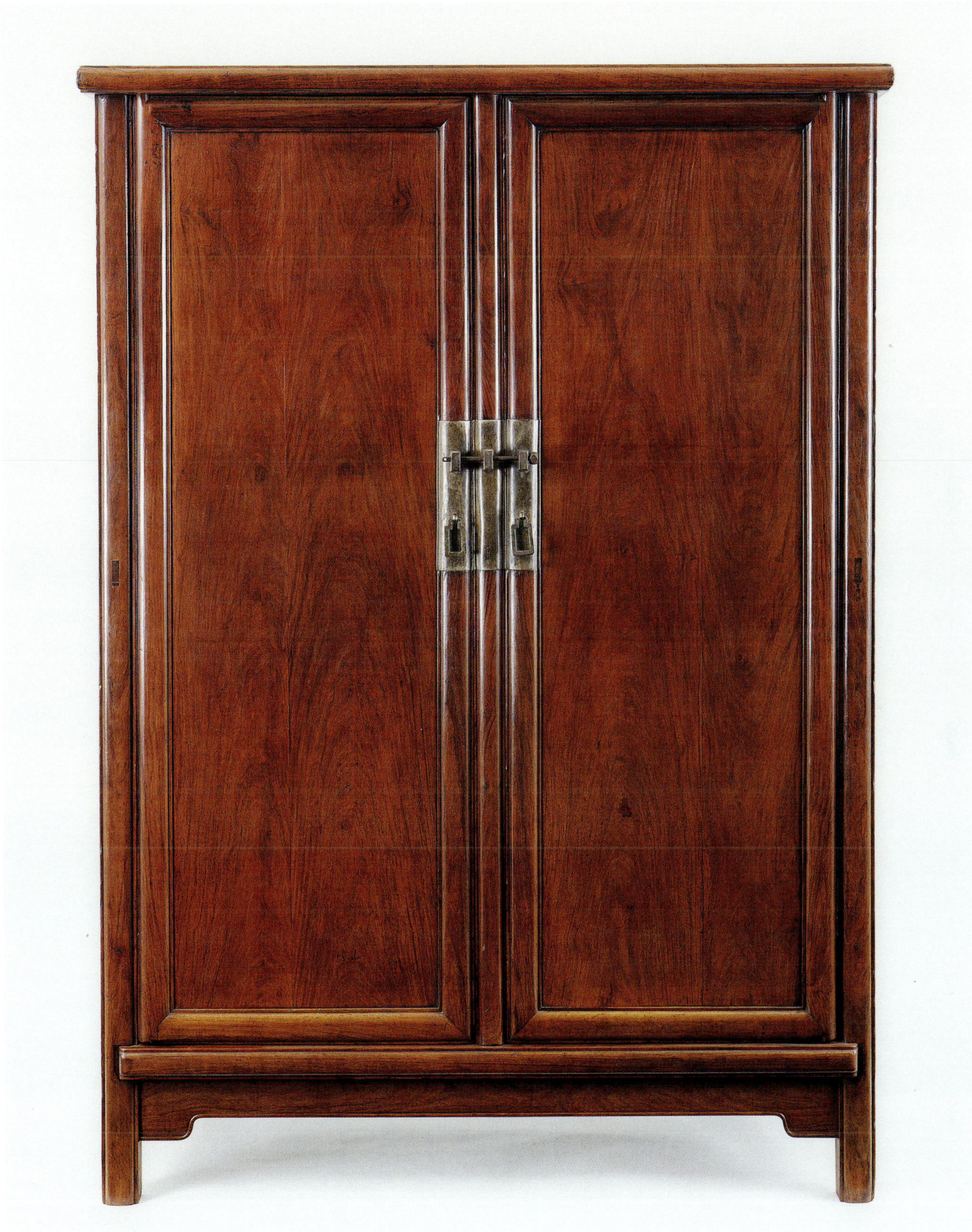

51

Cabinet

黄花梨方角櫃

Huanghuali
Early 18th Century
Jiangnan Region
97.5 x 46.5 x 145.5 cm H

This square-corner cabinet is handsomely styled and features highly figured *huanghuali* throughout, with single-piece bookmatched panels in the doors. The door and side panels are recessed within molded frames, a characteristic that appears with greater frequency during the early Qing period, and one that can also be seen as a refinement upon the earlier flush-panel tradition. The curvilinear aprons on front and sides are carved in relief with dragons and clouds. The interior is fit with a typical shelf/drawer unit. The short feet of this cabinet together with its overall proportions and size suggest that it was originally mated with a base stand.

A cabinet of similar style is illustrated in:
- Ecke, Gustav. *Chinese Domestic Furniture*, pl. 131.

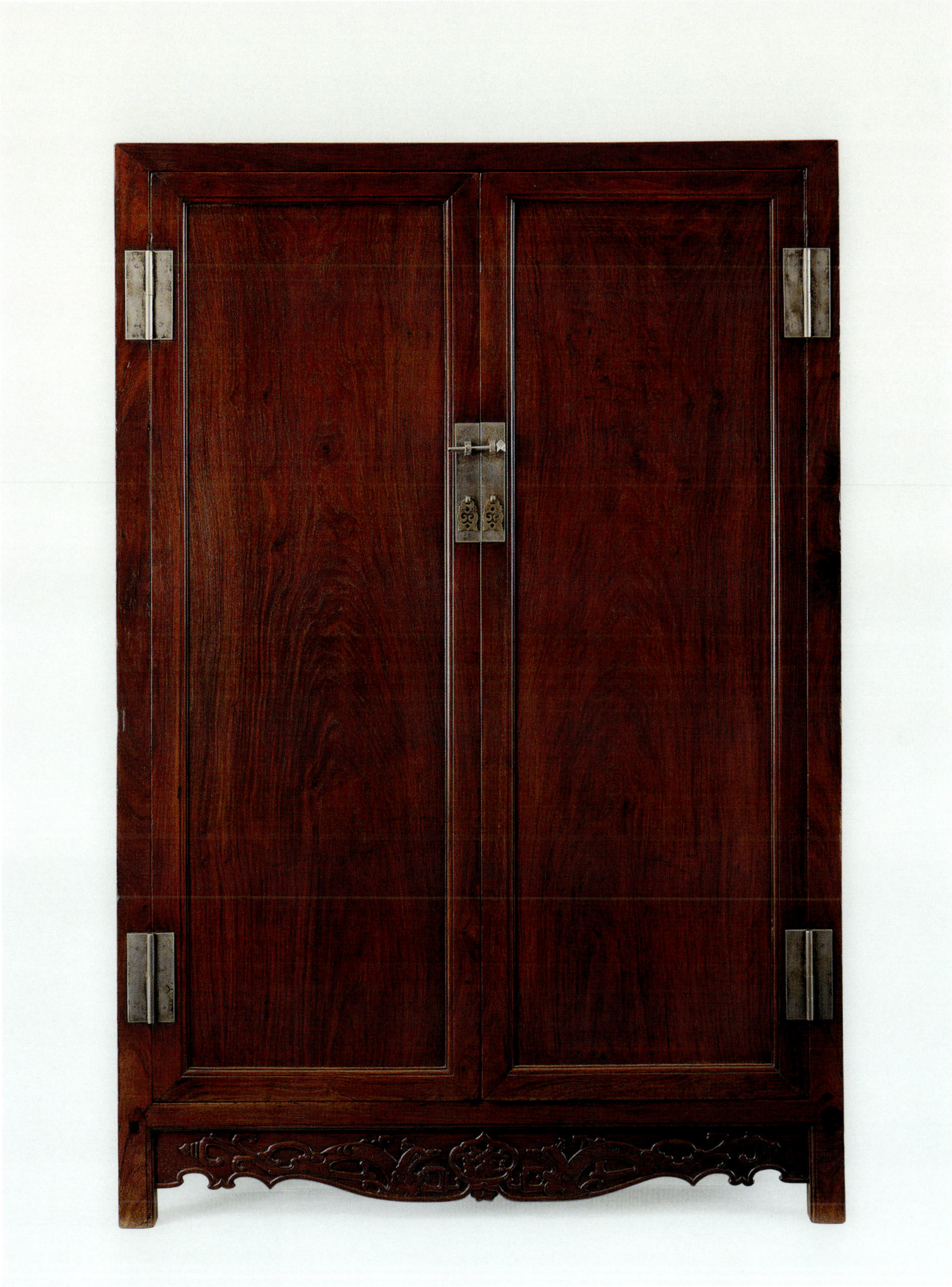

52

Cabinet

紫檀方角櫃一對

One of a Pair
Zitan, Huanghuali and *Nanmu*
18th Century
Beijing
95 x 53.5 x 177.5 cm H

These *zitan* square-corner cabinets exhibit exceptional workmanship. The frame members are subtly shaped with convex surfaces, and the large, smooth panels feature premium quality *zitan* with lustrous figure. *Nanmu* and *huanghuali* are employed as secondary materials. The door and side panels are each subdivided with three small *taohuan* panels that are exquisitely carved in relief with confronting dragons (see fig. 1, p. 10). The original hardware includes weighty door pulls inlaid with copper and white brass *yin-yang* motifs. The interior is fit with a traditional drawer/shelf unit, the drawers of which are fitted with gourds-shaped pulls with inlaid snowflake motifs.

Previously exhibited and illustrated in:

- National Museum of History. *Splendor of Style: Classical Furniture from the Ming and Qing Dynasties*, p. 165.

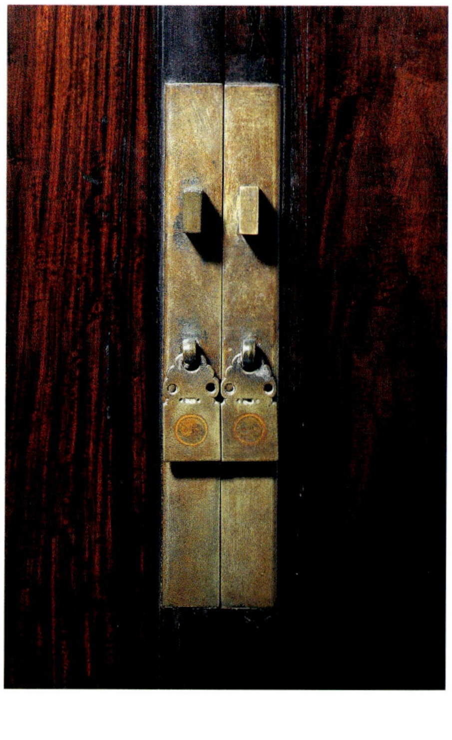

Door pulls

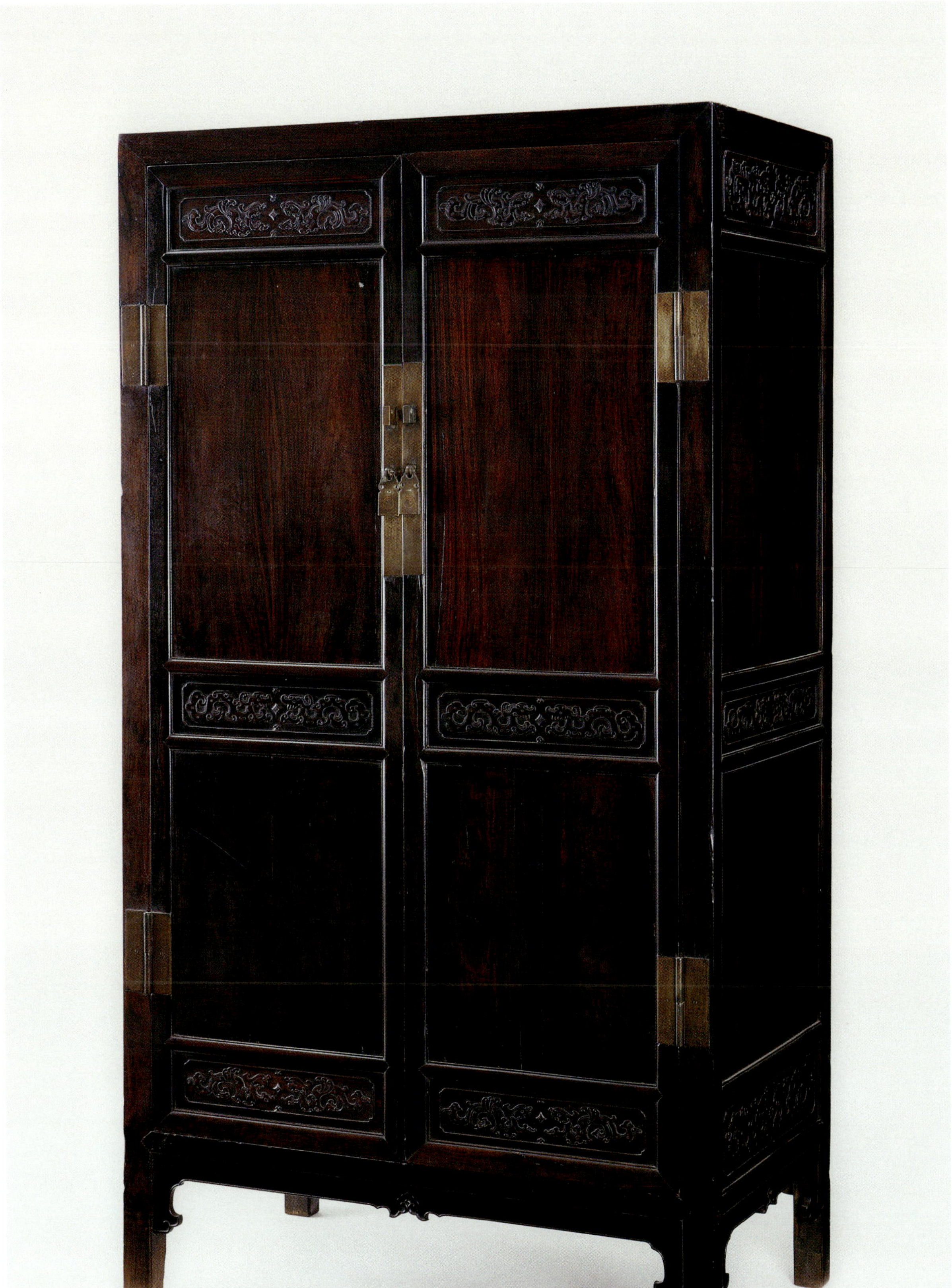

53

Cabinet with Lattice Doors
黄花梨透雕門方角櫃

Huanghuali
Late 18th/Early 19th Century
Jiangnan Region
105.5 x 47.5 x 198 cm H

This square-corner cabinet, which exhibits asymmetrical space division, may have been one of a pair. The door and side panels of the upper left compartment are pierced with angular scrolled dragons. The somewhat larger compartment on the upper right is fully enclosed. The interior of the large compartment below is arranged with a standard shelf and drawer unit, and its door panels are pierced with round openwork medallions.

The use of this unusual cabinet—whose depth is somewhat greater than average, and whose multi-sized compartments are also variously ventilated—suggests a specialized function.

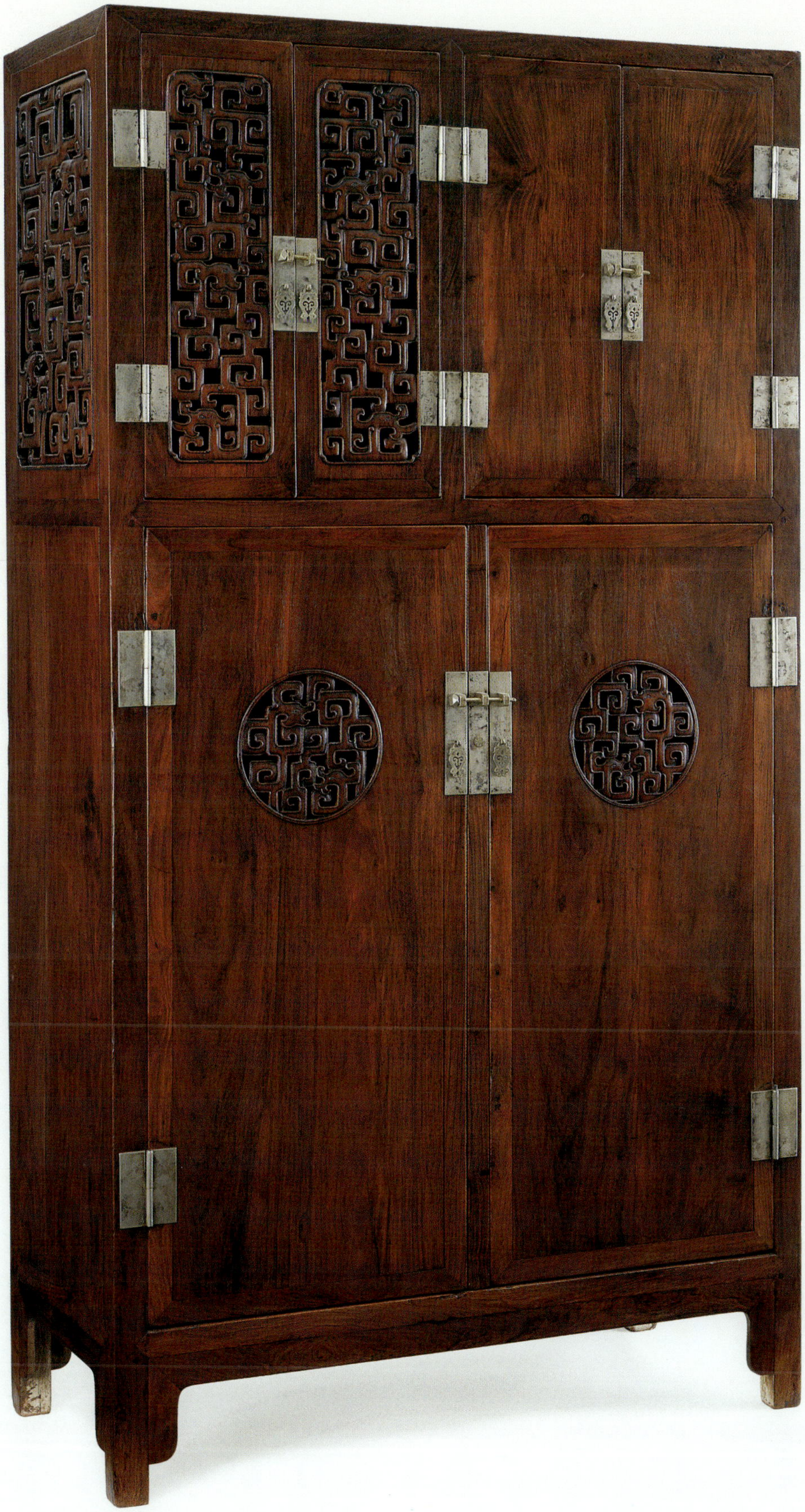

54

Bookshelf

黄花梨架格

Huanghuali
Late 18th Century
Jiangnan Region
110 x 51.5 x 175 cm H

This bookshelf unit exhibits minimal construction, with a single shelf at the base and a central drawer/shelf unit. In contrast with the otherwise austere form, an openwork railing around the shelf with drawers is carved with *ruyi* and flowers. When discovered, this bookcase had been resourcefully converted into a cabinet with panels nailed to the sides and back. It has since been restored; however, the outside of the frame members bears the scarred traces of more difficult times.

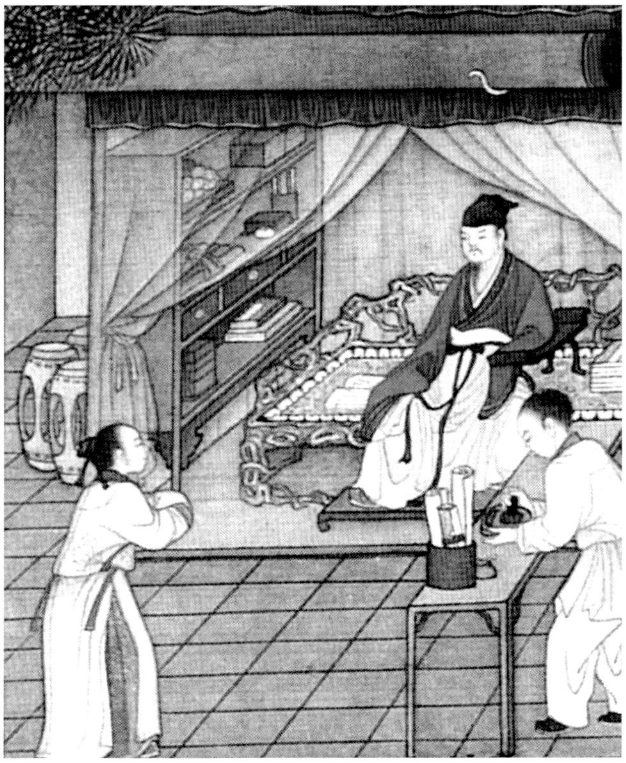

Bookcase. Detail from album leaf set Preservation of Righteousness *by Leng Mei, early 18th century.*

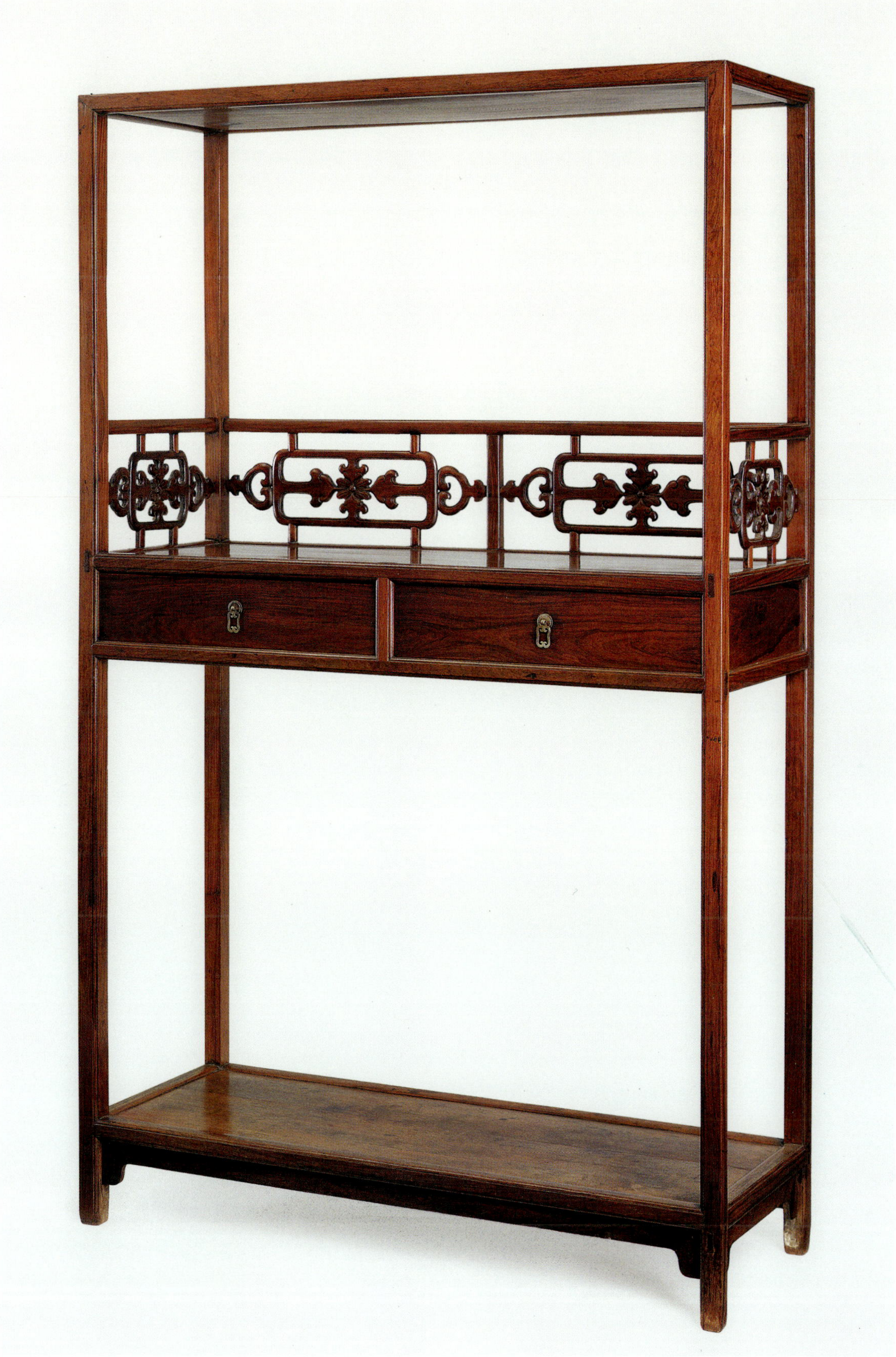

55

Small Cabinet

紫檀小方角櫃

Zitan
18th Century
Shanxi Region
57.5 x 34.5 x 69 cm H

This small cabinet is finely finished on all sides. The richly carved decoration contains imagery suitable for a young lady's apartment. The doors are carved in relief with birds and pomegranates, and phoenixes and peonies—symbols of femininity, fertility, birth of sons, and their potential emolument; below, a delicately styled apron is pierced with scrolling lotus and *ruyi*. Inside, drawers are also carved in relief with auspicious flowers.

Previously exhibited and illustrated in:

- National Museum of History. *Splendor of Style: Classical Furniture from the Ming and Qing Dynasties*, p. 163.

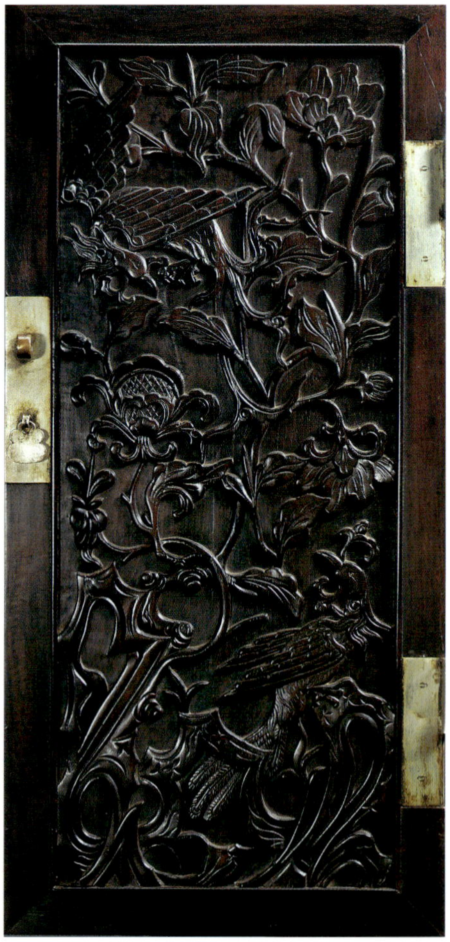

Detail of carved decoration

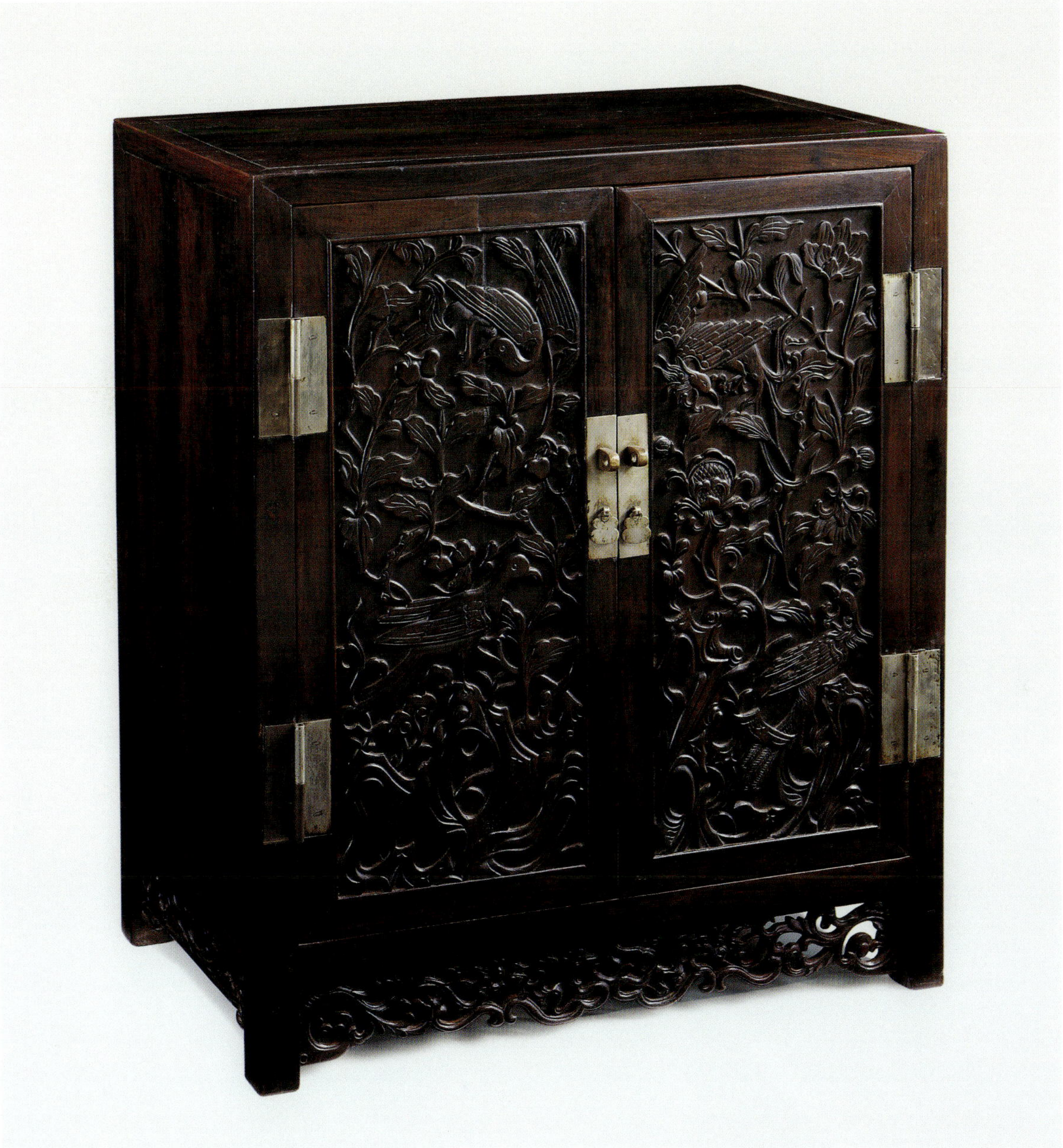

Screens & Lampstands

屏風燈檯

56

Table Screen

紫檀崁大理石小插屏

Zitan and Dali Marble
19th Century
Jiangnan Region
53 x 17.5 x 50 cm H

This small table screen exhibits a sleek 19th century style. The smoothly shaped frame members of dark *zitan* stand in elegant juxtaposition to the white Dali marble panel, whose mountainscape imagery appears as a brushed ink painting composed with minimalistic artistry.

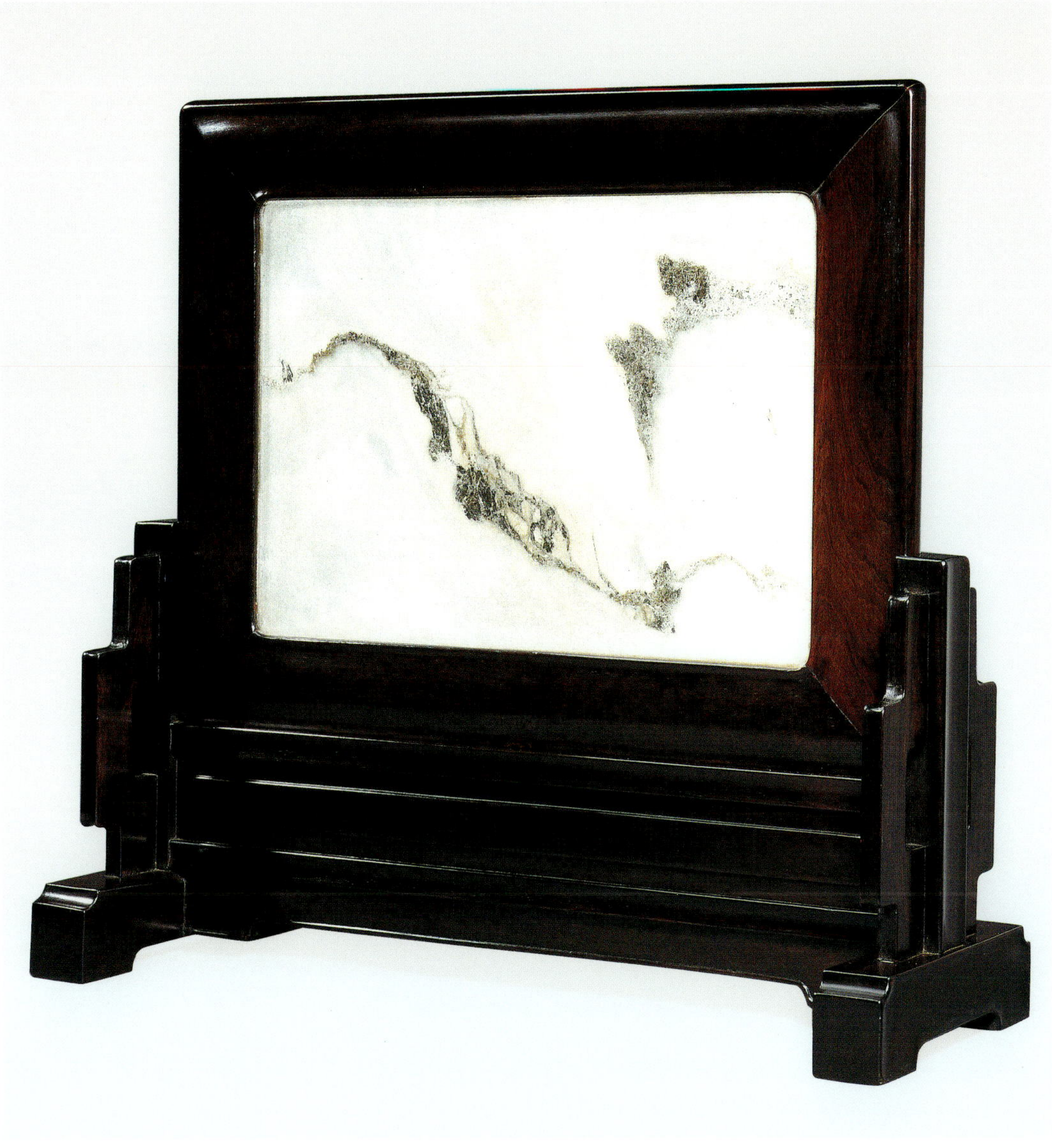

57

Table Screen with Mirror

紫檀貼皮插屏鏡子座屏

Zitan Veneer,
Hongmu and Glass
19th Century
North China
41.5 x 28 x 74 cm H

This table screen features a black lacquer panel with gold-painted decoration depicting bats, crabapple and peaches—a variant rebus for the traditional wish "Riches, Officialdom and Longevity" (*fu lu shou*). The opposite side of the screen panel is fit with a mirror that slides into place through an opening in the top and is cleverly concealed by a removable cap. Refined carving skill is evident in the openwork of the *taohuan* panel and the delicate relief work throughout. The broad faces of the frame members are laminated with veneers of *zitan* to a *hongmu* core (see fig. 9, p.17). This technique reflects the rarity of precious *zitan* during the late 18th and early 19th centuries.

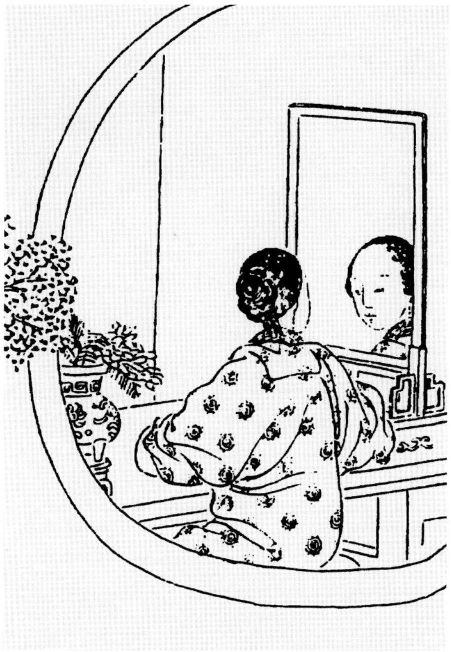

Table screen with mirror. Detail from woodcut illustration to Hong lou meng, *Qing Guangxu period (pub. 1889).*

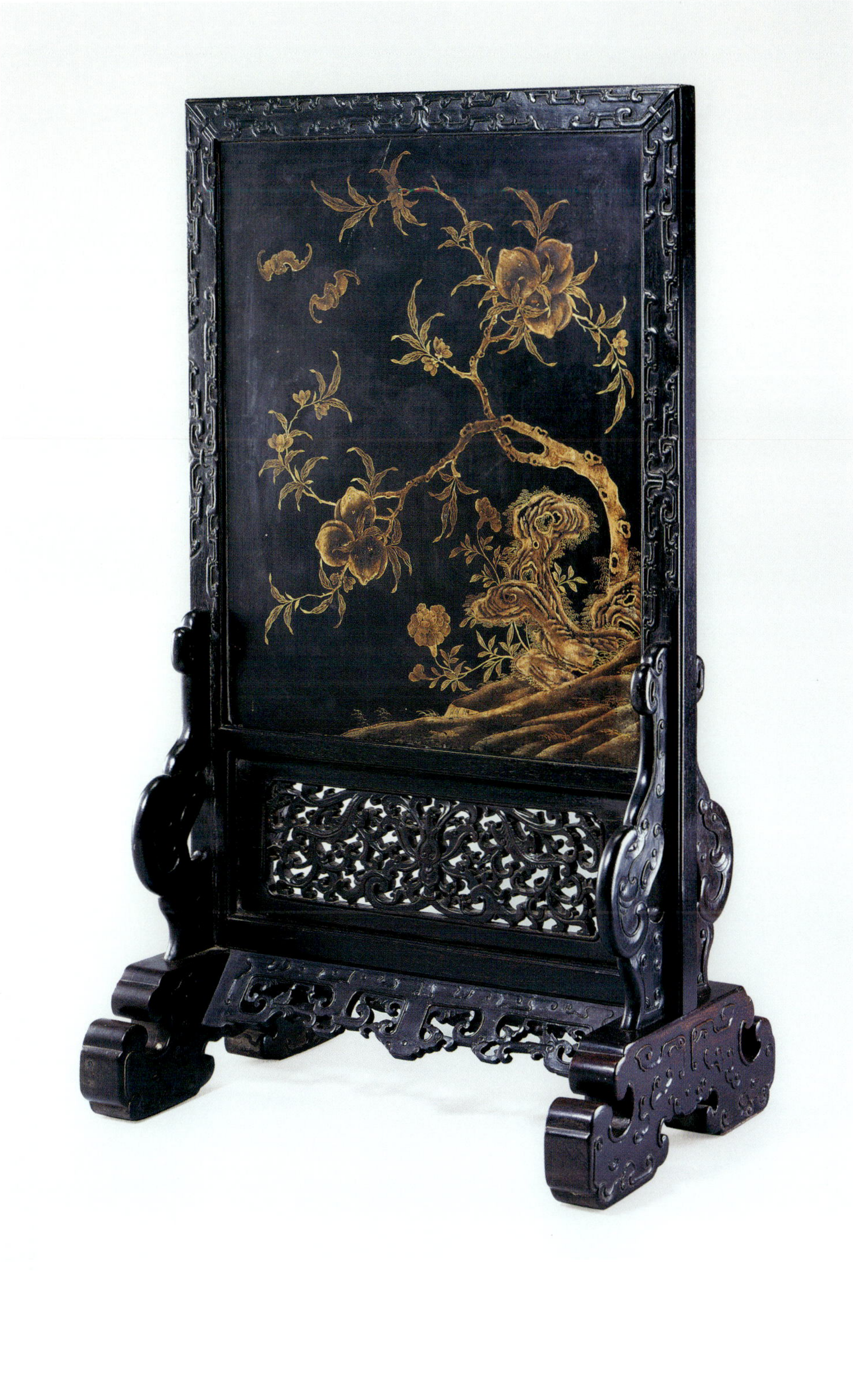

58

Standing Screen

紫檀插屏式透雕大座屏

Zitan
18th Century
Beijing/Tianjin
135 x 65 x 206 cm H

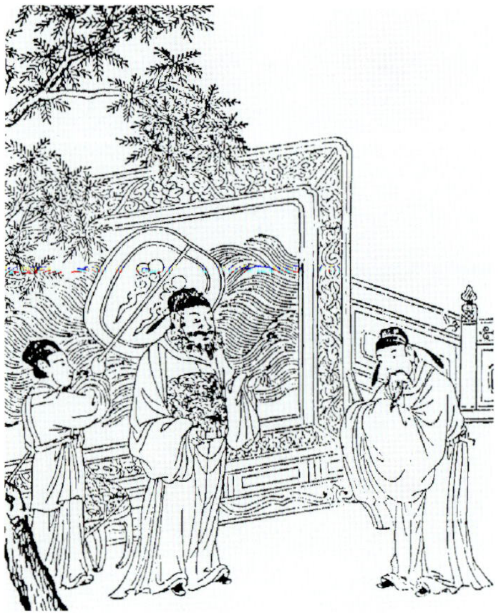

Large standing screen. Woodcut illustration from Yushi renfeng. *Ming Wanli period (d. 1620).*

The exquisite craftsmanship of this large standing screen suggests an origin at the Qing Imperial Workshops. Such screens traditionally housed paintings, calligraphy, decorative stone, and/or mirrors. Old restorations around the opening of the screen frame also indicate that the decorative panel was changed several times throughout its history.

The frame members of the removable screen are finely carved in relief with clouds, cranes and scrolling lotus, and the surrounding *taohuan* panels are both pierced and carved in fine relief with auspicious flowers and four-clawed dragons. The frame members on the front of the base are carved in relief with a *wanzi* diaper pattern; those on the base are more simply shaped with a convex molding. The central panel at the base is carved in relief with dragons; the others with auspicious floral designs—lotus, chrysanthemum, peony and *lingzhi*. The supporting post terminates with a lotus bud, and is flanked by replaced standing spandrels. Florid peonies decorate the aprons, and the feet are each sculpted with a lion toying with an embroidered ball.

Previously exhibited and published in:

- National Museum of History. *Splendor of Style: Classical Furniture from the Ming and Qing Dynasties*, p. 192.

Details: lion foot, detail of upper corner, detail of base panel:

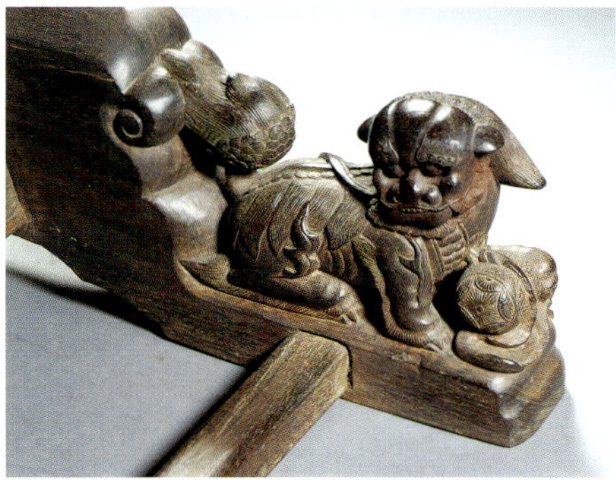

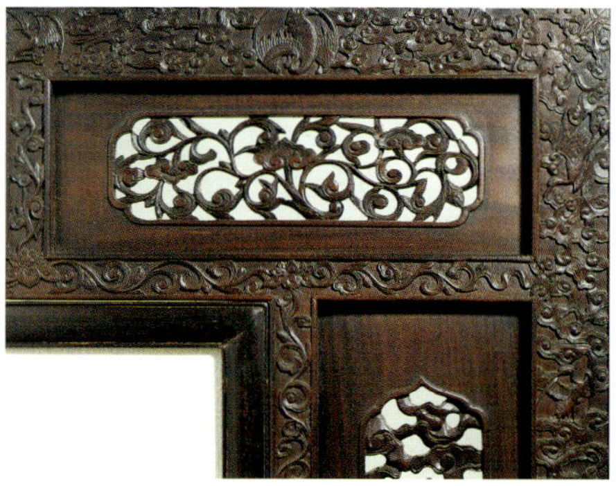

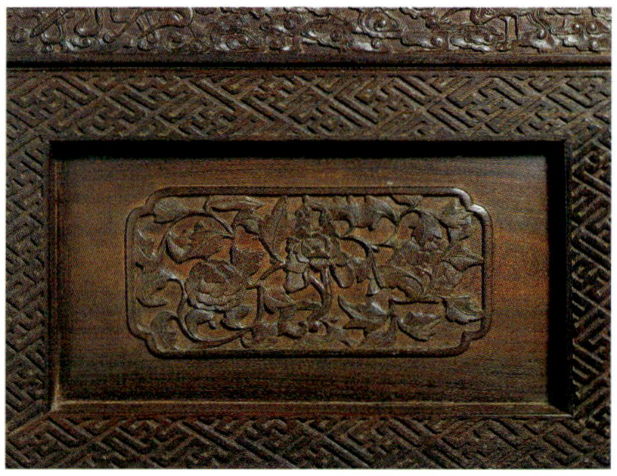

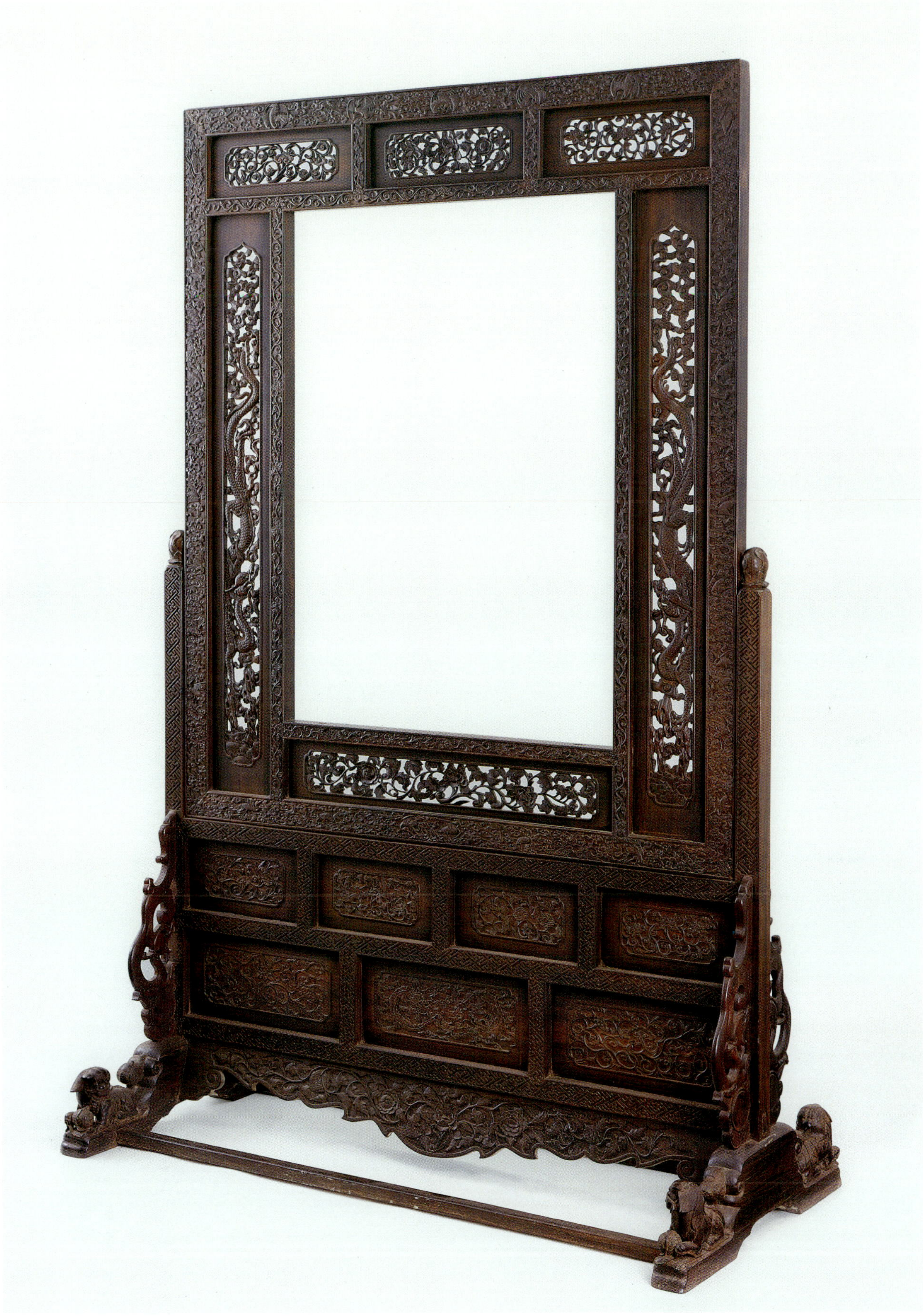

59

Eight-Panel Screen

黃花梨崁百寶八扇圍屏

Huanghuali and
Semi-precious Stone
Late 17th/Early 18th Century
North China
Each Panel 33.5 x 3 cm x 147 cm H

A number of large twelve-panel *huanghuali* screen sets are known that generally date from the 18th and 19th centuries. Visual reference material in paintings and woodcuts suggests that smaller six- and eight-panel screens were of more common use during the Ming period; an eight-panel screen pattern published in the Ming carpenters manual *Lu Ban jing* suggests a standard for the time. While perhaps once considerably more common, such screens are now relatively rare.

This screen is similarly constructed and detailed to the known *huanghuali* twelve-panel screens—similar molded frame members, related space division, and the same style of pierced openwork carving. Nevertheless, the quality of carving surpasses that which is commonly found in most twelve-panel screens. The pierced panels vibrate with *chi* dragons amongst curling clouds, all of which are finished on both sides in a smooth, polished style.

Medallions in various panels are carved in relief on one side with 'hundred antiques' motifs. This design, which was popularized during the Kangxi period asserted the assimilation of Confucian principles by the new Qing rulers through association with sacrificial rites, classical literature, and learning. The opposite side of the screen is also decorated antiquities as well as auspicious floral motifs, composed with colored inlays of carved soapstone and ivory. Regrettably, most of these inlays are now lost, although traces of the original inset designs are clear and distinct.

Similar twelve-panel screens are illustrated in :

- Wang Shixiang and Curtis Evarts. *Masterpieces from the Museum of Classical Chinese Furniture*, pl. 73.
- Jacobsen, Robert D. *Classical Chinese Furniture in the Minneapolis Institute of Arts*, pl. 54.

For further discussion on the history and use of such screens, see:

- Handler, Sarah. "The Chinese Screen: Movable Walls to Divide, Enhance, and Beautify," *Journal of the Classical Chinese Furniture Society* 3:3 (Summer 1993), pp. 4-31.

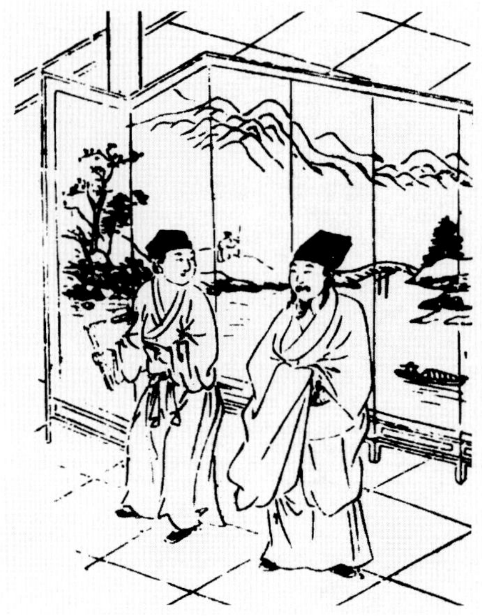

Eight-panel screen. Detail from woodcut illustration to Lu Ban jing, *Ming Wanli period (1573-1620).*

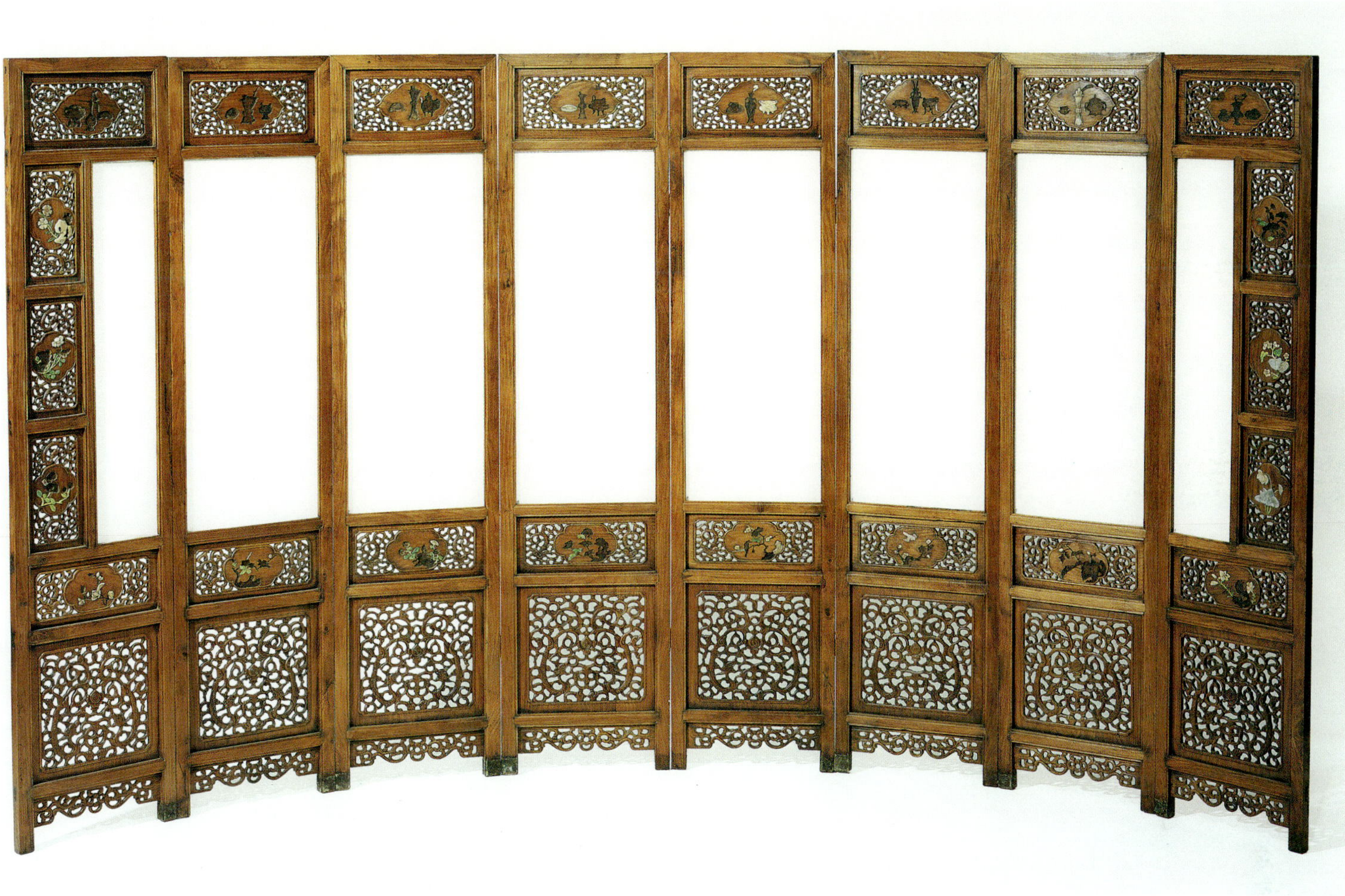

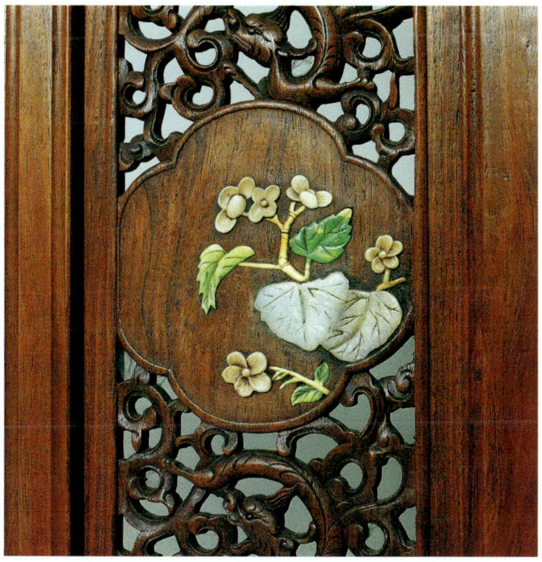

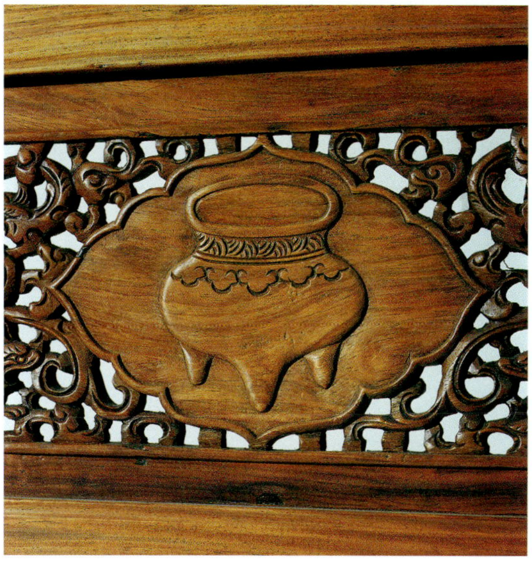

60

Six Screen Panels

黄花梨透雕隔屏六扇

Huanghuali
17th Century
North China
51 x 230 cm H

These richly decorated screen panels may have functioned as room dividers. Each screen is subdivided with three narrow and two large panels. The narrow frame members are unusually molded with wide, flat beading which flanks a central 'sword ridge' molding. The top panel of each contains a variant 'longevity' (*shou*) character flanked by auspicious mythical creatures. Other panels are variously decorated, each with scenes from ancient stories, mythical beasts, precious treasures, and birds and flowers. A curvilinear apron carved with scrolling grass is fit between the short feet at the base. The 'one-sided' carving is of exceptional quality; both subject matter and decorative style are closely related to that found amongst porcelain, lacquerware, and textiles dated to the late Ming period.

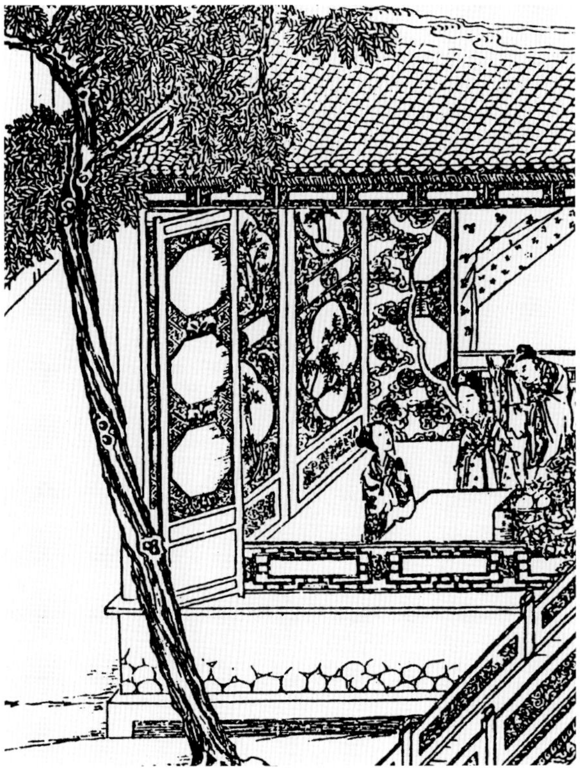

Screen panels. Detail from woodcut illustration to Hong lou meng, *Qing Guangxu period, 1879.*

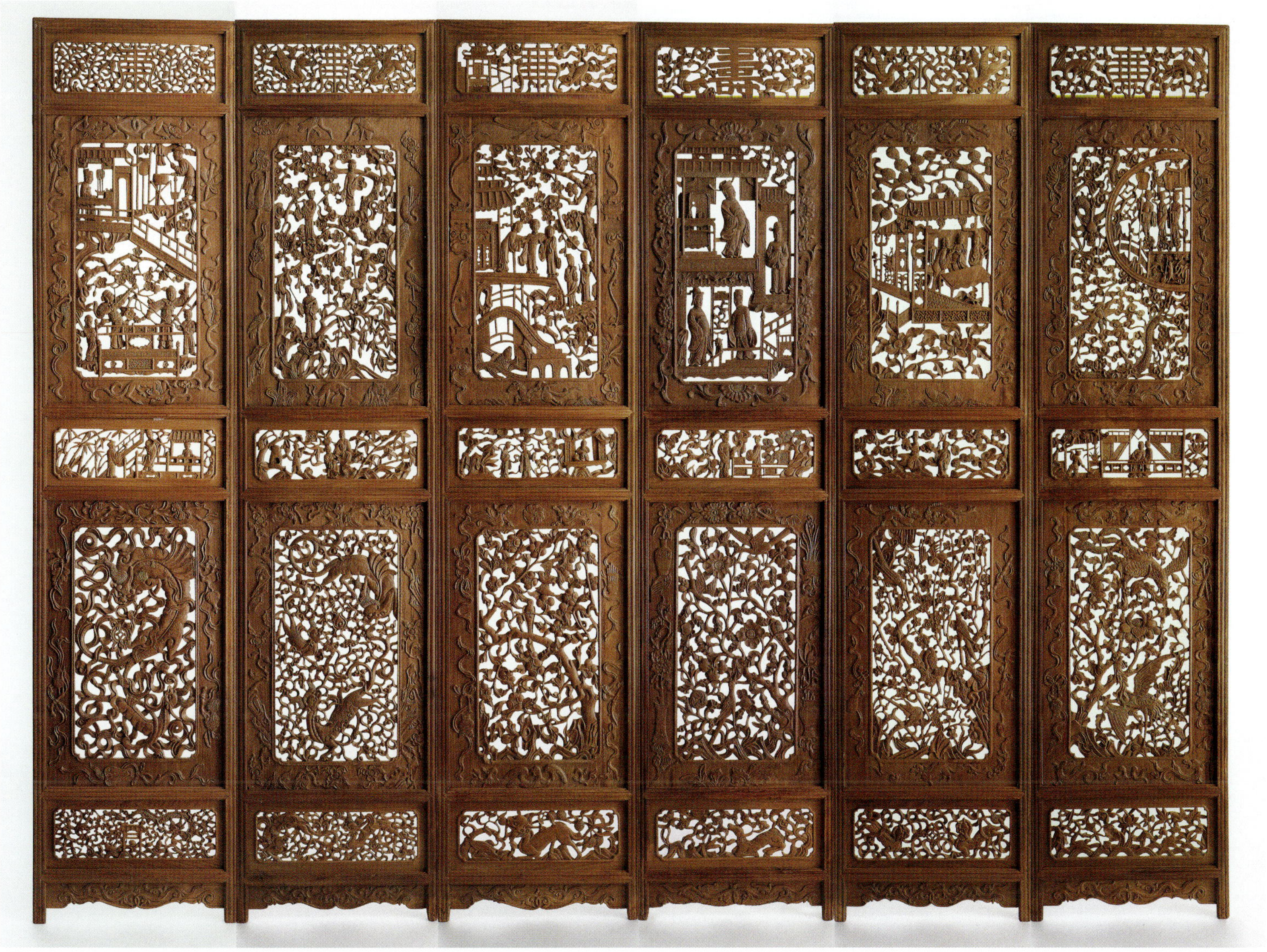

61

Pair of Lampstands

紫檀燈檯一對

Zitan
18th Century
North China
50 x 50 x 163 cm H

Once furnishing the Palace as well as grand households in great numbers, lampstands are today quite rare. The detail below is drawn from a handscroll illustrating the Yongzheng emperor's procession to offer sacrifices at the Xiannong Altar in the southern suburbs of Beijing, in which the artist has depicted over fifty lanterns set up along the route.

These lampstands are solidly constructed, and the precious *zitan* material from which they are made is of excellent quality. The square platform at the top is shaped with indented corners and its edge is molded to a half-round profile with beaded edges. Below, four hanging spandrels are carved in relief with scrolled *chi* dragons. The vertical post is square in section with indented corner beading; it rests on a disk at the base and tenons through the lapping base members. The large standing spandrels are also carved in relief with scrolled *chi* dragons. The feet on the base members are built up with laminations.

A matching pair of lampstands were published in:

- Sotheby's New York. *Important Chinese Furniture*, March 23, 1999, lot 37.

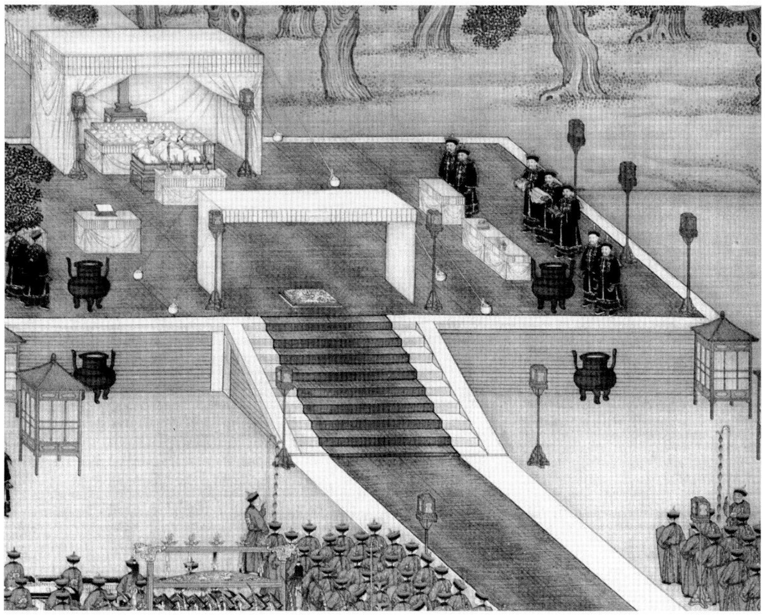

Lampstands. Detail from handscroll Offering Sacrifices at Xiannong Altar. *Anonymous, Yongzheng period (1723-1735).*

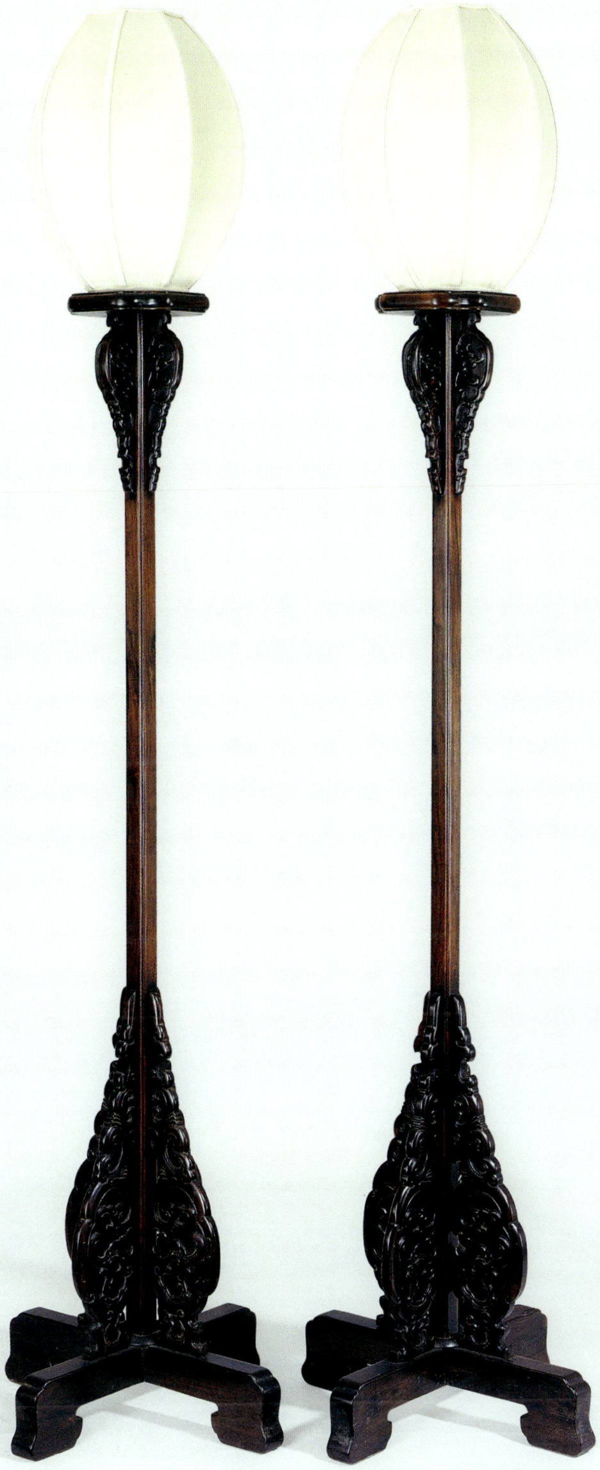

62

Ceremonial Lampstand

紫檀黃陽木燈檯

Zitan and Boxwood
18th Century
Beijing
178 cm H

This lampstand, which exhibits exquisite workmanship in fine materials, was likely intended for ceremonial use within a Buddhist context. The stand is easily disassembled into its component parts. The boxwood base is shaped as three elephant heads supporting a lotus leaf and pod, wherein the *zitan* post is seated. The boxwood top is also carved as three elephant heads supporting a sacred alms bowl carved in relief with rising cloud heads. The elephant heads are finely sculpted with ornamental mounts, and pendant streamers may well have hung from their upturned elephant trunks.

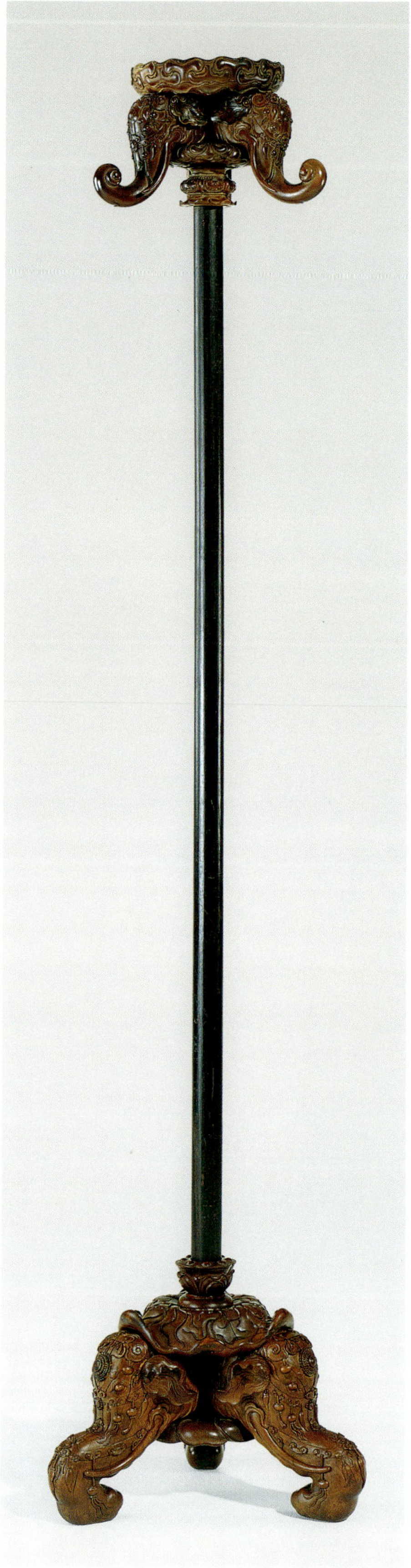

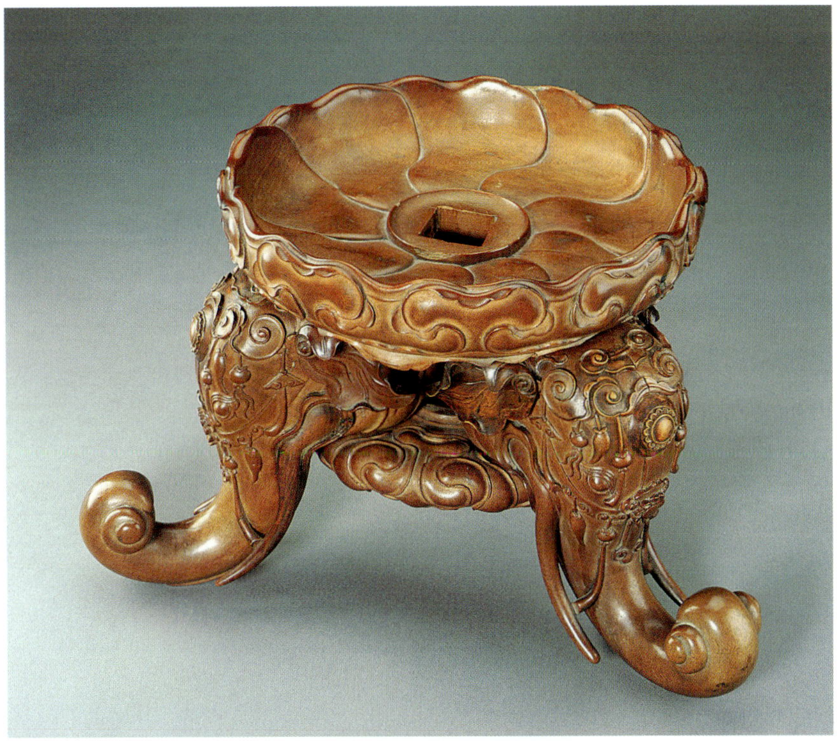

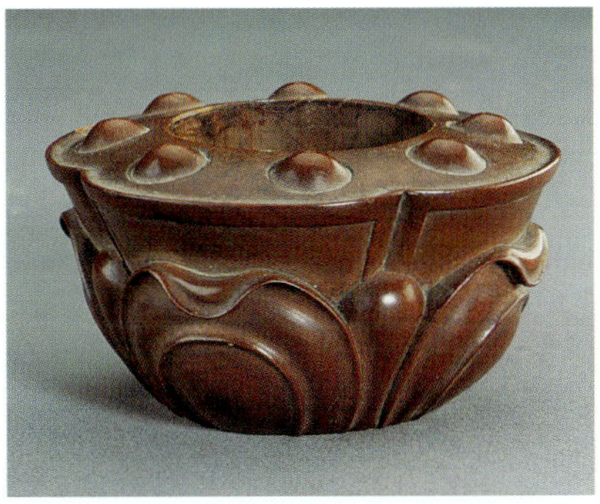

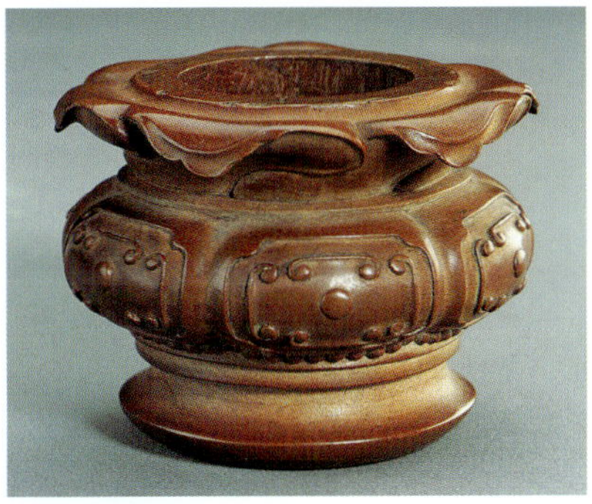

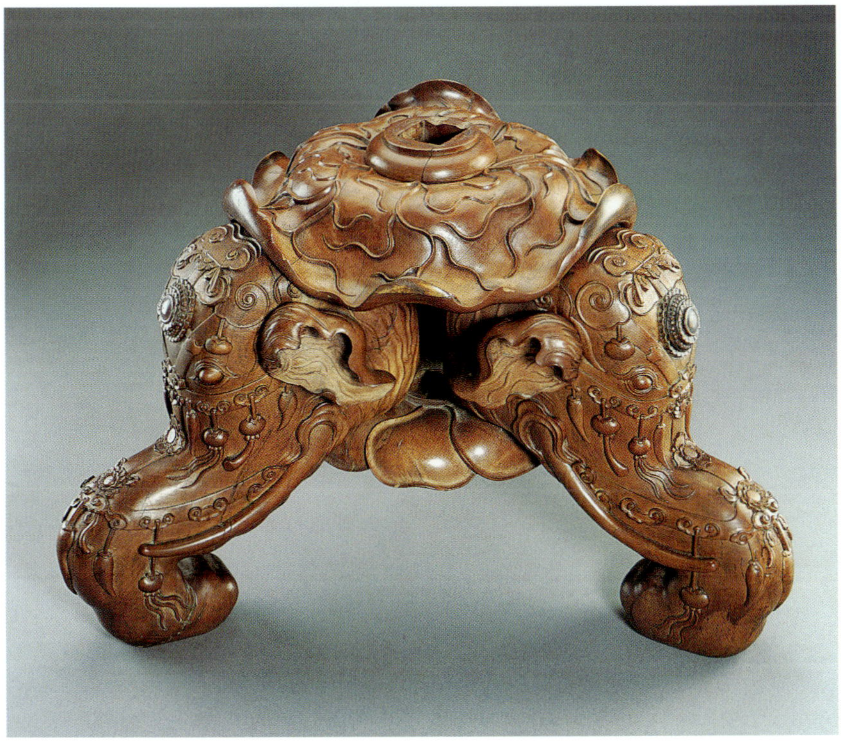

Miscellaneous

雜類完器

63

Tabletop Chest

黄花梨官皮箱

Huanghuali
18th Century
40 x 27 x 38.5 cm H

This Ming-style tabletop chest exhibits elegant design, refined workmanship, and select material, which is evident in the matched door panels of highly figured *huanghuali*. Flush square-corner hinges provide smooth, uninterrupted surfaces; the worn lockplates reveal an early brass-plating technique over a copper base. The interior is fit with seven multiple-sized drawers including full width drawers at the top and bottom, a large central drawer, and two narrow drawers on either side.

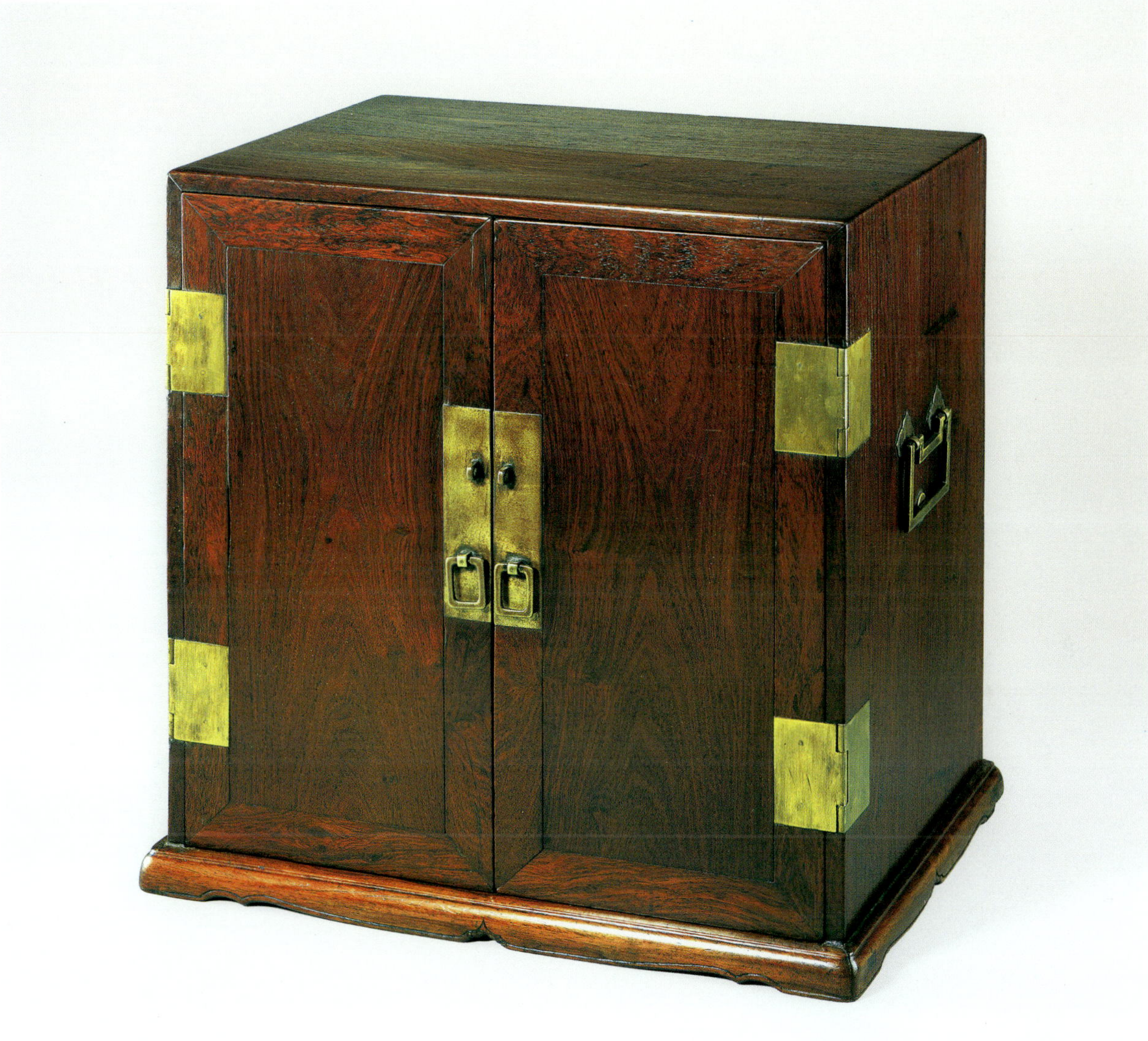

64

Tabletop Chest

黄花梨官皮箱

Huanghuali
18th Century
33 x 29 x 31 cm H

Refined workmanship is exhibited throughout this traditionally styled tabletop chest. The top features a single panel of *huanghuali*, and the doors panels are mirrored with matching grain. The original brass mounts have survived intact. The interior is fit with a typical arrangement of drawers.

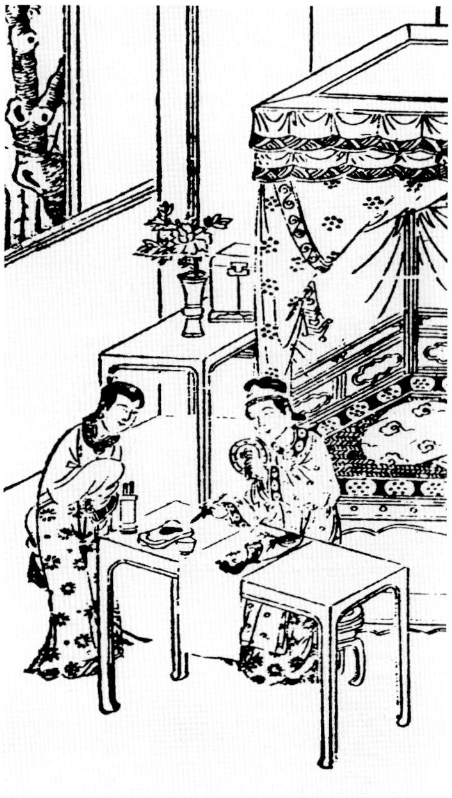

Dressing case. Detail from woodcut illustration to Linchuan simeng, *late Ming dynasty.*

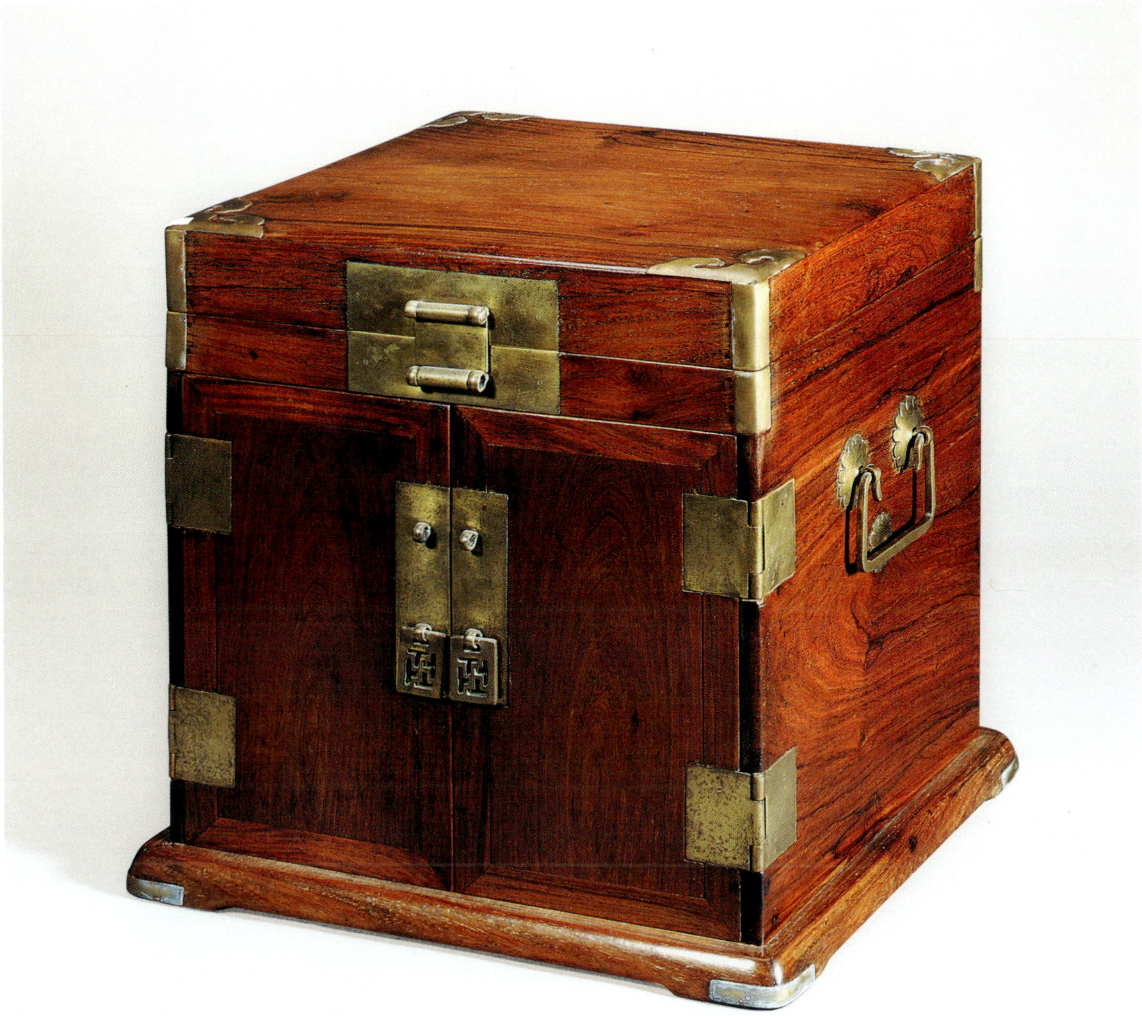

65

Dressing Case

黃花梨鏡架官皮箱

Huanghuali
18th Century
34.5 x 30.5 x 37 cm H

This cosmetic case exhibits a traditional form with a high, dome-shaped lid, beneath which, a folding mirror stand is fitted. The door panels are carved in relief with lantern-shaped medallions and stylized *shou* characters in a decorative style motif associated with the early Qing period. The paktong hardware is original, and the pulls are inlaid with copper and brass snowflake designs. Five drawers are concealed behind the doors.

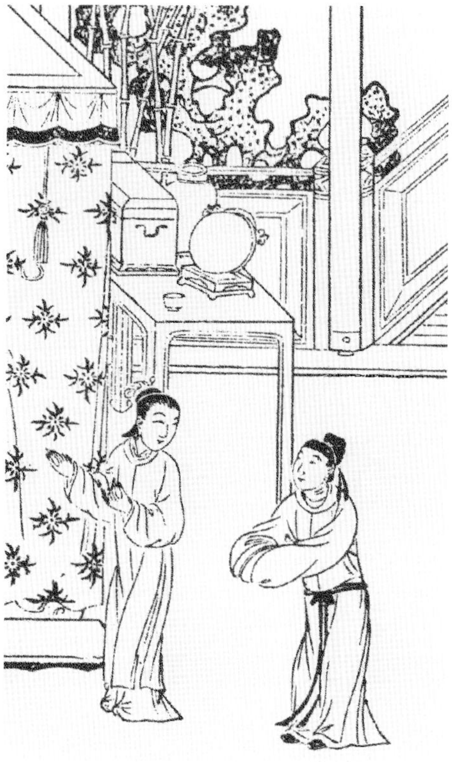

Dressing case and mirror stand. Detail from woodcut illustration to Qian'nu lihun, *Ming Wanli period (1573-1620).*

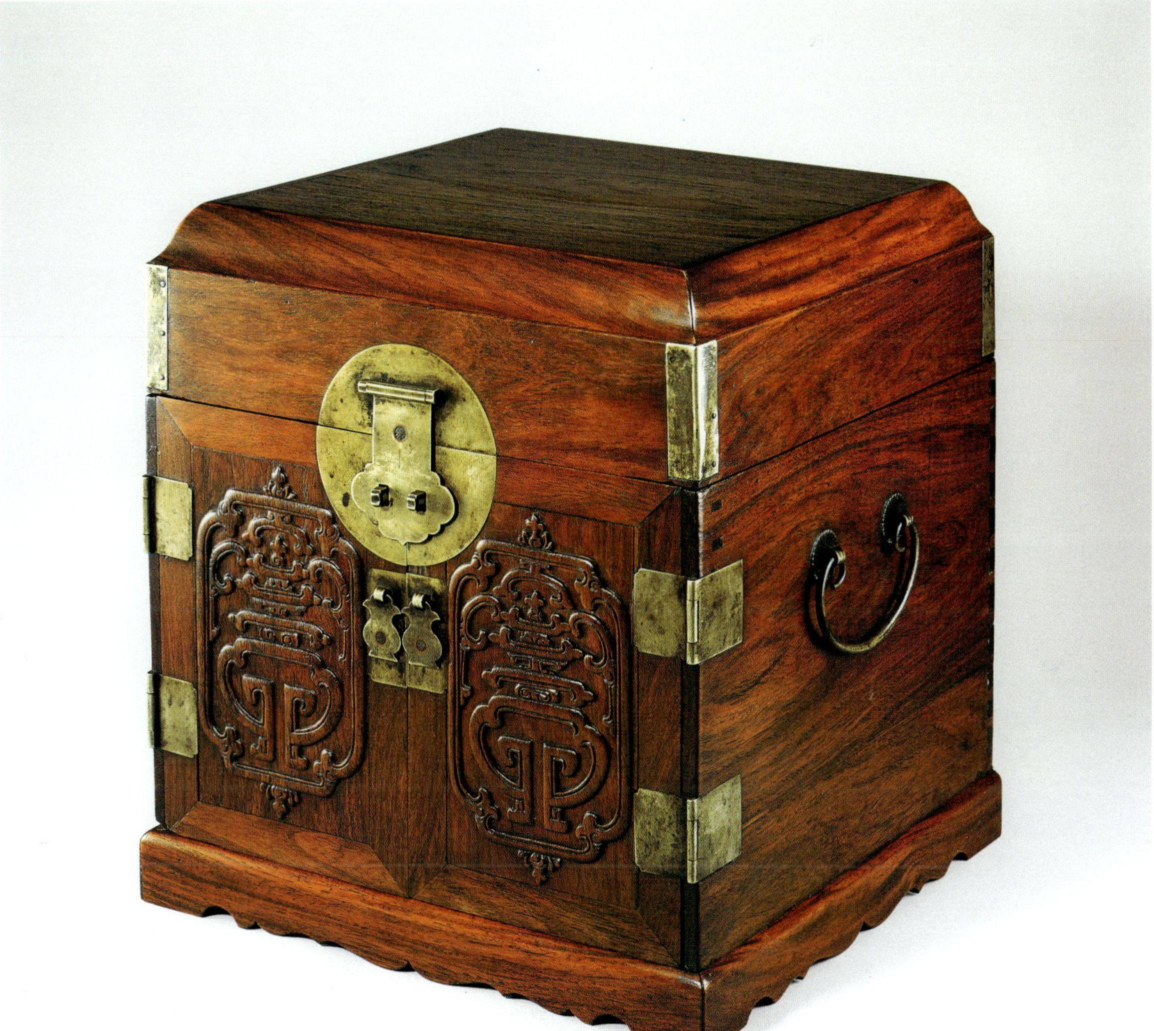

66

Dressing Case with Inlaid Decoration

黄花梨嵌百寶官皮箱

Huanghuali, Ivory, and
Semi-Precious Stones
18th Century
36 x 26 x 36 cm H

This *huanghuali* dressing case features auspicious inlaid decoration well suited for a young woman's dowry. The top of the case is decorated with birds, butterflies, dragonflies, pomegranate, and flowers (see fig. 9, p. 32). One side displays 'Buddha's hand' fruit, plum blossoms, birds, and butterflies; the other with peonies and butterflies. The door panels feature designs of the "Hundred Boys" with auspicious objects including the umbrella, plum blossoms, *ruyi*, crabs, and lanterns—all in a garden scene with clouds, rocks and bamboo. Stained ivory and bluish lazurite (*qingjin shi*) were employed for the decorative inlays.

The interior of the chest is fit with five drawers, each with pulls shaped in various cloud and *ruyi* patterns. The drawer faces are of *huanghuali*, while their interiors are of *tieli* wood.

Previously exhibited and published in:

- National Museum of History. *Splendor of Style: Classical Furniture from the Ming and Qing Dynasties*, p. 184.

A similarly styled chest possibly from the same workshop is published in:

- Bruce, Grace Wu. *On the Kang and between the Walls-the Ming Furniture quietly installed*, pl. 18.

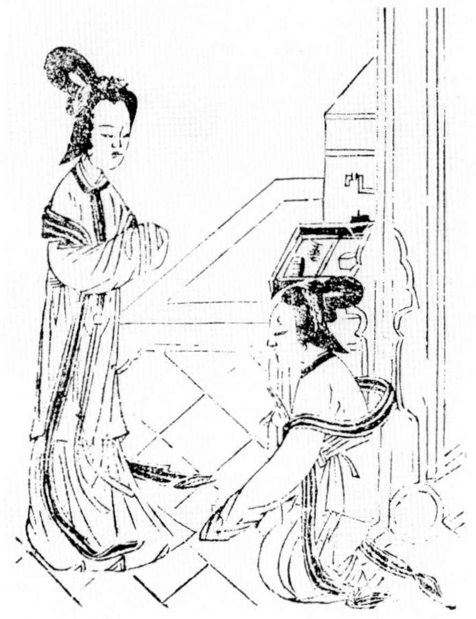

Dressing case. Detail from woodcut illustration to Yuzhai ji, *late Ming period.*

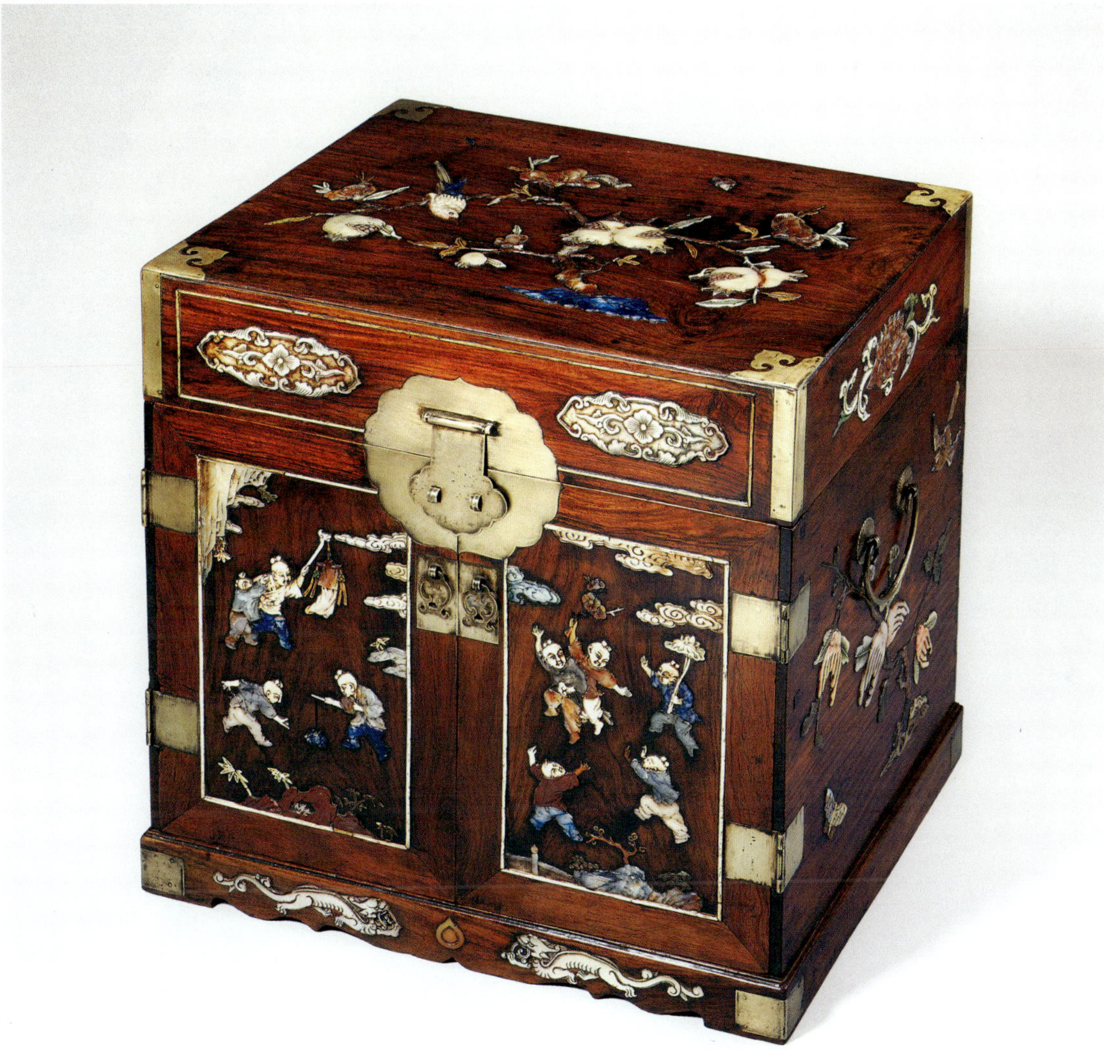

67

Cosmetic Case and Mirror Stand

黄花梨五屏鏡檯

Huanghuali
18th Century
North China
56 x 33.5 x 79 cm H

The throne-like screen of this cosmetic case is crested with dragon- and phoenix-heads. The top of each panel is finely carved in relief with cranes flying amongst clouds. The central panel is pierced with a promising scene illustrating a scholar rising from the sea on the head of a dragon and meeting a phoenix. The side panels feature auspicious flora—bamboo and *lingzhi*, chrysanthemums, peonies, and plum blossoms. A small balustrade surrounds the top of the base, and the front panels are carved with deer and *lingzhi*—symbols of emolument and longevity. The five panels, which are joined together on their backsides with small brass hooks, can be easily removed. The base was discovered in less fortunate condition, with missing doors that have since been replaced.

Mirror stands of closely related style are illustrated in:

- Hong Kong Museum of Art. *In Pursuit of Antiquities*, pl. 274.
- Jacobsen, Robert D. *Classical Chinese Furniture in the Minneapolis Institute of Arts*, pl. 64.
- Wang Shixiang. *Classic Chinese Furniture: Ming and Early Qing Dynasties*, pl. 164.
- Zhu Jiajin and Wang Shixiang. *Zhongguo meishu quanji Vol. 11*, p. 189.

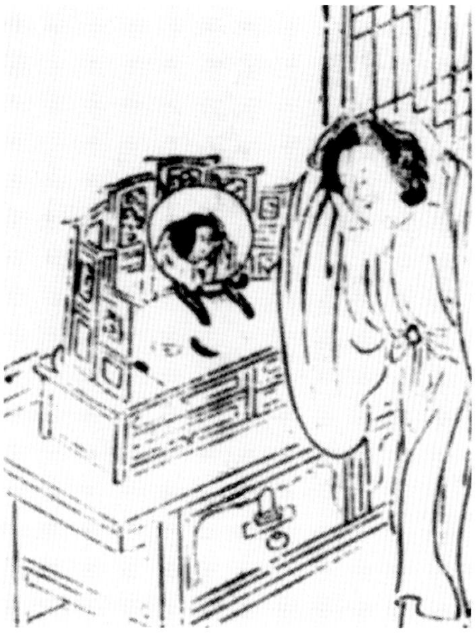

Mirror Stand. Detail from woodcut illustration to the carpenter's manual Lu Ban jing*, Ming Wanli period (1573-1620).*

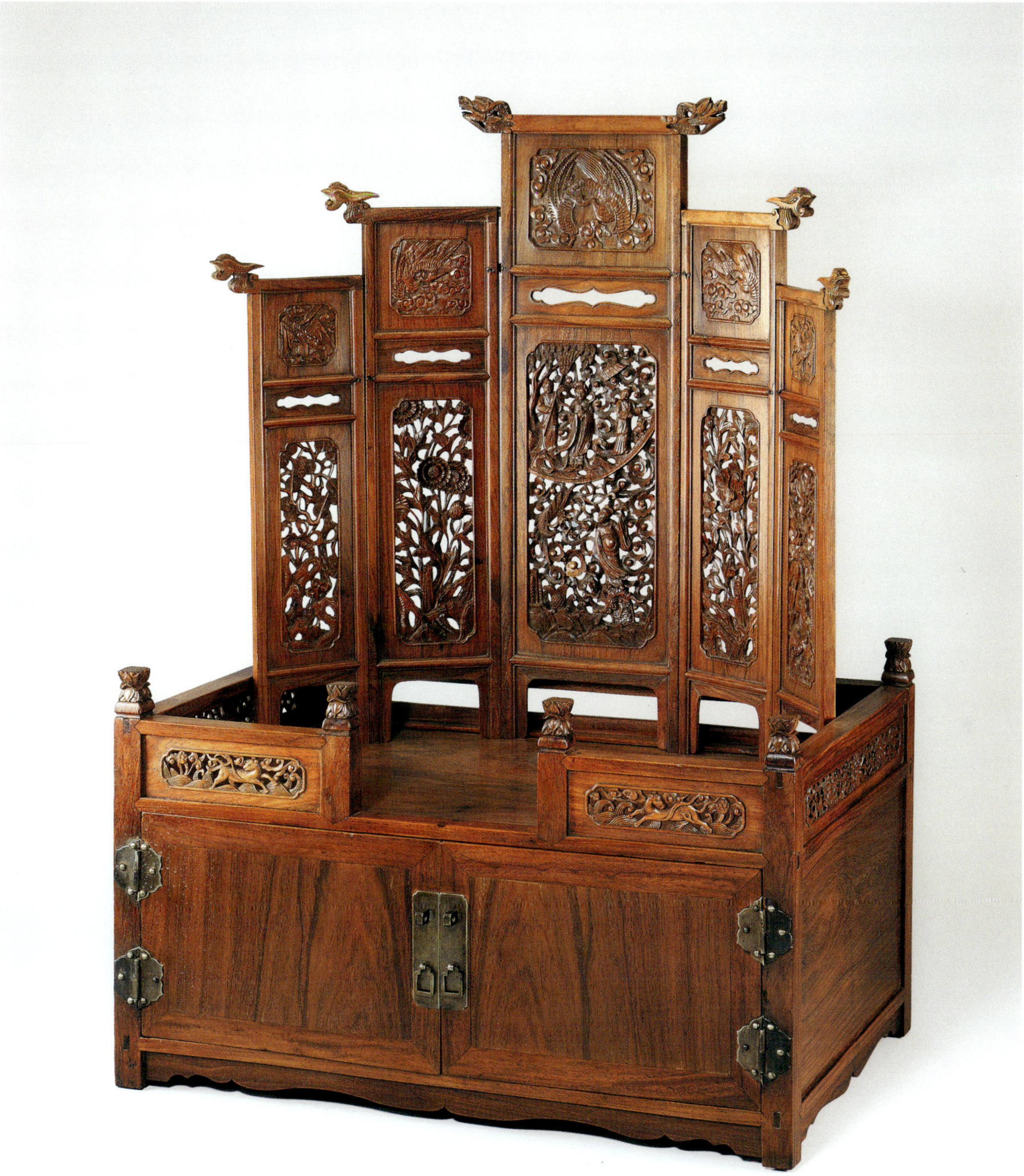

68

Cosmetic Case with Folding Mirror Stand

紫檀摺疊鏡箱

Zitan
18th Century
41.7 x 41.5 x 21.2 cm H

This cosmetic case exhibits a traditional early Qing style. Similar stands of *huanghuali* are somewhat more common, but those of *zitan* are rare.

The mirror support is hinged at the base with wood pivots and is fit with an adjustable angle support. A large bronze mirror with a polished surface was placed upon the lotus-shaped rest. Panels pierced with designs of *chi* dragons decorate its framework. Behind the hinged doors, the interior fit with drawers where cosmetics and jewelry were stored.

Mirror stands of related style are illustrated in:

- Hong Kong Museum of Art. *In Pursuit of Antiquities*, pl. 273
- Wang Shixiang. *Classic Chinese Furniture: Ming and Early Qing Dynasties*, pl. 162
- Wang Shixiang and Curtis Evarts. *Masterpieces from the Museum of Classical Chinese Furniture*, pl. 71.
- Yip Shing-Yiu and Grace Wu Bruce. *Chan Chair and Qin Bench: The Dr. S. Y. Yip Collection of Classic Chinese Furniture II*, pl. 65.

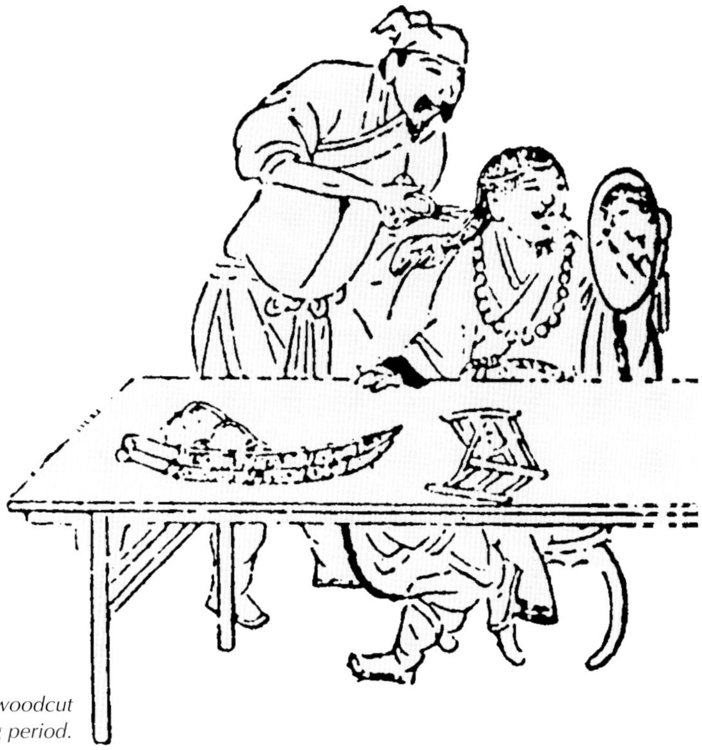

Folding mirror stand. Detail from woodcut illustration to Shui hu chuan, *late Ming period.*

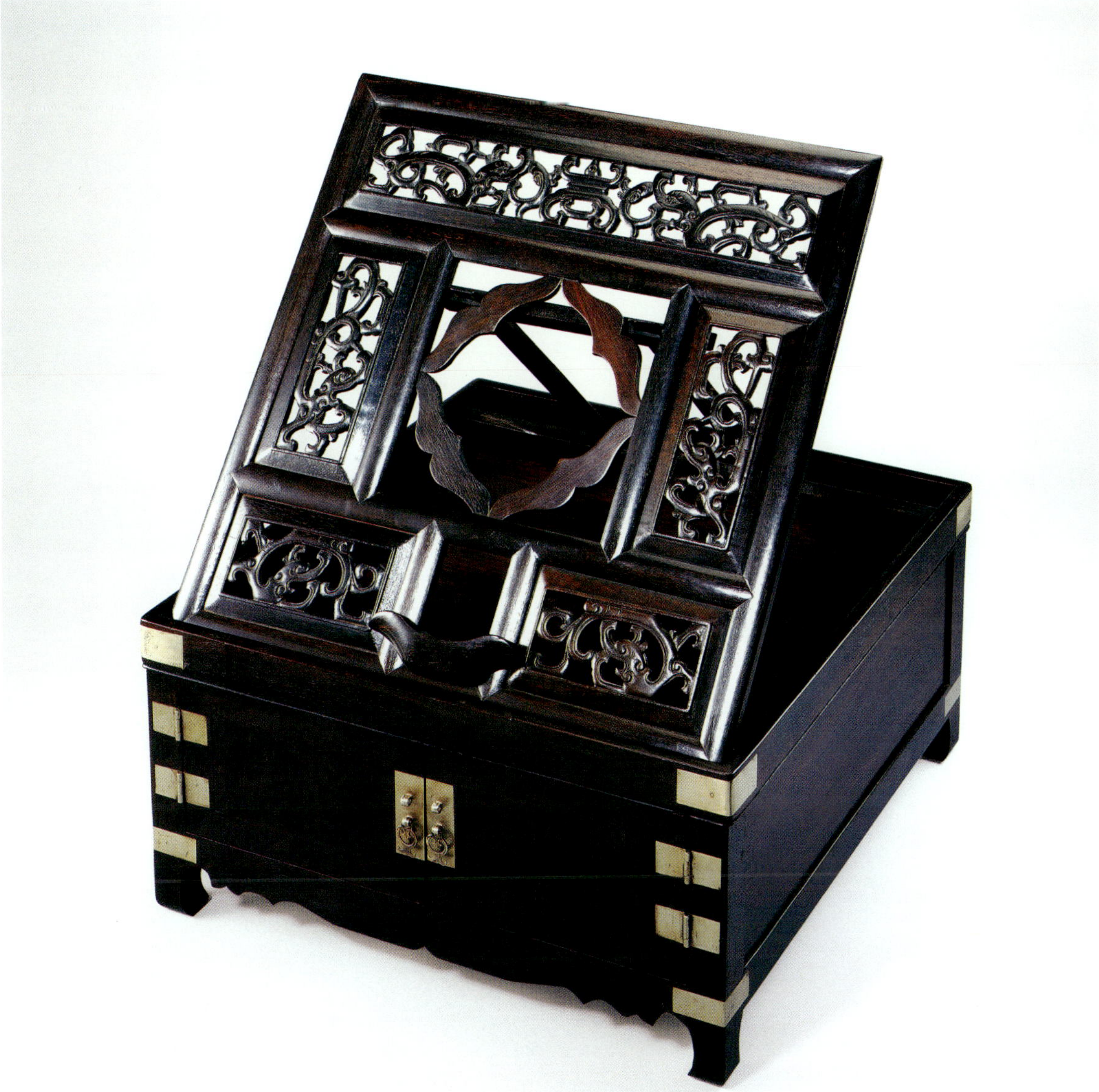

69

Cosmetic Case with Folding Mirror Frame

紫檀摺疊鏡箱

Zitan
19th Century
24.5 x 31 x 13 cm H
Open Height 34 cm

This compact, portable dressing case exhibits a mid-to-late Qing style that was popularized after the introduction of silvered-glass mirrors. Many such examples are found in the Shanghai Region. The smooth *zitan* surfaces and extent of metal mounts are masculine in style. The mirror is concealed under a hinged lid, which when opened, neatly folds into an upright position.

Similar examples are illustrated in:

- Ellsworth, Robert Hatfield. *Chinese Hardwood Furniture in Hawaiian Collections*, pl. 58.
- Tian Jiaqing. *Classic Chinese Furniture of the Qing Dynasty*, pl. 124.
- Ang, John Kwang-Ming. *The Beauty of Huanghuali*, p. 70.
- Beurdeley, Michel. *Chinese Furniture*, p. 171, pl. 229.

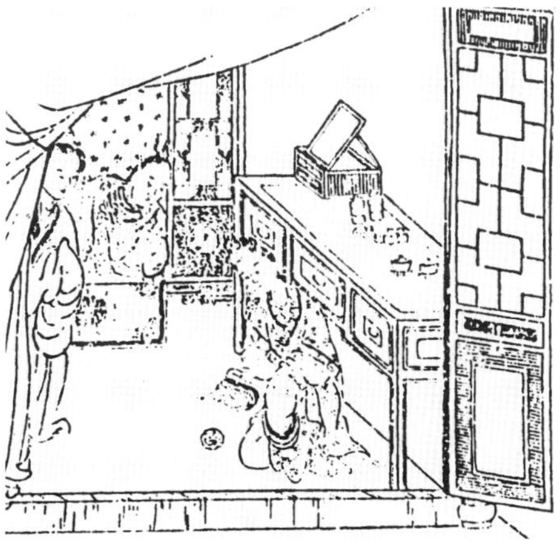

Dressing case with mirror. Detail from woodcut illustration to Shitou ji, *Guangxu period (1875-1908).*

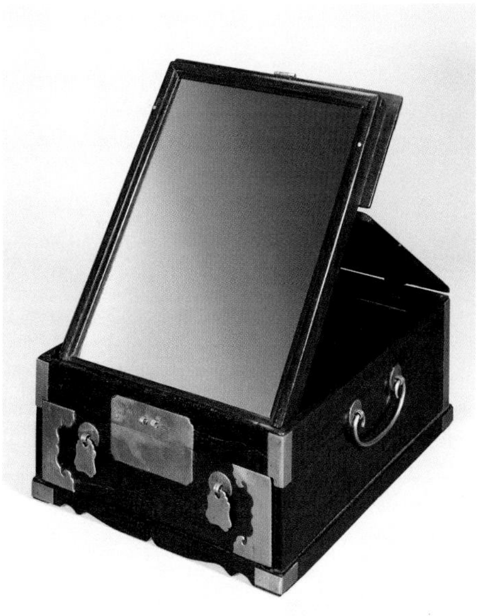

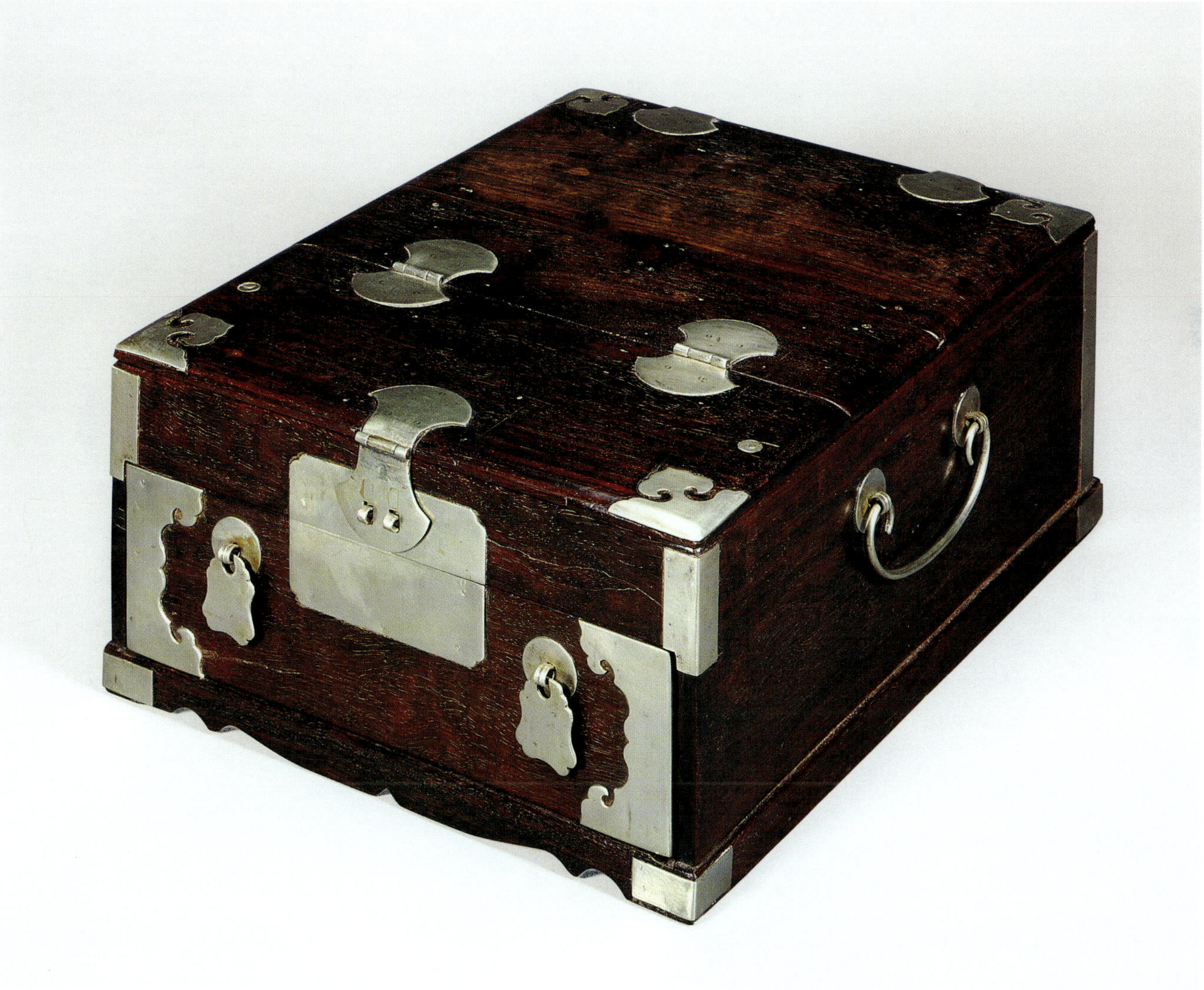

70

Tiered Carrying Case

紫檀提盒

Zitan and Ebony
18th Century
35 x 19 x 22 cm H

Tiered carrying cases were often used for bringing tasty snacks along on a visit. This example is of traditional size and construction; however, the use of *wumu* (ebony) is rarely encountered. The jet black *wumu* used for the frame members of the carrying rack stands in contrast to the reddish tonality of the *zitan* used for the tiered trays. Exquisite handling of this material is evident in its finely shaped beading and carved spandrels, the style of the latter resembling that of archaic jade carving. The material of the tiered trays is well matched, and the exposed dovetail construction is finely joined. *Tieli* was used for the tray bottoms.

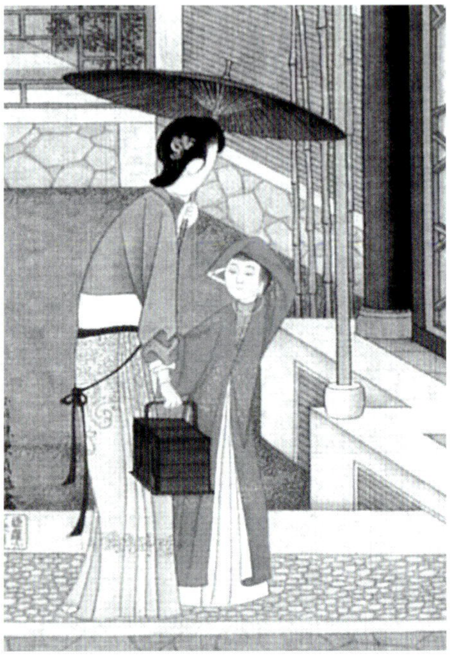

Foodbox. Detail from album leaf set Classical Ladies *by Jiao Bingzhen. Yongzheng period (1723-1735).*

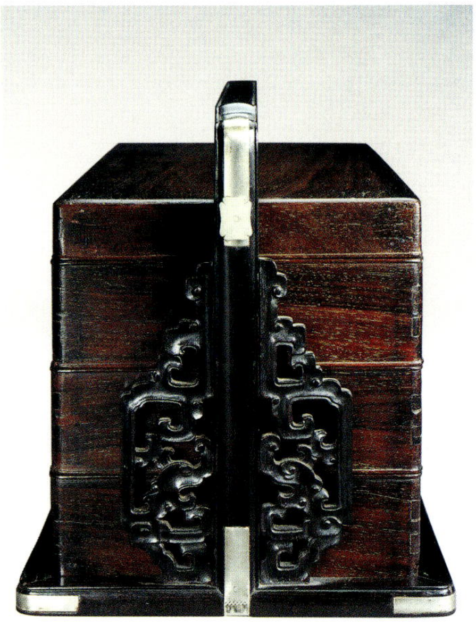

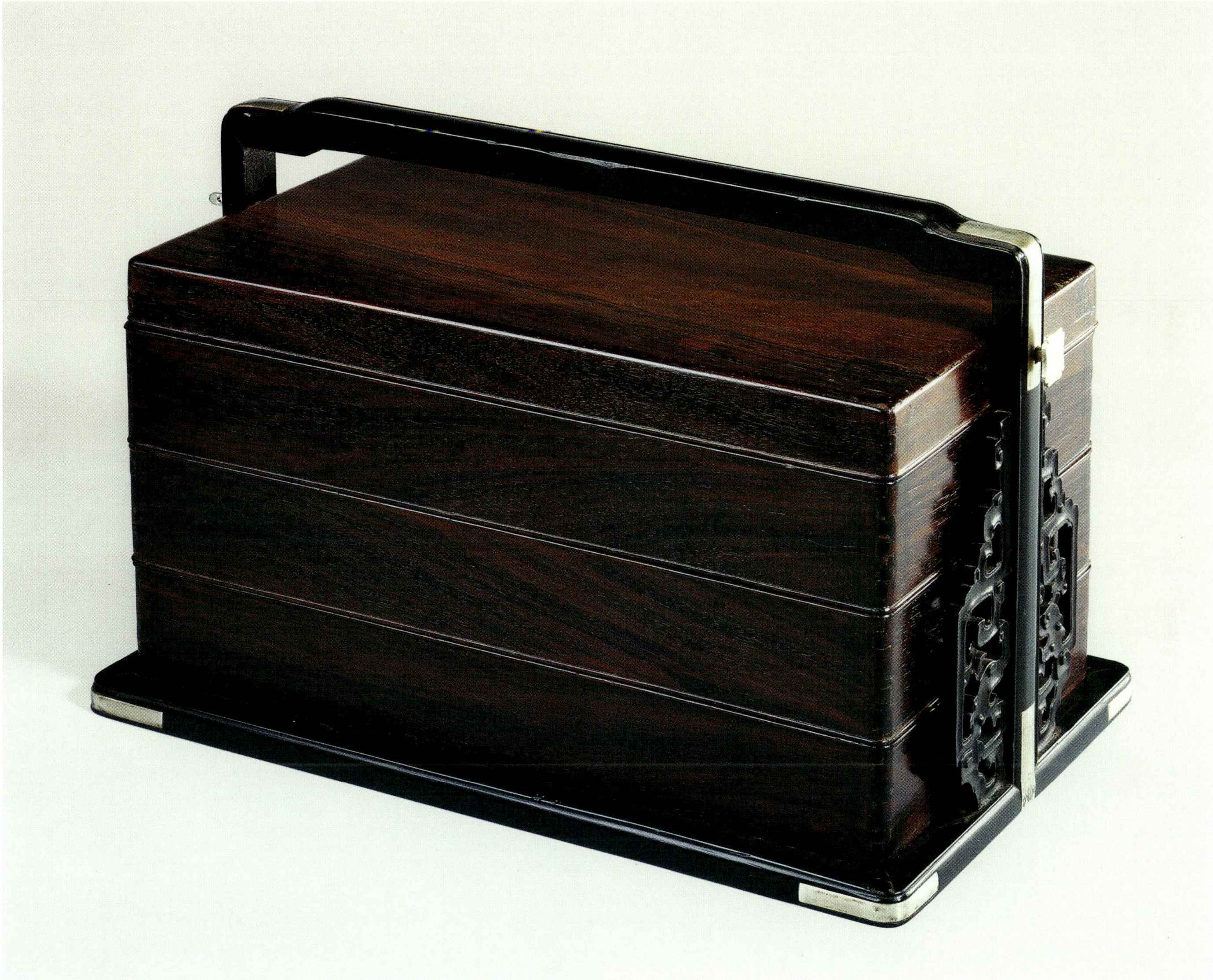

71

Portable Case

紫檀插門抽屜提盒

Zitan
18th Century
23 x 35 x 33 cm H

This portable case, which is fit with carrying handle attached to the top, exhibits a traditional Qing dynasty style. Such handy cases served multiple purposes; an early Qing handscroll illustrates use as an artist's toolbox (see illustration below).

This example is finely constructed with highly figured *zitan*, the front panel of which appears to have been specially selected for its rich, sunset imagery. The interior is fit with a tray and five drawers of various size. Although a few of the paktong mounts have been replaced, the chest has generally survived in excellent condition.

A *zitan* case of similar style and size is illustrated in:

- Bruce, Grace Wu. *Zitan furniture from the Ming and Qing dynasties*, pl. 16.

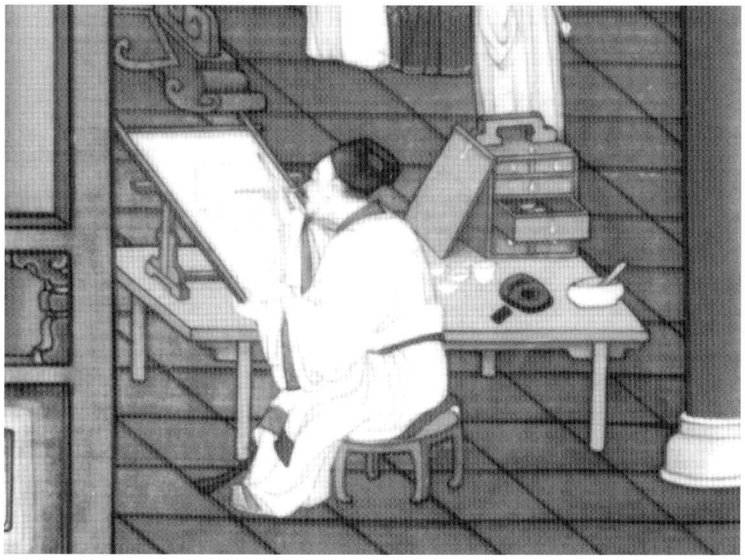

Stationery case with drawers and removable front cover. Detail from handscroll by Leng Mei (active 1703-1717), Eighteen Beauties of the Han Palace at the Break of Spring. *National Palace Museum, Taipei.*

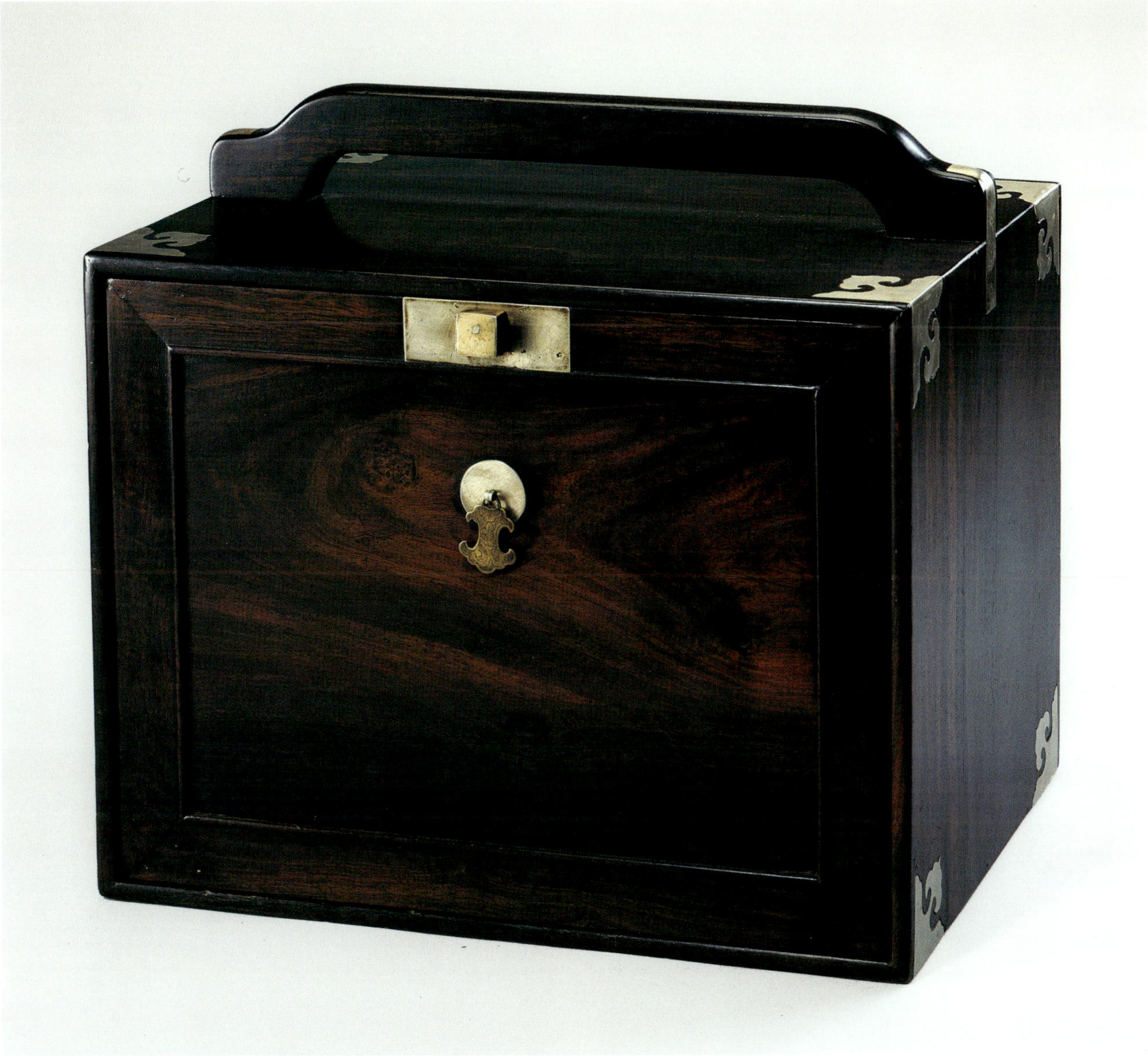

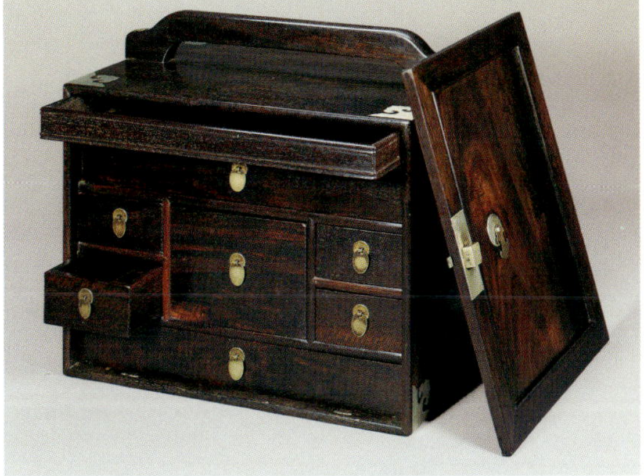

72

Portable Case

紫檀癭木插門抽屜提盒

Zitan, Burl, and *Nanmu*
Late 18th/Early 19th Century
23.5 x 33 x 32.5 cm H

This portable case is also of a traditional Qing dynasty style; however, its use of material and interior configuration are rarely seen. The handle and frame of the front panel are made from *zitan*; the casework, the front panel, and the drawer fronts are made of burlwood; the drawer interiors, *nanmu*. Drawers aside, the interior space also houses a tray and a lidded burlwood box. The case is well preserved with its original yellow brass hardware, and retains a lovely aged patina.

Cases of similar style are illustrated in:

- Bruce, Grace Wu. *Zitan furniture from the Ming and Qing dynasties*, pl. 13.
- Yip Shing-Yiu and Grace Wu Bruce. *Chan Chair and Qin Bench: The Dr. S. Y. Yip Collection of Classic Chinese Furniture II*, pl. 59

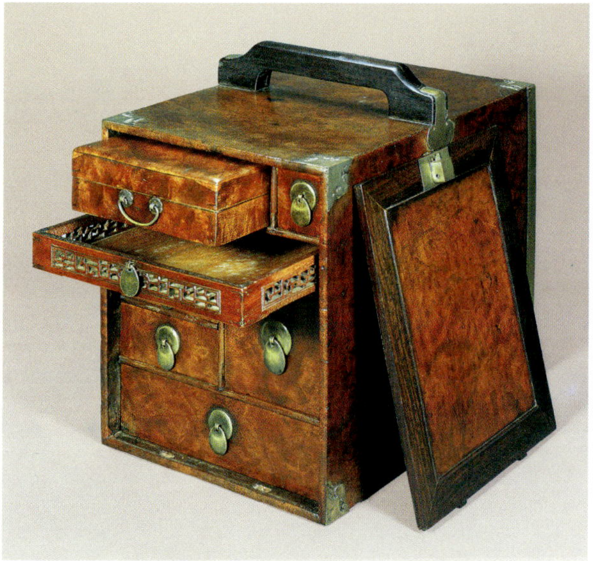

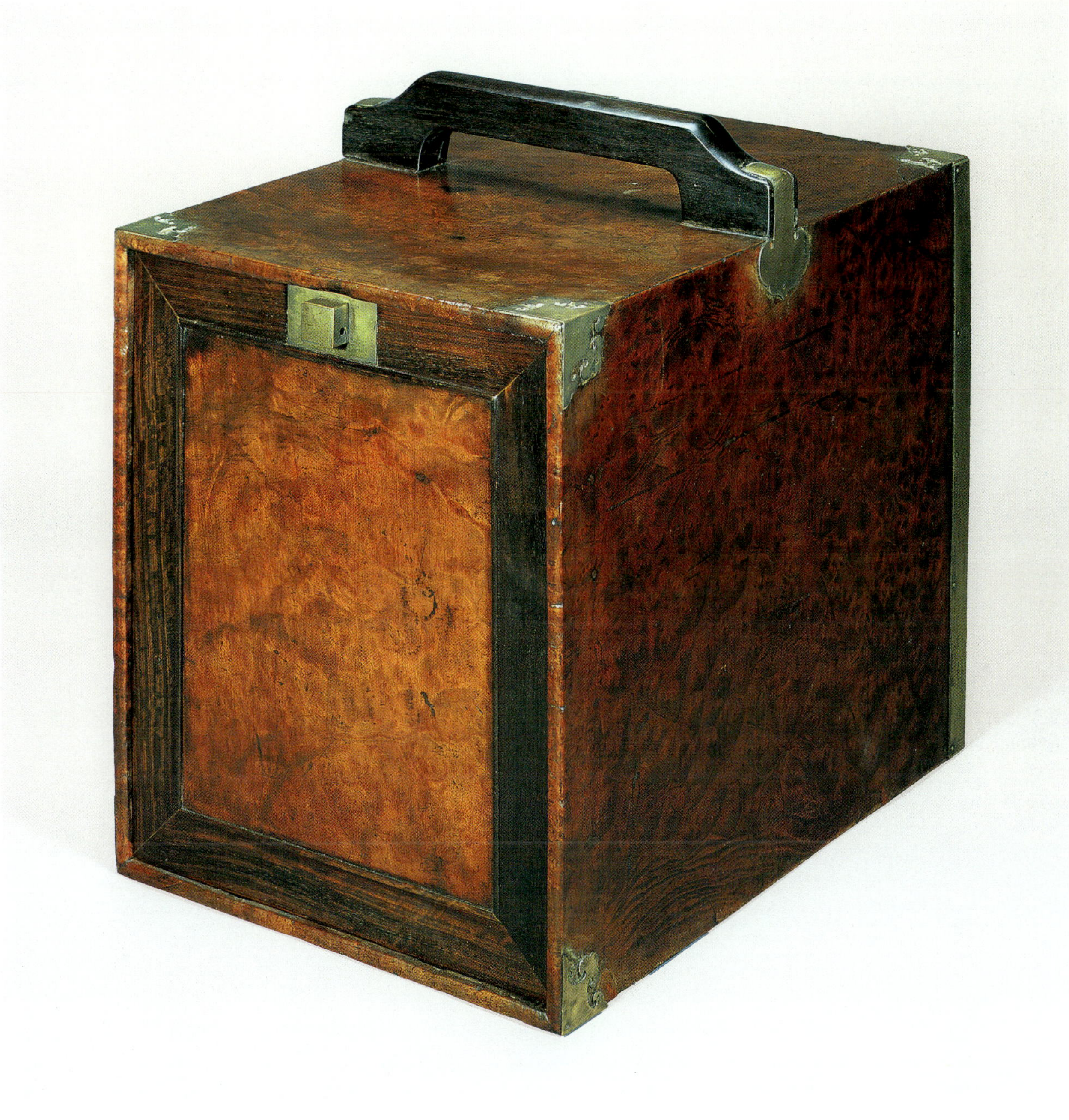

73

Box with Sliding Cover

紫檀匣

Zitan
18th Century
26.5 x 14 x 11.5 cm H

Small boxes of fine construction and precious materials were variously used for the safekeeping of rare treasures, storage of stationery implements, or the presentation of small gifts.

This box is of a traditional style with a semi-concealed lid that slides in and out from one end. The box is completely constructed of *zitan* with exceptional tiger-striped figuring in the side panels.

A red lacquer box of similar size and construction that was excavated from an early Ming tomb demonstrates the longstanding tradition of this style.

- Zhu Jiajin, Xia Gengqi, eds. Zhongguo qiqi quanji: 5 Ming, pl. 2.

74

Book Box with Sliding Cover

黄花梨書匣

Huanghuali
Late 17th/Early 18th Century
29 x 19 x 11.5 cm H

This book box of plain style was made with highly figured *huanghuali*. The sliding cover features rippling grain patterns that shimmer with a luminescent quality. The surfaces reveal rounded wear and even patination.

The inscription on the lid reads *Guwen Yuan Jian* (Profound Investigations into the Classics), the title of a series of essays selected by the Emperor Kangxi (pub. 1685) and compiled by Xu Qianxue, a noted *jinshi* scholar official of the early Qing period. This storage box was likely one of several used to store the 64 *juan* series.

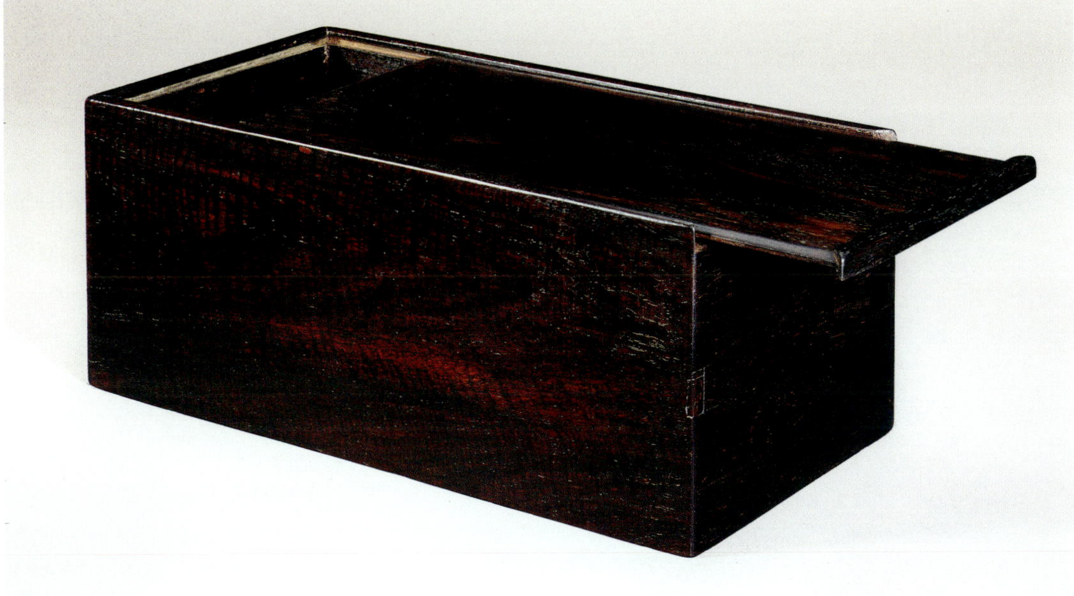

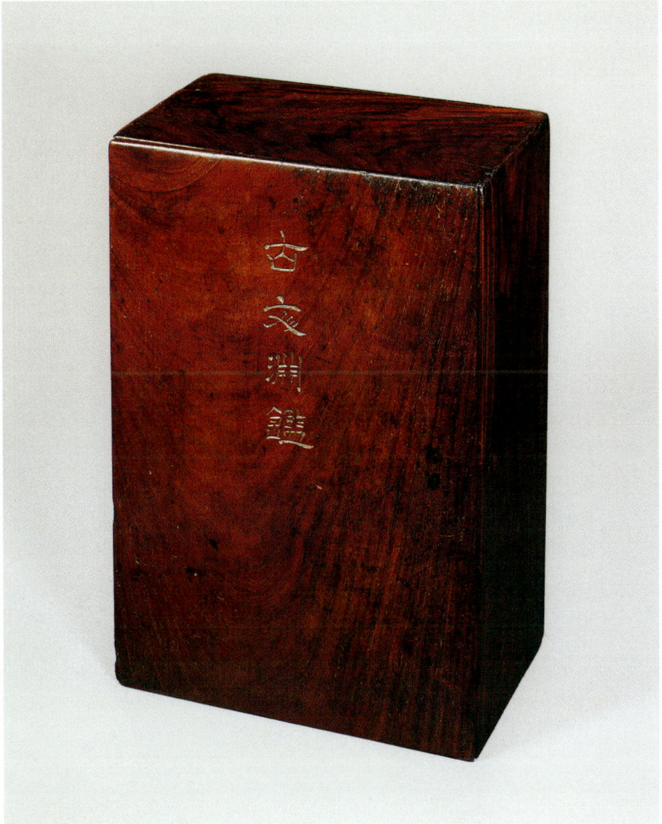
古文淵鑑

75

Small Lidded Box

黄花梨小箱

Huanghuali
18th Century
21 x 14 x 15 cm H

This small, lidded box is of traditional style and charming character. The interlocked pattern of fine dovetail joinery is visible along each upright corner. The striated grain patterns of the *huanghuali* have aged to a lovely, mellowed hue, and the original metal mounts have survived intact with a softly worn patination.

76

Small Lidded Chest

黄花梨箱

Huanghuali
Late 18th/Early 19th Century
40.5 x 23 x 17 cm H

The detail from the woodcut illustration below portrays the Emperor Taizu of the Song dynasty rewarding palace ladies for their services with silk and silver, who will return to their distant homes with gifts transported in small chests.

This small chest is of traditional form, standard size, and plain style. The construction is made from relatively thin panels of *huanghuali* with highly striated patterning; *tieli* was used for the bottom panel. The mated edges of the lid and box are raised with a wide, flat beading. The original hardware has survived intact.

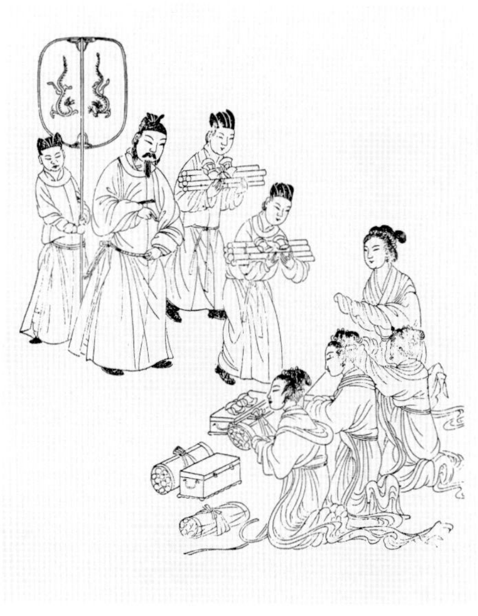

Presentation boxes. Detail from woodcut illustration to Yangzheng tujie, *late Ming period.*

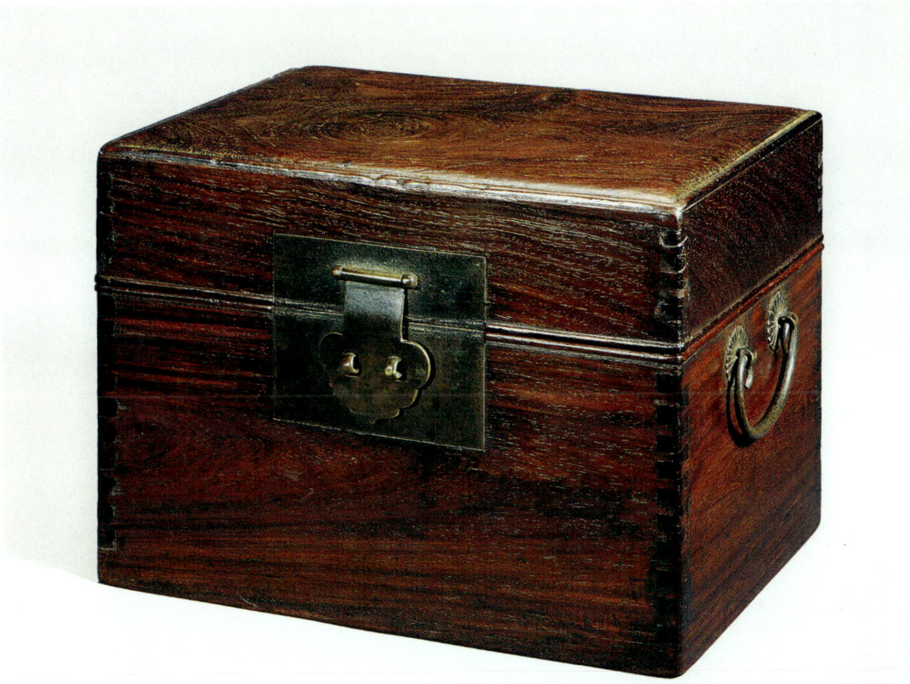

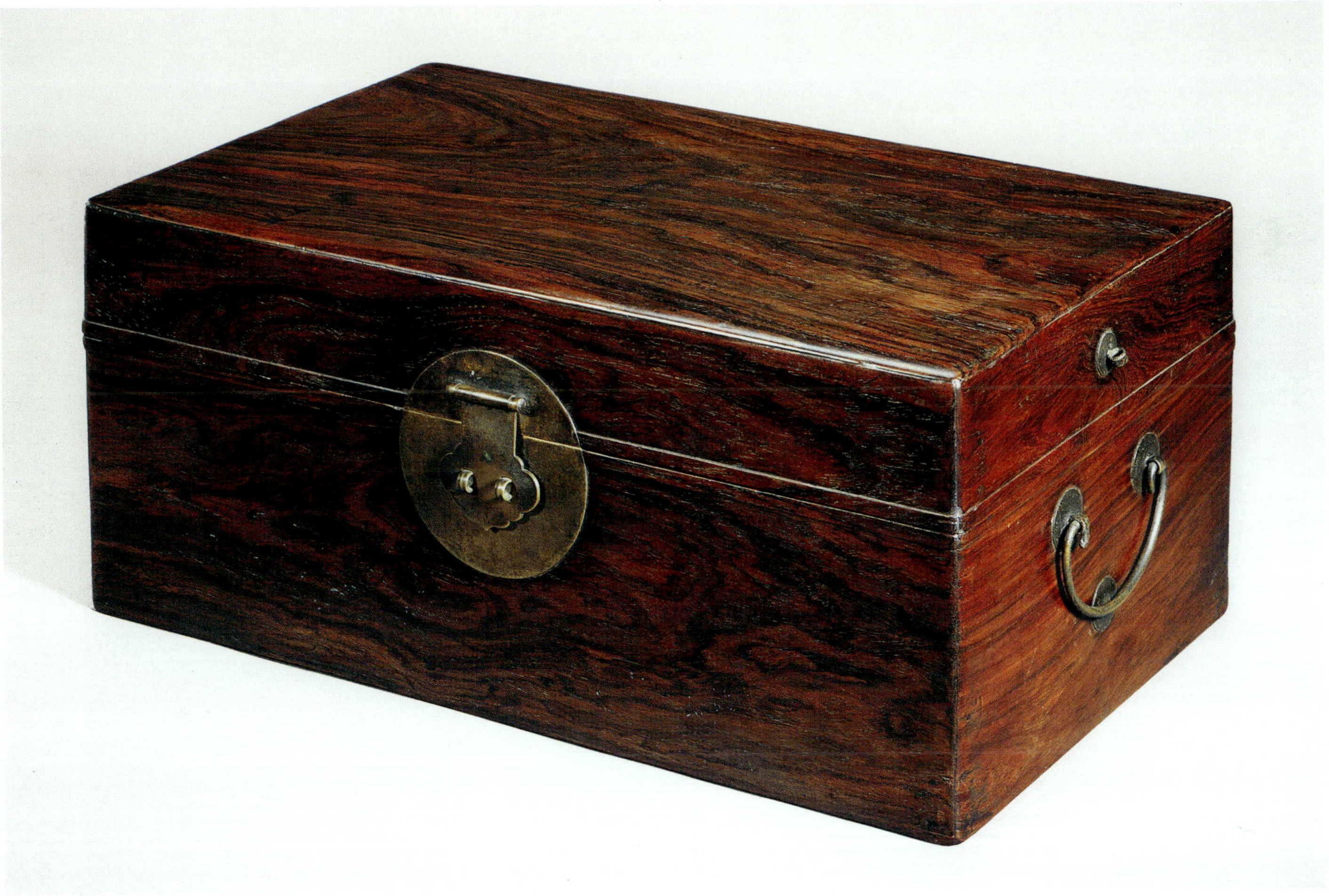

77

Lidded Chest with Inlaid Decoration

黃花梨嵌百寶箱

Huanghuali and
Semi-Precious Stone
17th Century
37 x 20.5 x 14 cm H

Auspicious patterns inlaid with semi-precious stones decorate the top, sides, front and back of this *huanghuali* case. The lid is decorated with a dragon, phoenix, and mixed precious treasures including a lute, chime, lozenge, silver bar, gourd, and *ruyi*. The front of the chest is decorated with cherry blossoms and tea flowers; the sides, lotus and magnolias, and; the back, with narcissus, chrysanthemums and antiquities.

The chest is otherwise of traditional form and standard size, with beading around the matched edges of the lid and chest. Exposed dovetail joinery along the four vertical corners appears contrasted to the refined decorative style. The original hardware has survived and the lockplate exhibits a rarely seen quatrafoiled *ruyi* pattern—a decorative pattern more commonly associated with ancient artifacts.

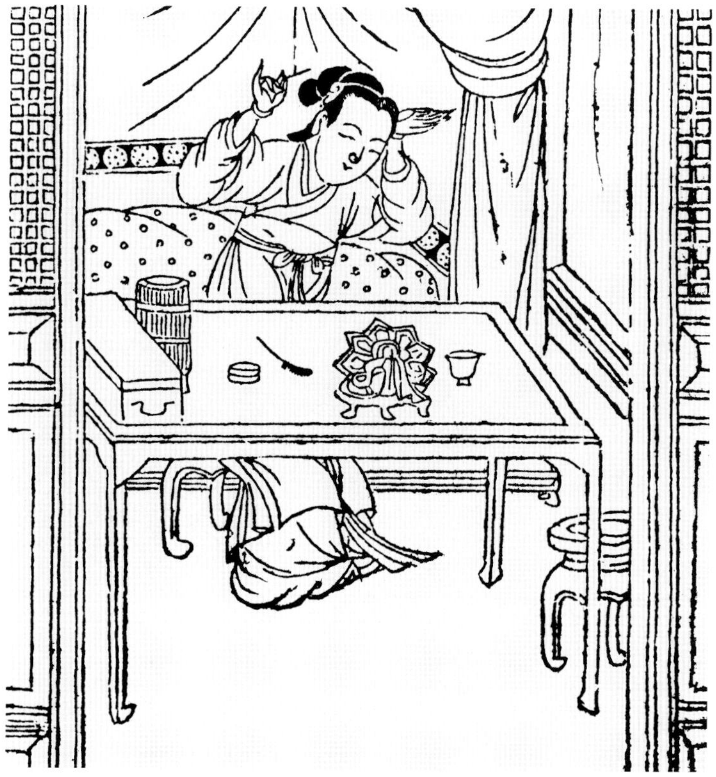

Dressing case. Detail from woodcut illustration to Pipa ji, *late Ming period.*

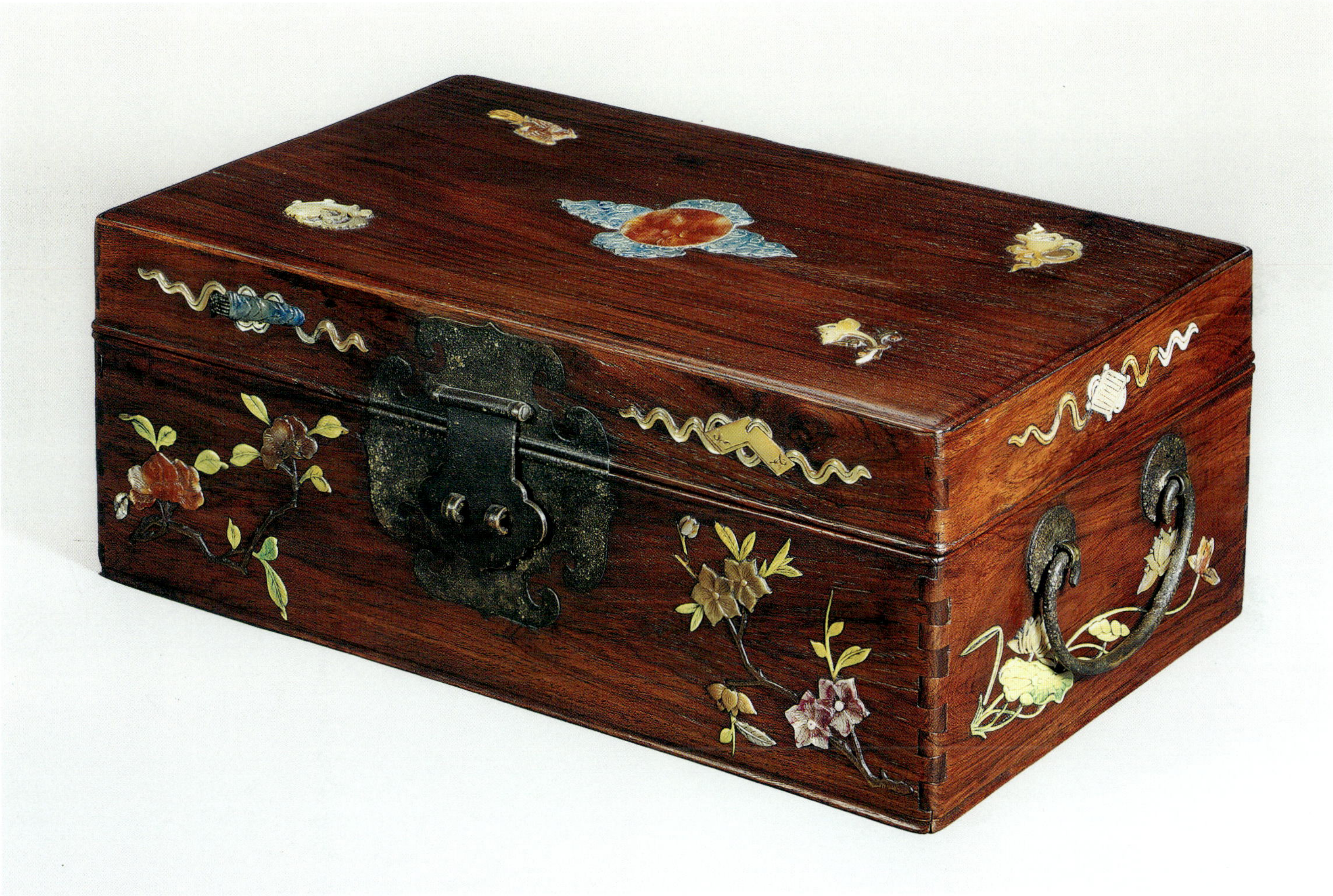

78

Lidded Chest

紫檀箱一對

One of a Pair
Zitan
Late 18th/Early 19th Century
44 x 26 x 22 cm H

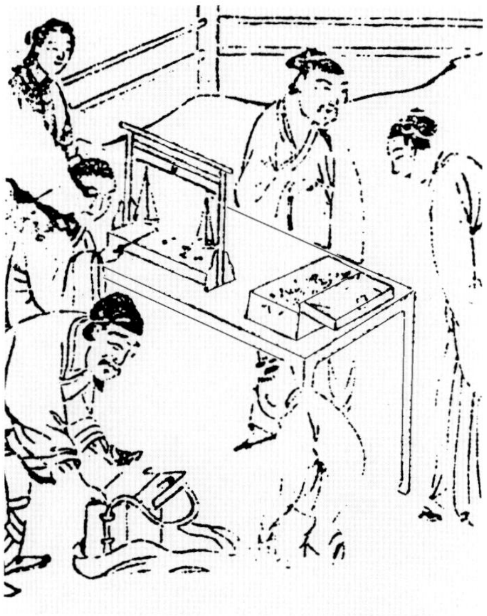

Money chest. Detail from woodcut illustration to Xing shi heng, *Ming Tianqi period (1621-1627).*

Similar chests are often seen in book illustrations as money chests. These small chests are sturdy constructions made from thick panels of *zitan*. A wide beading is shaped around the lid and top of the chest, the raised design of which also continues through the foliate-shaped lockplates. The original brass mounts include rarely seen bail handles of Western style that are cast with stops that prop the handles outright for easy lifting. The interior of each chest is fit a shallow *zitan* tray. Inked inscriptions corresponding to #10 and #15 suggest that these two were originally a large group.

79

Lidded Chest

紫檀箱

Zitan
17th Century
46 x 24 x 21 cm H

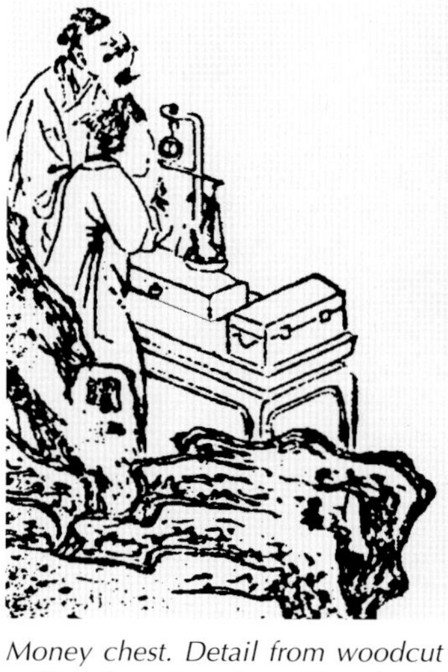

Money chest. Detail from woodcut illustration to Shen luan jiao chuanqi, *early Qing period.*

This simply styled chest exhibits solid construction with exposed dovetail joinery. The timber is a fine quality *zitan* of uniform deep brownish-black color, and the surfaces are age-worn and rich with patination. Most of the original paktong hardware is heavily patinated with pitted and scaled encrustation.

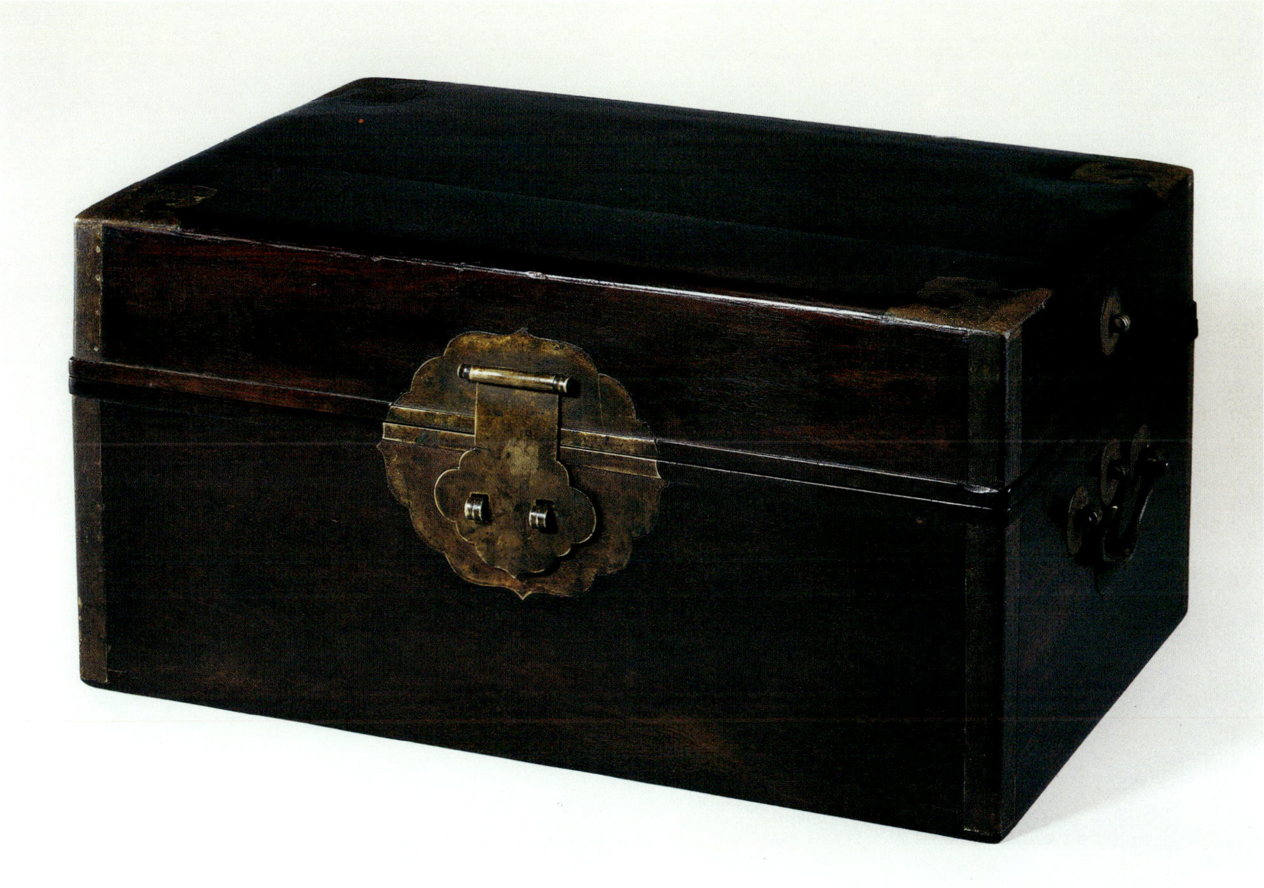

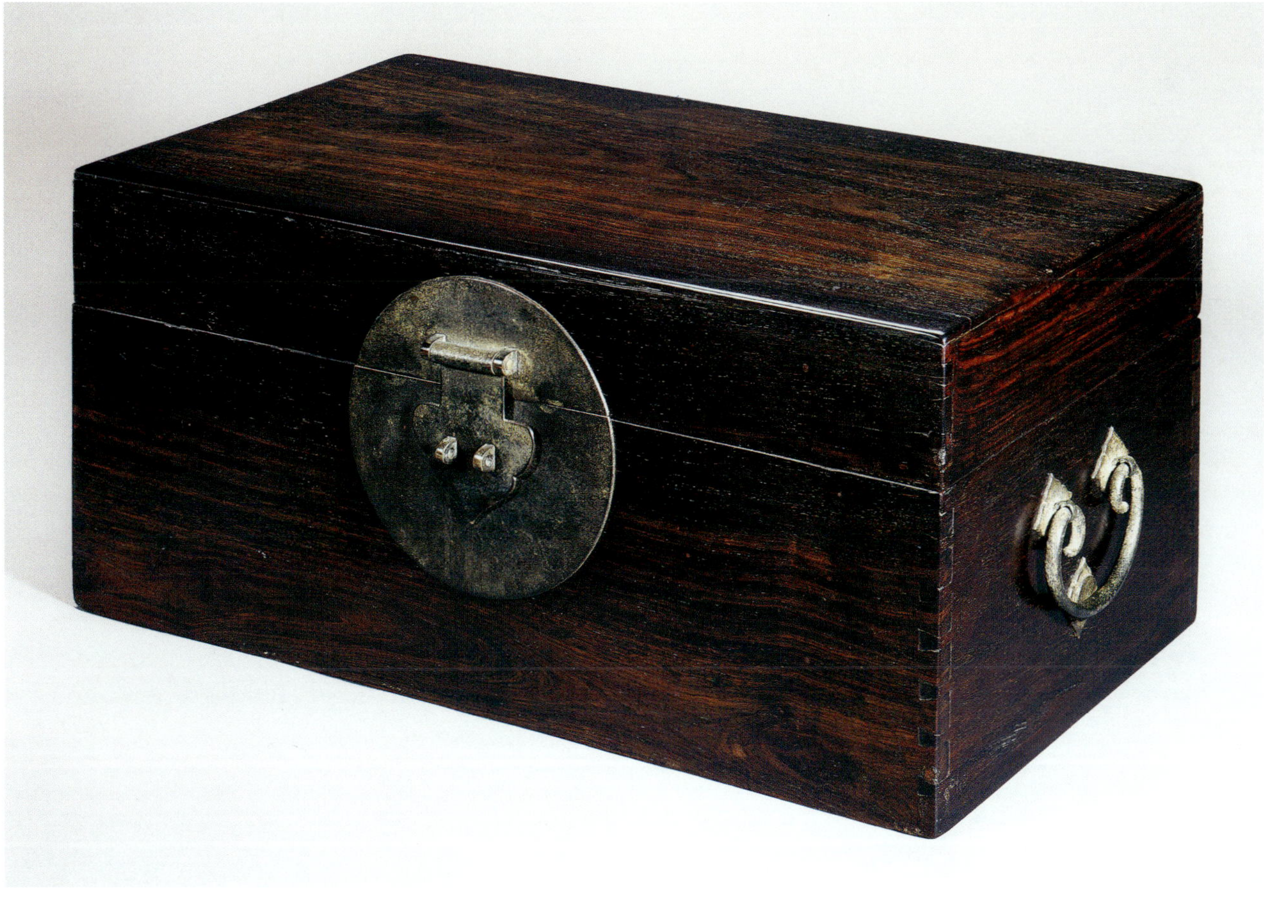

80

Lidded Sutra Chest

黃花梨纏蓮花佛經箱

Huanghuali
17th Century
43 x 24 x 23.5 cm H

Buddhist inspiration is evident in the lotus flower and scrolling tendril patterns that embellish the front of this sutra chest. The integrated decoration of the incised metalwork also reflects a unified expression—and one that is rarely seen due to the high degree of specialization amongst the various artisan trades. The *huanghuali* panels are carved in relief, while the brass lockplate and hinges demonstrate the more rarely seen incised-and-hammered techniques. The other surfaces are plain without decoration, and the bottom of the box is fit with a panel of *nanmu*—a timber traditionally associated with book storage due to its insect repelling characteristics.

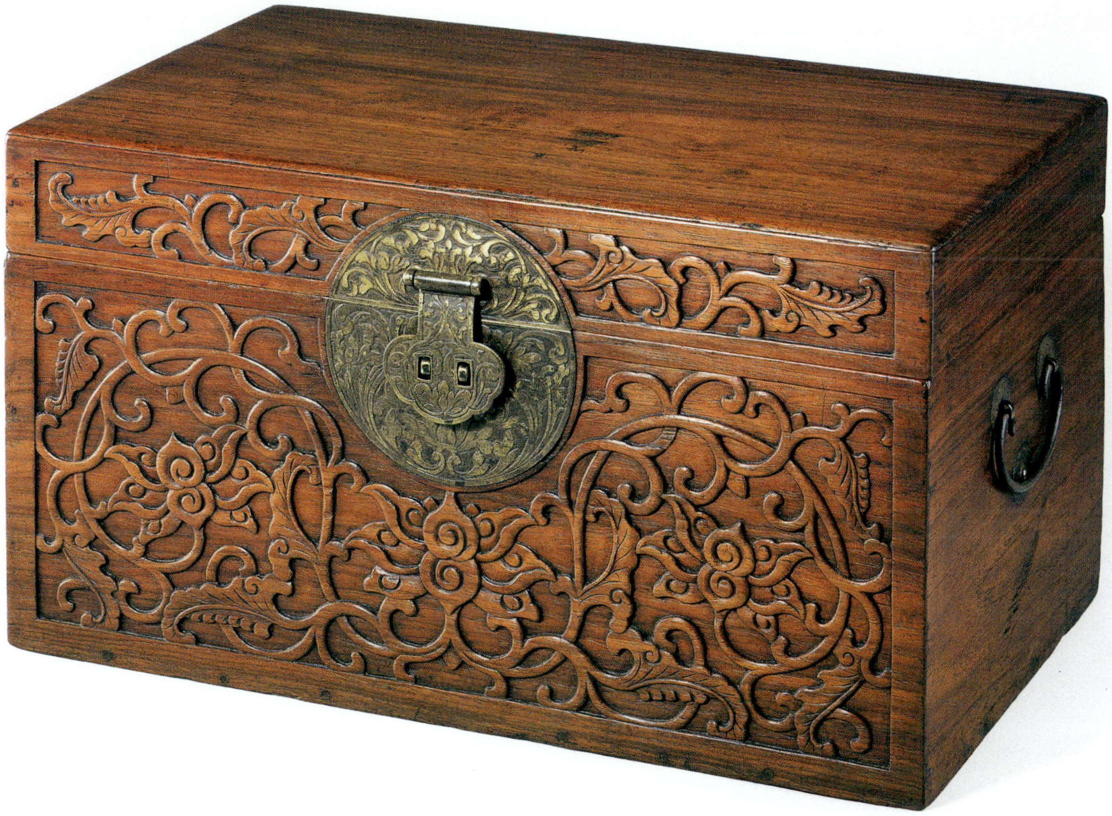

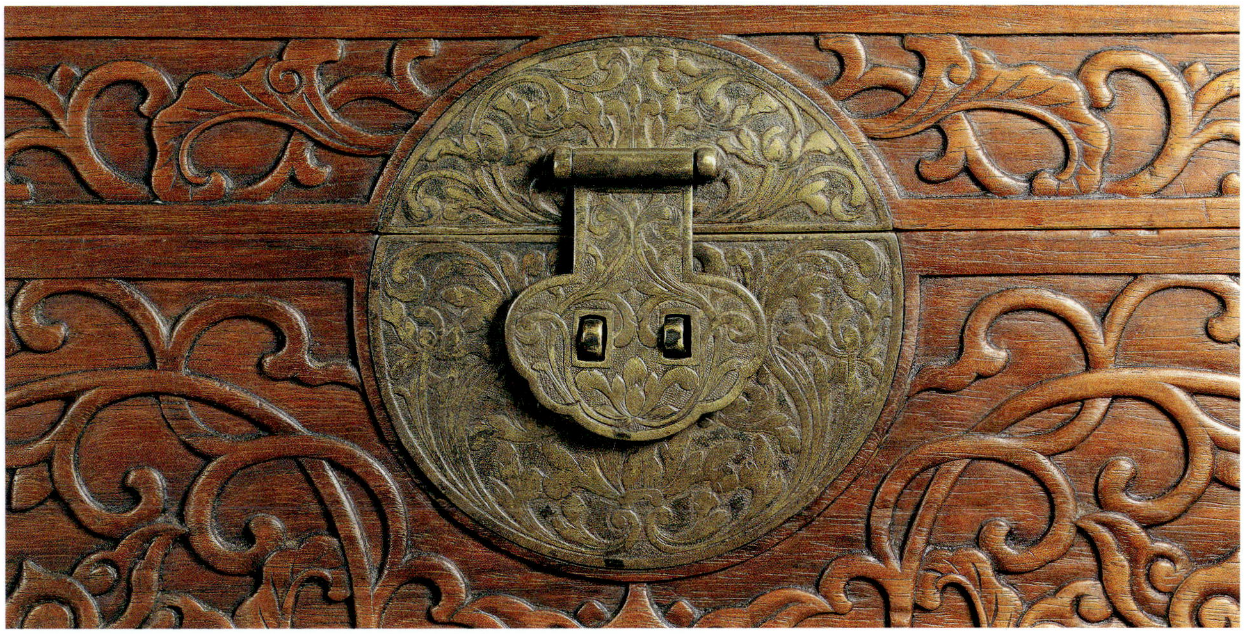

81

Lidded Clothing Chest with Inlaid Decoration

黃花梨嵌百寶衣箱

Huanghuali
18th Century
60.8 x 46 x 23 cm H

This *huanghuali* chest is decorated with composite inlays of mother-of-pearl as well as other semi-transparent precious materials. The single panel top of the chest features imagery of birds, magnolias and bamboo; the front, peonies and birds; the sides, birds with peaches and pomegranates; and the back, birds and plum blossoms—all favorite motifs for dowry furniture. A number of the original inlays that had fallen out have been restored with mother-of-pearl.

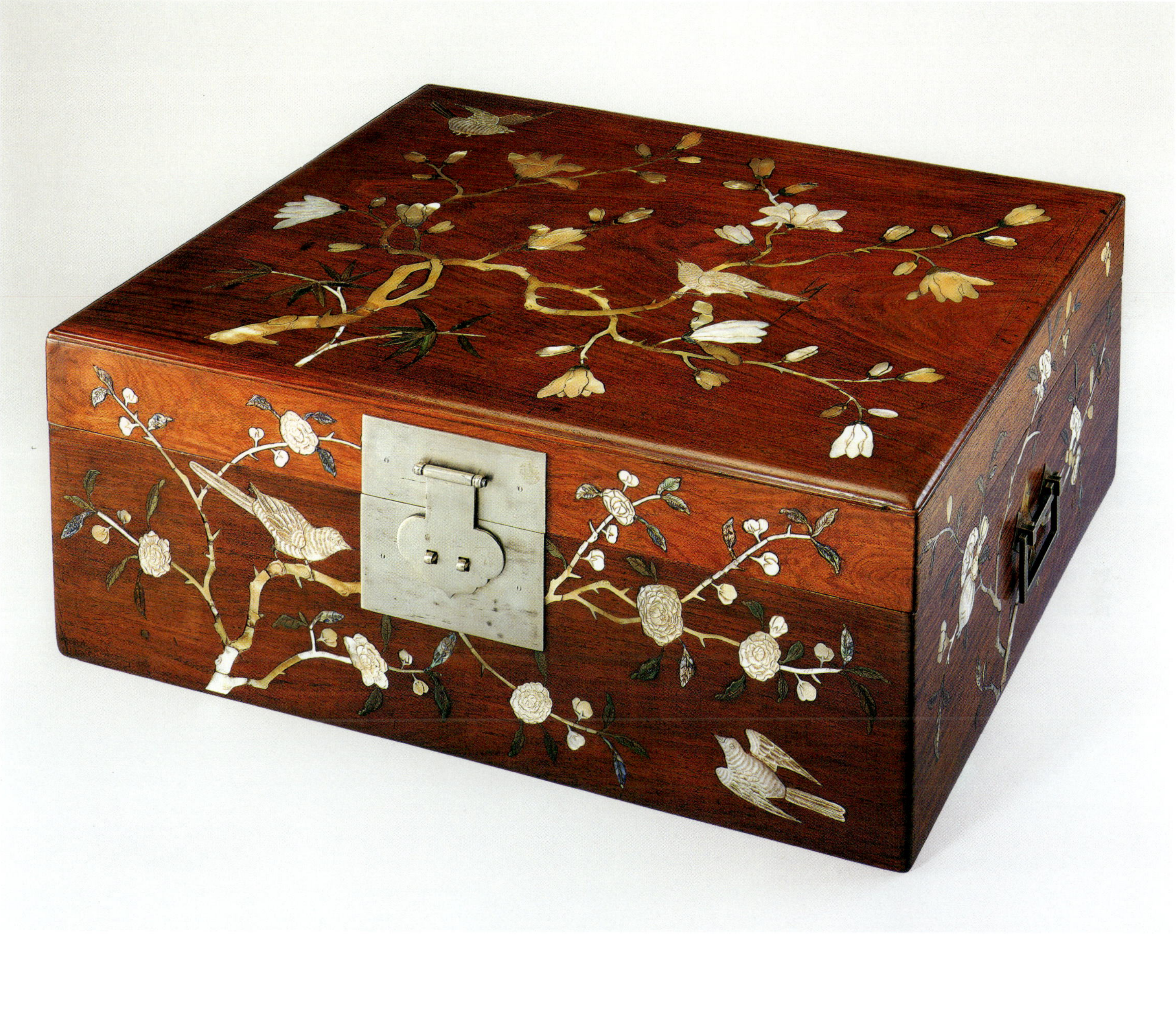

82

Double-Sixes Gameboard

紫檀雙陸盤

Zitan
16th Century
47 x 28 x 8.5 cm H

The dice game 'double sixes' was highly popular amongst the Tang period aristocracy. Seventeenth and eighteenth century tables fit with similar gameboards also demonstrate a tradition that continued into the late Ming and early Qing periods. However, by the mid-Qing period, the game had fallen out of fashion; today, little is understood of the actual rules.

This gameboard is constructed as a deep-sided tray. It is made from high quality *zitan*; the bottom, constructed with two richly patterned boards. Most of the original ivory inlays have been replaced. Given the long history of the game, the somewhat arbitrary dating of this piece may be a conservative attribution.

Similar examples are illustrated in:

- Ang, John Kwang-Ming. *The Beauty of Huanghuali*, p. 86.
- Bruce, Grace Wu. *The Dr. S. Y. Yip Collection of Classic Chinese Furniture*, pl. 62.
- Wang Shixiang and Curtis Evarts. *Masterpieces from the Museum of Classical Chinese Furniture*, pl. 91.

For a more complete discussion on the game of 'Double Sixes' see:

- Chen Zengbi. "Double Sixes." *Journal of the Classical Chinese Furniture Society* 2:3 (Summer 1992), pp. 48-55.

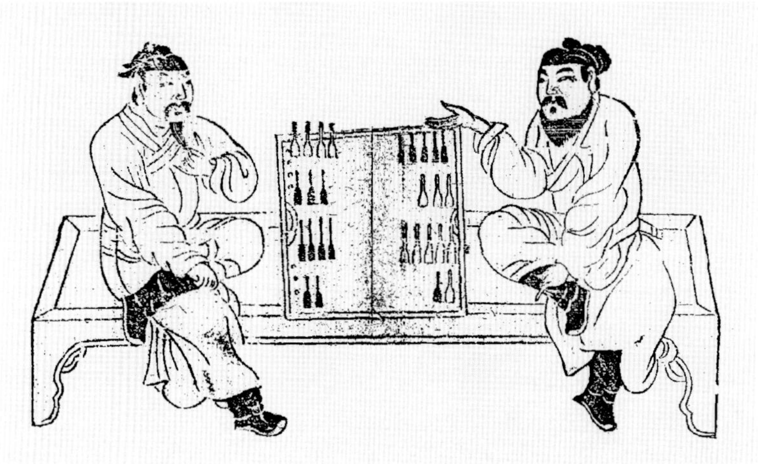

Double Sixes. Woodcut illustrations from Pu shuang *by Hong Zun, Song dynasty.*

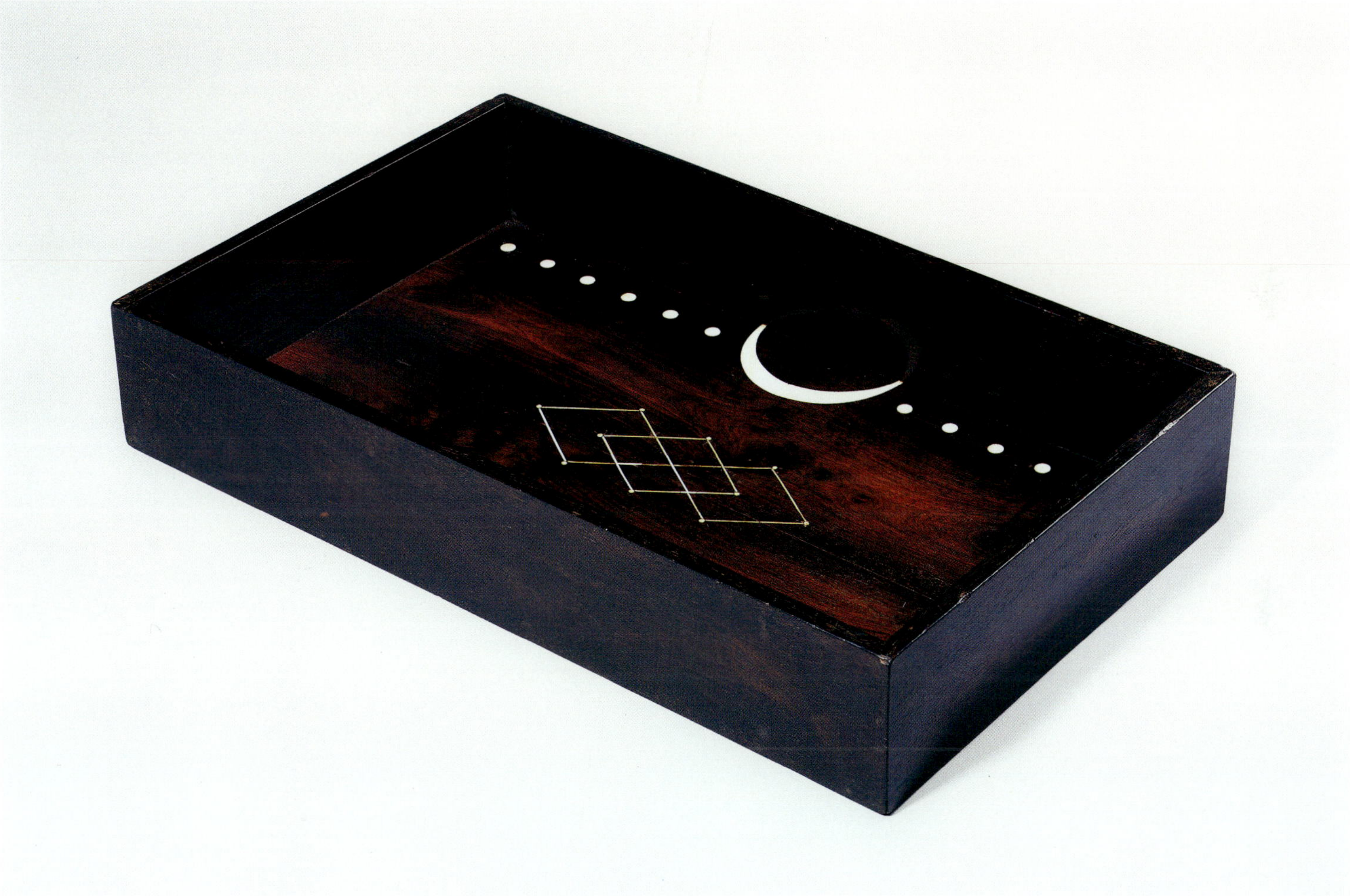

83
Serving Tray
紫檀茶盤

Zitan
18th Century
35.5 x 35.5 x 2.5 cm H

Such trays were used for serving tea and small delicacies; they also were used on the desk to contain stationery items. This *zitan* square tray exhibits refined workmanship and select material. The side panels are delicately pierced with a fine pattern of lines linked with ovals—a design motif that expresses the theme of 'limitless continuity.'

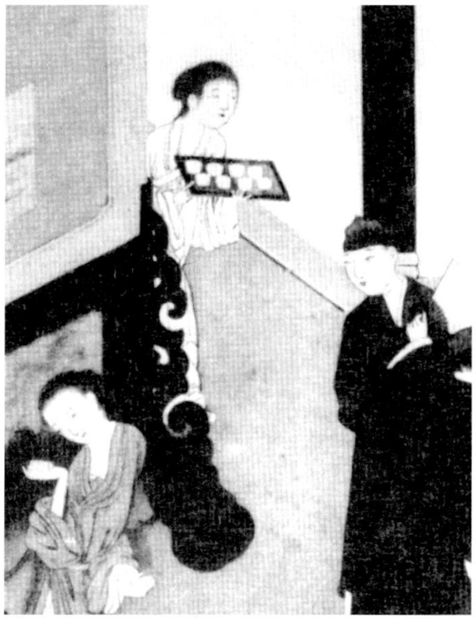

Service tray. Detail from album leaf set Bai mei tu *depicting scenes from the novel* Jin Ping Mei*, early 18th century.*

84
Stationery Tray with Drawers
紅木文具抽屜盤

Hongmu
Late 19th Century
35.5 x 29.5 x 5.5 cm H

This stationery tray houses two shallow drawers suitably sized for small brushes and ink sticks. Conceal behind these 'pull-less' drawers is a pivoting arm; as one drawer is pressed slightly inward, the other drawer is pushed outward. The drawer fronts are incised with narcissus flowers and a seal script inscription, and the two sides of the tray are incised with a poem. Accordingly, the design and carving was the work of Zhou Qizhang (*hao* Zhu Shi Shan Ren), an artist from northwestern Fujian province. The inscription is dated to 1889.

Stationery trays of similar design are illustrated in:
- Ellsworth, Robert Hatfield, *Chinese Furniture: One Hundred Examples from the Mimi and Raymond Hung Collection*, pl. 93.
- Lo, Kai-Yin, ed., *Classical and Vernacular Chinese Furniture in the Living Environment*, pl. 37,
- Tian Jiaqing. *Classic Chinese Furniture of the Qing Dynasty*, pl. 127.

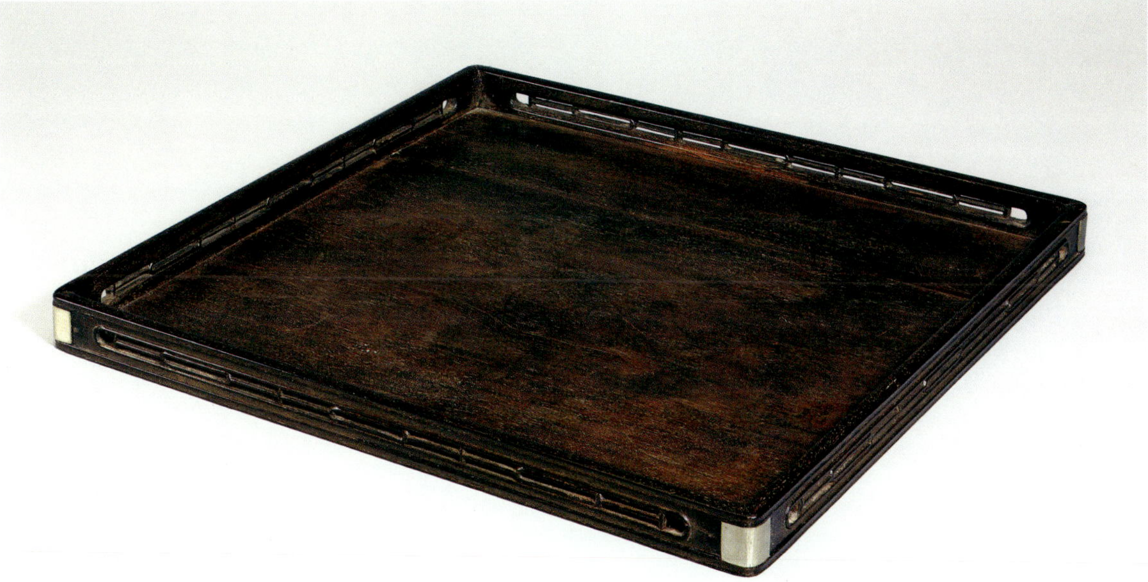

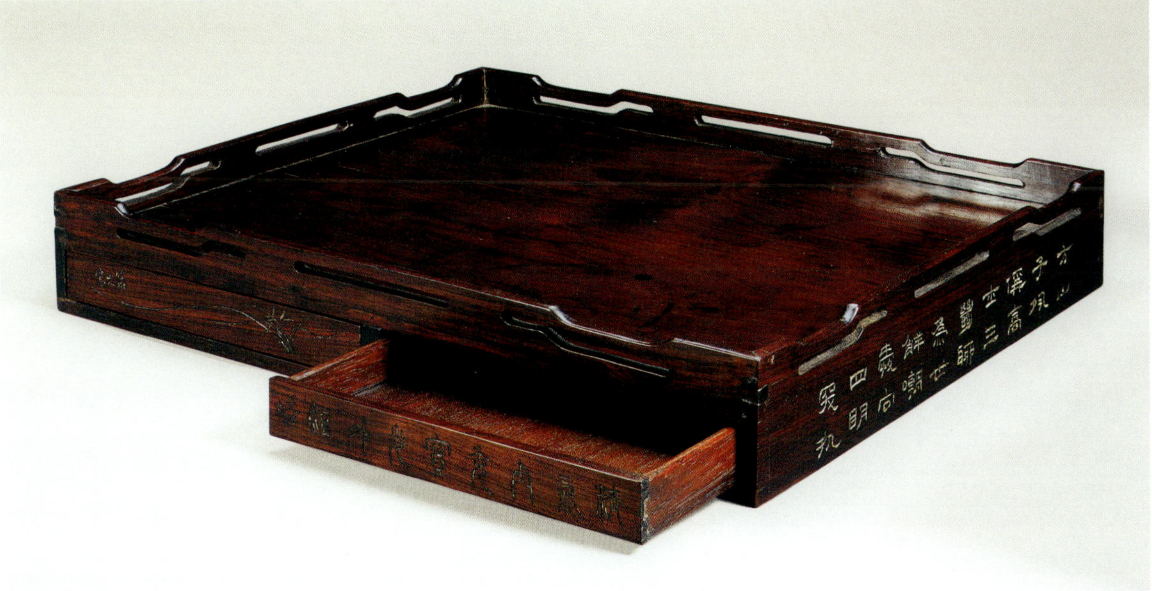

85
Incense Tool Holder
紫檀莇瓶

Zitan
18th Century
4.5 cm Diameter x 11 cm H

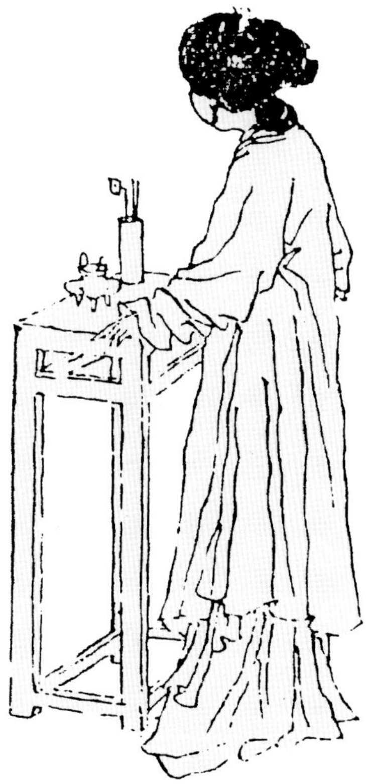

Incense tool holder. Woodcut illustration to Sanguo huaxiang, *Qing Guangxu period, 1881.*

Incense tools included a pair of chopsticks for manipulating the burning incense, and a long-handled spade for grooming the incense ash. This cylindrical holder is bored with a deep hole for supporting incense tools. It has been shaped to a foliate profile, and the top and bottom are carved in relief as five-petaled plum flowers.

Similar examples are published in:
- Tsang, Gerard and Hugh Moss. *Art of the Scholars Studio*, pls. 114, 234.

86
Table Stand
紫檀穀腿几

Zitan
18th Century
42.5 x 24 x 13.5 cm H

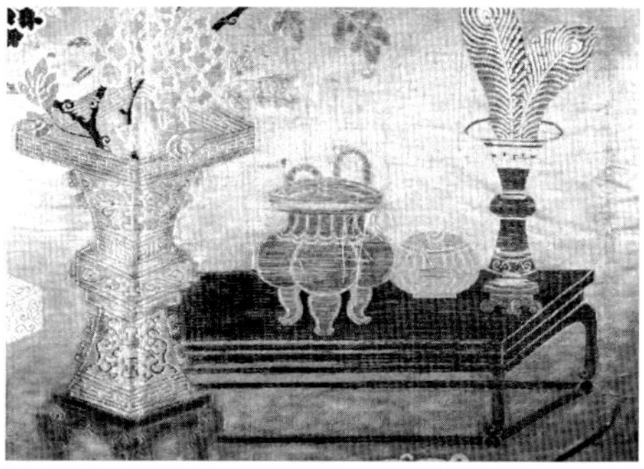

Table Stand. Detail from silk brocade textile. 17th Century, Chinese.

This table stand exhibits refined '*zitan* workmanship' with delicate beading around the edge of the frame, elegantly shaped indented corners, and finely molded surfaces. Such stands were used to elevate precious treasures or as a platform for incense accoutrements.

A stand of similar style is illustrated in:
- Jacobsen, Robert D. *Classical Chinese Furniture in the Minneapolis Institute of Arts*, pl. 84.

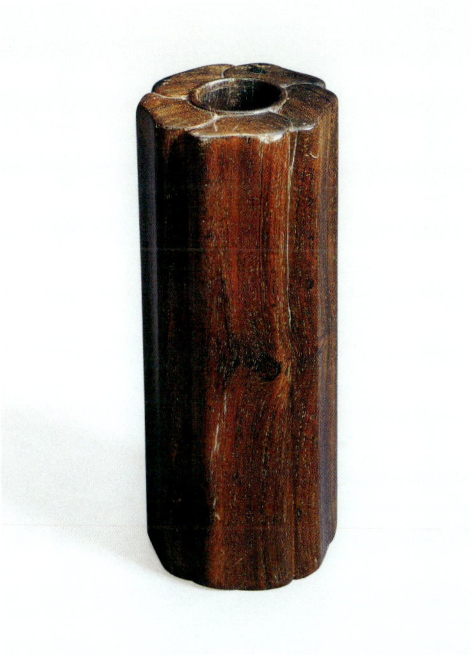

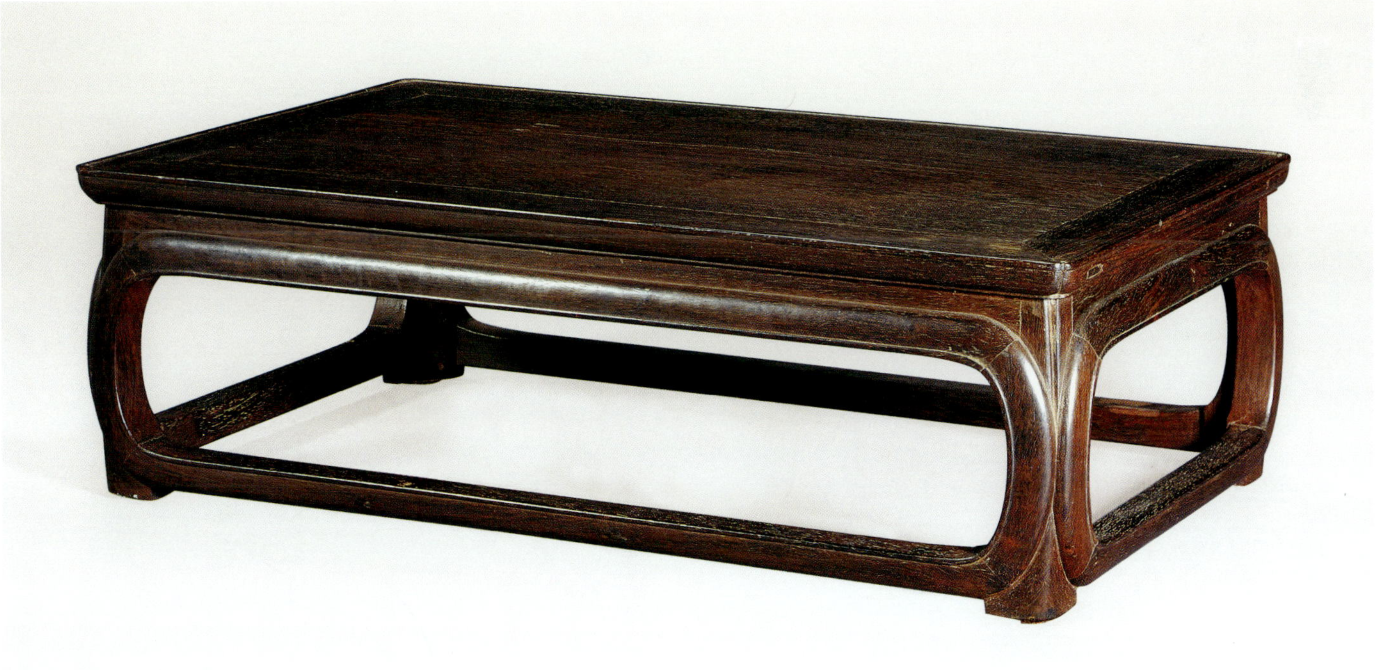

87

Small Precious Treasures Shelf Stand

紫檀多寶格几

Zitan
19th Century
39 x 17 x 23 cm H

Art objects and curiosities of ranging size, as well as stationery implements can be displayed upon this multifunctional shelf unit. The thin-cut panels of *zitan* are uniformly textured and notably dense. The end panels are pierced and carved with auspicious bat-and-chime (*fuqing*) and *chi* dragon motifs.

88

Small Precious Treasures Shelf Stand

紫檀多寶格几

Zitan
19th Century
35-47 x 19 x 25 cm H

This unique tabletop shelf unit is comprised of three tiered platforms for the display of precious objects. The lowest platform may be extended or withdrawn, providing alternative display configurations for variously sized objects. The angular scrolled framework is finely worked with concave surfaces imitating the style of archaic jades.

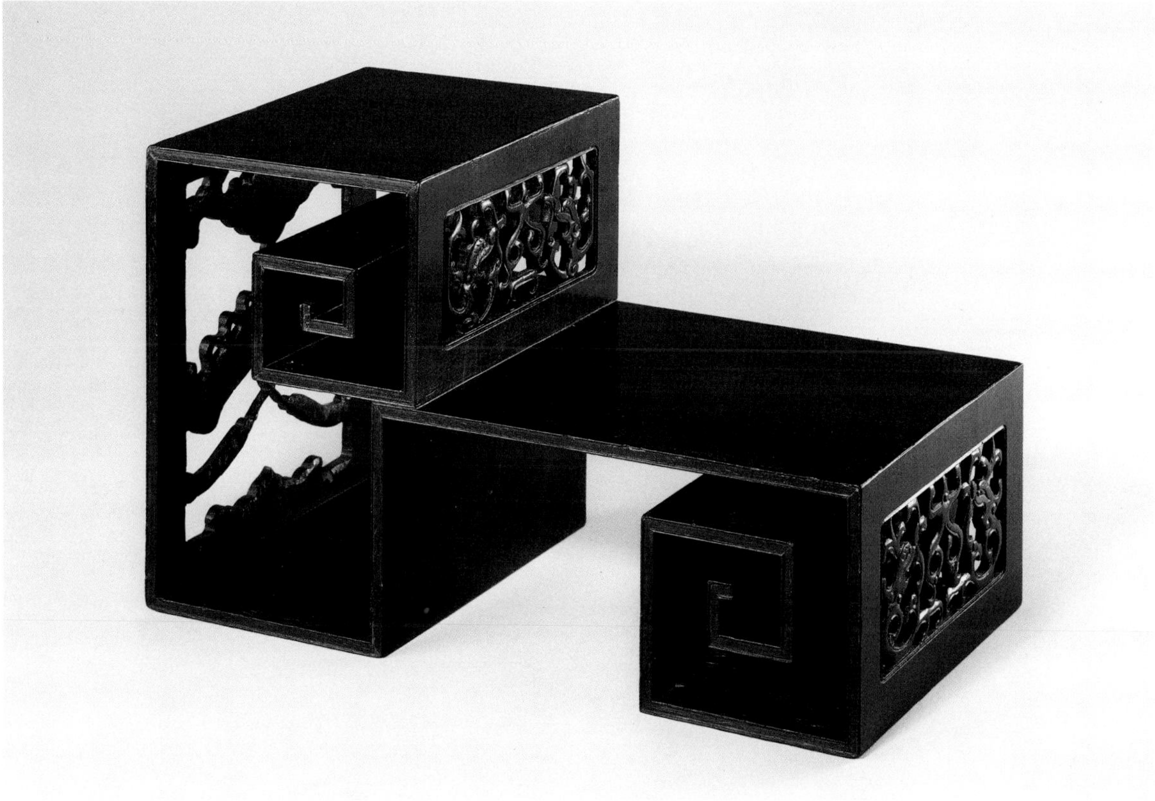

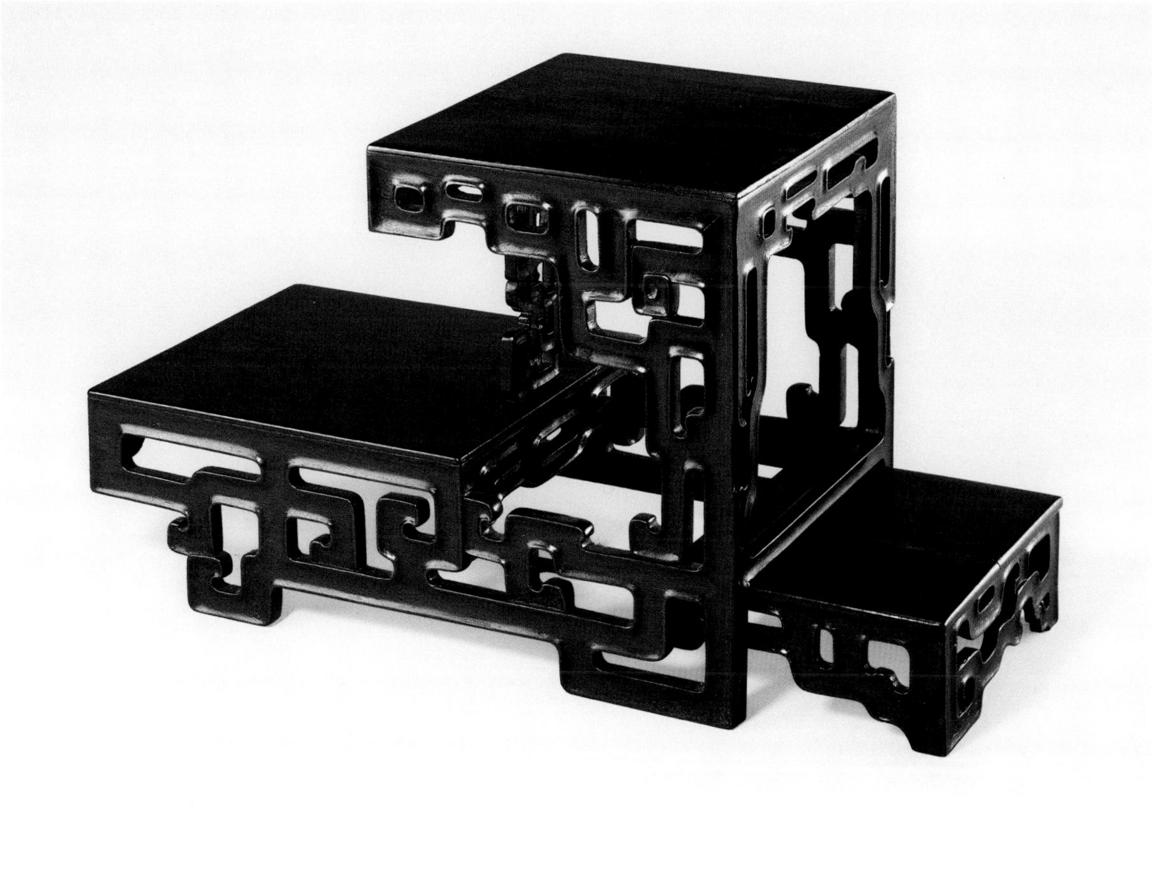

89

Clappers

紫檀蓮花板

Zitan
18th Century
25 x 6 x .8 cm Thickness (each)

Clappers are percussion instruments used in the performance of traditional Chinese music and opera. Made of dense *zitan*, these clappers produce a sharp, crisp tone. The surfaces are uniformly worn from extensive use. The three clappers are loosely tied together with a silk cord that is looped through holes drilled at the ends.

Clappers of similar style are illustrated in:

- William Watson, *Chinese Ivories from the Shang to the Qing*, pl. 235.

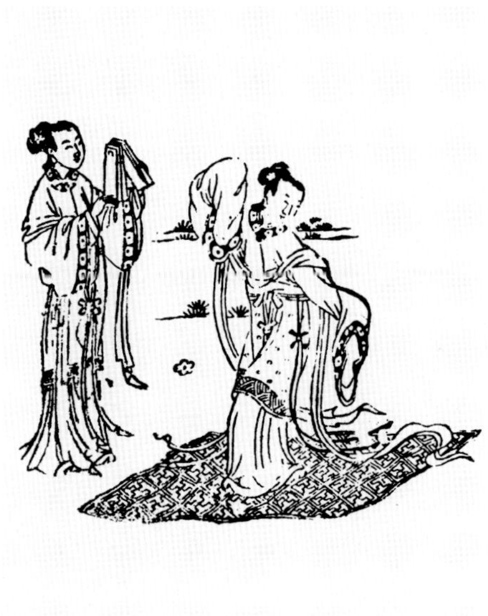

Clappers. Detail from woodcut illustration to Xiuru ji, *late Ming period.*

90

Small Drum

硬木小鼓

Hardwood
16th/17th Century
14.5 x 11 x 7 cm H

The outside of this small drum is carved in relief with various animals including horses, sheep, lions and elephants; the base is pierced and carved with the Daoist Immortal Liu Hai standing on a three-legged toad. A drum skin was originally attached through a series of holes penetrating through the rim to the interior.

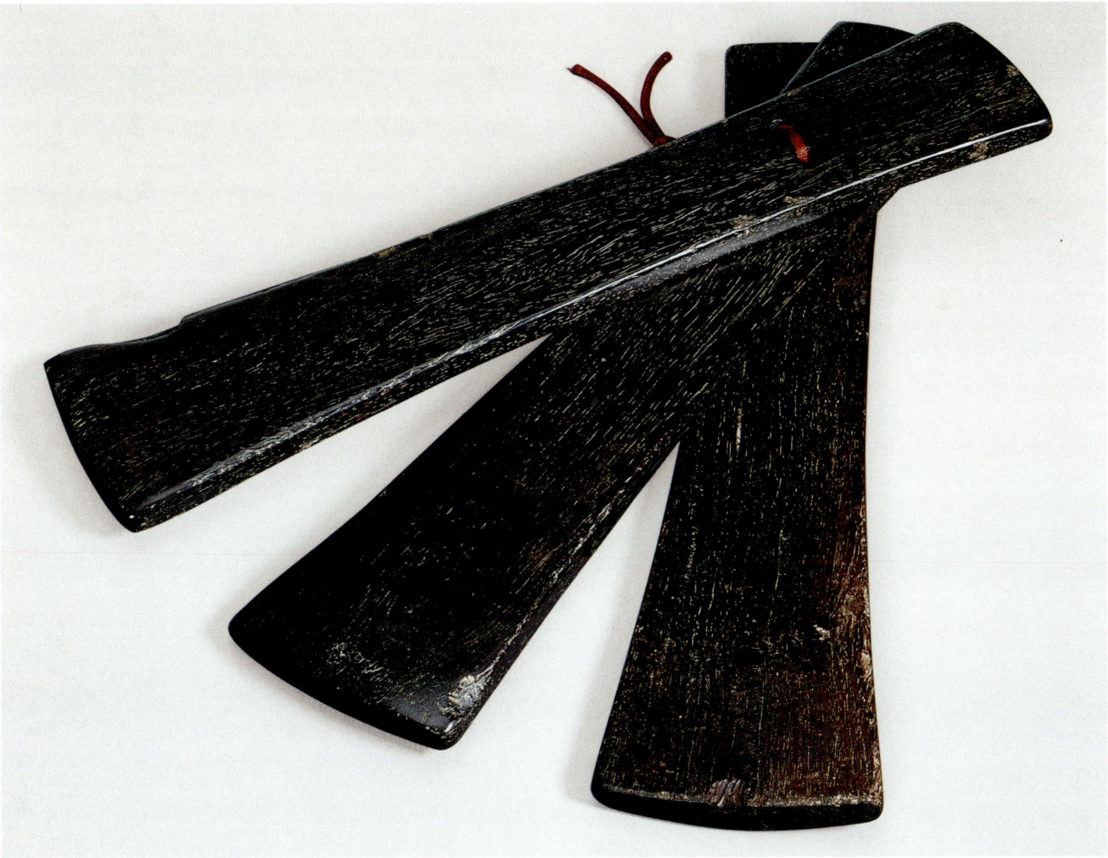

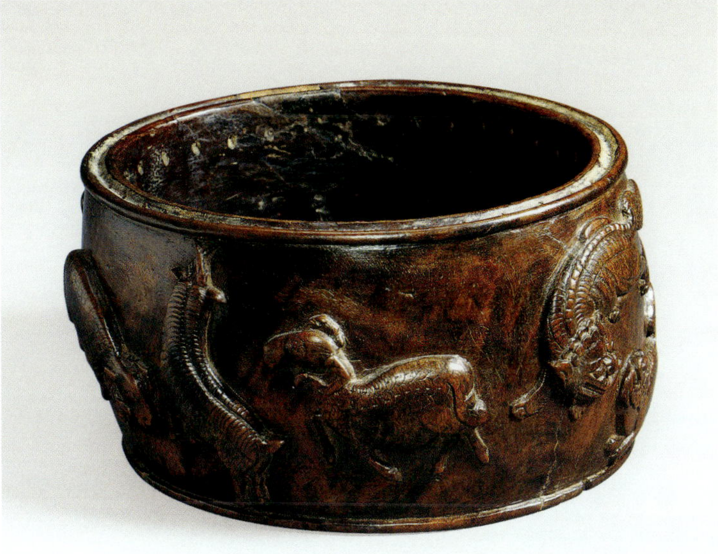

91

Cylindrical Box with Zodiac Animals

硬木十二生肖盒

Hardwood and Ivory
19th Century
5.3 cm Diameter x 9.5 cm H

This cylindrical box contains a set of twelve zodiac animals. The box of yet unidentified hardwood is finely shaped with ribbed moldings; the aged surface is rich with patination. The zodiac animals are each carved from ivory as small pendants with flattened backs.

92

Massage Roller

紫檀象牙按摩滚筒

Zitan and Ivory
18th Century
11 cm W x 18 cm L

Ancient traditions of massage have continued into modern times, and similarly styled massage tools can be purchased in Chinese markets today. This massage roller is made from precious *zitan* and ivory. The lobed ivory roller has aged to a warm golden tonality. The cylindrical handle is finely shaped from *zitan* to a foliate profile, which appears as a flower petal on the butt of the handle. A thick brass wire shaped to fit into the handle and through the center of the roller completes the assembly.

A similar example made from *huanghuali* wood is illustrated in:
- Ang, John Kwang-Ming. *The Beauty of Huanghuali*, p. 89.

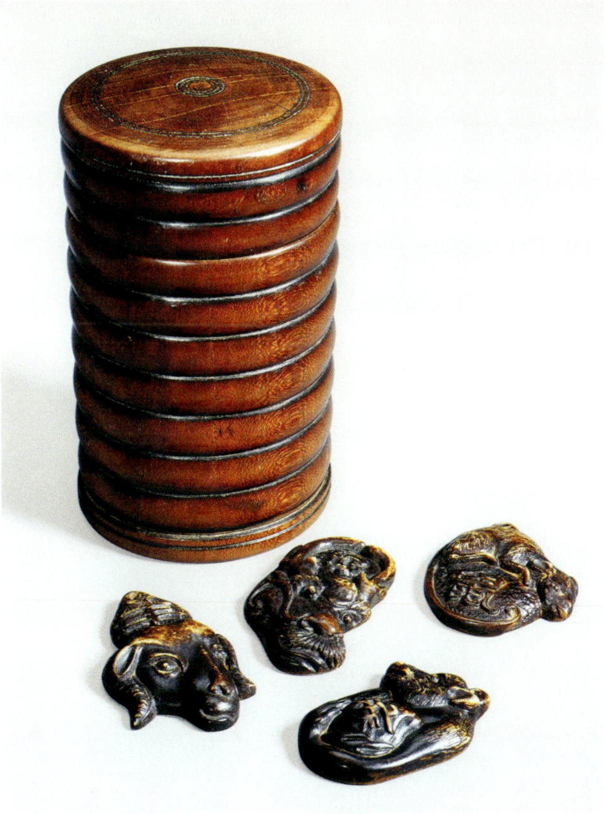

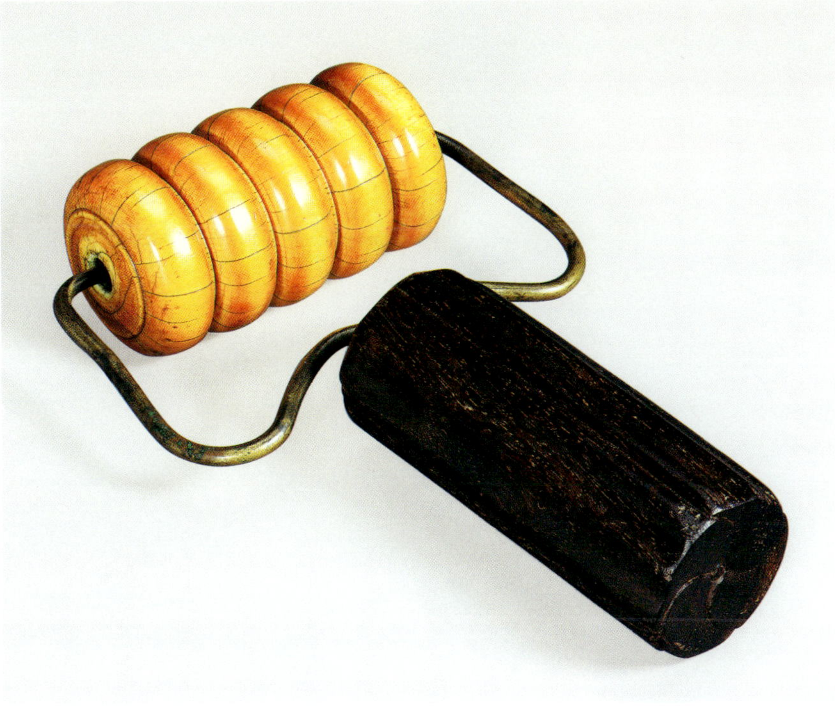

93

Tea/Wine Pot Caddy

黃花梨紅木茶壺桶

Huanghuali and *Hongmu*
19th Century
20 cm Diameter x 28.5 cm H

The *huanghuali* base of this caddy is shaped like a brushpot, to which winged handles have been attached. The lid, which is made from darker *hongmu*, is fit with a handle and locks into position with a clever securing device. The elegantly shaped wings and fluted surfaces of the vessel exhibit refined workmanship.

Similar tea caddies made from precious hardwoods are illustrated in:

- Yip Shing-Yiu and Grace Wu Bruce. *Chan Chair and Qin Bench: The Dr. S. Y. Yip Collection of Classic Chinese Furniture II*, pl. 39.
- Tsai C. Y. Zitan: *The Most Noble Hardwood*, p. 203

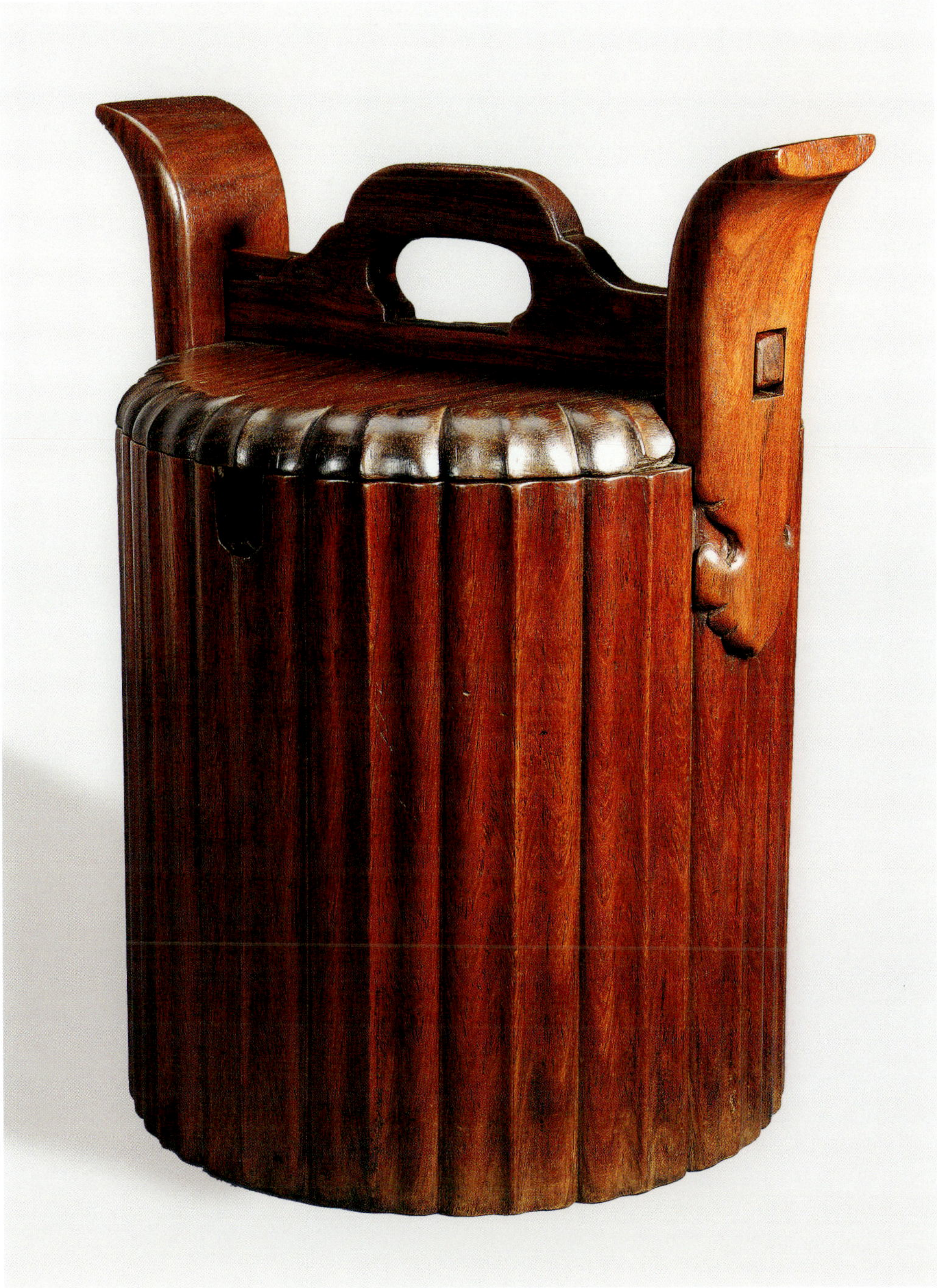

94

Balance Stand

紫檀天平架

Zitan
18th Century
62.5 x 22.5 x 80.5 cm H

In an age where crude silver was used as currency for exchange, the balance was necessary for determining specific weight. Finely produced with precious *zitan*, this balance stand exhibits a traditional form evident during the late Ming period; however, its refined decorative style places it in the early Qing period. This balance beam terminates with dragons carved in relief whose heads turn back to face each other. Elegantly styled spandrels and standing spandrels lightly reinforce the rack and its supporting posts. The base is fit with two drawers, of which the upper is specially configured for storage of the original balance beam and trays, now replaced. The drawers are fit with sliding locks to which miniature locks can be secured.

Similar balance stands are illustrated in:

- Ang, John Kwang-Ming. *The Beauty of Huanghuali*, p. 73.
- Bruce, Grace Wu. *Ming Furniture*, p. 32.
- National Museum of History. *Splendor of Style: Classical Furniture from the Ming and Qing Dynasties*, p. 202.
- Wang Shixiang and Curtis Evarts. *Masterpieces from the Museum of Classical Chinese Furniture*, pl. 96.

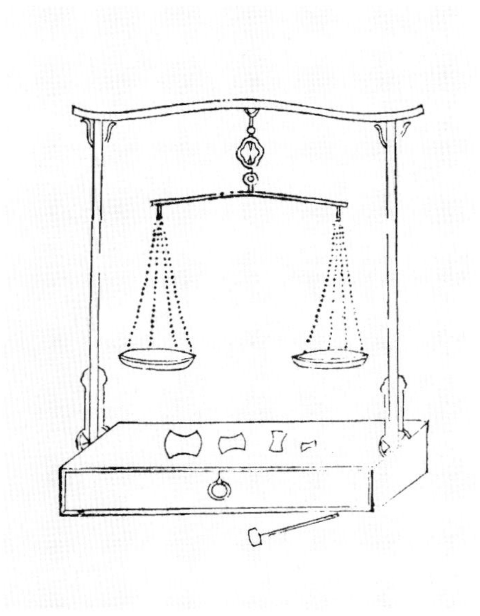

Balance Stand. Woodcut illustration from the encyclopedia Sancai tuhui, *Ming Wanli period (pub. 1607).*

95

Portable Hand Balance

紫檀秤錘盒

Zitan, Ivory and Brass
18th Century
33.5 L x 7.5 W

Portable hand balances were also used throughout China for weighing out goods as well as silver. Those made of precious materials are rare. The spoon-shaped case of this piece is made from *zitan*, the surface of which bears silver wire studs marking out the auspicious characters '*Xinglong*' (prosperity) at the top; the trademark '*Dun ji*' reads across the mid-section. The case pivots open where a graduated ivory balance, brass weight and tray are neatly fit.

Similar example are published in:

- National Museum of History. *Splendor of Style: Classical Furniture from the Ming and Qing Dynasties*, p. 203.
- Zhu Jiajin, Xia Gengqi, eds. *Zhongguo qiqi quanji: 5 Ming*, pl. 152.

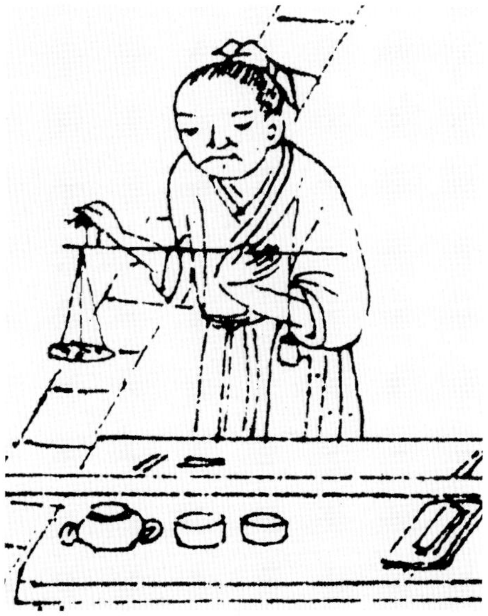

Handheld balance. Woodcut illustration to Mofa jiyao, *Qing dynasty.*

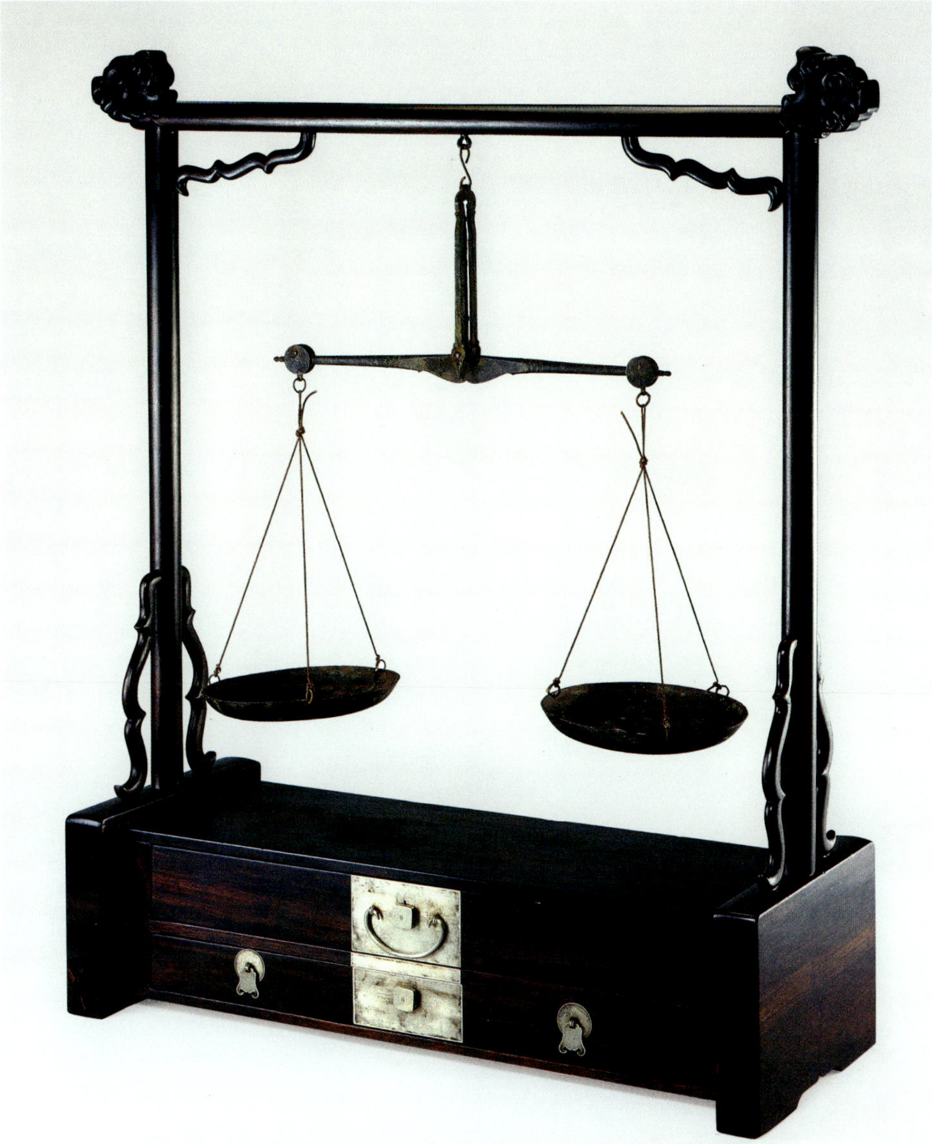

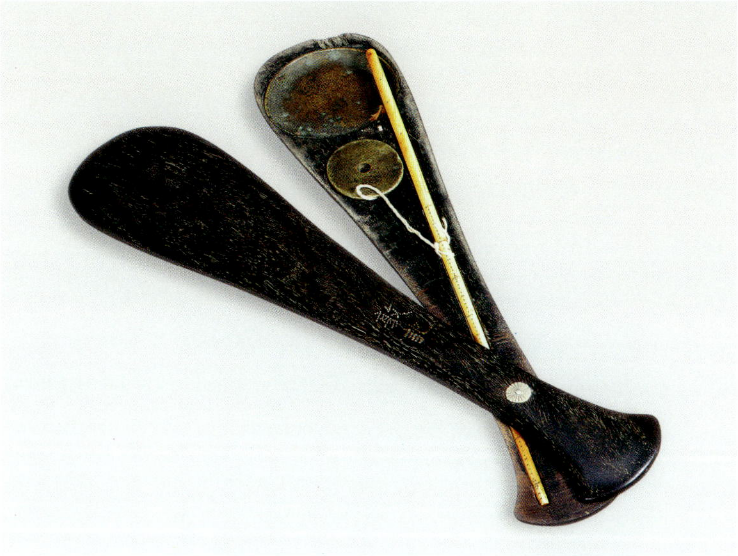

96

Carriage Harness Mount

紫檀嵌琺琅裝飾品馬騾鞍

Zitan
18th Century
Shanxi
32.5 x 25 x 15 cm H

Similar mounts are still in use in rural areas of modern China where they are strapped onto the back of a mule and serve as a harness for a cart. This mount is finely crafted from precious *zitan*. Within a hierarchical Confucian society, the use of *zitan* for such a functional object reflects that manner in which rank, prestige, and wealth were externalized through ostentatious display.

The front of this mount is decorated with auspicious lions. Four unusual brass plaques each feature an inlaid enamel bats motif; an additional bat carved in relief on the back thus signifies the Five Happinesses (*wufu*). A finely carved twisted rope pattern is raised in relief along the edges of the cross members and pads. This piece has survived with a lovely, worn patination.

Similar examples are illustrated in:

- Christie's, NY. *Important Chinese Furniture Formerly the Museum of Classical Chinese Furniture Collection*, lot 86.
- Bruce, Grace Wu. *Dreams of Chu Tan Chamber and the Romance with Huanghuali Wood: The Dr. S. Y. Yip Collection of Classic Chinese Furniture*, pl. 63.
- Tsai C. Y. *Zitan: The Most Noble Hardwood*, p. 191

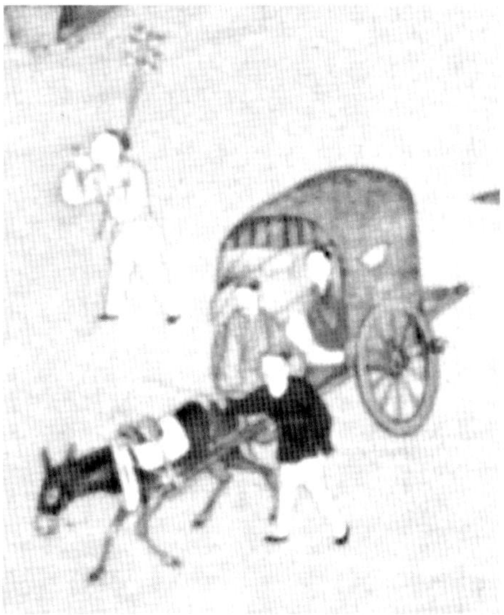

Saddle. Detail from the hanging scroll Peace for the New Year *by Ding Guanpeng, Qing Qianlong period (1735-1795). National Palace Museum, Taipei.*

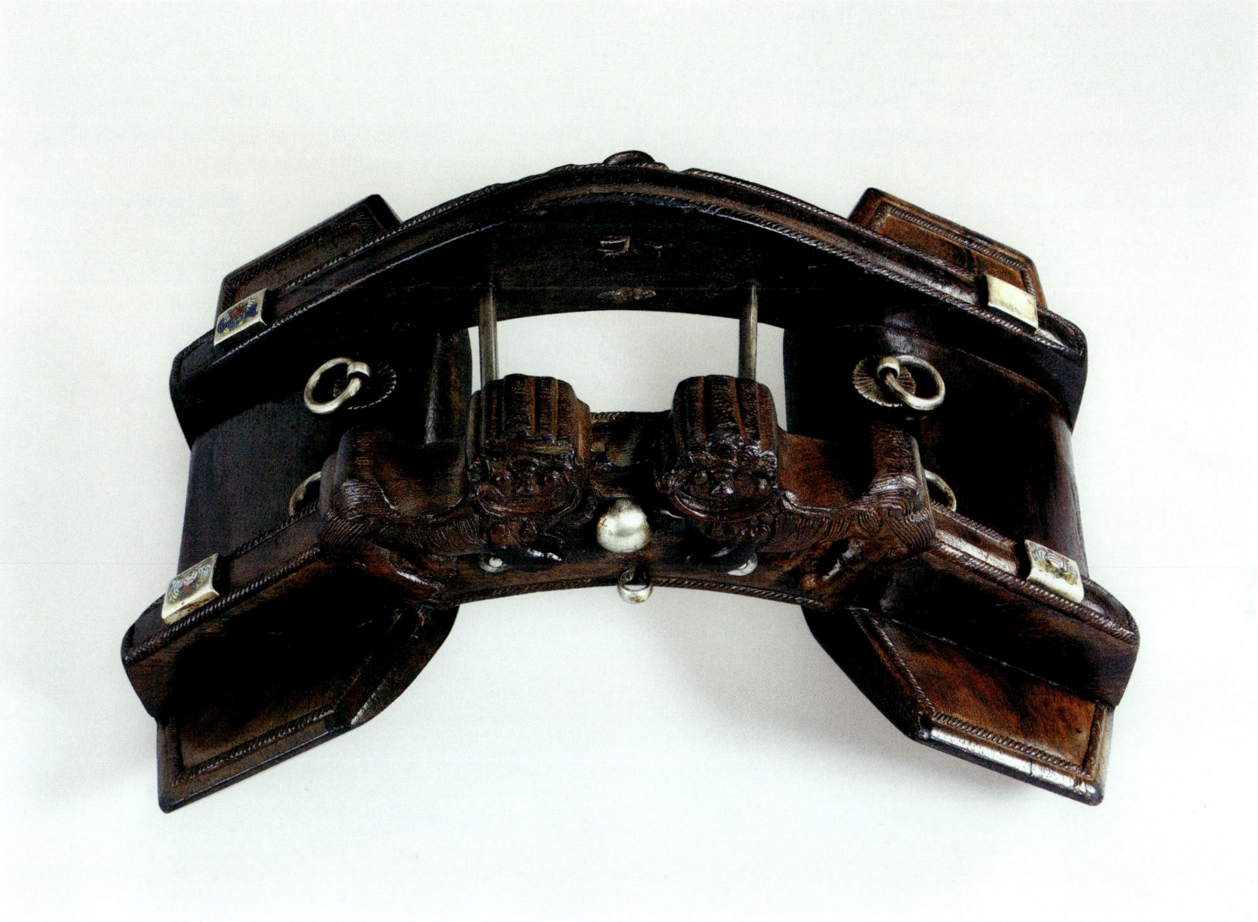

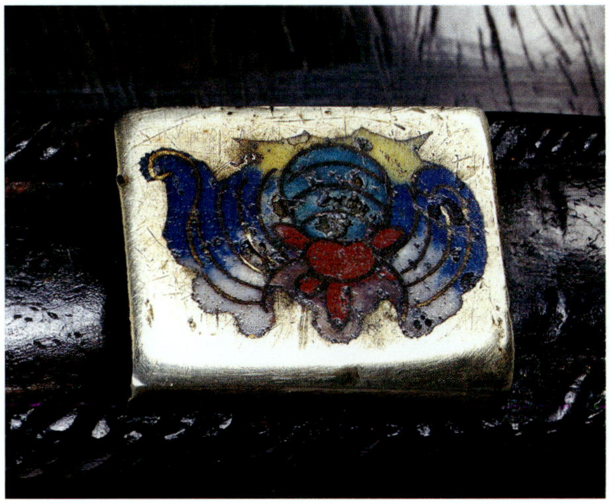

Brushpots

筆筒

97

Small Brushpot with Fitted Base

紫檀地座小筆筒

Zitan
17th Century
8.5 cm Diameter x 14.5 cm H

The body of this small brushpot is finished with a plain smooth surface, which under strong light reveals deep red-colored pigmentation and finely textured pores. The top of the rim is shaped with a concave molding, and a wide, flat beading is shaped around the edge. The square base fitted to the bottom stands on *ruyi*-shaped feet.

A *zitan* brushpot of similar form, varying in the style of its round, convex-edged base, was excavated from a Wanli period (1573-1620) tomb in the Shanghai, Baoshan region (see fig. 5, p. 38).

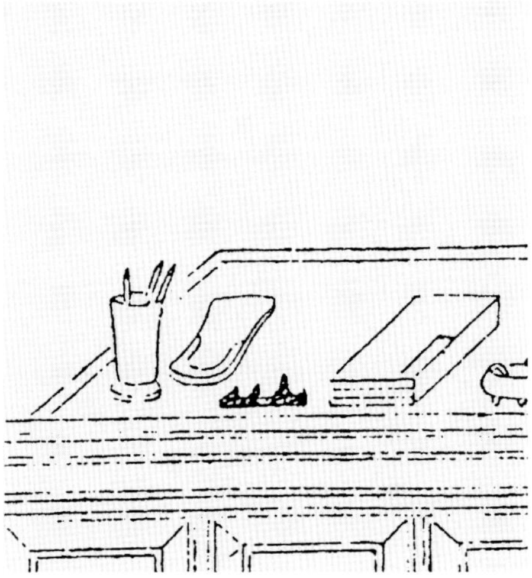

Brushpot. Detail from woodcut illustration to Chongjiao jinyin ji, *late Ming period.*

98

Small Carved Brushpot with Fitted Base

紫檀雕三友小筆筒

Zitan
17th Century
9 cm Diameter x 13 cm H

This small brushpot was modeled to a naturalistic form, and the surfaces carved in a relief *applique*-style with branches of pine, bamboo, and prunus. The 'Three Friends of Winter' motif and the style in which it is carved are both typical of 17th century decoration. The base, which is also finely carved in a foliate style, is fit to the bottom and stands upon three cloud-shaped feet. The *zitan* is finely textured and rich with deep-red pigmentation.

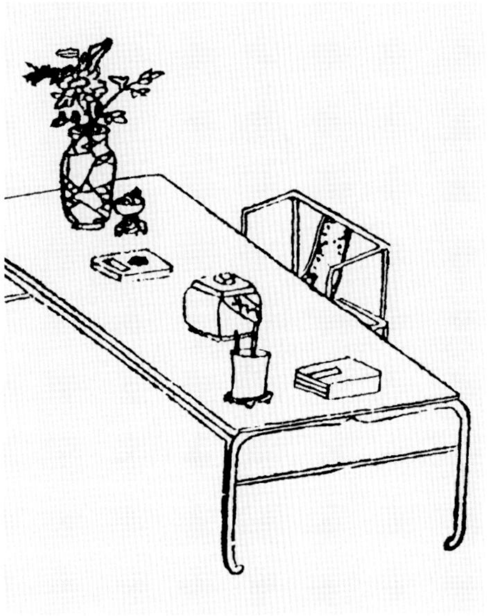

Brushpot. Detail from woodcut illustration to Chun dengmi ji, *late Ming period.*

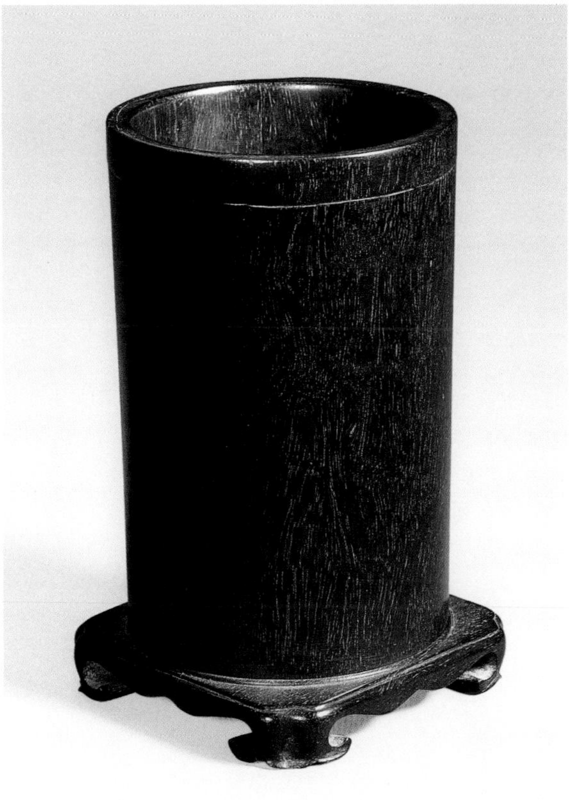

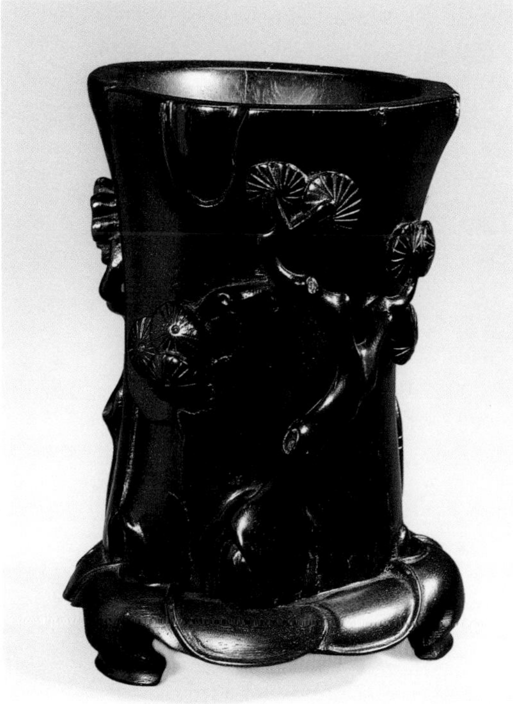

99

Hexagonal Brushpot with Fitted Base

黄花梨地座筆筒

Huanghuali
17th Century
17 cm Diameter x 18.5 cm H

The single-piece body of this brushpot is hexagonal in shape with indented corners, and the overall form tapers slightly from the top toward the base. The rim is accented with a wide, flat beading. The separate, round base is inserted into the bottom; its convex edge is carved in relief with twisted and knotted rope pattern that corresponds to the hexagonal design above, and three feet are shaped at the bottom. The surface reveals natural aging and patination.

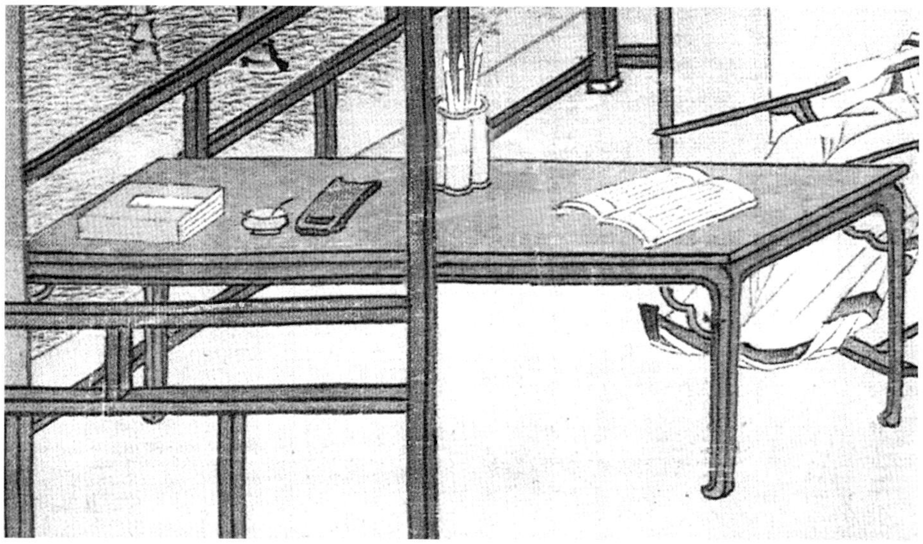

Brushpot. Detail from hanging scroll by Qiu Ying, Ming 16th century. National Palace Museum, Taipei.

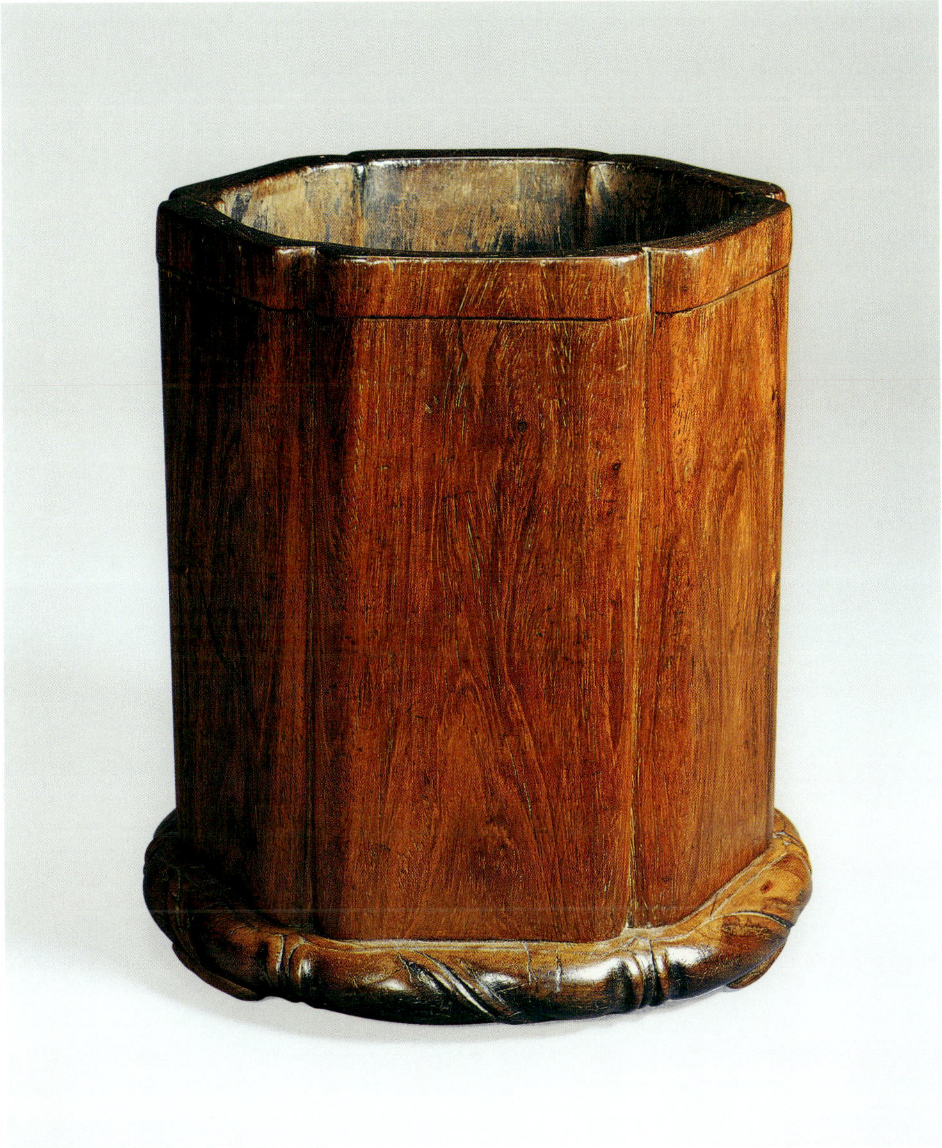

100

Brushpot/Scrollpot with Base Stand

黃花梨地座筆筒

Huanghuali
17th Century
25.5 cm Diameter x 24 cm H
Stand 27.5 x 27.5 x 5 cm H

This large brushpot, or scrollpot, is shaped to a subtly waisted form. Although mellowed from age, the grain patterning is active with lively striations and abstract figuring. The smooth-polished surfaces, which reveal patination and minor wear, are relatively clean and recently repolished. The independent *xumi*-style base is shaped from a single piece of wood and is comprised of a circular concave-molded waist/receptacle mated to a square platform. The classically styled platform is shaped with indented corners and *kunmen* openings that turn into cloud-scrolled feet.

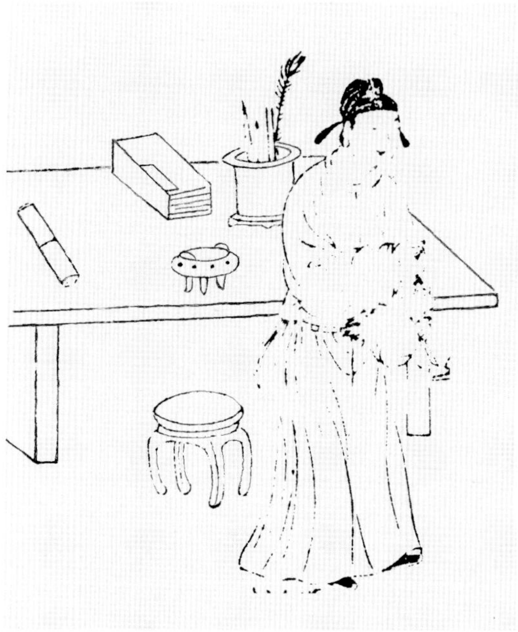

Brushpot. Detail from woodcut illustration to Yu he ji, *late Ming period.*

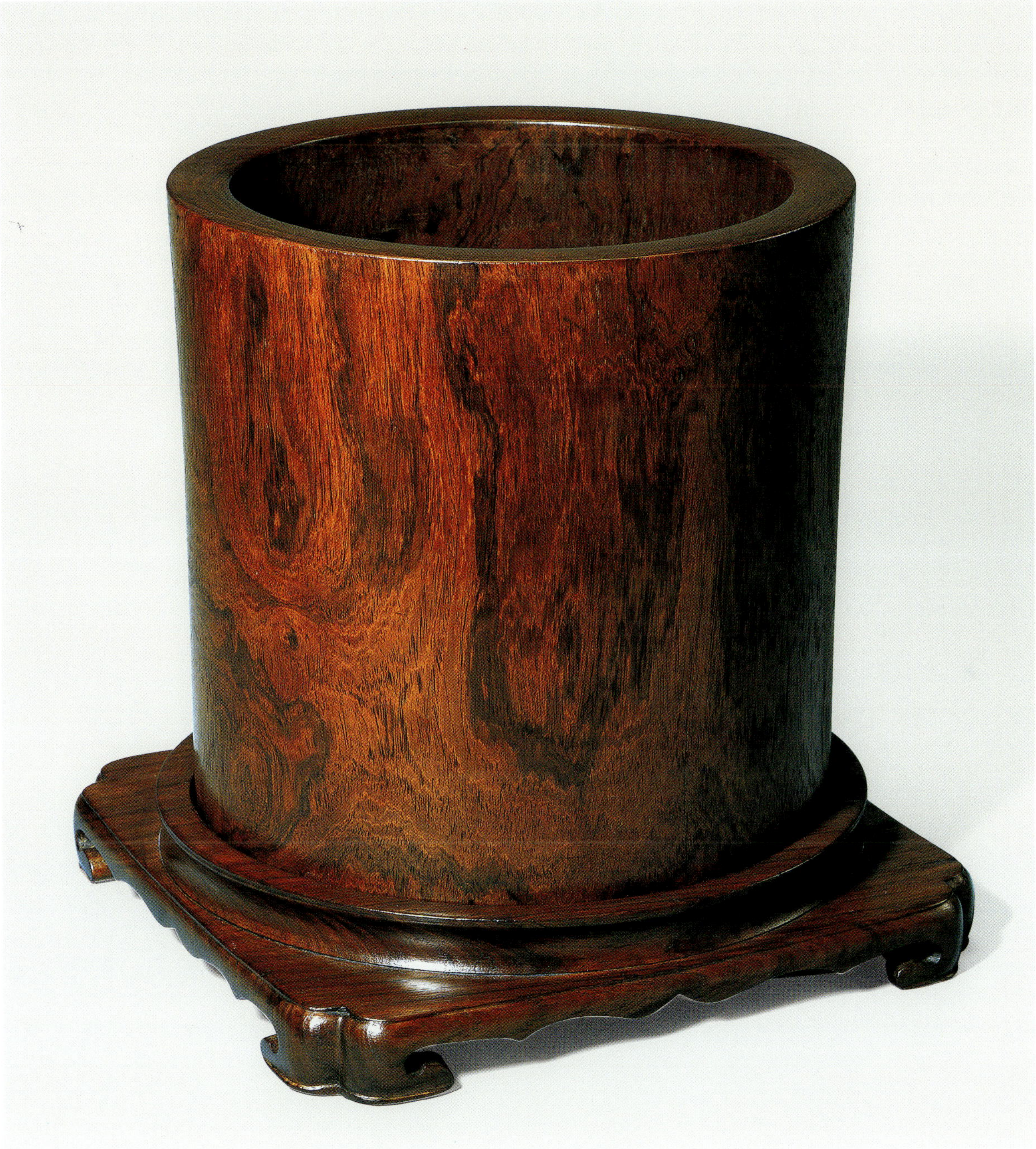

101

Brushpot

紫檀筆筒

Zitan
18th Century
11 cm Diameter x 13 cm H

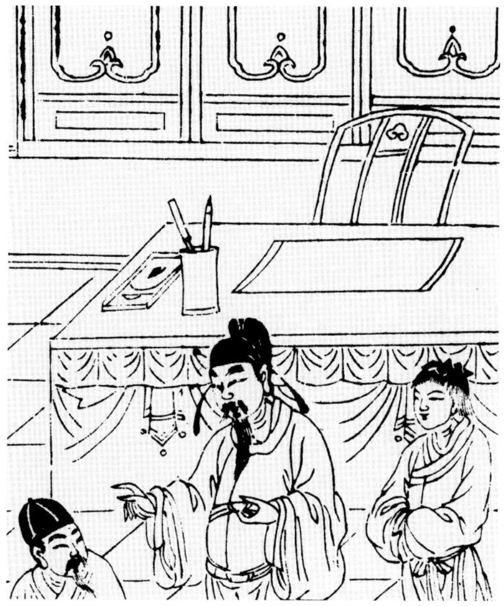

Brushpot. Detail from woodcut illustration in Ruishi liangyin, *Ming Chongzhen period (1628-1644).*

The body of this small brushpot has a slightly waisted profile. To the otherwise plain, smooth body is a subtly incised line around the base. The surface exhibits age through its softly worn patina. Strong light does not diminish the natural darkness of the material, but highlights the 'crab-claw' patterning of the open pore structure. The separate, inserted bottom is slightly recessed to create a rimmed foot.

102

Brushpot with Beaded Rim and Base

黃花梨筆筒

Huanghuali
18th Century
13 cm Diameter x 14 cm H

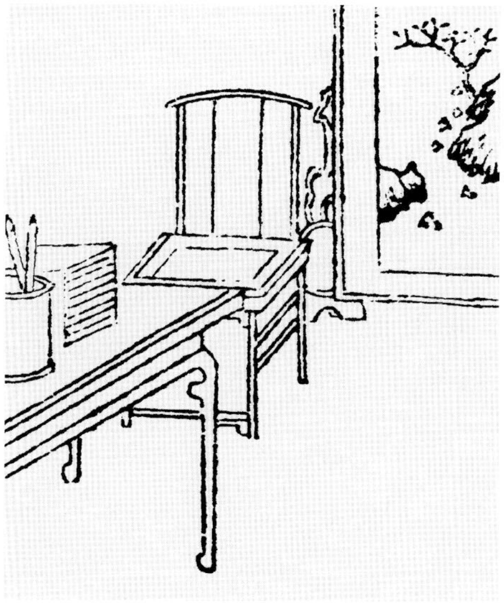

Brushpot. Detail from woodcut illustration to Yu lun pao, *late Ming period.*

This brushpot exhibits refined workmanship. The rim is neatly styled, flaring out from the inside and finishing with a thin beaded lip; the base is accentuated with a broad, raised beading. The grain patterns of the figured *huanghuali* wood are mellowed with age and reveal a rich, warm patination. The inserted base is slightly recessed, leaving a foot rim.

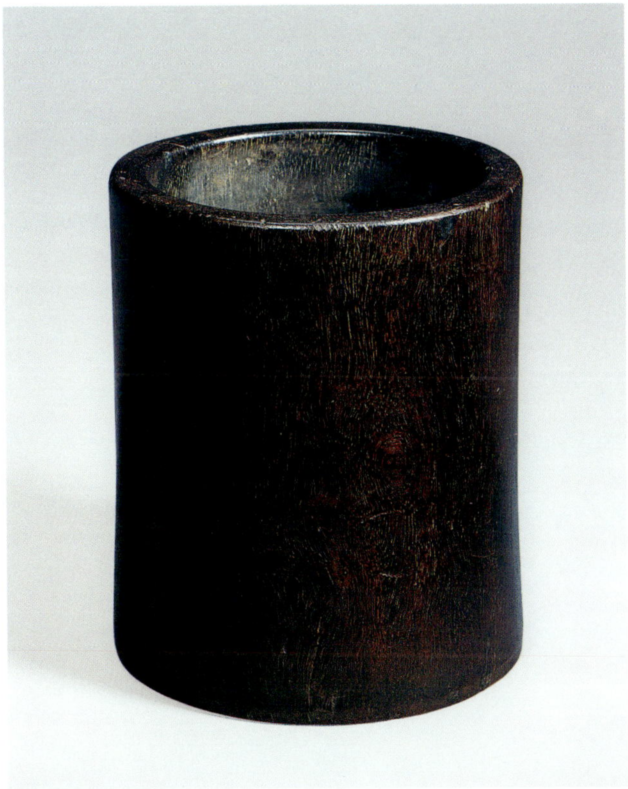

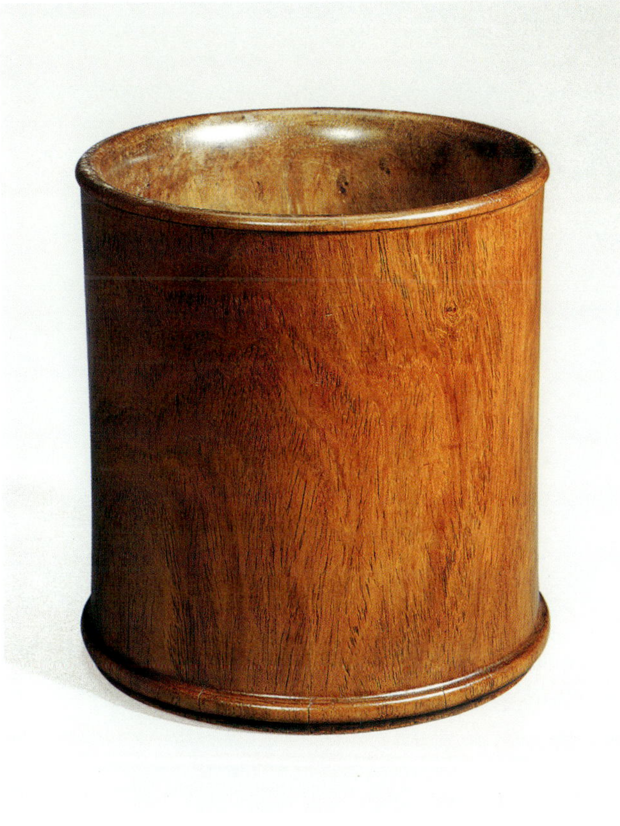

103
Brushpot
黄花梨筆筒

Huanghuali
18th Century
13.5 cm Diameter x 14.5 cm H

The waisted profile of this *huanghuali* brushpot accentuates the natural figure whose dark layered striations appear as mountainous peaks rising one after another. The surface is patinated and reveals wear from age. The flat bottom is fit with a round, core plug.

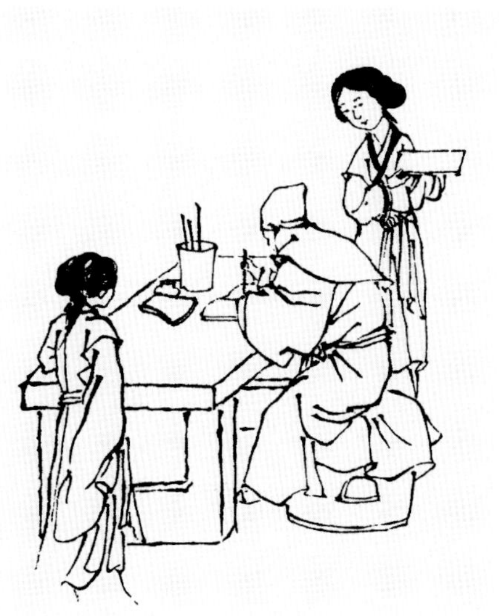

Brushpot. Woodcut illustration to Sanguo huaxiang, *Qing Guangxu period.*

104
Brushpot with Inscription
鐵力木有陰雕款筆筒

Tieli
18th Century
15 cm Diameter x 14.5 cm H

The body of this medium-sized brushpot is shaped to a slightly waisted as well as tapered form. The richness of finely figured tieli with a whorling grain pattern is revealed on one side; the opposite side is incised with a poetic inscription in clerical script, which may be read as:

Why use the mountains and pines
    to slip into anonymity
When one cup of the joyful libations
    will quiet the passions.
The ancients were so principled in
    the art of long life
Thus today must be so deserving of
    oblivious intoxication.

The exterior surface has a rich and warm patination, and reveals the wear of natural age. The interior surface reveals tool marks from the uneven turning of a primitive wood lathe. The flat bottom is fit with a round, core plug.

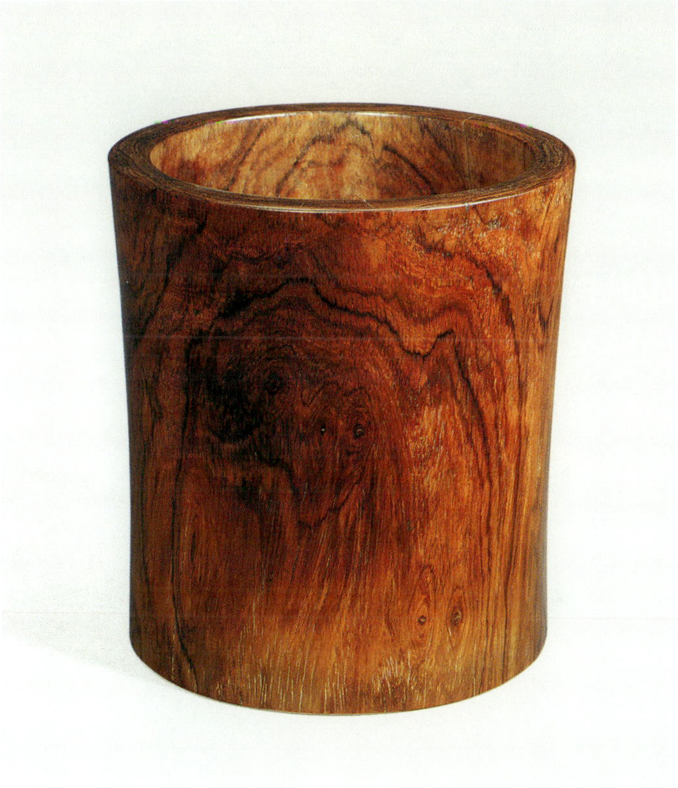

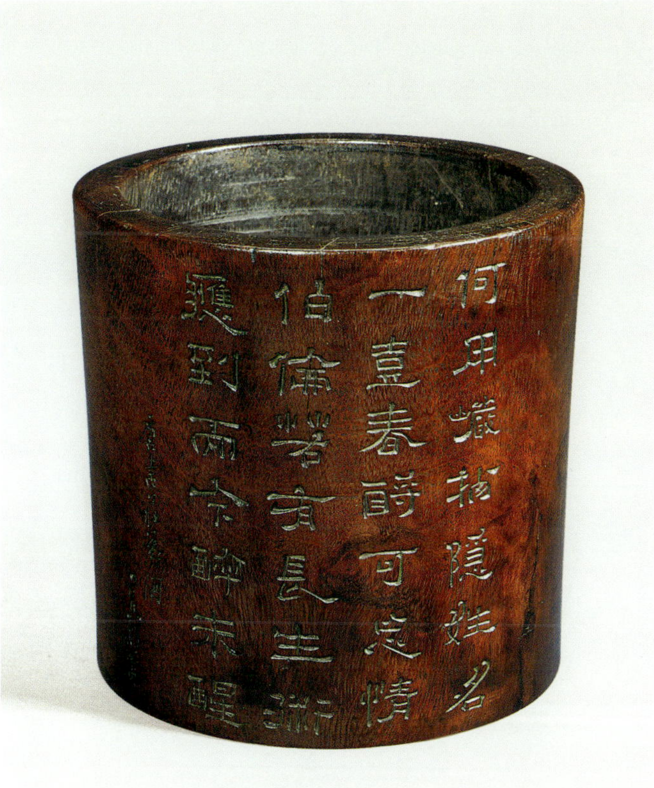
何用巖栖隱姓名
一壺春酎可忘情
伯倫若有長生術
應到而今醉未醒

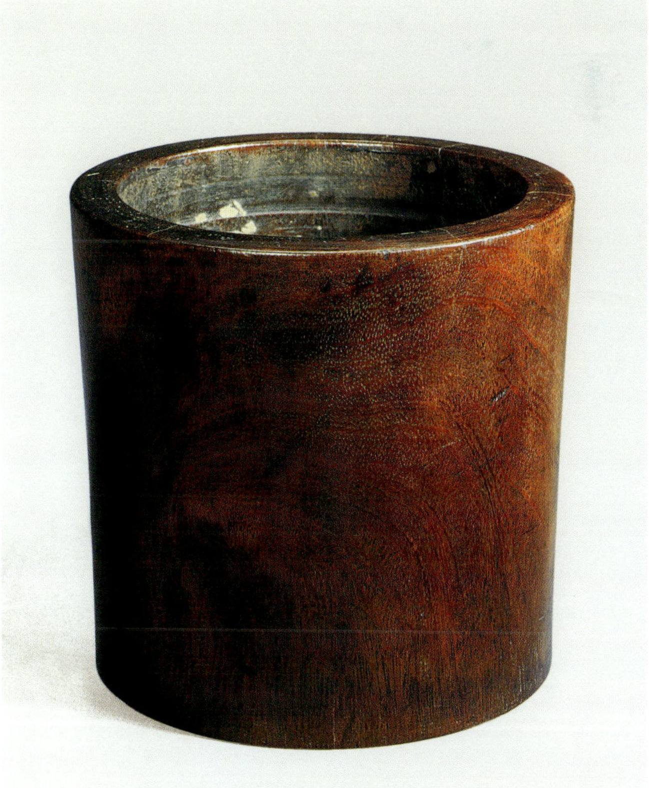

105

Brushpot

黄花梨筆筒

Huanghuali
18th Century
15.5 cm Diameter x 17.8 cm H

This uniquely shaped brush pot has a bellied-jar form with a turned out lip above and beaded base below. The original lacquer finish on the exterior surface has mellowed to a lovely patination; the interior also retains an aged lacquer surface. The bottom is a separate insertion.

Previously exhibited and published in:

- National Museum of History. Splendor of Style: *Classical Furniture from the Ming and Qing Dynasties*, p. 205.

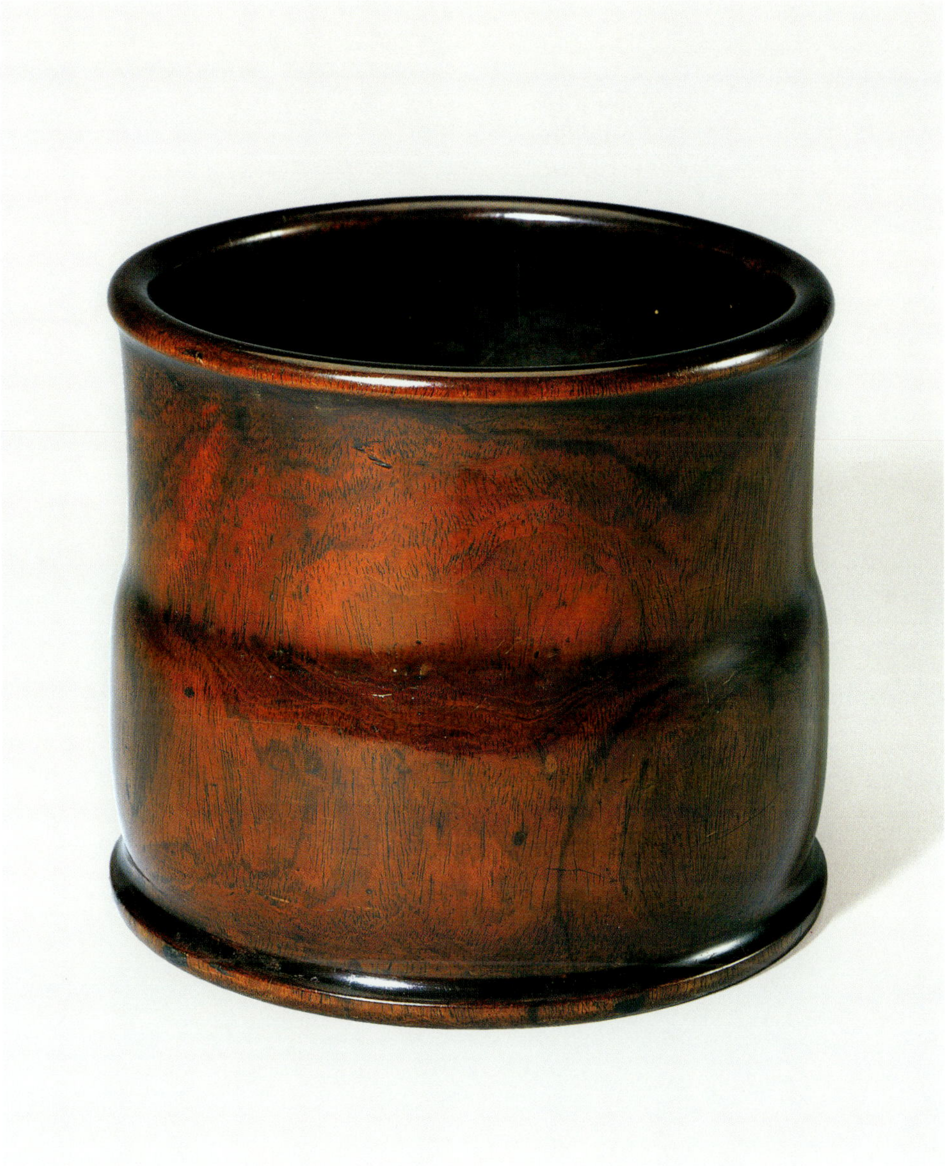

106

Brushpot

黃花梨筆筒

Huanghuali
18th Century
17.8 cm Diameter x 17.5 cm H

This brushpot exhibits refined craftsmanship and quality material. Fine beading is shaped along both the lip and the base. The otherwise plain surfaces reveal the exquisite figuring and shimmering grain patterns of select *huanghuali*. Three feet are shaped at the base, and the bottom is fit with a separate insertion.

A *hongmu* brushpot of similar style and size closely is illustrated in:

- Wang Shixiang and Curtis Evarts, *Masterpieces from the Museum of Classical Chinese Furniture*, pl. 98.

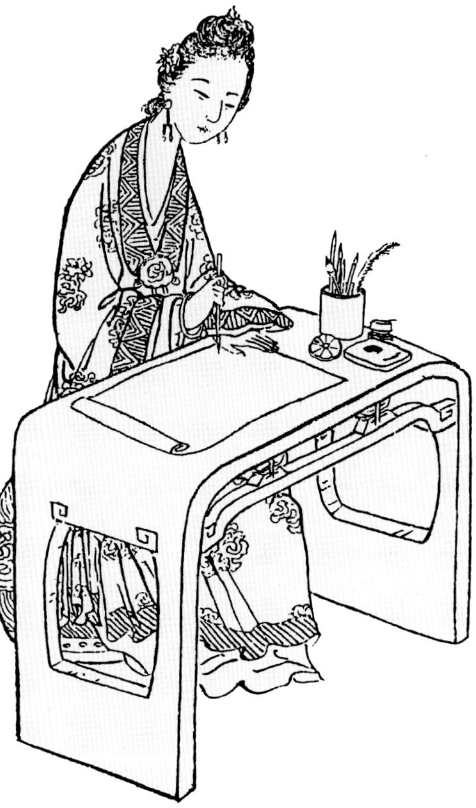

Brushpot. Woodcut illustration to Shitou ji, *Qing Guangxu period (1875-1908).*

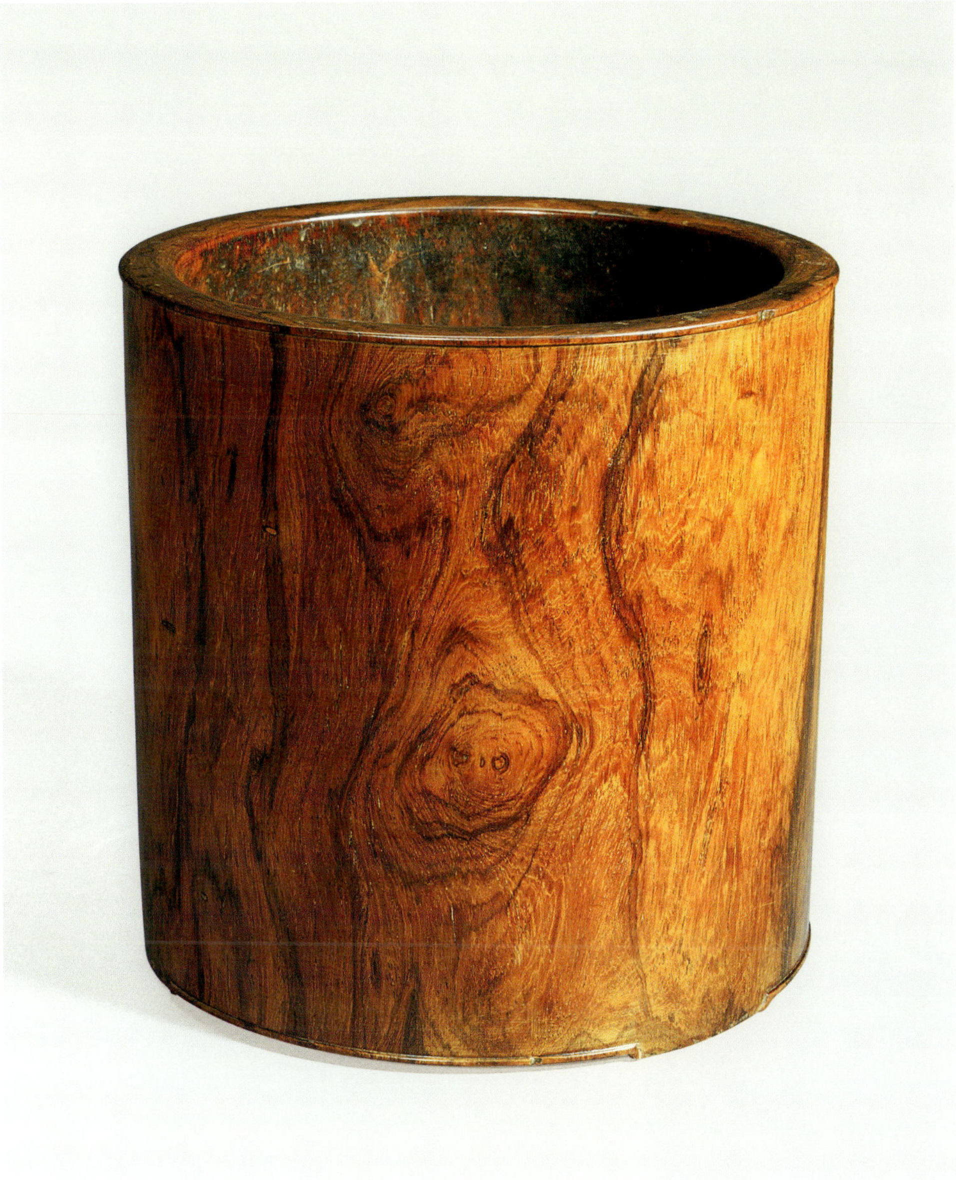

107

Brushpot with Inscription

紫檀有陰雕款筆筒

Zitan
19th Century
18 cm Diameter x 16.5 cm H

The body of this medium-sized brushpot is shaped to a slightly waisted profile with smooth surfaces. The material is exceptionally dense, finely textured, and under strong light reveals striated grain patterns and shimmering reddish-golden tonalities. The open pores also exhibit 'crab-claw' patterning and 'golden-thread' (*jinsi*) flecks. The concave-shaped bottom is fit with a round, core plug.

One side bears a poetic inscription that alludes to the virtues of the past. The four, seven-character stanzas are arranged in vertical rows of four and three. The characters are crisply incised in clerical script, which are further highlighted with a bronze-toned pigment.

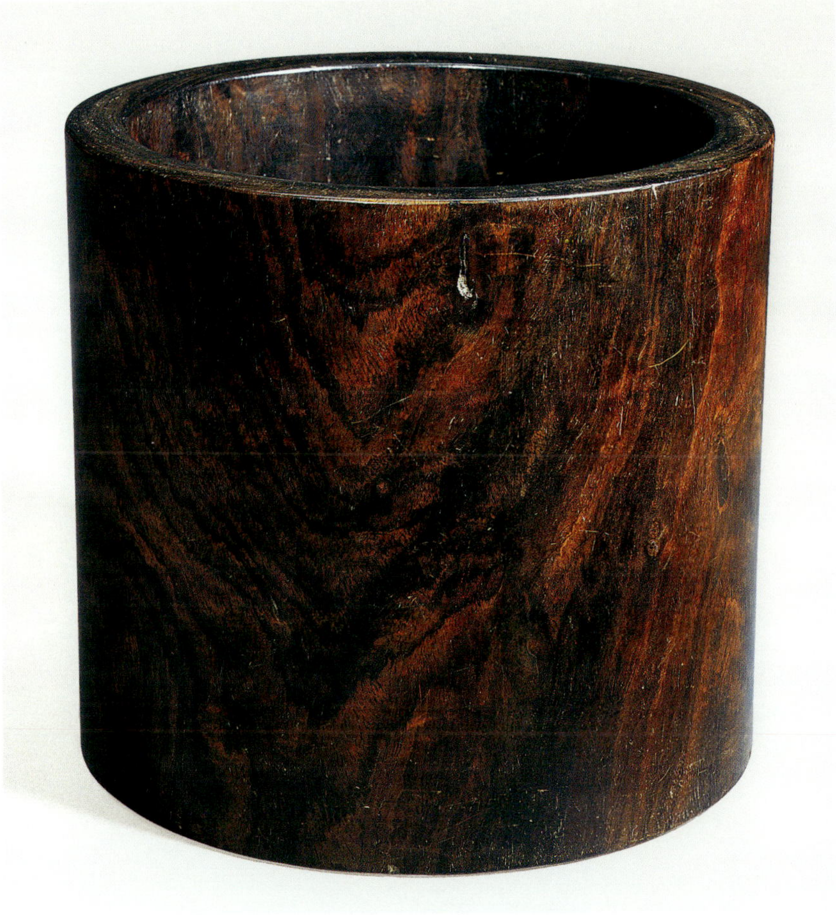

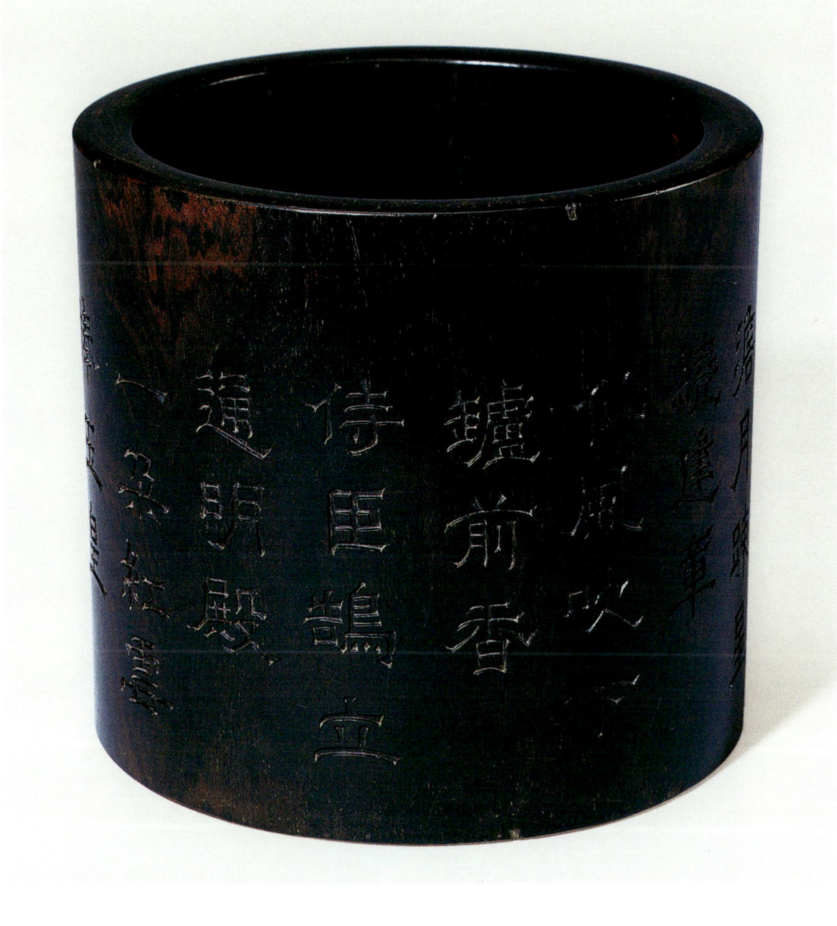
鑪前香
侍臣鵠立
通明殿
一朵紅雲

108

Brushpot with Ink Inscription

黄花梨有墨款筆筒

Huanghuali
17th Century
23 cm Diameter x 21 cm H

This large brushpot is shaped with a slight waist and is otherwise plain without tooled decoration. The entire surface also bears the unusual traces of a lengthy brushed ink inscription around a large central *shu* (book) character. The lightly cleaned surface retains both the deep patination and traces of the inscription that penetrated to stain the surface of the wood. The concave-shaped bottom is fit with a round, core plug.

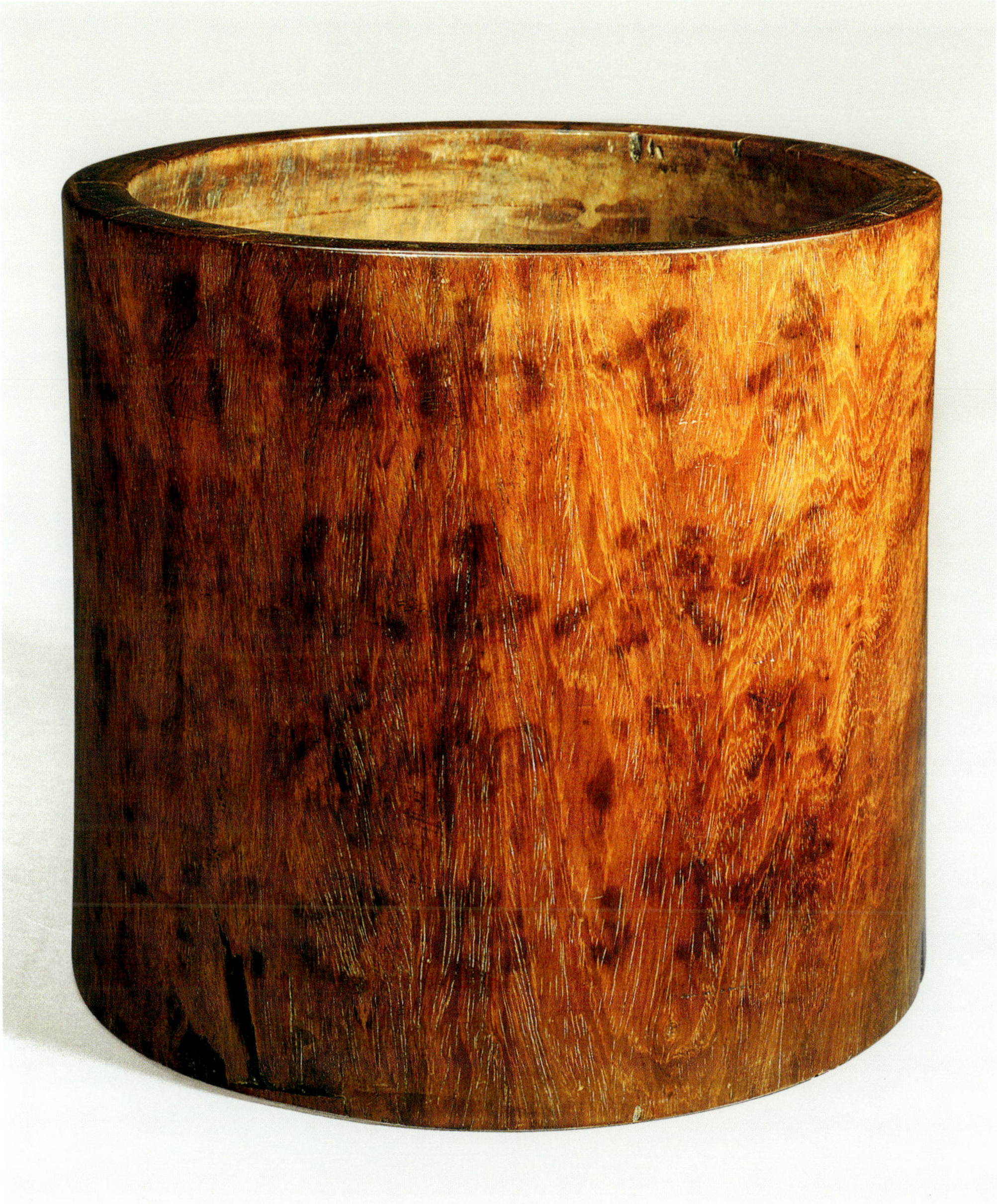

109

Scrollpot

癭木筆筒

Burlwood
18th Century
26 cm Diameter x 27.5 cm H

This large scrollpot is shaped with straight sides. The light-colored wood has a lovely warm-toned patina, and the unusual grain patterning is splashed with mottled figuring. The interior retains a thick lacquer coating. The flat bottom is fit with a round, core plug.

Previously exhibited and published in:

- National Museum of History. *Splendor of Style: Classical Furniture from the Ming and Qing Dynasties*, p. 206.

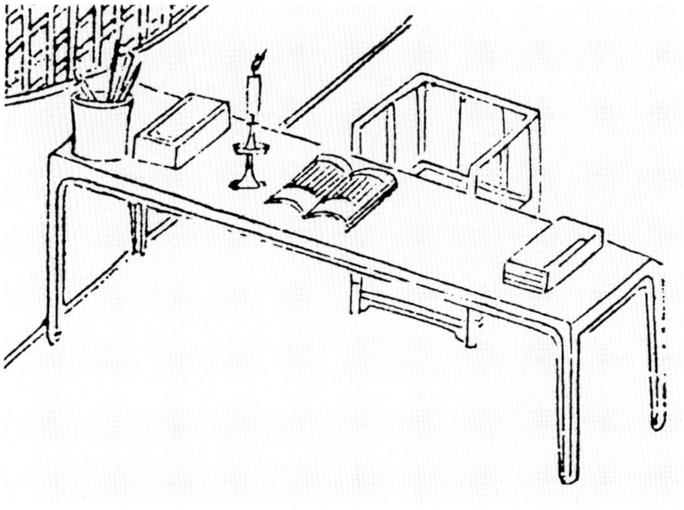

Brushpot. Detail from woodcut illustration to Lie guo zhi chuan, *Ming Wanli period (1573-1620)*

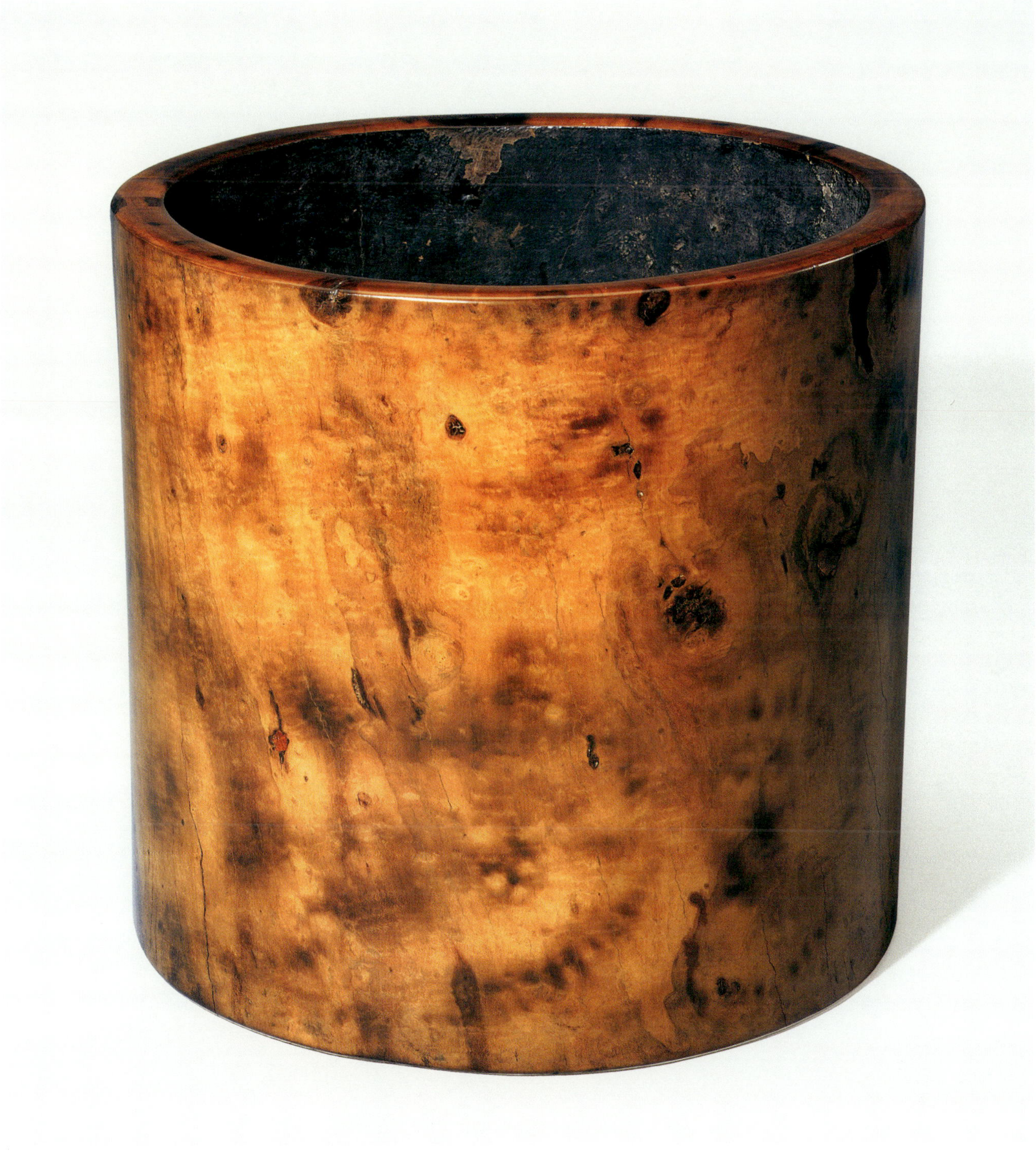

110

Scrollpot

紫檀筆筒

Zitan
20th Century
27 cm Diameter x 23 cm H

The body of this large brushpot is shaped with a relatively thick wall (2.7 cm) to a slightly waisted form. The light-toned *zitan* has a translucent, shimmering surface, which reveals golden tones when exposed to bright light. The surface bears little patination or traces of natural wear from age. The flat bottom is fit with a round, core plug.

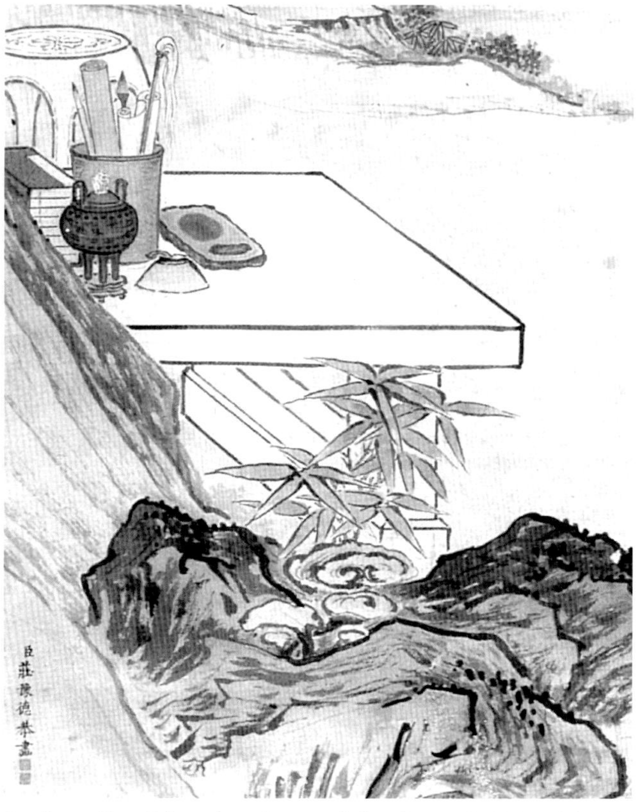

Brushpot. Detail from hanging scroll 'Landscape in Winter' *by Hu Gui, 18th century.*

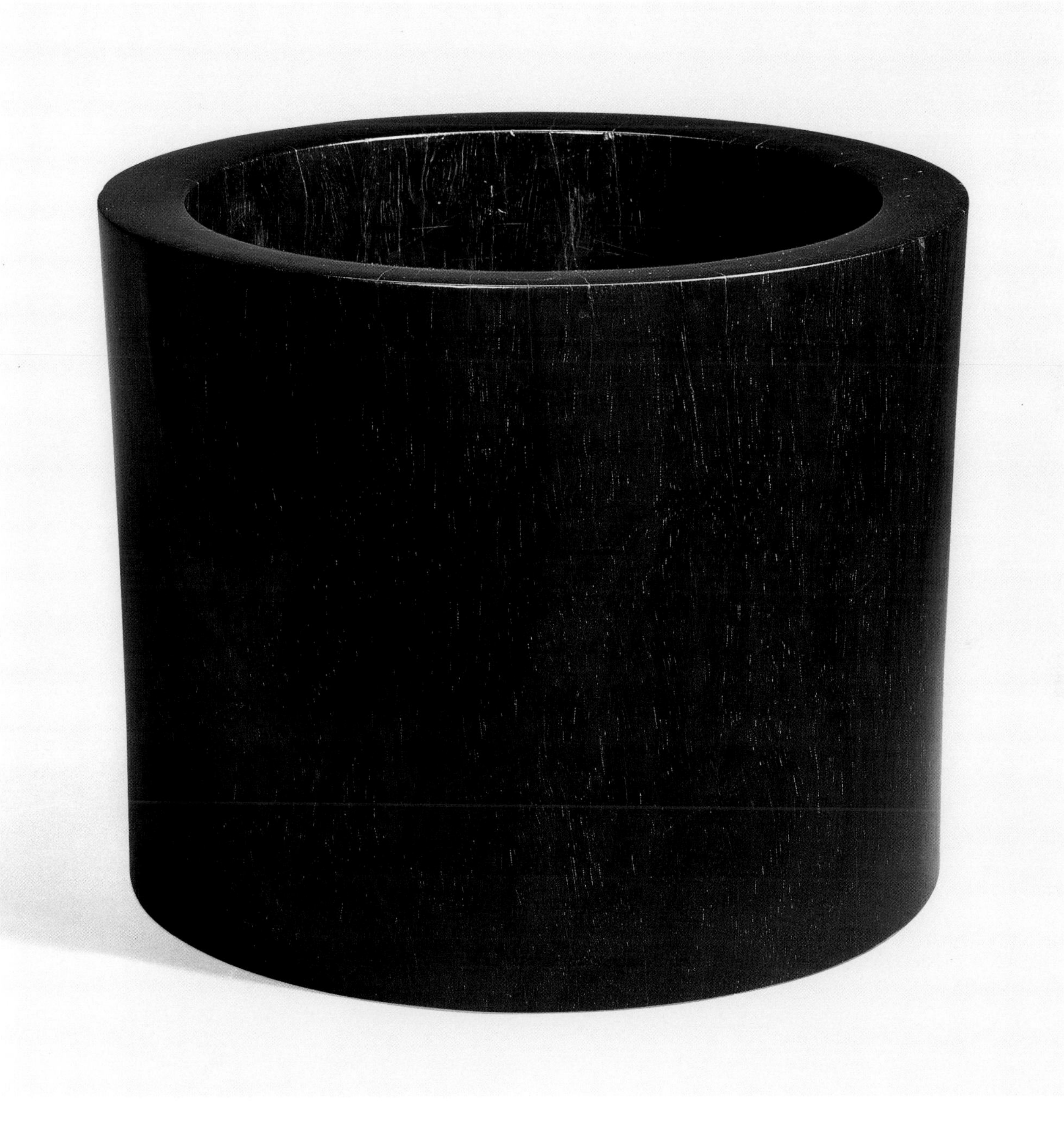

111

Scrollpot

紫檀筆筒

Zitan
18th/19th Century
31.3 cm Diameter x 27 cm H

The body of this scrollpot is shaped with a slight waist. The *zitan* has a translucent, shimmering surface, which reveals lighter golden tones when exposed to bright light. The surface has been cleaned but reveals age-worn patination. The flat bottom is fit with a round, core plug.

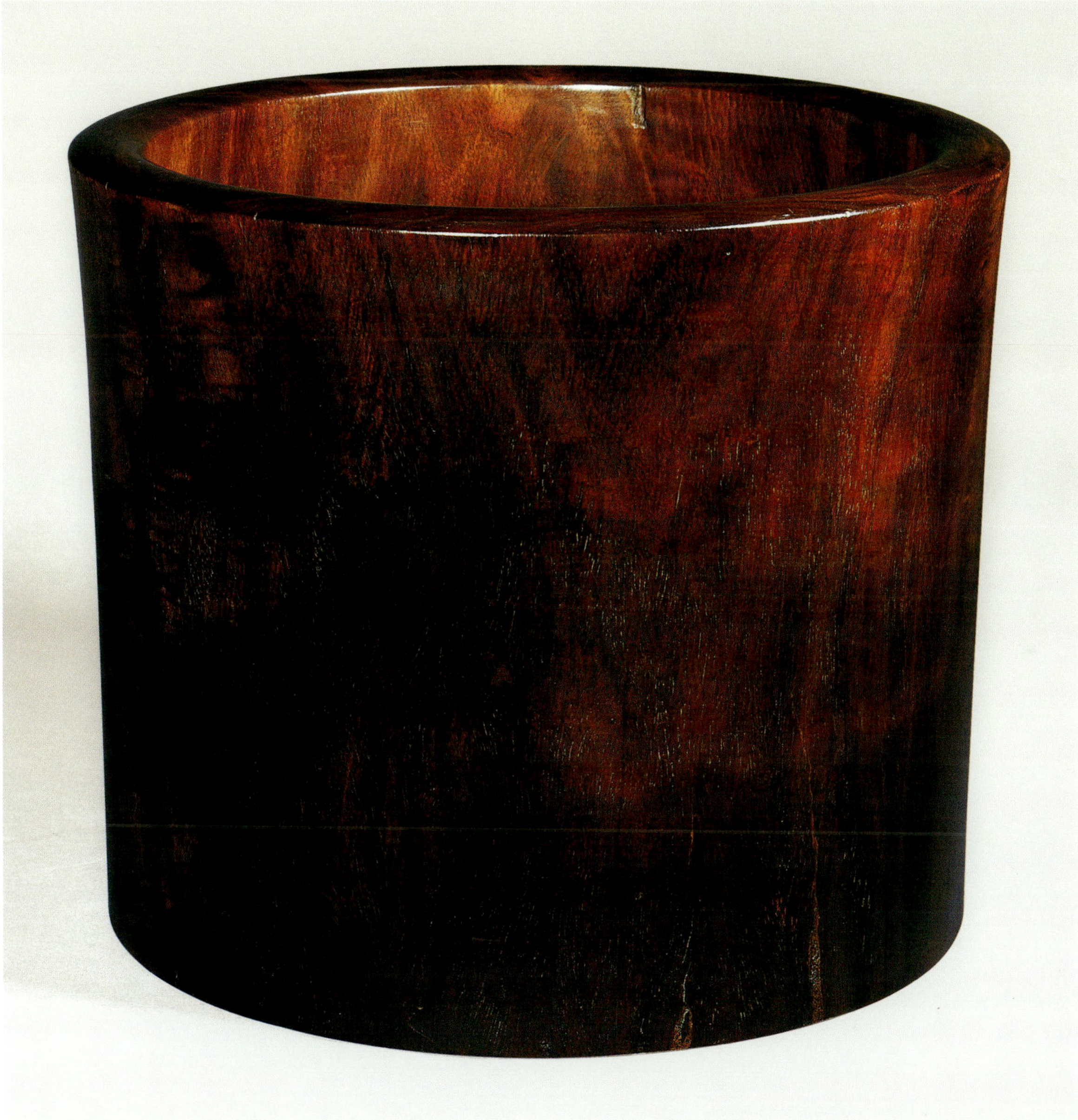

112

Scrollpot

黄花梨筆筒

Huanghuali
17th Century
36 cm Diameter x 24.5 cm H

This massive scrollpot is shaped with walls measuring 3.2 centimeters thick; the solid bottom measures 5.0 centimeters in thickness. The body is shaped to a slightly waisted profile with smooth surfaces. The surfaces have been cleaned but reveal natural age and patination. Traces of red lacquer on the inside suggest that the interior was originally neatly coated.

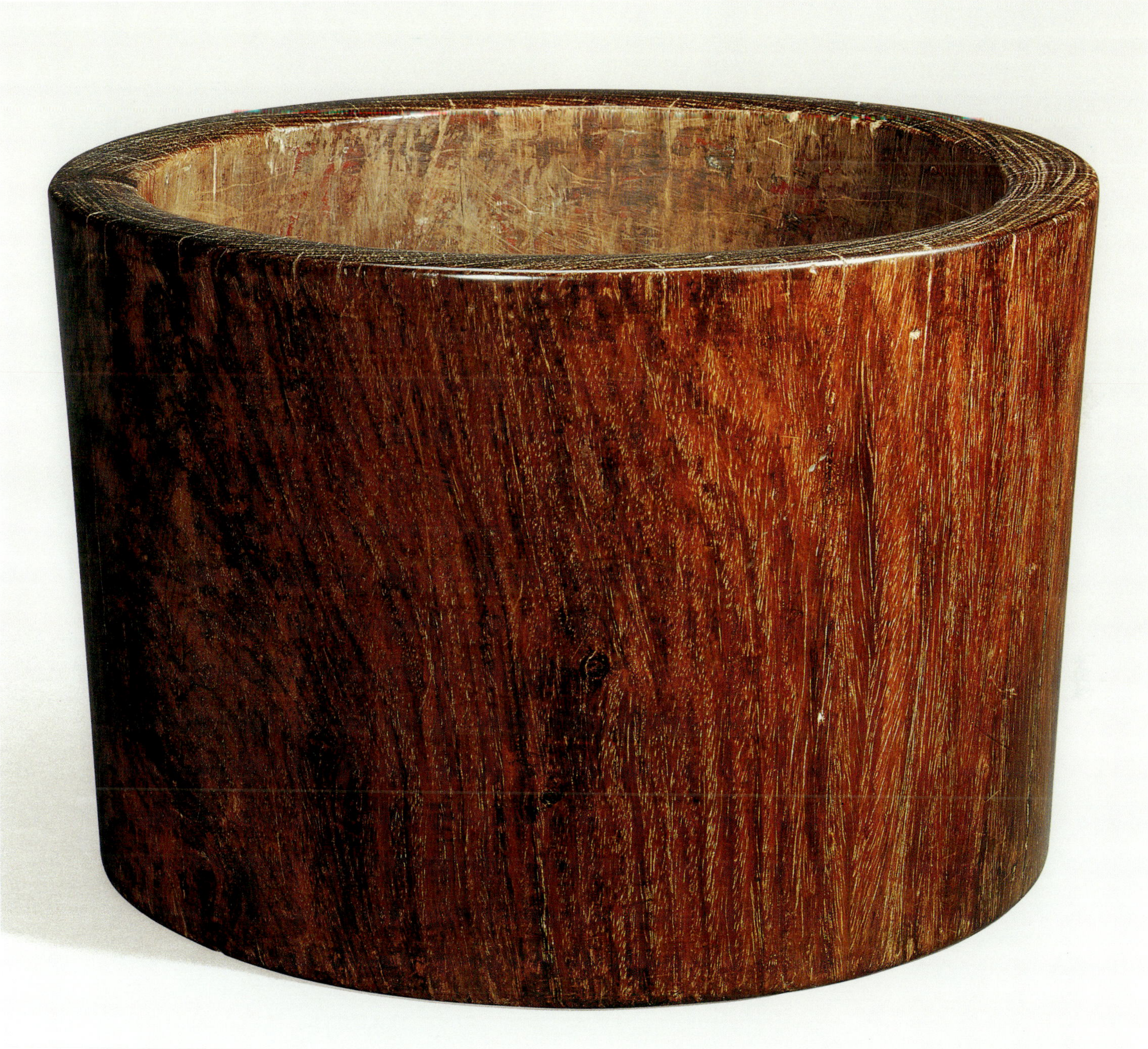

113

Pine Tree Brushpot

紫檀仿松筆筒

Zitan
19th Century
18.5 cm Diameter x 19.5 cm H

This brushpot is shaped with relatively thick walls from dense *zitan* of coffee-brown tonality. This natural color, combined with artistic carving, imparts the rustic impression of a weathered pine tree. A small patch of ingrown sapwood was exploited by the artisan carver, who highlighted the defect in order to imitate the scarred inner tissue of a pine tree. The polished exterior surface retains some patination, and the interior surface bears traces of an old lacquer coating. The flat bottom is fit with a round, core plug.

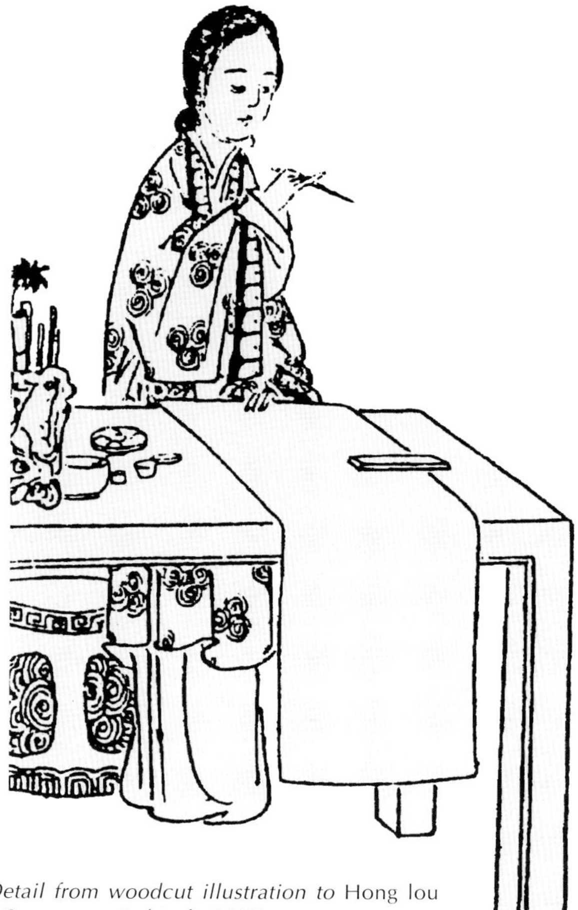

Brushpot. Detail from woodcut illustration to Hong lou meng, *Qing Guangxu period (pub. 1889).*

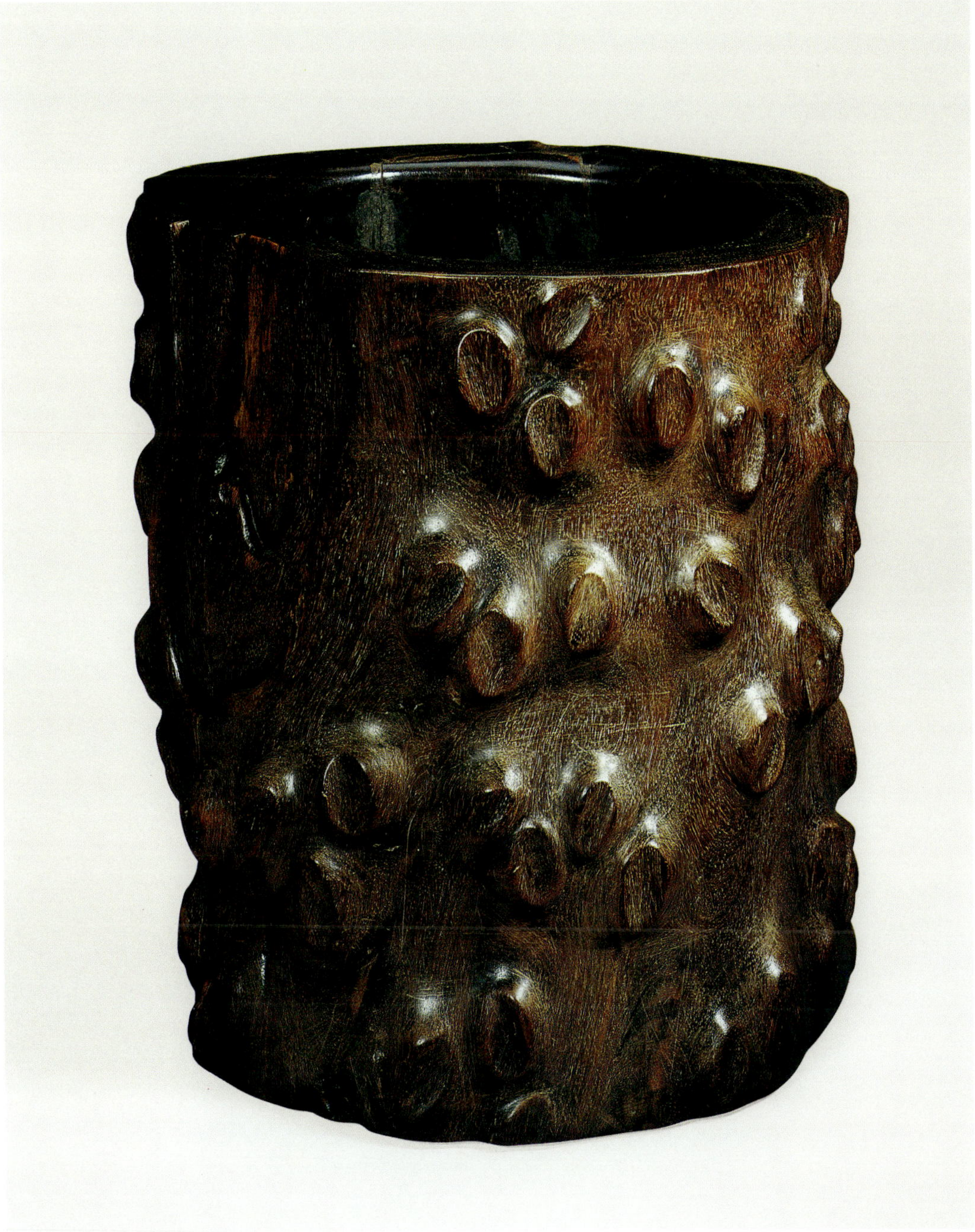

114

Pine Tree Brushpot

黄花梨仿松筆筒

Huanghuali
19th Century
24 cm Diameter x 19.5 cm H

This large brushpot is carved to resemble the rough, natural surface of a pine tree trunk, the artifice of which is further enhanced by the natural coffee-brown color of the timber. The patinated surface reveals the natural wear of age. The flat bottom is fit with a round, core plug.

A similarly styled example is illustrated in:
- Ang, John Kwang-Ming. *The Beauty of Huanghuali*, p. 87.

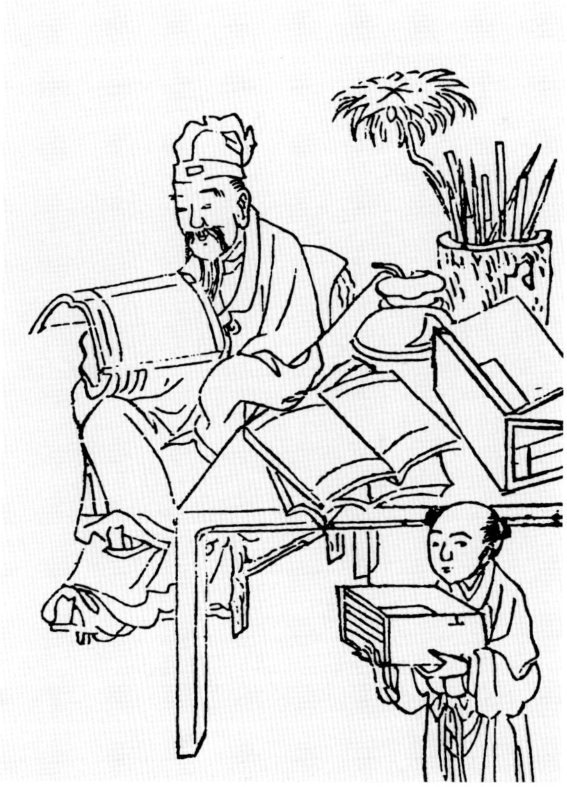

Brushpot. Detail from woodcut illustration to Xiyou ji, *Qing Qianlong period (pub. 1758).*

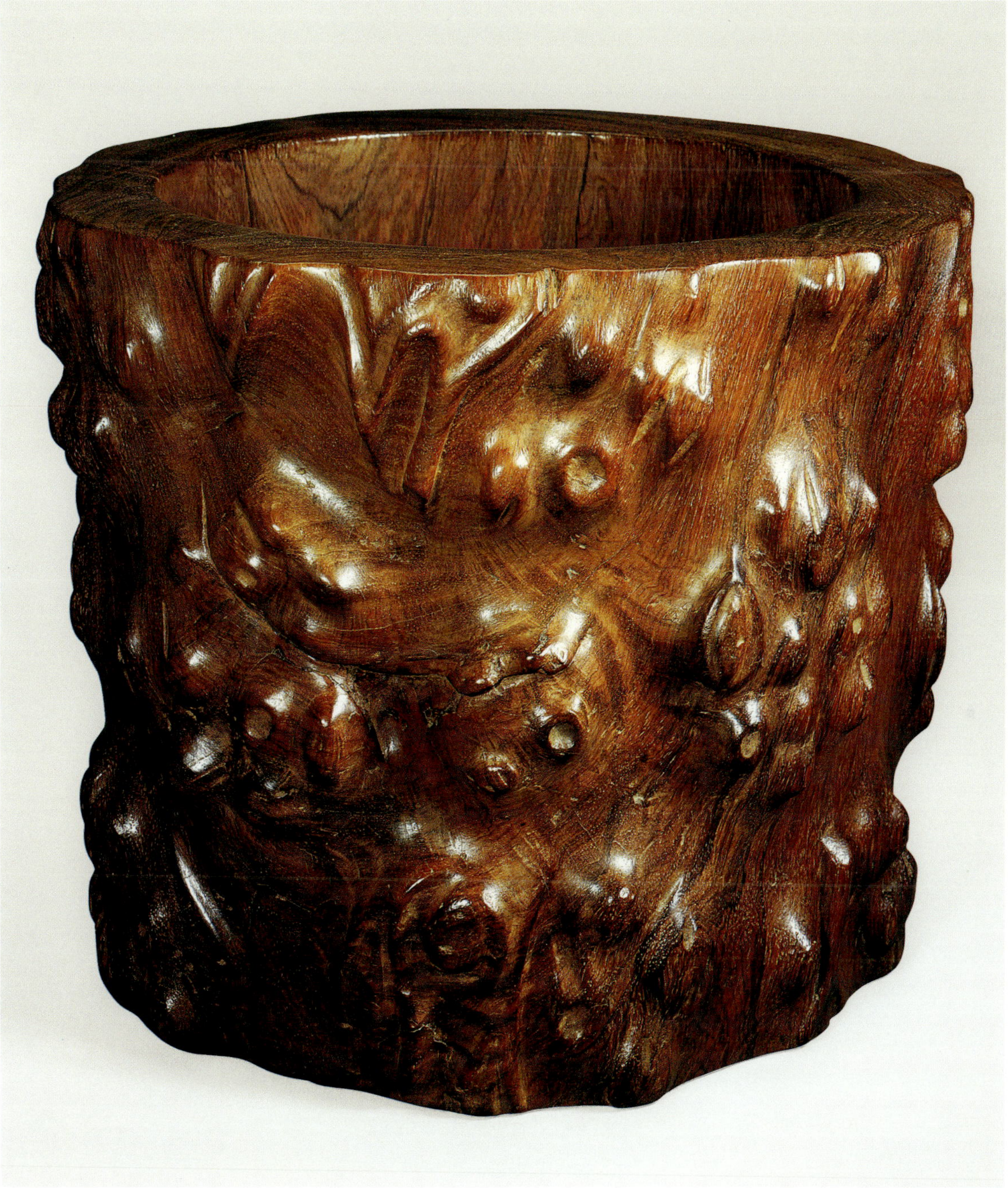

115

Large Root-Shaped Pot

柞榛木樹莨筆筒

Zhazhen Wood
18th Century
33 cm Diameter x 37 cm H

This unusually styled pot is sculpted to resemble a tree trunk of undulating section. Its rather small, yet deep opening precludes use as a scrollpot or brush pot, but rather appears more suited as a decorative vessel for long-stemmed objects (see illustration below). The lower section is girdled with flourishing mass of convoluted growth, which appear in the form of stylized flowers and *lingzhi* fungus. The separate base stand is carved with cloud patterns.

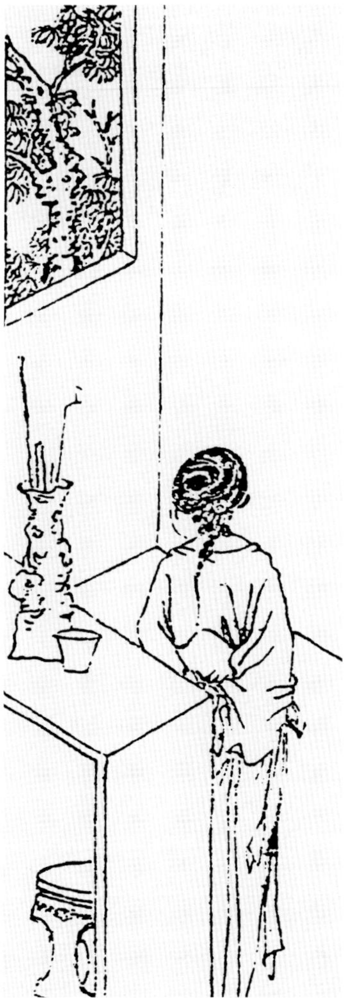

Root vessel. Woodblock print from Hong lou meng, *Qing Guangxu period (pub. 1882).*

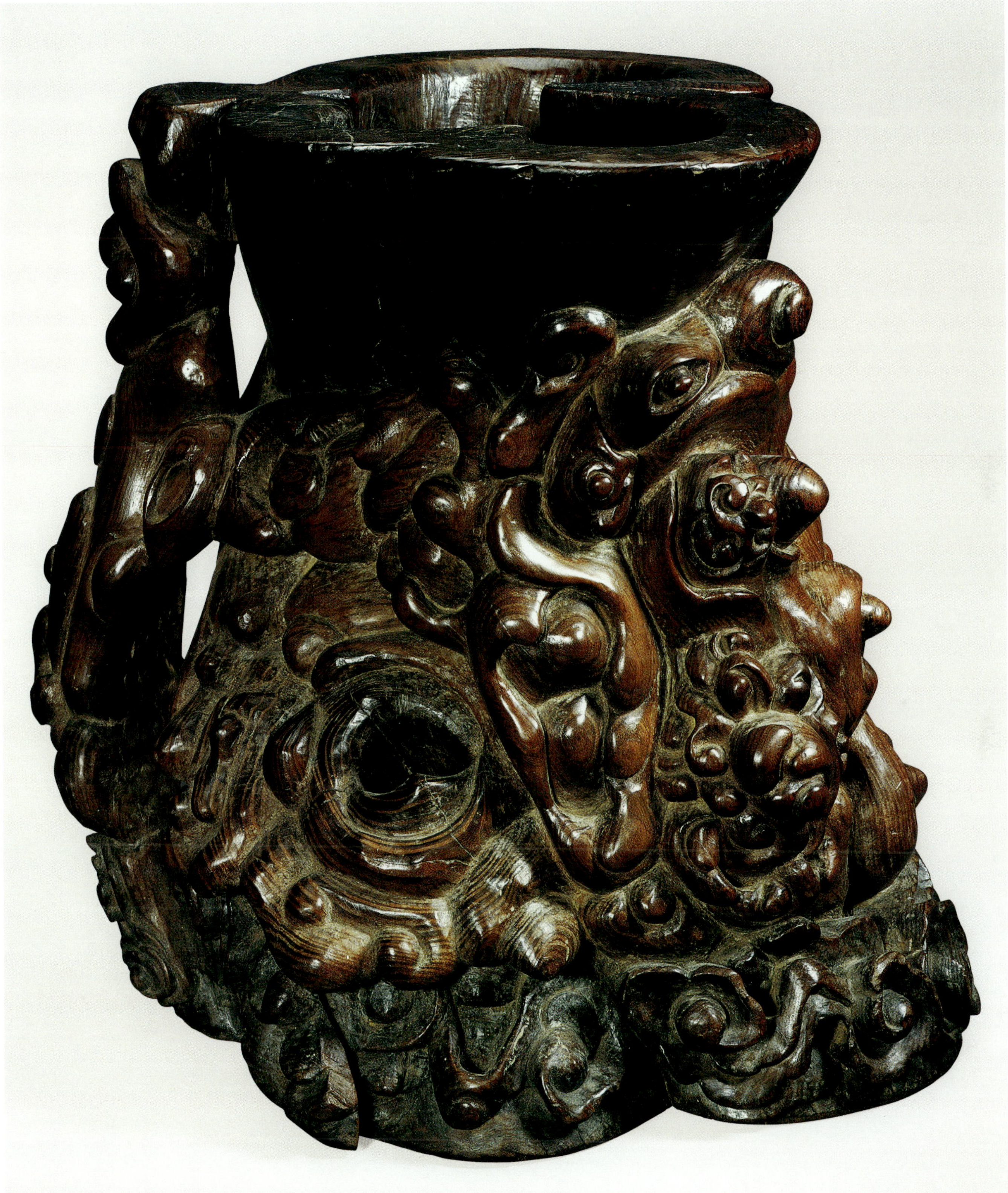

116

Large Pine Tree Scroll / Brushpot

雜木仿松筆筒

Coniferous Softwood
18th Century
35 x 28 x 38 cm H

The surface of this large tree-trunk-shaped pot is worked to resemble the knubby bark of some varieties of pine trees. A concave molded rim of hardwood trims the opening at the top. The otherwise bottomless pot sits on a separate softwood base of waisted style, which is shaped with *kunmen* openings and hoof feet.

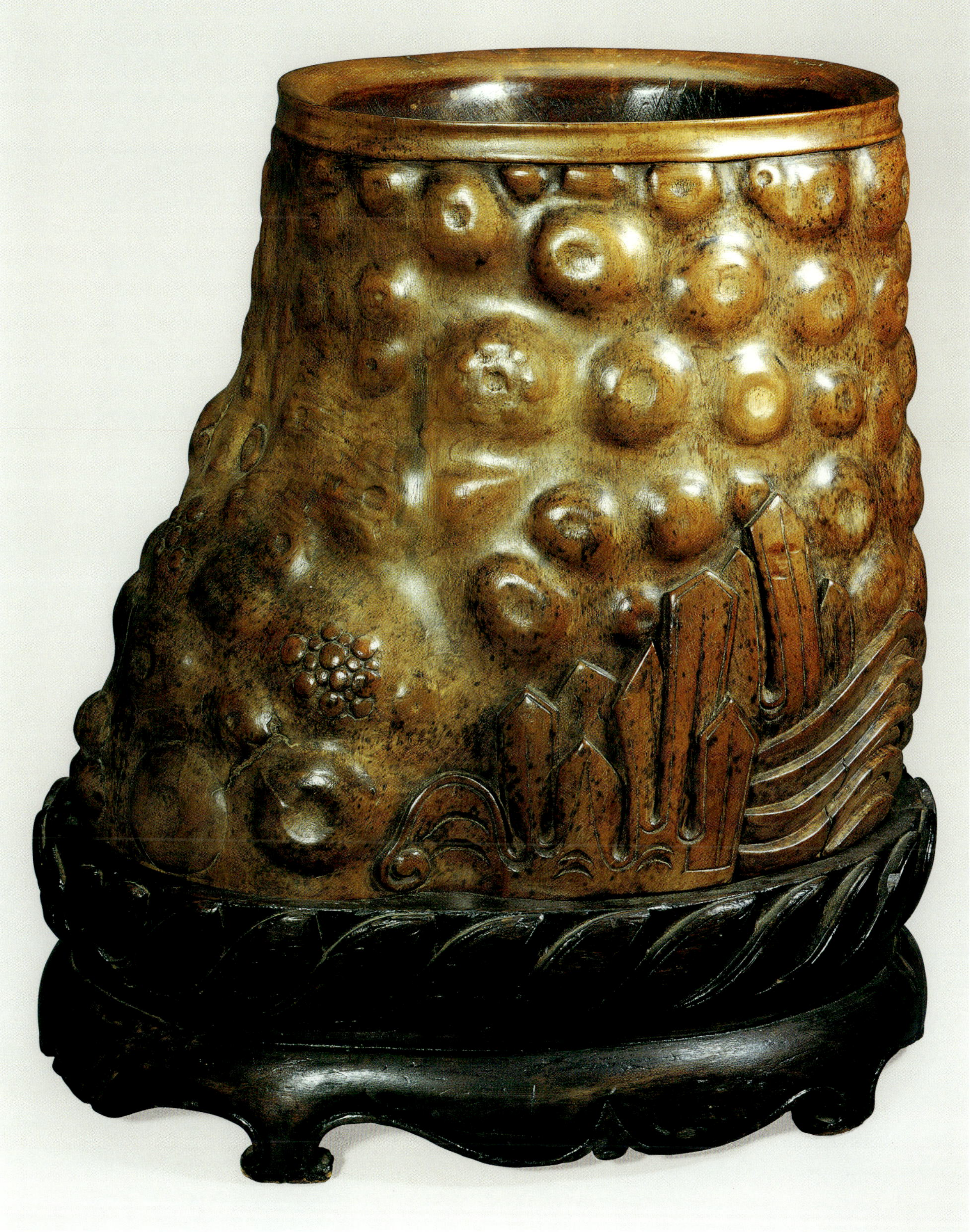

117

Brushpot with Zhouzhi Inlay

紫檀嵌百寶筆小筒

Zitan
17th Century
9.7 cm Diameter x 12.7 cm H

This small brushpot features an inlaid garden landscape scene. The compact composition depicts a plum tree with twisted, gnarled trunk rooted in a rocky outcropping along a waterside. *Lingzhi* and grasses appear freshly sprouted on the ground, and two butterflies flutter above the blossoming plum flowers—auspicious rebuses for longevity and immaculate beauty. New growth at the tip of the plum branches is realistically highlighted with a green hardstone, foretelling of fresh leaves yet to sprout. Silver wire was used to impart the smooth ripples of the watery foreground.

While many of the so-called Zhouzhi works use artificially stained ivory to achieve a multi-colored effect, these inlays are naturally colored stones, including malachite, turquoise, and coral. The *zitan* body flares slightly out towards the top, and the flat bottom is fit with a recessed, round, core plug.

Brushpots with similar inlay work are published in:

- Tsai C. Y. *Zitan: The Most Noble Hardwood*, pp. 169, 171, 173, 175.
- Clunas, Craig. *Chinese Carving*, p. 62, fig. 71.

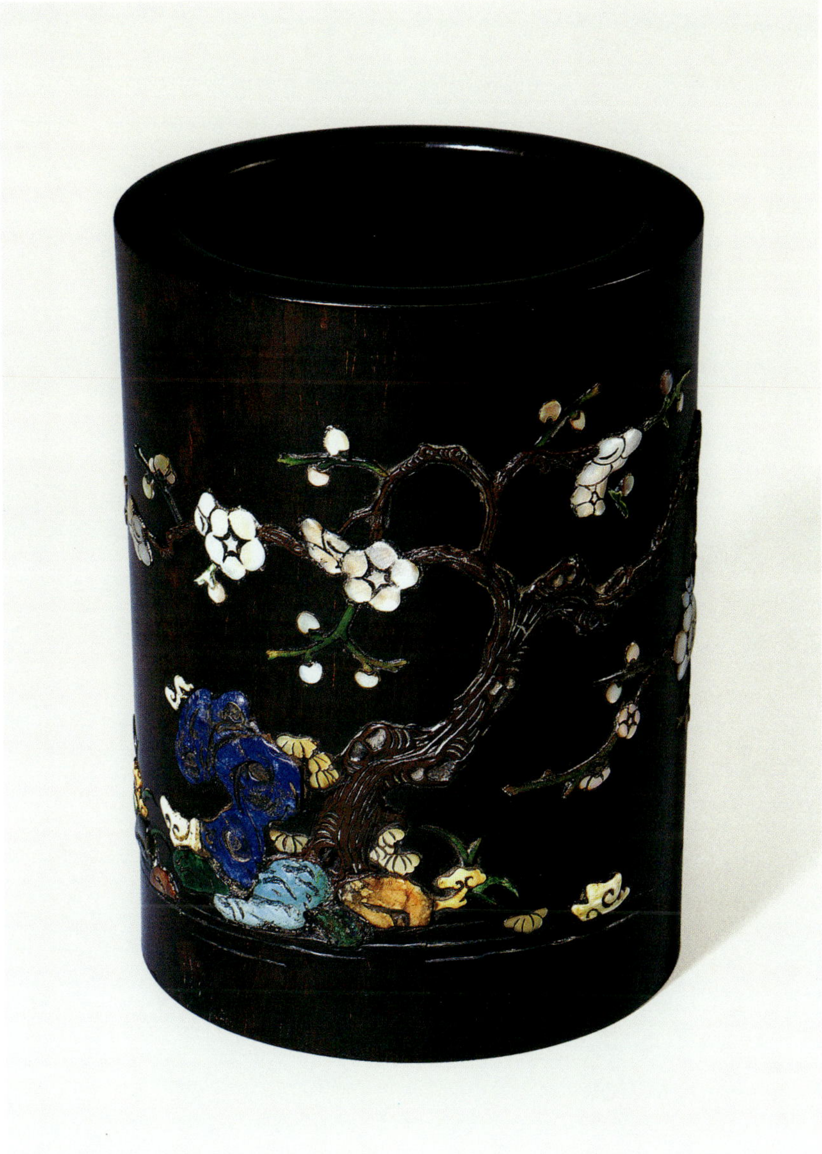

118

Foliate-style Brushpot with Floral and Dragon Designs

黄花梨花式雕龍筆筒

Huanghuali
17th/18th Century
17 cm Diameter x 18 cm H

This brushpot, carved as layered petals, appears as a blossoming flower. The outer petals frame relief-carved *chi* dragons and auspicious magnolia, begonia, and tea flowers. While plain brushpots are known to have been reworked in this popular style, the original work is here evident in the uniform patination of inner and outer surfaces, and the softly rounded wear of the relief. Three feet are shaped about the base perimeter, and a separate piece is inserted as the bottom.

A similar example is illustrated in:

- Ang, John Kwang-Ming, *The Beauty of Huanghuali*, p. 88.

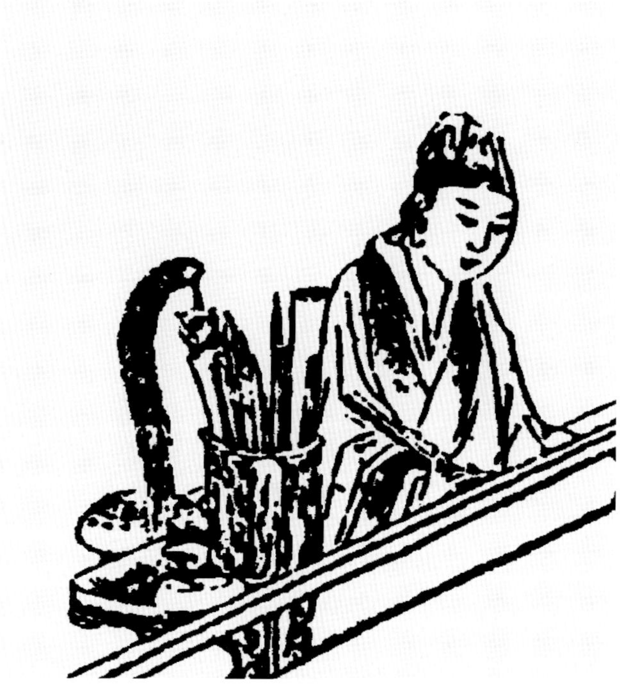

Brushpot. Detail from Woodcut illustration to Hong lou meng, *Qing dynasty, Guangxu period (pub. 1879).*

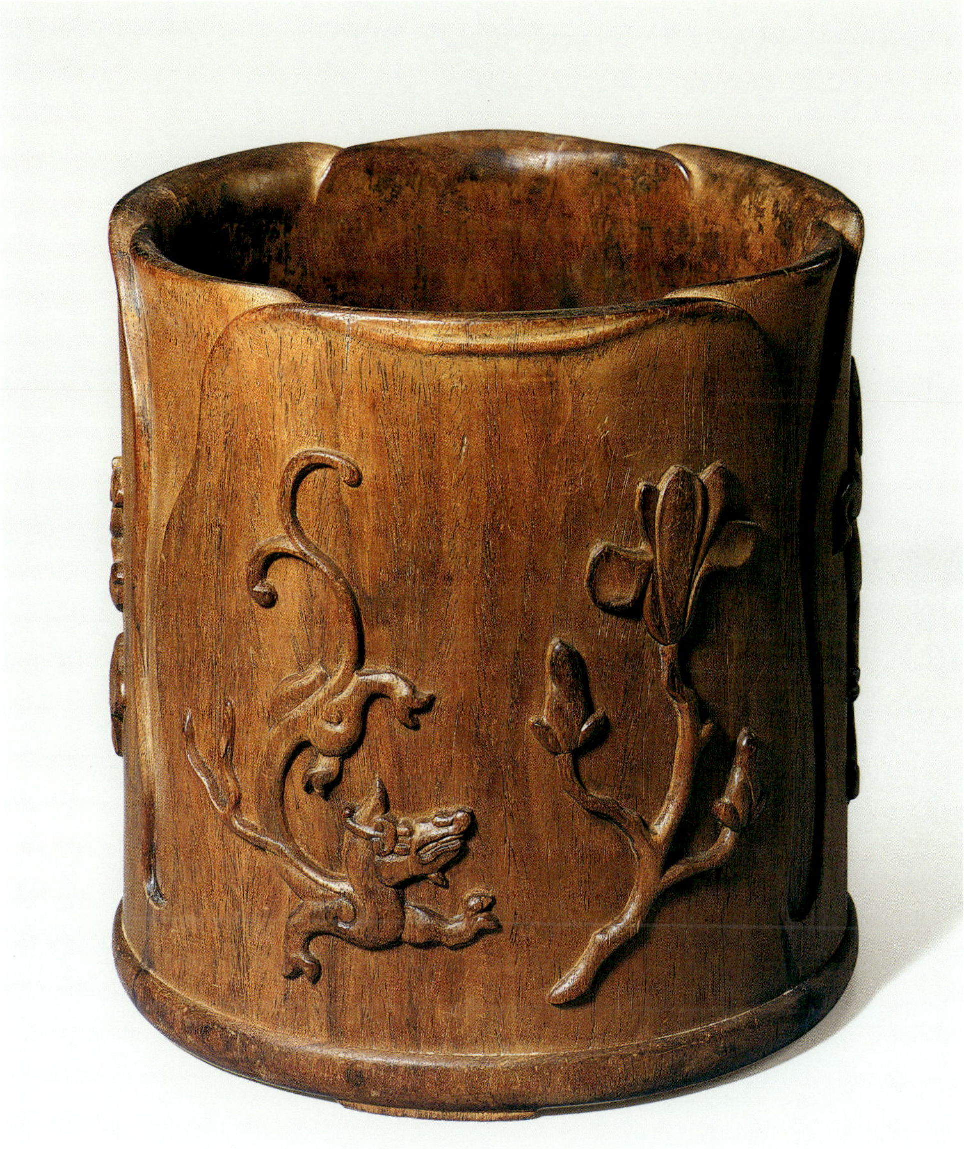

119

Wicker-Style Brushpot

黄花梨仿編藤筆筒

Huanghuali
18th Century
18 cm Diameter x 17 cm H

The imitation of lesser materials in more precious materials reached unprecedented heights during the Qianlong period—a phenomenon that is reflected in the rare and unusual 'basket weave' style of this *huanghuali* brushpot. The entire surface is patterned with relief and incised carving to simulate that of woven reed. The aged surface bears lovely patination. The flat bottom is fit with a round, core plug.

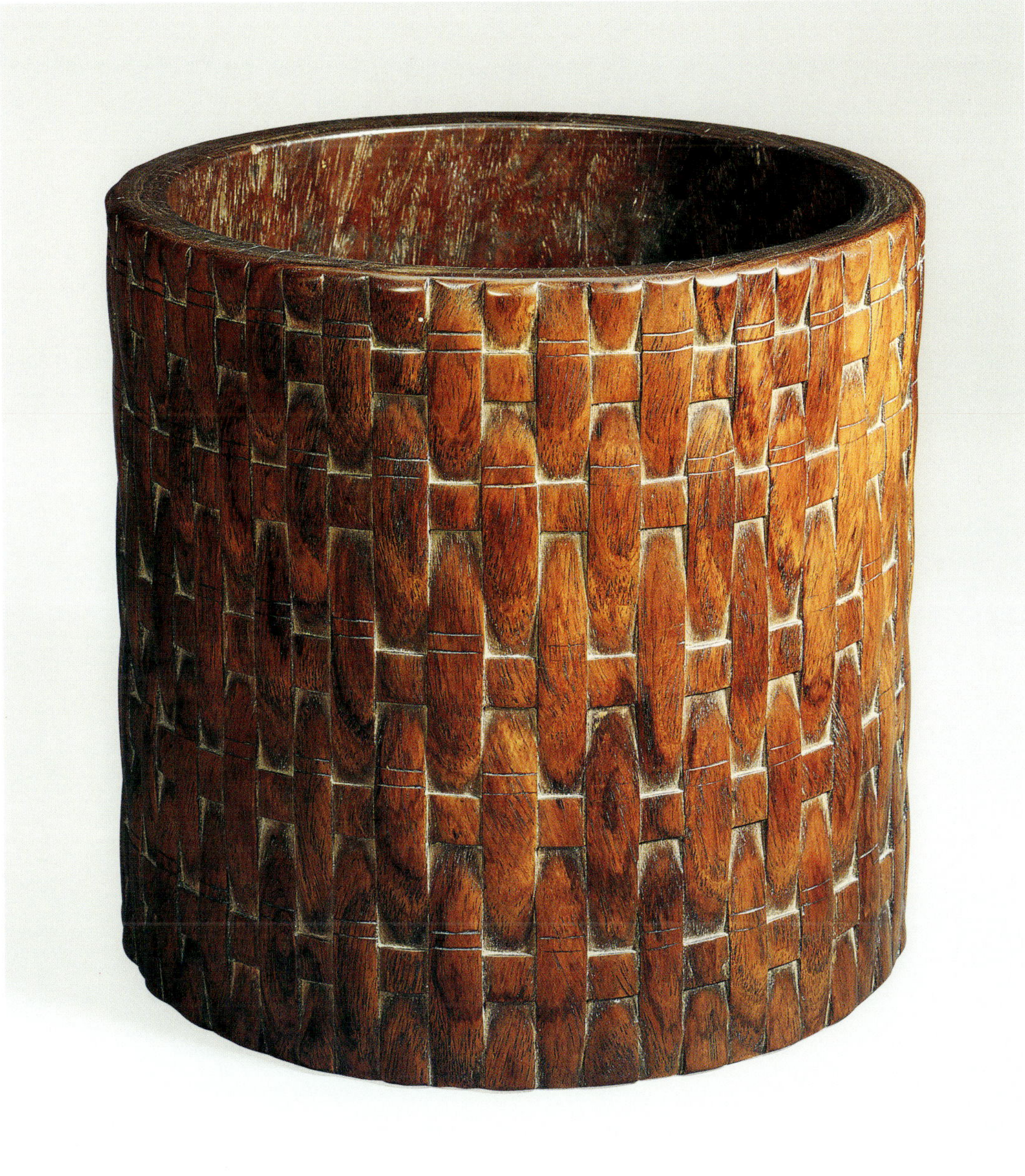

120

Bamboo-Style Brushpot

黃花梨仿竹筆筒

Huanghuali
18th Century
21 cm Diameter x 20 cm H

This brushpot imitates a section of large diameter bamboo. The surface molded with broad concave-shaped bands that are bordered with raised, nodular-shaped rings. The solid base has a dished-out bottom, leaving a foot rim around the perimeter.

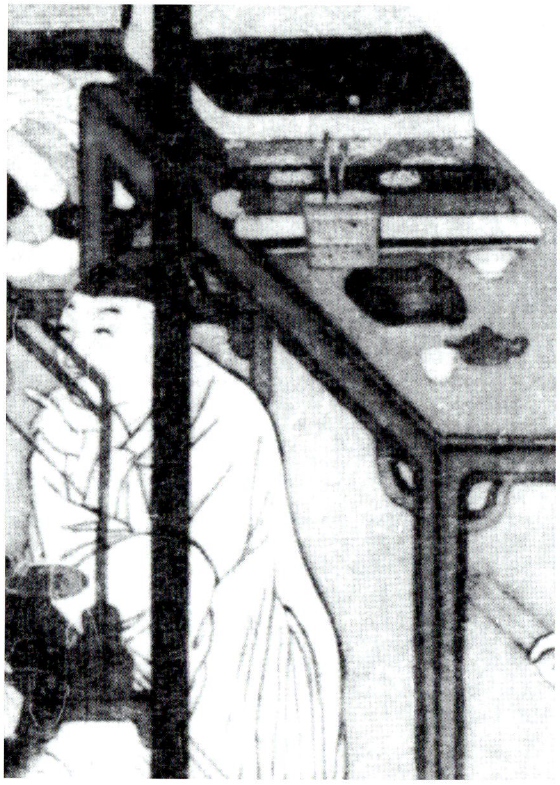

Brushpot. Detail from album leaf set Bai mei tu *illustrating scenes from the novel* Jin Ping Mei*, early Qing period.*

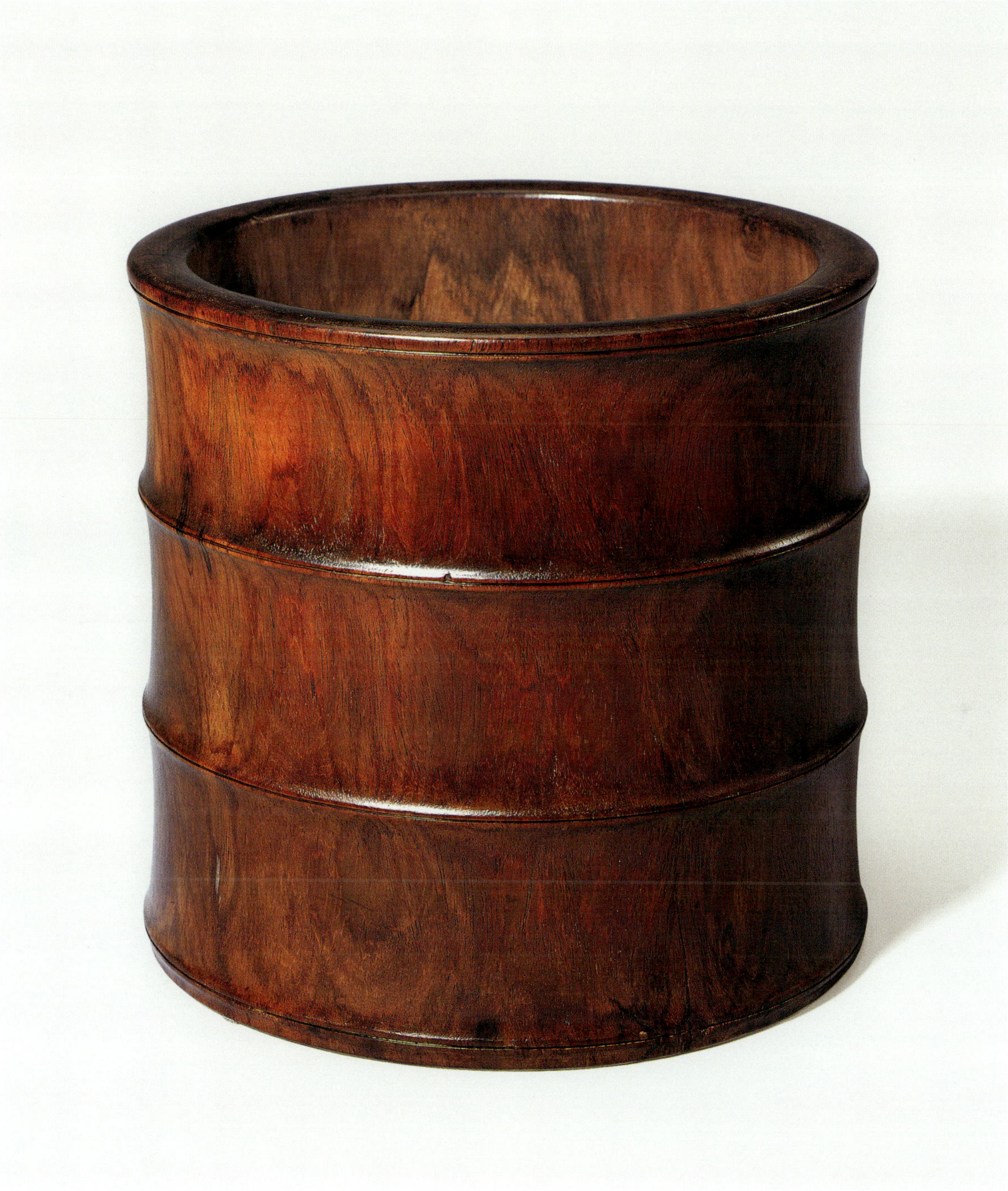

121

Brushpot with Relief Carving

黃花梨雕人物筆筒

Huanghuali
18th Century
20 cm Diameter x 18.5 cm H

The surface of this brushpot is carved in relief with the unusual scene of an inebriated lady in repose upon a garden bench; complementary lines of poetry incised in running script read "Drunken Repose in the Peony Garden." The body of the brushpot is otherwise shaped with a slight waist. The material, which is heavily striated with streaking and mottled markings ranging from dark brown to lighter, coffee-brown tones, may be a borderline variety of *huanghuali*. The slightly concave bottom is fit with a round, core plug.

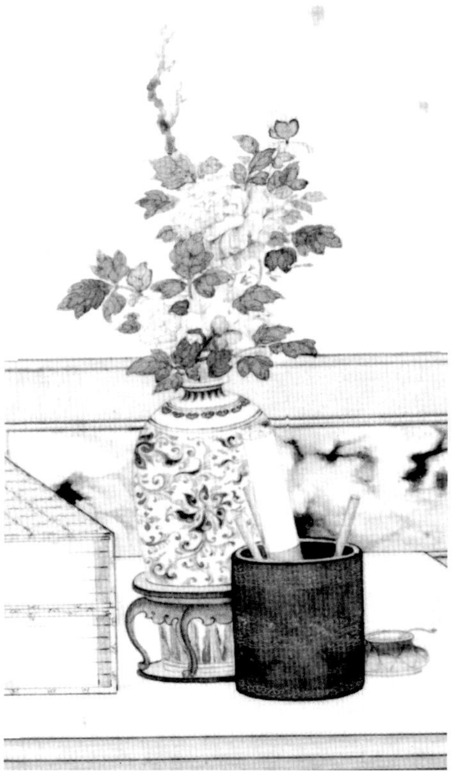

Brushpot. Detail from painting by Ding Guanpeng, Qing Qianlong period (1735-1795). National Palace Museum, Taipei.

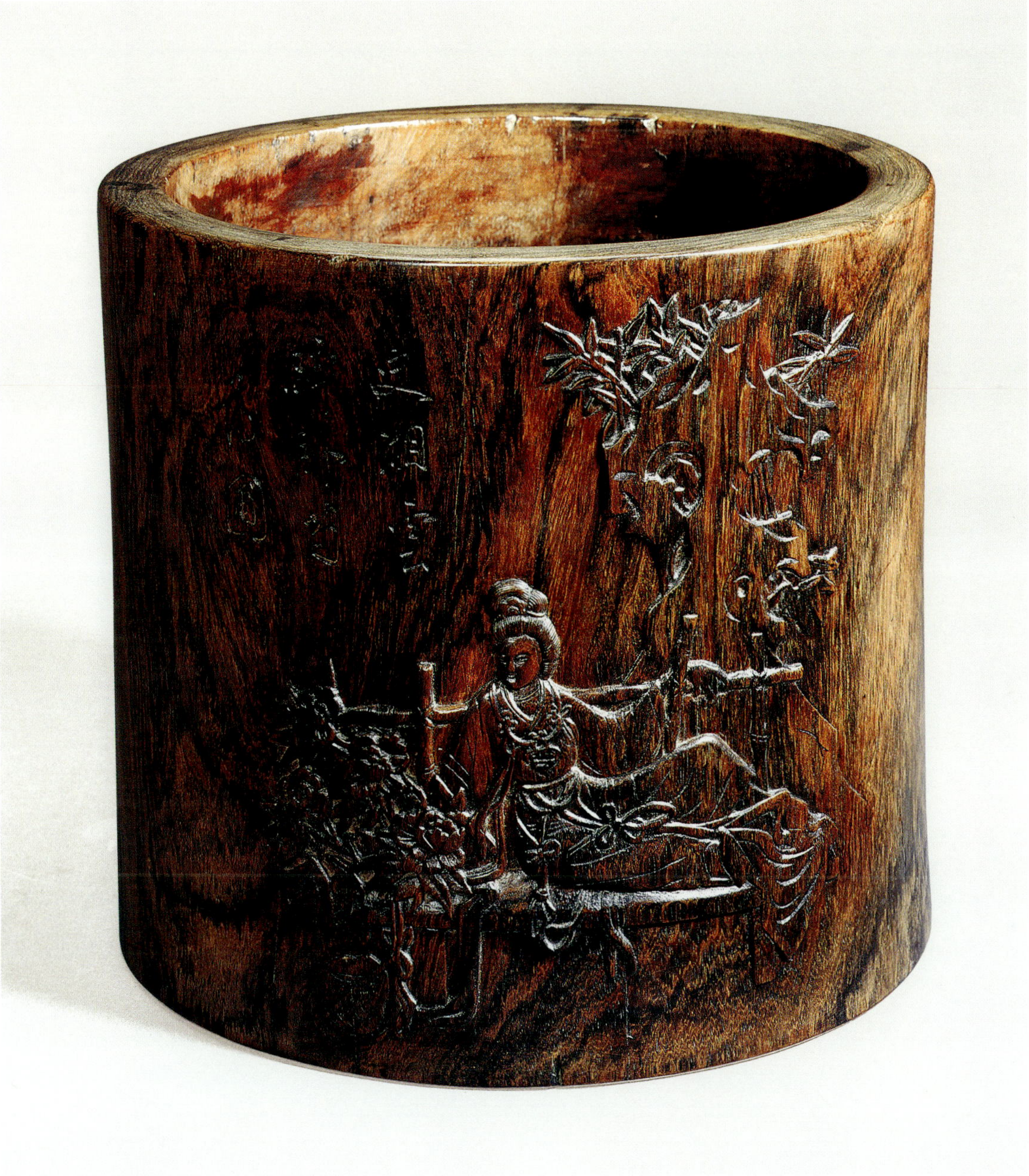

122

Brushpot with Dragon Carving

紫檀雕龍筆筒

Zitan
18th Century
15 cm Diameter x 15.5 cm H

Of probable Imperial origin, magnificent soaring dragons decorate the surface of this brushpot in masterly relief carving. A five-clawed dragon assumes a formal, frontal position. Dragons to either side are writhing through the cloud and waves. The rim is bordered with incised keyfret pattern. The surfaces bear soft-worn patination. The flat bottom is fit with a round, core plug.

The *zitan* brushpot with *huanghuali* base illustrated below is also carved with a similar decorative theme, but clearly exhibits an earlier style, attributed by Wang Shixiang and Zhu Jiajin to the Jiajing period (1522-1566), or possibly earlier. This piece may well have provided inspiration for the piece in the Liang Yi Collection, whose dragon decoration is more typical of the mid-Qing period and was executed with very fine relief carving.

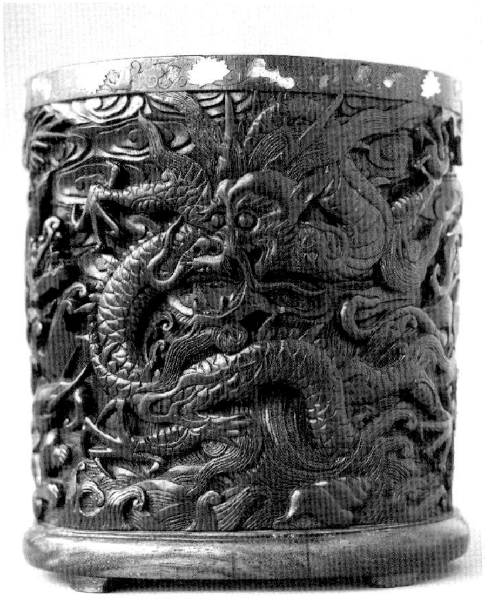

Brushpot with dragon carving. Zitan *and* huanghuali. *14.6 cm dia. x 16.5 cm H. Ming. After* Zhongguo meishu quanji Vol. 11.

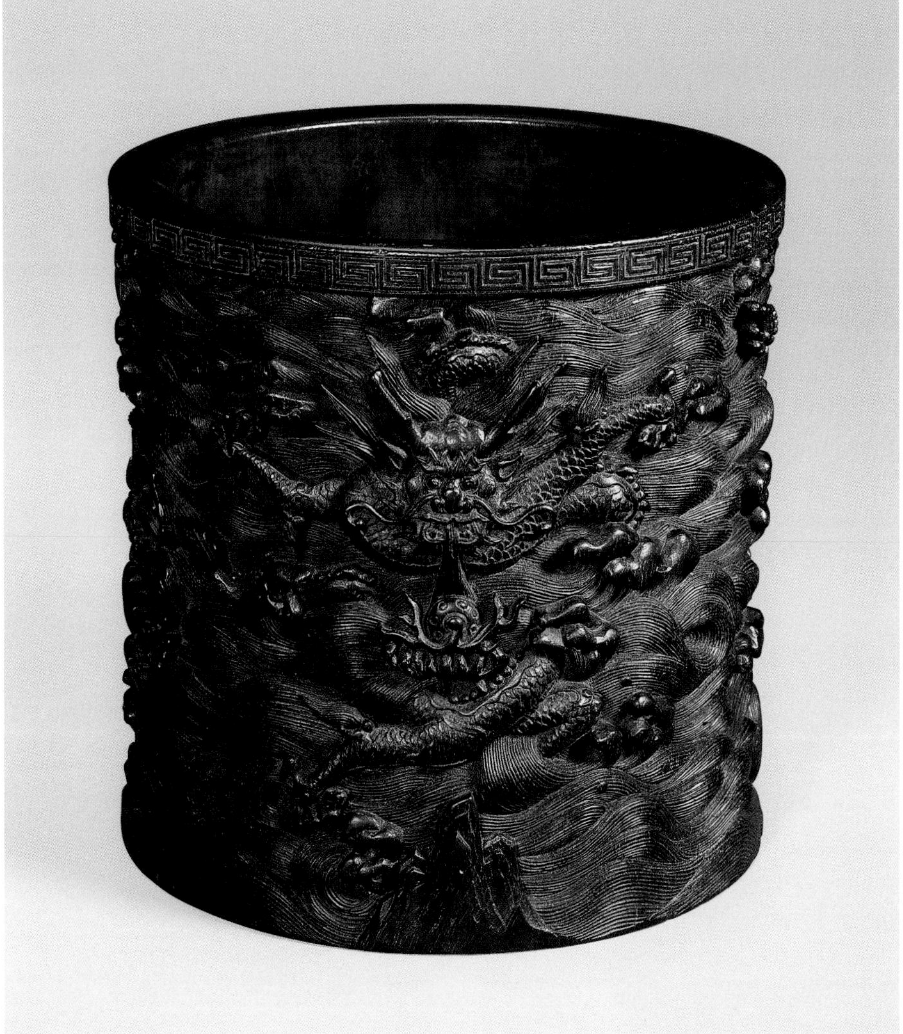

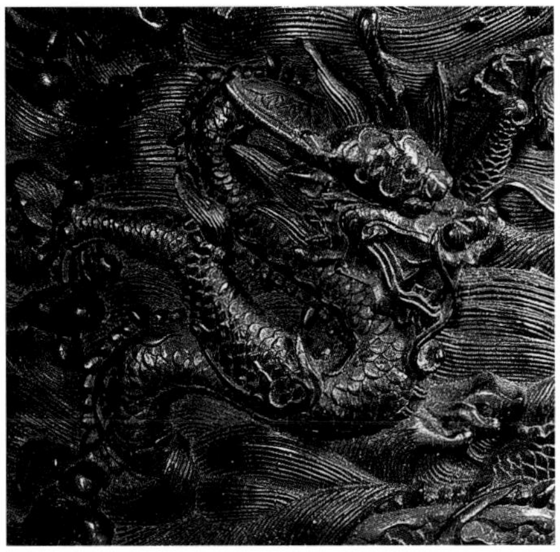

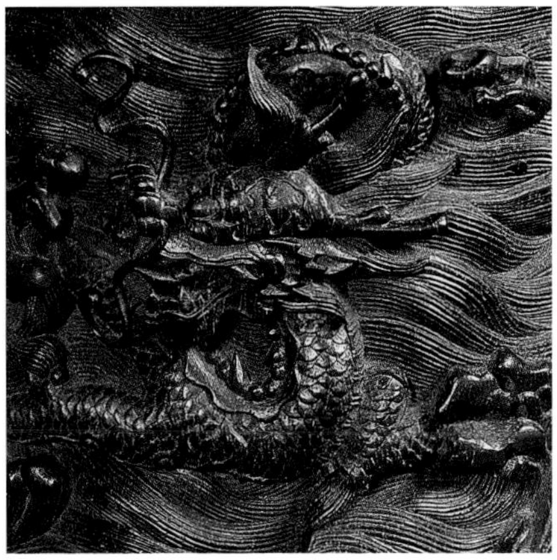

Bibliography

Bibliography

- Ahern, Captian George P. *Compilation of Notes on the Most Important Timber Tree Species of the Philippine Islands*. Manila: Forestry Bureau, 1901.
- Ang, John Kwang-Ming. *The Beauty of Huanghuali*. Taipei: ArtAsia, 1995.
- Berliner, Nancy. *Beyond the Screen: Chinese Furniture of the 16th and 17th Centuries*. Boston: Museum of Fine Arts, Boston, 1996.
- Beurdeley, Michel. *Chinese Furniture*. Tokyo, New York and San Francisco: Kodansha International, 1979.
- Bruce, Grace Wu. *Dreams of Chu Tan Chamber and the Romance with Huanghuali Wood: The Dr. S. Y. Yip Collection of Classic Chinese Furniture*. Hong Kong: New Island Printing Co. Ltd., 1991.
- ______. *Ming Furniture*. Hong Kong: Grace Wu Bruce Co., Ltd., 1995.
- ______. *On the Kang and between the Walls-the Ming Furniture quietly installed*. Hong Kong: Grace Wu Bruce Co., Ltd., 1998.
- ______. *Zitan furniture from the Ming and Qing dynasties*. Hong Kong: Grace Wu Bruce Co., Ltd., 1999.
- Cai Yi-An. *Qingdai guangshi jiaju* (Chinese furniture in Cantonese style). Hong Kong: 8 Dragons Publishing, 1993.
- Cao Xueqin. *Honglou Meng* (Dream of the Red Mansion). 3 vols. Taipei: Zhongguo gudian xiaoshuo xinkan, 1996.
- Chen Zengbi. "Double Sixes." *Journal of the Classical Chinese Furniture Society* 2:3 (Summer 1992), pp. 48-55.
- Chi Jo-hsin. "Zhou Zhu yu Zhouzhi gongyi" (Chou Chu and the Craftsmanship of Chou Chih works). *International Colloquium on Chinese Art History*. Taipei: National Palace Museum, 1991, pp. 657-679.
- China Guardian. *Classical Chinese Furniture*. Beijing, October 27, 1999.
- Christie's, NY. *Important Chinese Furniture Formerly the Museum of Classical Chinese Furniture Collection*. New York, September 19, 1996.
- Clunas, Craig. "Furnishing the Self in Early Modern China." Catalogue essay in *Beyond the Screen: Chinese Furniture of the 16th and 17th Centuries*. Boston: Museum of Fine Arts, Boston. 1996, pp. 21-53.
- ______. *Chinese Carving*. Victoria & Albert Museum: London, 1996.
- ______. *Superfluous Things: Material Culture and Social Status in Early Modern China*. Urbana and Chicago: University of Illinois Press, 1991.
- David, Sir Percival. *Chinese Connoisseurship, The Ko Ku Yao Lun, The Essential Criteria of Antiquities*. London: Faber and Faber, 1971.
- *Dongtian qinglu* (Song, mid 13th century). Huang Binhong, Deng Shi eds. *Meishu Congshu*, Vol, 5, Shenzhou gouguangshe, 1947.
- Ecke, Gustav. *Chinese Domestic Furniture*. Rutland, Vermont: Charles E. Tuttle, 1962.
- Ellsworth, Robert Hatfield. *Chinese Furniture: One Hundred Examples from the Mimi and Raymond Hung Collection*. New York, 1996.
- ______. *Chinese Furniture, Hardwood Examples of the Ming and Early Ch'ing Dynasties*. New York: Random House, 1970.

- ______. *Chinese Hardwood Furniture in Hawaiian Collections*. Honolulu: Honolulu Academy of Arts, 1982.
- Evarts, Curtis. "From Ornate to Unadorned: A Study of a Group of Yokeback Chairs." *Journal of the Classical Chinese Furniture Society* 3:2 (Spring 1993), pp. 24-33.
- ______. "A Pair of Zitan Southern Official's Hat Armchairs." *Journal of the Classical Chinese Furniture Society*, 1:4 (Autumn 1991), pp. 4-9.
- ______. "The Furniture Maker and the Woodworking Traditions of China." Essay in Berliner, Nancy. *Beyond the Screen: Chinese Furniture of the 16th and 17th Centuries*. Boston: Museum of Fine Arts, Boston, 1996, pp. 52-75.
- Gao Lian. *Zunsheng bajian* (Eight Discourses on the Art of Living) (ca 1591). Wenyuange Siku quanshu, vol. 871. Taiwan shangwu yinshuguan.
- Gu Yongqi. "Zitanmu de banzhi yu dingming" (The identification and terminology of zitan). *Shoucangjia* (Collectors) 34, 1999:2 pp. 40-42.
- Handler, Sarah. "The Chinese Screen: Movable Walls to Divide, Enhance, and Beautify." *Journal of the Classical Chinese Furniture Society* 3:3 (Summer 1993), pp. 4-31.
- Hong Kong Museum of Art. *In Pursuit of Antiquities*. Urban Council of Hong Kong, 1995.
- Jacobsen, Robert D. *Classical Chinese Furniture in the Minneapolis Institute of Arts*. Minneapolis Institute of Arts, 1999.
- Lee, Yu-kuan. *Oriental Lacquer Art*. New York and Tokyo: Weatherhill, 1972.
- Lin, Lina. *Special Exhibition of Furniture in Paintings*. Taipei: National Palace Museum, 1996.
- Lo, Kai-Yin, ed. *Classical and Vernacular Chinese Furniture in the Living Environment*. Hong Kong: Yungmingtang, 1998.
- Ma Weidu. "Chenmu yongsu de zitan jiaju" (Elegant zitan furniture). *Shoucangjia* (Collectors) 21, 1997:1, 24-27
- National Museum of History. *Splendor of Style: Classical Furniture from the Ming and Qing Dynasties*. Taipei, 1999.
- Nicholas Grindley. London, November 1999.
- Palace Museum Ancient Architecture Department. *The Illustrated Catalogue of the Architecture and Decoration of the Imperial Palace: Interior Design*. Beijing: Forbidden City Publishing House, 1995.
- Pu Anguo. *Ming Qing Sushi Jiaju* (Suzhou-style furniture from the Ming and Qing dynasties). Hangzhou: Zhejiang sheying chubanshe chu ban faxing, 1999.
- ______. *Zhongguo Hongmu Jiaju* (Chinese Hongmu Furniture). Hangzhou: Zhejiang sheyin chubanshe, 1996.
- Qian Yong. *Fuyuan conghua* (preface dated 1825). Biji xiaoshuo da guan 2:5.
- Qu Dajun. *Guangdong xinhua* (New Remarks on Guangdong), Hainan wenmu (Figured woods from Hainan). Zhonghua shuju chuban, 1985.

- Schafer, Edward H. "Rosewood, Dragon's Blood, and Lac." *Journal of the Classical Chinese Furniture Society* 1:4 (Autumn 1991), pp. 64-70. (Originally published in *Journal of the American Oriental Society*, vol. 77, no. 2 [April-June 1957].)
- Shanghai Museum. *Chinese Ming and Qing Furniture Gallery*. Shanghai: Shanghai Museum, 1996.
- Shanghai shi wenwu guanli weiyuanhui. "Shanghai Baoshan Ming Zhu Shoucheng fufu hezang mu." *Wenwu* 1992:5, pp. 63-65.
- Shoso-in Office. *Treasures of the Shoso-in: The North Section*. Tokyo: Asahi Shimbum Publishing Co., 1987.
- Sotheby's New York. *Important Chinese Furniture*, March 23, 1999, Sale 7277.
- Sze, Mai-Mai. *The Tao of Painting: A Study of the Ritual Disposition of Chinese Painting*. New York: Pantheon Books, 1956.
- Tian Jiaqing. *Classic Chinese Furniture of the Qing Dynasty*. Hong Kong: Phillip Wilson Publishers Ltd., 1996.
- ______. "Zitan and Zitan Furniture." *Orientations*, December 1994. pp. 43-49.
- *Tian shui bing shan* (A Record of the Waters of Heaven Melting the Iceberg). Biji xiaoshou daguan. Taipei: Xinxing shuju, 1978, Vol. 6:6.
- Tsai C. Y. *Zitan: The Most Noble Hardwood*. Taipei: My Humble House Publications, 1996.
- Tsang, Gerard and Hugh Moss. *Art of the Scholars Studio*. Hong Kong: The Oriental Ceramic Society of Hong Kong, 1986.
- Tu Long. *Qi ju ji fu qian*. (Notes on Utensils and Clothing for Daily Life) (published 1606). Meishu congshu, er ji, di jiu ji, Shenzhou, 1937.
- ______. *Wenfang qiju qian*. (Notes on Utensils for the Studio) (published 1606). Meishu congshu, er ji, di jiu ji, Shenzhou, 1937.
- Wang Shixiang and Curtis Evarts. *Masterpieces from the Museum of Classical Chinese Furniture*. San Francisco: Tenth Union, 1995.
- Wang Shixiang. *Classic Chinese Furniture: Ming and Early Qing Dynasties*. Translated by Sarah Handler and the Author. Hong Kong: Joint Publishing Company, 1986.
- ______. *Connoisseurship of Chinese Furniture*. 2 vols. Hong Kong: Joint Publishing (H.K.) Co., Ltd., 1990.
- ______. *Xiushilu jieshou* (An introduction to the Ming dynasty lacquer manual Xiushilu). Beijing: Wenwu chubanshe chuban faxing, 1998
- Wang Shixing. *Guang zhi yi* (preface dated 1597). Biji xiaoshuo daquan, Taipei: Xinxing shuju, 1978.
- Watson, Ernest. *The Principal Articles of Chinese Commerce*. Shanghai, 1930.
- Watson, William, ed. *Chinese Ivories from the Shang to the Qing*. The Oriental Ceramic Society and the British Museum; London, 1984.
- Wen Zhenheng. *Zhangwuzhi* (Treatise on Superfluous Things). 12 *juan*.

Compiled ca. 1620. Annotated edition by Chen Zhi. Nanjing: Jiangsu kexue jishu chubanshe, 1984.

- Xie Kun. *Jinyu suosui*. Meishu congshu, Shenzhou guoguangshe, 1947, Vol.14, 3:8.
- Yip Shing-Yiu and Grace Wu Bruce. *Chan Chair and Qin Bench: The Dr. S. Y. Yip Collection of Classic Chinese Furniture II*. Hong Kong: The Chinese University of Hong Kong, 1998.
- Zhang Dexiang. "Zhongguo gudai jiaju muzhi de shibie ji jianding yiyi" (The discernment and appreciation of antique Chinese furniture woods, Part 1). *Shoucangjia* (Collectors) 27, 1998:1, pp. 20-23.
- Zhang Yan. *Yangzhou qiqi shi* (History of Yangzhou Lacquerware). Jiangsu sheng kexue jishu chubanshe, 1995.
- Zhu Jiajin and Wang Shixiang. *Zhongguo meishu quanji* Vol. 11. Gongyi meishu bian. Beijing: Wenwu chubanshe, 1988.
- Zhu Jiajin and Xia Gengqi, eds. *Zhongguo qiqi quanji*: 5 Ming. Fujian: Fujian meishu chubanshe, 1995.
- Zhu Jiajin. "Yongzheng nian de jiaju zhizao kao" (A Study of the Yongzheng Imperial Furniture Workshops). *Mingjia tan jianding*. Beijing: Zijincheng chubanshe, 1995, pp. 353-363.